CANONICAL THEISM

CANONICAL THEISM

A Proposal for Theology and the Church

Edited by

William J. Abraham

Jason E. Vickers

Natalie B. Van Kirk

WILLIAM B. EERDMANS PUBLISHING COMPANY

GRAND RAPIDS, MICHIGAN / CAMBRIDGE, U.K.

Published 2008 by

Wm. B. Eerdmans Publishing Co.

2140 Oak Industrial Drive N.E., Grand Rapids, Michigan 49505 /

P.O. Box 163, Cambridge CB3 9PU U.K.

Printed in the United States of America

12 11 10 09 08   7 6 5 4 3 2 1

Library of Congress Cataloging-in-Publication Data

Canonical theism: a proposal for theology and the church /
edited by William J. Abraham, Jason E. Vickers, Natalie B. Van Kirk.

    p.   cm.

    Includes bibliographical references.

    ISBN 978-0-8028-6238-9 (pbk.: alk. paper)

    1. Church. 2. Theology.   I. Abraham, William J. (William James), 1947-
II. Vickers, Jason E.   III. Kirk, Natalie B. Van.

BV600.3.C36   2008

262.001 — dc22

                                                    2007043607

www.eerdmans.com

With grateful thanks to

   William S. Babcock
      and
   Schubert M. Ogden

*whose gifts and dedication to the arts of teaching and thinking
well have shaped each of us*

Contents

PART III

Acknowledgments

In bringing this volume to press we gladly acknowledge the help received. Robin Lovin, as dean of Perkins School of Theology, Southern Methodist University, provided splendid encouragement and vital financial assistance for meetings in the early stages. Evan Abla rendered invaluable help in securing the indices; likewise Heather Oglevie in proofreading. The team at Eerdmans was outstanding: Jon Pott and Reinder Van Til in their enthusiasm for the project; Jennifer Hoffman in the editorial process. We also want to thank Vladimir Grigorenko, the iconographer at St. Seraphim Orthodox Cathedral in Dallas, for permission to use the beautiful icon that appears on the cover.

Introduction

William J. Abraham

Canonical theism is both a vision of church renewal for the twenty-first century and a long-haul, intergenerational theological project. It is not one more speculative exercise in inventing new but irrelevant ideas. It is unrepentantly a robust intellectual effort to retrieve neglected elements of Christian conviction and practice that will reenergize the church and change the world. It is unapologetically driven by work in the academy. It is shamelessly committed to providing resources for the awakening and sustaining of spiritual life for local Christian congregations. It is enthusiastically committed to crossing the standard divisions that have kept Christians apart and proposes to do so by transcending the conventional categories of debate and conversation. It is firmly rooted in personal faith in the gospel of God in Jesus Christ, leans on the help of the Spirit, and loves the church as a precious gift of grace. It is aggressively committed to rigorous investigation and to the art of persuading critics and friends. In this essay I shall set the scene for what follows by situating the project in various ways, by indicating its central concerns, and by mapping what lies ahead.

Situating the Project

The Situation in Theology

Liberal Protestants are still trying to hold on to some crucial academic centers of power, but they are at the end of the line and have been ousted by their own more radical children and grandchildren. Evangelicals are looking for deeper roots and wider commitments, but they are currently hitting out in all directions, and not least at each other, to find an elusive consensus. Roman Catholicism is taking stock after Vatican II, but it is internally divided on the best way forward. Orthodoxy is searching for its own voice after the cruelty of persecution, but it is sorely tempted to withdraw from debate until it knows who are its real friends and enemies. Pentecostalism is coming of age intellectually, but it is unsure if it will really find a hearing in the church as a whole. Liberation theology has lifted up the plight of the poor and oppressed and still views itself as the best game in town, but it has fallen into a shrill moralism and for the most part has exhausted its resources. Karl Barth is making a comeback, but his disciples are in danger of falling into a barren scholasticism, and he is likely to suffer the same fate as Aquinas in the early twentieth century, that is, there are so many competing readings of his work that he may be more admired than emulated. In canonical theism we look not to the work of individual genius, or to a party slogan, or to an arresting theme, but to the resources of the whole church as the way ahead.

The Situation in Philosophy

Both the analytical and continental traditions have rediscovered religion. The dogmas of modernity have been challenged to the core. While many still look to science as the paradigm of rationality, most still want to find a place for human agency and the humanities. In epistemology, foundationalism has become something of a demon to be exorcised on the spot, but there is no agreement on where to go next. The chaos seems to have created space; there is a chastened if still very guarded openness to faith. In canonical theism we welcome the pause for breath and intend to find our own voices (note the plural) in this arena.

The Situation in Culture and Politics

Capitalism has triumphed economically and politically, yet it fails as a comprehensive vision of human existence. The shadow of Marxism continues to flourish underground in much cultural theory, but the death camps have killed it off as a live option. The search for a Third Way in politics has flourished in the hands of Tony Blair but it has faltered in the

United States, at least for the moment. Fundamentalism within Christianity and aggressive forms of Islam have entered the political arena with a vengeance. Claims to possess divine revelation are back on the table, but we have lost the art of adjudicating them. In the absence of serious argument and the arts of persuasion it is natural to turn to violence to resolve the disputes that inevitably arise. Terrorism has now replaced oppression as the challenge to address, but many think that the glut of material on terrorism is a form of intellectual blackmail that will be readily exploited on the right. In canonical theism we believe that this is not a time for paranoia or breast-beating; it is a time to engage in robust proclamation and mission. Political and cultural life will continue to be tumultuous and violent; we need resources that have outlasted the vicissitudes of culture and politics, and we think they are readily available.

The Situation in the Churches

The West has become a new mission field, especially in Europe. The gradual erosion of faith, much of it fueled by the church's own leaders and guides, is now visible for all to see. The effort to make a virtue of this erosion by looking for a religionless Christianity and a secular society has proved ephemeral and fruitless. At best the church in Europe now faces indifference and ambivalence; at worst it faces hostility.

In the United States the church is officially preoccupied politically with sexual politics, but underneath there has been a significant rebirth of interest in faith in parts of the mainline churches across the board. The conventional distinctions between mainline and evangelical no longer hold; evangelicals are often mainline and mainline is increasingly evangelical. Europeans have long looked on the United States as a century behind in the inevitable decline of faith in the modern world, but this was a projection of their own pessimism and sorrowful self-confidence. American religion, an inch deep and a mile wide, continues to flourish. There is in the United States a unique appropriation of the Christian faith that defies easy analysis and that confounds the prophets of doom; it may not always be pretty, but it is persistent, resilient, and invariably interesting.

In the Third World the spread of Pentecostalism and charismatic forms of evangelicalism is now rightly getting the attention it deserves. The information on this has been around for over a decade, but we do not ow if recent efforts at getting the word out will be integrated into the hard-drive of the media and of cultural memory. There are small signs that the church in the West is absorbing critical elements of this extraordinary renewal, but most of it is heavily disguised in order to avoid the censorship of ecclesial bureaucrats who talk pluralism but practice exclusion. Pentecostalism in the West is something of a joke that is all too readily and continuously available on national television; outside the West it is a volatile, energetic phenomenon more like early Methodism than modern Fundamentalism.

In canonical theism we believe that the best days of the church may yet be ahead of us, but we cannot proceed into the future without all that the Holy Spirit has given to us in resources. We make no grand claims to be the theology of the future, for we have seen that movie run its course at the academic box-office too often to be fooled even by our own optimism. Nor do we dare play at prophesying rosy days ahead, for the prospects of a new Dark Ages cannot be definitively ruled out. Yet we believe that the time is ripe for a fresh venture in Christian theology that will honor the life of the church, identify the critical mistakes that have crippled us for centuries, and contribute to a recovery of intellectual nerve.

The Contribution of Canonical Theism

In canonical theism we believe that the church cannot face the challenges that lie ahead without rethinking the internal ordering of its own life and without its intellectual leaders and teachers reconceiving their fundamental theological vocation.

We welcome the intense interest in various forms of orthodoxy, but we are convinced that we are destined to repeat some of the destructive mistakes of the past if those committed to orthodoxy do not come to terms with some crucial conceptual and material discoveries that lie to hand. Liberal Protestantism has become a sect that can only survive as a parasite on the wider church. Pentecostalism and evangelicalism will dissolve into forms of ecclesial mutiny and liberal Protestantism if they do not find a bigger horizon in which to operate. Roman Catholicism can make its deepest contribution as a leaven in the whole, but only if it relativizes its epistemological commitments. Orthodoxy must find a way to revisit its own best insights in the patristic period and fully acknowledge the work of God outside its walls. Mainline Protestantism has extraordinary resources, but its more moderate and conservative constituencies need to retrieve the heart and soul of the faith and regraft this into its missional initiatives in evangelism and social service.

The details of our main proposals and our reasons for pursuing them will be laid out in the theses and essays that follow but for now suffice it to say this. For canonical theism the core of the faith is not scripture, or creed, or liturgy, or this or that great voice from the past, and the like. The core is the great gift of medicinal salvation mediated through the great canonical heritage of the church, a marvelous, manifold, developmental work of the Holy Spirit before and after Pentecost. Even to speak of a core is dangerous because it suggests there is one thing we can name and seize upon when what is at issue is a manifold network of resources that require careful appropriation and reception. Yet we do have a name and a tangible set of proposals that should enable the newcomer to begin wrestling with what we propose. The heart of our proposal is that the church developed not just a canon of scripture or of doctrine but a manifold canonical heritage that really can do the job intended by God across space and time.

This canonical heritage has primacy over everything else: over philosophical and epistemological theory, over cultural analysis, and over political theory. Within the latter, that is, within the trio of philosophy, cultural studies, and political theory, we are convinced that epistemological work is primary and indispensable. Epistemological theories have been at the heart of modernity. They were conceived, nurtured, and developed mostly by Christian intellectuals. While intended to save the ship, epistemological theories have flooded its engine rooms, found their way down every corridor, and have clogged up the ventilation system. They have also spoiled the food, making it all too dry and salty. Put plainly, epistemological theorizing (much of it amateurish and dripping with self-confidence) has led to the colossal erosion of the faith of the church both formally and materially.

Epistemological problems require epistemological solutions, so the difficulties that arise at this level can only be cured by better epistemological work. Theologians who lean on political and cultural analysis that cooks the books in philosophy and epistemology will be like accountants who fiddle the figures: they will eventually be caught out by events; they undermine the institutions they serve and whose welfare should be their primary concern. Hence we have no intention of accepting the current obituary notices that cleverly disguise their own epistemological dogmas in funeral orations or that conceal their wares under the cover of hermeneutics. To repeat, epistemological problems require epistemological solutions.

Yet we insist that all our philosophical work is secondary to the primary commitments of faith. There is indeed a paradox here. We do have a metaphilosophical thesis to hand, but it is liberating not constricting in its import. The point can be pressed most persuasively historically: the church was wise to keep its philosophical commitments as midrash. It was right to bet the store on its complex ontology, on its carefully developed creed, on its diverse practices, on the beauty of its worship, on the intrinsic shine of its saints, on the modest identification of its best teachers, on its culturally sensitive iconography, and the like. There are many ways to name this manifold treasure of materials, practices, and persons; our term for it is the canonical heritage of the church. Despite the brokenness of the church and the constant struggle for fidelity, the diverse components of this heritage have survived the welter of cultural, political, and philosophical worlds it has inhabited, and they are available for retrieval and reuse today. Moreover, the church has within its members the creativity to develop all sorts of theories and interests that are more than adequate to meet its needs and to respond to the intellectual challenges of the day.

Mapping the Road Ahead

The essays that follow are the fruit of a collaborative project that has been pursued for more than five years. It is precisely because the ideas pursued here are beyond the scope of any one scholar that we count ourselves extremely fortunate in gaining the interest, encouragement, and help of the friends who have contributed to this volume. There has been no effort to form an official school, no attempt to impose an agenda on others, and no entry requirements for participation in the conversation. It simply has happened that all of us in one way or another have found the ideas developed in and around the theme of canonical theism interesting and worthy of exploration. In our collaboration together there has been no constraints beyond those of standard academic work in discussion or writing; each has brought his or her own skills and convictions; and each has been free to follow the evidence where it leads. Each is responsible only for the material that shows up under his or her authorship. There is a unity to our work as a whole, but we have no illusions about being comprehensive.

It will become immediately clear that we have come to accept fresh ways of thinking and speaking about old topics that are usually housed in discussions about the church, scripture, tradition, reason, experience, and the like. More controversially, we have reworked the idea of canon so that it has connotations and intellectual aspirations that are radically different from its standard usage. Fresh ways of formulating old problems and new ways of thinking about perennial theological issues require new ways of speaking. Thus the transformation of old linguistic categories and the invention of new ones are inescapable. We trust that the reader will be patient in coming to terms with these innovations. Rather than provide new definitions we prefer to allow the changing conceptual landscape to emerge naturally in our treatment of the issues that detain us. It helps, of course, to have a roadmap; hence, what follows is a very brief preview of how the book as a whole unfolds.

The group met biannually for a period of three years at Perkins School of Theology, beginning with a conversation around the theses that appear below. This is clearly the natural place for the reader to begin.

Part I provides the meat of the book by describing and explaining the central components of the canonical heritage of the church. There are seven essays in all, beginning with one that explicitly relates the canonical heritage to the work of the Holy Spirit. The six essays that follow explore the crucial components of the canonical heritage of the church that we want to retrieve and reinstate over time in the life of the church.

After a more personal essay on the emergence of canonical theism, Part II extends a series of olive branches to differing communities within contemporary Christian theology. The second insists on the primacy of the doctrine of the Trinity in understanding the content of the Christian faith, an issue of pivotal concern to all Christians. The third engages *The Philokalia*, a pivotal text of Orthodoxy. The fourth tackles the issue of papal infallibility, obviously a topic dear to the heart of Roman Catholicism. The fifth explores a fresh vision of the authority of scripture, a matter of continuing concern to mainline Christianity. The sixth interacts with historical scholarship about Jesus, a matter of enormous concern to most theologians, but especially to liberal Protestants. The last explores the potential connections of our central proposals with evangelicalism.

Part III offers three essays that begin charting the implications of canonical theism for theological education, systematic theology, and the life of the church as a whole.

What we have here is the beginning of a conversation together that is far from over and that will continue into the future. The authors come from various disciples: theology, philosophy, history, and biblical studies. Each of us has our own research interests that sometimes do and sometimes do not dovetail with our work here. We come from a great variety of ecclesial backgrounds and are passionately interested in making whatever modest contribution we can to our church communities. We came together serendipitously; all of us except one have been deeply connected in one way or another with Perkins School of Theology at Southern Methodist University; the lone exception has ties that are indirect but no less substantial for that. We believe that theology is a wonderful discipline and count ourselves fortunate indeed to have been placed by providence in and around Perkins.

We value the legacy of open, rigorous inquiry that has been central to the Graduate Program in Religious Studies at Southern Methodist University from its inception. The dedication to William S. Babcock and Schubert M. Ogden represents our deep appreciation for their work in the Graduate Program in Religious Studies across the years. The material proposals developed are very different from the ideas that animated folks at Southern Methodist University a generation ago, but we do not see ourselves departing from the legacy of scholarship and intellectual virtue we inherited from an amazing band of pioneers. We represent in many ways a radical departure from the material claims of the recent past, but there are deep continuities of spirit and style that we intentionally cherish. As things presently stand, we are but one slice of an intellectual community that has many different voices who are passionate in articulating their own positions, who are generally honest and forthright in conversation, and who seek to be rigorous in their work as a whole. It would give us great joy if others were to find our ruminations illuminating, provocative, and sufficiently substantial and challenging to merit their attention and criticism.

Canonical Theism: Thirty Theses

WILLIAM J. ABRAHAM

THESIS I:

Canonical theism is a term invented to capture the robust form of theism manifested, lived, and expressed in the canonical heritage of the church. It is proposed as both a living form of theism and a substantial theological experiment for today. We can explicate it further by distinguishing it from other forms of theism and by indicating more clearly how it is related to the canonical heritage of the church.

THESIS II:

Canonical theism is to be distinguished from mere theism, philosophical theism, process theism, open theism, classical theism, and consensual theism.

THESIS III:

It differs from mere theism in being much more robust; thus it is unapologetically trinitarian in form and content.

THESIS IV:

It differs from philosophical theism, say, Anselmic or perfect being theism, in that it is derived from the canonical heritage of the church rather than developed from philosophical sources.

THESIS V:

Canonical theism differs from process theism in that it has no stake in the theism advanced by process philosophers and theologians are free to examine the claims of process theism on merit.

THESIS VI:
The same principle applies *mutatis mutandis* to present attempts to develop the form of open theism that is currently being articulated by some American evangelicals. Canonical theists are free to examine the claims of this form of theism on its merits and to either reject it or to accept it as additional midrashic extension of their theism.

THESIS VII:
Canonical theism differs from classical theism in that the latter is a historical notion drawn from the history of ideas and used to designate a strong monotheism with impassibilist connotations. Canonical theism is first and foremost trinitarian; and, while it readily absorbs the classical attributes of monotheism, the commitment on passibility is modest and complex.

THESIS VIII:
Canonical theism differs from the consensual theism of, say, Thomas Oden, in two ways. First, it is skeptical of the claim that there exists a consensus across the patristic era, Roman Catholicism, magisterial Protestantism, evangelical orthodoxy, and the like. While there are clear elements of overlap between these groups, there are very serious differences that challenge the claim of consensus. Second, canonical theism focuses on the public, canonical decisions of the church existing in space and time across the first millennium.

THESIS IX:
Canonical theism is intimately tied to the notion of the canonical heritage of the church. The church possesses not just a canon of books in its Bible but also a canon of doctrine, a canon of saints, a canon of church fathers, a canon of theologians, a canon of liturgy, a canon of bishops, a canon of councils, a canon of ecclesial regulations, a canon of icons, and the like. In short, the church possesses a canonical heritage of persons, practices, and materials. Canonical theism is the theism expressed in and through the canonical heritage of the church.

THESIS X:
The canonical heritage of the church came into existence through the inspiration of the Holy Spirit. The Holy Spirit was active in motivating, energizing, guiding, directing, and overseeing their original production in the church.

THESIS XI:

The canonical heritage of the church functions first and foremost soteriologically. It operates as a complex means of grace that restores the image of God in human beings and brings them into communion with God and with each other in the church. Each component is primarily an instrument to be used in spiritual direction and formation.

THESIS XII:

The canonical heritage through which canonical theism is mediated is not in and of itself an epistemology, nor is it meant to serve as an epistemology. It is not a handbook on how to resolve disputes about rationality, justification, warrant, knowledge, and truth.

THESIS XIII:

The ongoing success of the canonical heritage of the church depends on the continuing active presence of the Holy Spirit working through the relevant persons, practices, and materials.

THESIS XIV:

The canonical heritage of the church is to be received in genuine repentance and lively faith. The effective operation of the various components depends on an open and contrite heart and a readiness to practice the light of God that one encounters.

THESIS XV:

Generally speaking, the various components of the canonical heritage have their own distinctive role in the economy of faith. Thus, the scriptures do not do the job of the creed, and the creed does not do the job of the episcopate, and the episcopate does not do the work of baptism, and so on. Each has its own function in the healing and restoration of the human soul.

THESIS XVI:

While the various elements in the canonical heritage work ideally together, there is a fair degree of over-determination, for there is overlapping in their particular purposes. When one is missing or improperly used, others can take up the spiritual slack. Thus the icons can marvelously convey the content of the gospel and the teaching of scripture.

THESIS XVII:
Canonical theism's vision of canon differs from the standard Western vision of canon in two ways. First, it extends canon beyond the canon of scripture or the Bible. Here it draws on the original meaning of canon as a "list." Second, it eschews conceiving canon as an epistemic criterion, relocating canon within the church rather than within the field of epistemology and philosophy. In canonical theism canon is construed fundamentally as a means of grace, a way through which the Holy Spirit reaches and restores the image of God in human agents.

THESIS XVIII:
On the surface, commitment to canonical theism appears to involve a turn to Roman Catholicism and a move away from Protestantism. This is false. Both Protestantism and Roman Catholicism work with a radically epistemic conception of canon; and they restrict canon to scripture. Magisterial Protestantism tries to work with the canon of scripture alone. Roman Catholicism adds tradition, the magisterium, and papal infallibility understood in epistemic terms as the means whereby the meaning of the canon is to be rightly understood. Hence epistemology rather than soteriology is primary in the conception and reception of canon in both Protestantism and Roman Catholicism.

THESIS XIX:
Although canonical theism is clearly compatible with Eastern Orthodoxy, it is unclear how far the Eastern church articulates any substantial vision of the canonical heritage of the undivided church.

THESIS XX:
Canonical theism emerges as an option within Protestantism and is proposed as a healing theological option within Protestantism. It can readily be seen as a fresh reappropriation of the patristic tradition for today. It invites Protestantism to a radical revision of its internal commitments. It is unclear how far this is possible given the constitutive elements of Protestantism. Perhaps canonical theism is essentially post-Protestant at its core and cannot be absorbed within Protestantism. At its conception canonical theism arose out of a deep, even searing, dissatisfaction with current forms of liberal and conservative Protestantism. However, there is no reason in principle why canonical theism cannot preserve and even enhance the best insights and fruits of the Protestant traditions across the centuries.

THESIS XXI:

Canonical theism gives intellectual primacy to ontology over epistemology. We find ourselves meeting God, discovering our sinfulness, encountering redemption, struggling with evil, immersed in suffering, and the like. We are initiated into the faith of the gospel, baptized, enter the church, experience the presence and power of the Holy Spirit, and are converted to a life of holiness. We encounter these phenomena without having an epistemology to hand, without necessarily figuring out how to deal with the questions about truth, rationality, justification, and knowledge that conventionally arise. Nor do these phenomena require us to have an epistemology before we engage in them. Hence ontology is logically prior to epistemology. Without the ontology the epistemology is likely to be thin, wooden, and inappropriate.

THESIS XXII:

The canonical heritage generates rigorous epistemological reflection and theorizing. Such work needs to be pursued at the highest intellectual level. There is no drawing back from the epistemology of theology into some kind of naive credulity or a shutting down of the questions of meaning and justification rightly raised by philosophers in the twentieth century. Canonical theists are interested in pursuing the implications of epistemologies compatible with canonical theism for the understanding of the history of the church and the study of scripture. Canonical theism may lead to the development of epistemological insights that have overtones for all of human thought and existence that are as yet unidentified and unexplored.

THESIS XXIII:

Canonical theists have no stake per se in foundationalism as an epistemological position. Canonical theism is open to a whole variety of epistemological options, whether foundationalist or coherentist, internalist or externalist, evidentialist or non-evidentialist. These matters are to be pursued with rigor and appropriate sophistication as needed.

THESIS XXIV:

In the epistemology of theology, special attention should be given to epistemic suggestions already present in the canonical heritage of the church. These have often been obscured from vision when canon has been construed as a criterion and when epistemology has been conceived along internalist lines.

THESIS XXV:

No single epistemological vision should be offered or sanctioned as canonical in the church. This can be spelled out in two ways. First, various and internally competing epistemological visions and theories are compatible with the content of the canonical heritage. Second, the various epistemological assertions, comments, and suggestions found in the canonical heritage do not constitute a full-dress, comprehensive epistemological vision.

THESIS XXVI:

Epistemological insights and theories have a place as teaching tools in the church and as part of the work of evangelism and apologetics. People naturally ask epistemological questions within and without theology, and their questions deserve to be taken seriously. Knowing when and how to introduce epistemological issues and materials is a matter of delicate pedagogical judgment.

THESIS XXVII:

The history of the canonical heritage throws light on the history of epistemology. Some of the most interesting epistemology in the West has been evoked by theological disagreement, even though in the secularization of the academy this has been lost from view in the histories of epistemology. Canonical theists are interested in fresh ways of understanding the history of epistemology, not least in identifying and exploring epistemic insights that have been forgotten or ignored. They are especially interested in the place of theism in the history of epistemology, exploring the role posited for God in debates about rationality, justification, and knowledge.

THESIS XXVIII:

The continuity between the canonical faith of the church beyond the first millennium and the ecclesial communities that arise thereafter is an open question. Clearly, different configurations of Christianity have preserved and effectively deployed much of the canonical heritage in their own way and manner. Witness, for example, the varied way in which the doctrine of the Trinity has been preserved in hymnody in non-creedal traditions. Questions of continuity and discontinuity should be addressed with a generous disposition.

THESIS XXIX:

The canonical heritage of the church constitutes a bedrock commitment for Christians as a whole. We need to approach the various Christian churches and denominations not in terms of one element of the canonical heritage as constitutive of Christian identity but in terms of how far they have owned the various components of the canonical heritage. This prohibits an all or nothing judgment, with one group automatically in and another group automatically out. We will have to work with judgments of proportion and degree.

THESIS XXX:

All epistemological proposals, like papal infallibility, scriptural infallibility, and the Methodist Quadrilateral, should be treated as midrash, secondary to the primary constitutive commitments of the church as a whole. Hence we need not give up our epistemological theories, but they do have to be decanonized if we are to secure the unity of Christians. This is where the rub is going to come hard for many. Perhaps the epistemological positions could be canonical for sub-groups within the church as a whole, while not being at all canonical for the whole church. Radical decanonization of epistemologies of theology is the preferred option.

PART I

Medicine of the Holy Spirit:
The Canonical Heritage of the Church

Jason E. Vickers

In many respects, canonical theism re-envisions both theology and church from top to bottom. At the heart of this re-envisioning of theology and church, the careful reader will discover a summons to retrieve the *full contents* and, even more important, the *originating purpose* of the canonical heritage of the church. Having said this, we anticipate that many persons will be uneasy with what we identify as the full contents of the canonical heritage of the church. For example, some may be formally or officially reticent to embrace canonical images and saints. Moreover, there may be disputes about what belongs in the canon of sacraments. Further, there are sure to be disagreements over the canon of episcopacy. We are well aware that such differences exist, and we will be delighted if canonical theism provokes serious and patient dialogue concerning the contents of the canonical heritage of the church.

There is a real sense in which retrieving the originating purpose of the canonical heritage of the church is a higher priority for canonical theists than reaching ecumenical consensus regarding the normative contents of the canonical heritage. Thus, in our view, the success or failure of canonical theism has primarily to do with the degree to which it aids in the recovery of a particular understanding of the originating purpose of the canonical heritage of the church. To state the matter succinctly, canonical theists believe that ecclesial canons are first and foremost gifts of the Holy Spirit in and through which the Holy Spirit is present and at work in the life of the church. More specifically, we believe that the canonical heritage of the church is like a grand medicine chest, the contents of which the Holy Spirit uses to bring about the healing of the world.

In this chapter, I will fill out canonical theism's vision of the originating purpose of the canonical heritage of the church by identifying three characteristic aspects of the presence and work of the Holy Spirit in and through ecclesial canons: (1) the *generosity* and *creativity* of the Holy Spirit, (2) the *therapeutic* nature of the work of the Holy Spirit, and (3) the *freedom* of the Holy Spirit. These are not, of course, the only aspects of the presence and work of the Holy Spirit to which canonical theists are committed. These are, however, the aspects that help to clarify both the way in which canonical theism differs from much modern theology and the way in which canonical theism is a strategy for the renewal of theology and the church today. Moreover, as we will see, these are the aspects that show how canonical theism might be successful quite apart from procuring any ecumenical consensus regarding the normative contents of the canonical heritage of the church.

The Canonical Heritage of the Church and the Generosity of the Holy Spirit

At the heart of canonical theism is a deep conviction that the materials, persons, and practices that comprise the canonical heritage of the church are gifts of the Holy Spirit. Thus canonical theists are in agreement with Irenaeus when he says,

> God established in the Church the apostles, the prophets, the doctors *and all the other effects of the working of the Spirit* in which those who do not run to the church do not share. . . . Where the Church is, there is also the Spirit of God and where the Spirit of God is, there are also the Church and all grace. And the Spirit is truth.[1]

Straightway, we need to stress that we recognize in Irenaeus's remark a dialectical and mysterious tension. On the one hand, there are *in the church* special "effects of the working of the Holy Spirit in which those who do not run to the church do not share." For canonical theists such special effects include but are not necessarily limited to liturgy, scripture, creeds and doctrine, the sacraments, episcopacy, images, and saints and teachers. On the other hand, while we regard these things as special effects of the presence and work of the Holy Spirit in the church, we do not take

---

1. Irenaeus, *Adv. haer.* 3.24.1; emphasis mine.

this to mean that the Holy Spirit is only present and at work in the church. On the contrary, we are open to a generous reading of Irenaeus's comment that "where[ever] the Spirit of God is, there are also the church and all grace." For canonical theists, the very plentitude of the canonical heritage of the church suggests that the Holy Spirit is by nature both generous and creative. Accordingly, we have no interest in restricting the presence and work of the Holy Spirit to the canonical heritage of the church.

Similarly, when it comes to the presence and work of the Holy Spirit in the visible church, canonical theists do not wish to restrict the effects of the Spirit to the ecclesial canons that have emerged across the centuries, i.e., canons of scripture, liturgy, images, sacraments, saints, and the like. Once again, we are sympathetic with Irenaeus when he says, "It is impossible to say how many charisms the church receives throughout the world from God in the name of Jesus Christ who was crucified under Pontius Pilate."[2] Thus we are prepared to recognize a range of charismatic gifts that may not be accorded official canonical status in most traditions. Two examples of such gifts are worth mentioning. Canonical theists are open to the charismatic practices of prophecy and demon exorcism for which there is abundant testimony throughout the history of the early church.[3] The fact that in some parts of the church today these gifts are not often evident or acknowledged is, in our judgment, no reason to dismiss them prematurely.

It should be clear by now that, at the heart of canonical theism, there is a deep commitment to the notion of the *generosity* and *creativity* of the Holy Spirit in both the church and the world at large. That said, canonical theists are especially interested in those effects of the presence and work of the Holy Spirit that have consistently manifested themselves in various materials, persons, and practices in the life of the church across the centuries. Otherwise put, canonical theists are especially interested in those effects of the presence and work of the Holy Spirit which, because of their persistence and power in the life of the church, acquired canonical status early on.

From the standpoint of canonical theism, the varied and dynamic nature of these canonical materials, persons, and practices reflects the generosity and creativity of the Holy Spirit. The Spirit is present and at work in written texts, in oral tradition, in visual images, in symbols and in sacra-

---

2. Irenaeus, *Adv. haer.* 2.32.4.

3. On demon exorcism, for example, see Justin Martyr, *Dialogue with Trypho* 85.2.

ments, in the work of the liturgy, in episcopal oversight, and in living persons such as saints and teachers. In short, the Spirit gives generously and creatively a dynamic range of gifts so that the church lacks nothing that she could need or ask for.

It is precisely in stressing that the full range of canonical materials, persons, and practices should be seen as effects of the presence and work of the Holy Spirit that canonical theism hopes to foster renewal in theology and the church today. Thus canonical theists resist the tendency that we perceive in some modern Protestant theology to focus almost exclusively on the presence and work of the Holy Spirit in and through the canon of scripture. Similarly, we resist the tendency that we perceive in some Catholic theology to focus almost exclusively on the presence and work of the Holy Spirit in the sacraments and the episcopacy. Likewise, we resist the tendency in some charismatic-Pentecostal theology to overemphasize the presence and work of the Holy Spirit in the unique charismatic gift of speaking in tongues.

In our judgment, the tendency, where prevalent, to over-emphasize the presence and work of the Holy Spirit in particular ecclesial canons or gifts has led to the spiritual impoverishment of the church by divesting it of the fullness of the generosity and creativity that characterizes the presence and work of the Holy Spirit. For example, in traditions that ignore or even reject the power of images, visually oriented persons are robbed of any deep awareness of or sensitivity to the presence and work of the Holy Spirit in and through images. Similarly, in traditions that ignore or reject the canon of saints, persons who learn best from observing examples set by other persons are robbed of any deep awareness of or sensitivity to the presence and work of the Holy Spirit in and through the saints. Further, in "anti-liturgical" or "low-church" traditions, persons who are oriented naturally to symbolism are left uninformed of the presence and work of the Holy Spirit in images, in hymns, and in the sacraments.

At this stage, we anticipate objections that it is primarily Protestant traditions which have divested the church of the fullness of the Spirit's gifts in the canonical heritage. For example, most Protestant traditions do not recognize a canon of saints or a canon of images, and many Protestant traditions can appear to have rather low views of the liturgy and the sacraments (including ordination). By contrast, Eastern Orthodox and Catholic churches have maintained most, if not all, of the canonical materials, persons, and practices mentioned above.

To this objection, canonical theists have two things to say. First, we are convinced that the rather drastic thinning out of the canonical heritage that occurred early on in Protestantism was a serious overreaction for which Protestant traditions continue to suffer theologically and spiritually to this day. We especially regard as a gross overreaction the overt and subtle forms of iconoclasm that have characterized much of Protestantism from the very beginning.[4]

Second, while we acknowledge that the Orthodox and Catholic traditions have maintained most, if not all, of the canonical heritage of the church, we want to raise additional concerns about a potential loss of the *therapeutic* function of canonical materials, persons, and practices on the one hand, and a potential loss of the *freedom* of the Holy Spirit on the other. It is only in taking up these concerns that the applicability of canonical theism to Eastern Orthodox traditions and to Catholicism will become clear.

The Therapeutic Nature of the Work of the Holy Spirit

While canonical theists are concerned to stress the generosity and creativity of the Holy Spirit, they are equally concerned to stress *the therapeutic nature of the work of the Spirit* both generally and particularly in and through the canonical heritage of the church. Thus, while canonical theists regard the loss of the fullness of the canonical heritage of the church as a regrettable development within Protestantism, we regard as an equal if not greater problem the loss of emphasis on the therapeutic nature of the Spirit's presence and work in and through ecclesial canons *as primary*.[5] In

---

4. For an excellent account of iconoclasm in early English Protestantism, see Eamon Duffy, *The Stripping of the Altars: Traditional Religion in England 1400-1580* (New Haven: Yale University Press, 1992). Also see John Phillips, *The Reformation of Images: Destruction of Art in England, 1536-1660* (Berkeley: University of California Press, 1973).

5. We celebrate the recent increase of theologians from a wide variety of ecclesial communions who stress the therapeutic nature of the presence and work of the Holy Spirit. For example, see Ellen T. Charry, *By the Renewing of Your Minds: The Pastoral Function of Christian Doctrine* (New York: Oxford University Press, 1997). Also see Vigen Guroian, "Divine Therapy," *Theology Today* 61:3 (October 2004): 309-21. Finally, we regard the recent revival of interest in the work of Yves Congar as contributing to the renewal of a therapeutic vision of the presence and work of the Spirit. For example, see John Webster, "Purity and Plentitude: Evangelical Reflections on Congar's *Tradition and Traditions*," *International Journal of Systematic Theology* 7:4 (October 2005): 399-413. Also see Elizabeth T. Groppe, *Yves Congar's Theology of the Holy Spirit* (New York: Oxford University Press, 2004).

our judgment, the loss of emphasis on the therapeutic nature of the Spirit's work as primary has occurred in highly specific ways in both Protestantism and Catholicism. Moreover, we sense that something similar can occur in a more subtle way in Orthodoxy.[6]

What do mean when we say that there has been a loss of emphasis within both Protestantism and Catholicism on the therapeutic nature of the work of the Holy Spirit as primary? From the standpoint of canonical theism, there is a tendency in both Protestantism and Catholicism to appeal to the work of the Holy Spirit in particular canonical materials, persons, or practices as epistemic criteria that demonstrate either the truthfulness of each tradition or the validity of each church. Thus there is a tendency among Protestants to appeal to the Spirit's inspiration of the scriptures as an epistemic criterion that secures the truthfulness of the scriptures and, subsequently, the validity of Protestant churches.[7] We see this most especially in the immense time and energy that Protestant theologians have expended in the modern period on the development of doctrines of inspiration and inerrancy.[8]

Similarly, Catholic theologians often appeal to the presence and work of the Holy Spirit in sacraments and in episcopacy to secure the truthfulness of the Catholic tradition and the validity of the Catholic Church. We see this most especially in the development of the doctrine of papal infallibility.[9] Likewise, some Pentecostal-charismatics are prone to appeal to the activity of the Spirit in giving supernatural gifts such as the gift of speaking in tongues as validation for either their tradition or their church.

At this stage, it needs to be stressed that canonical theists do not deny that the Holy Spirit inspired prophets and apostles to write the scriptures. Nor do canonical theists deny that the Holy Spirit is present and at work in the church through sacraments and the episcopacy. For that matter, canonical theists are open to the possibility that scripture or the episcopacy might, with sufficient modifications, have a role to play in the epistemology of theology. For example, scripture might be able to function

---

6. The attendant danger here is the notion that it is precisely the possession of the fullness of the canonical heritage of the church that secures the legitimacy of the Orthodox tradition and church.

7. For an extended account of this, see my essay on canonical theism and the epistemology of theology in this volume.

8. See Douglas Koskela's contribution in this volume.

9. See Mark Powell's contribution in this volume.

epistemically when its relationship to a genuinely epistemic concept like divine revelation is spelled out carefully.[10]

The problem is that, from the standpoint of canonical theism, the canons of scripture and episcopacy in particular have been made to function within modern Protestantism and Catholicism *primarily* as epistemic criteria. As a result, their therapeutic function as charismatic gifts of the Holy Spirit has often been obscured or lost altogether. In a penetrating analysis of this development, the nineteenth-century Russian Orthodox theologian Alexei Khomiakov notes that, in both Catholic and Protestant theology in the modern period "authority became external power" and "knowledge of religious truths [was] cut off from religious life."[11]

For canonical theists, the epistemic conception and use of ecclesial canons in modern theology is problematic in at least two ways. First, appeals to ecclesial canons as epistemic criteria have been and continue to be a major source of division and disunity in the church. Thus Protestants who appeal to the canon of scripture as the only acceptable epistemic criterion in theology necessarily find themselves disunited from Catholics who appeal to scripture, tradition, and the presence and work of the Holy Spirit in episcopacy as authorizing the Catholic tradition and church. The same holds, of course, the other way around. Similarly, Pentecostals who appeal to the gifts of tongues as the distinguishing mark of true Christianity or the true church necessarily disunite themselves from Christian traditions which either do not possess or which do not emphasize this gift. On all sides, appeals to particular gifts of the Spirit as epistemic criteria have been and continue to be the source of division and disunity within the ecumenical church.

Second, the epistemic conception and use of ecclesial canons is most regrettable precisely because it tends to obscure the therapeutic power of

---

10. For the relationship between scripture and divine revelation, see the following works by William J. Abraham: *Crossing the Threshold of Divine Revelation* (Grand Rapids: Eerdmans, 2006); *Divine Revelation and the Limits of Historical Criticism* (Oxford: Oxford University Press, 1982); *The Divine Inspiration of Scripture* (Oxford: Oxford University Press, 1981).

11. As quoted by John Meyendorff in "Doing Theology in an Eastern Orthodox Perspective," in *Eastern Orthodox Theology: A Contemporary Reader,* ed. Daniel B. Clendenin (Grand Rapids: Baker Academic, 2003), 87. The original quotation can be found in English in A. E. Morehouse's translation of Khomiakov's *Quelques mots d'un chretien orthodoxe sur les confessions occidentals.* For Morehouse's translation, see Alexander Schmemann, ed., *Ultimate Questions* (Crestwood, NY: St. Vladimir's Theological Seminary Press, 1975).

the Spirit's many and varied gifts to the church. In our view, canonical materials, persons, and practices are effects of the Spirit's presence and work in the church, the primary aim of which is nothing less than the restoration of persons to God, not epistemic justification for theological traditions or ecclesial communions. The obscuring of this primary purpose has been spiritually disastrous in a variety of ways.

For example, the obsession with epistemology invariably involves extracting from the whole of the canonical heritage the one or two ecclesial canons deemed most appropriate for epistemic use in theological argument. Such a move not only changes the function of the ecclesial canons to be extracted, but it also significantly weakens the charismatic power of the canonical heritage as a whole. In our view, canonical materials, persons, and practices are therapeutically most effective when functioning together. Thus Athanasius is right when he argues that, in order to be theologically and spiritually beneficial, the reading of the scriptures must be accompanied by the imitation of the lives of the saints. He says,

> But for the searching and right understanding of the Scriptures there is need of a good life and a pure soul, and for Christian virtue to guide the mind to grasp, so far as human nature can, the truth concerning God the Word. One cannot possibly understand the teaching of the saints unless one has a pure mind and is trying to imitate their life.[12]

Similarly, consider Nicholas Cabasilas's marvelous description of the way in which prayers, psalms, scriptures, and the Eucharist work together in the context of the liturgy. He writes,

> The prayers turn us towards God and obtain for us pardon for our sins; the psalms make God look favourably upon us, and draw to us that outflowing of mercy which is the result of such propitiation. . . . As for the lessons from the Holy Scripture, which proclaim the goodness of God, and his love for men, but also the severity of his justice and judgment, they instill in our souls the fear of the Lord, enkindle in us love for him, and thereby arouse in us great eagerness and zeal for

---

12. Athanasius, *De Incarnatione Verbi Dei* 57. It is worth noting that, at roughly the same time Athanasius was developing a list of canonical scriptures, he was also writing the *Life of Anthony.* Thus one can see Athanasius's conviction concerning the importance of a close connection between reading scripture and imitating the saints informing his own work as a theologian in a very deep way.

the observance of his commandments. All these things, which make the souls of both priest and people better and more divine, make them fit for reception and preservation of the holy mysteries, which is the proper aim of the liturgy.[13]

In line with their stress on the primacy of the therapeutic function of ecclesial canons, canonical theists are drawn to the image of the Holy Spirit as divine physician. The image of the Holy Spirit as divine physician affects and supports a fundamental shift in our thinking about the characteristic activity of the Holy Spirit. Instead of restricting our thinking to quasi-epistemic activities such as the inspiration of the scripture writers, the rich and powerful image of the Holy Spirit as physician invites us to focus on the Spirit's work in comforting, healing, enabling, empowering, renewing, and restoring to life. For that matter, on the image of the Holy Spirit as divine physician, even the activity of inspiring is not simply jettisoned or forgotten. On the contrary, it is transformed from a quasi-epistemic activity into a therapeutic one.

Thus canonical theists do not view the inspiration of the Holy Spirit primarily as a doctrine designed to secure the truthfulness of scripture. Instead, we think of inspiration in a way that is compatible both with the image of the Holy Spirit as physician and with the etymological sense of the term, namely, to breathe into, to excite, to make alive, or to animate. On this view, even the work of the Holy Spirit in inspiring is designed primarily to bring human persons to newness of life. Consequently, whether the Holy Spirit inspired the scripture writers in the traditional quasi-epistemic sense is not nearly as important from the standpoint of canonical theism as whether the Holy Spirit inspires persons reading the scriptures today, making them truly alive unto God and to one another.

In addition to transforming the way we think about the characteristic activity of the Holy Spirit, the image of the physician and the metaphor of healing immediately bring to mind the specific activity of prescribing medicine. This is most appropriate and helpful. Canonical theists conceive of the canonical heritage of the church as a grand medicine chest full of prescriptions that have the power to cure all that ails human persons spiritually, intellectually, emotionally, physically, and morally. The medicines are, as we have seen, the materials, persons, and practices that make up the

---

13. Nicholas Cabasilas, *A Commentary on the Divine Liturgy*, trans. J. M. Hussey and P. A. McNulty (London: SPCK, 1983), 26. For more on the healing power of the liturgy, see Paul Gavrilyuk's essay in this volume.

canonical heritage, including scripture, images, sacraments, episcopacy, teachers and saints, liturgy, doctrine, and so on.

That the Holy Spirit would provide such a dynamic range of medicines should hardly come as a surprise. After all, human physicians often give multiple prescriptions for common physical ailments. For example, a doctor might prescribe an antibiotic, rest, and a decongestant for the flu. Given the far more complex nature of humanity's spiritual disease, we find it fitting and natural that the Holy Spirit would provide a whole host of prescriptions aimed at the restoration of our created nature. Speaking of the priestly care for the body of Christ, John Chrysostom rightly calls our attention to that body's greater susceptibility to disease than physical human bodies and therefore to the comparative greatness of its need for healing, saying,

> People who are keen for athletic fitness need doctors and trainers and a careful diet and continual exercise and any amount of other precautions. For the neglect of a small detail in these matters upsets and spoils the whole scheme. Then what about those whose vocation it is to look after this Body which has to contend, not against flesh and blood, but against unseen powers? How can they keep it spotless and sound, unless they possess superhuman wisdom and fully understand the treatment suitable for the soul? *Or do you not realize that that Body is liable to more diseases and attacks than this flesh of ours, and is infected more quickly and cured more slowly?*[14]

At this stage, it is crucial to note that, while canonical theists maintain that the Holy Spirit gives a variety of medicines for our healing, we also acknowledge that each medicine has its purpose. For example, Chrysostom goes on to hint at the differences between the ways that saints effect healing in the body of Christ and the ways that priests and teachers heal through the use of words. He writes,

> In adopting the best possible way of life, you may be spurred on to emulation by someone else's example; but when it is false doctrine that the soul is suffering from, words are urgently needed, not only for the safety of the Church's members, but to meet the attacks of outsiders as well.[15]

---

14. John Chrysostom, *Six Books on the Priesthood*, trans. Graham Neville (Crestwood, NY: St. Vladimir's Theological Seminary Press, 2002), 114; emphasis added.

15. Chrysostom, *Six Books on the Priesthood*, 115. For more on the healing power of

Similarly, we do not expect the canon of scripture to facilitate healing in the same way that canonical images do so.[16] John of Damascus captures aspects of the difference between the ways in which scripture and other written materials bring healing on the one hand and the ways in which images bring healing on the other, saying,

> For just as the words edify the ear, so also the image stimulates the eye. What the book is to the literate, the image is to the illiterate. Just as words speak to the ear, so the image speaks to sight; it brings understanding.[17]

Later, in a powerful passage that depicts the church as a "spiritual hospital" and that calls attention to the way in which the canon of saints and martyrs often works collaboratively with the canon of images, John further illustrates the unique way that images bring healing. He writes,

> What more conspicuous proof do we need that images are the books of the illiterate, the never silent heralds of the honor due the saints, teaching without use of words those who gaze upon them, and sanctifying the sense of sight? Suppose I have few books, or little leisure for reading, but walk into the spiritual hospital — that is to say, a church — with my soul choking from the prickles of thorny thoughts, and thus afflicted I see before me the brilliance of the icon. I am refreshed as if in a verdant meadow, and thus my soul is led to glorify God. I marvel at the martyr's endurance, at the crown he won, and inflamed with burning zeal I fall down to worship God through His martyr, and so receive salvation.[18]

Nor do we expect images to bring healing in precisely the same way that the eucharist does or the eucharist to bring healing in the exact manner of the episcopacy.[19] Yet we also maintain that the Holy Spirit works in

---

doctrine, see Paul Gavrilyuk's chapter on scripture and the *regula fidei* in this volume. For the healing power of teachers, see the relevant chapter by Horace Six-Means.

16. For the ways in which images bring healing, see Natalie B. Van Kirk's chapter on images in this volume.

17. John of Damascus, *On the Divine Images,* trans. David Anderson (Crestwood, NY: St. Vladimir's Theological Seminary Press, 1980), 25.

18. John of Damascus, *On the Divine Images,* 39.

19. For the ways in which eucharist brings healing, see Natalie B. Van Kirk's chapter on the sacraments in this volume. For the healing power of the episcopacy, see William J. Abraham's chapter in this volume.

and through the various canonical materials, persons, and practices toward a common goal, namely, to make us "partakers of the divine nature."[20] If this goal is to be achieved, however, then it is not enough for the Holy Spirit to be present and at work in the canonical heritage of the church. On the contrary, if we are to become "partakers of the divine nature," then the Holy Spirit must be present and at work in us. Otherwise put, canonical theists are committed to a doctrine of the divine indwelling of the Holy Spirit. We need to say a word or two about this commitment before taking up the freedom of the Spirit.

For canonical theists, the divine indwelling of the Holy Spirit is the necessary condition that must be met if human persons are to become partakers of the divine nature. Even here the canonical heritage of the church plays a crucial role. Thus divine indwelling is generally understood mysteriously to occur in baptism. For example, speaking of baptism, Basil of Caesarea says,

> The water receives our body as a tomb, and so becomes the image of death, while the Spirit pours in life-giving power, renewing in souls which were dead in sin the life they first possessed. This is what it means to be born again of water and Spirit: the water accomplishes our death, while the Spirit raises us to life. . . . Through the Holy Spirit comes our restoration to Paradise, our ascension to the Kingdom of heaven, our adoption as God's sons, our freedom to call God our Father, our becoming partakers of the grace of Christ, being called children of light, sharing in eternal glory, and in a word, our inheritance of the fullness of blessing, both in this world and the world to come.[21]

It is important to notice the way that Basil piles up the metaphors in relation to the work of the Spirit in baptism. Clearly, when the Spirit comes, persons are no longer the same. On the contrary, persons are ontologically different. On the one hand, to be sure, they remain human. On the other hand, however, they are more than human. Having been raised from death to life with Christ by the power of the Holy Spirit, their lives are now eucharistically oriented to the source from which they came, namely, the Father.

The other important thing to notice is that Basil develops what we might call a doctrine of mutual indwelling. On the one hand, Basil speaks

20. 2 Pet. 1:4.
21. Basil of Caesarea, *De spiritu sancto* 15.35-36.

of the Holy Spirit dwelling in persons. On the other hand, Basil argues that we also dwell in the Holy Spirit. Thus Basil depicts the Holy Spirit as "a place in which people are sanctified."[22] Of course, what should be clear by now is that the result of this mutual indwelling is the elevation of human persons to God. In these passages from Basil, for example, we find ourselves being restored, adopted, calling upon God, sanctified, made partakers of grace, sharing in glory, and ascending to heaven. Of all the gifts that come with the indwelling of the Holy Spirit, however, Basil clearly regards *theosis* or deification as the most important. He writes,

> From this comes knowledge of the future, understanding of mysteries, apprehension of divine things, distribution of wonderful gifts, heavenly citizenship, a place in the choir of angels, endless joy in the presence of God, becoming like God, *and the highest of all desires, becoming God*.[23]

At this stage, an astute observer might point out that an irreducible element of becoming "partakers of the divine nature" is knowledge of God. Indeed, the doctrine of divine indwelling is closely associated with a doctrine of divine illumination in the tradition. We can see this close connection in Basil, who says,

> If we are illumined by divine power, and fix our eyes on the beauty of the image of the invisible God, and through the image are led up to the indescribable beauty of its source, it is because we have been inseparably joined to the Spirit of knowledge. . . . "No one knows the Father except the Son, and no one can say 'Jesus is Lord' except in the Holy Spirit." Notice that it does not say *through* the Spirit but *in* the Spirit. . . . [The Spirit] reveals the glory of the Only-Begotten in Himself, and He gives true worshippers the knowledge of God in Himself. The way to divine knowledge ascends from one Spirit through the one Son to the one Father. Likewise, natural goodness, inherent holiness and royal dignity reaches from the Father through the Only-Begotten to the Spirit.[24]

This is, however, a vastly different sort of knowledge than the knowledge sought by theologians who ask ecclesial canons to function primarily

---

22. Basil of Caesarea, *De spiritu sancto* 26.62.
23. Basil of Caesarea, *De spiritu sancto* 9.23; emphasis added.
24. Basil of Caesarea, *De spiritu sacnto* 18.47; emphasis original.

as epistemic criteria rather than as means of grace. One way to capture this difference is to say that, in and through the canonical heritage of the church, we come to know God "personally," and that through coming to know God personally, our natures are healed and restored, even enhanced. As Basil so eloquently puts it, "[The Spirit] does not reveal [knowledge] to them from outside sources, but *leads them to knowledge personally*."[25]

The Freedom of the Holy Spirit

Having stressed the therapeutic nature of the Spirit's presence and work in the canonical heritage of the church, we come now to the last feature of the vision of the Holy Spirit shared by canonical theists. From the standpoint of canonical theism, the presence and work of the Holy Spirit is characterized by *freedom*. Thus canonical theists do not wish to restrict in any sense the way in which the Holy Spirit can and does work to bring about the healing and restoration of human persons and human communities to God. The Holy Spirit may work in powerful ways through scripture to bring about the healing and restoration of some persons and communities. Similarly, the Holy Spirit may work therapeutically in and through the sacraments to restore persons in other communities. Still yet, the Holy Spirit may work through images, saints, doctrine, or even the episcopacy to bring about the renewal and re-creation of human persons. Indeed, from the standpoint of canonical theism, the presence of the Holy Spirit penetrates and sustains the whole of creation and is therefore free to use any aspect of creation to restore persons and human communities to God.[26]

At this juncture, some readers are likely to inquire about whether those churches that recognize and make use of the full range of canonical materials, persons, and practices are somehow in a better position vis-à-vis

25. Basil of Caesarea, *De spiritu sancto* 18.47; emphasis added. Basil's remarks here are epistemologically fascinating. On the one hand, canonical theists are interesting in developing further the epistemological dimensions of the work of the Holy Spirit. On the other hand, canonical theists have no interest in canonizing the epistemic proposals that may result from such work. For more on this, see my chapter on canonical theism and the primacy of ontology.

26. For the relationship between the Holy Spirit and creation, see Jürgen Moltmann, *God in Creation: A New Theology of Creation and the Spirit of God* (Minneapolis: Fortress Press, 1993).

the presence and work of the Holy Spirit. Here, canonical theists wish to say two things. On the one hand, we wish to encourage those churches who have neglected some of the canonical materials, persons, and practices to reconsider the ways in which the Spirit might be present and at work in the whole of the church's canonical heritage. For example, we would celebrate if some Protestant traditions were to rediscover the ways in which the Holy Spirit can be and is present in images and saints.

On the other hand, we refuse to say that those churches which lack some of the canonical materials, persons, and practices are necessarily deficient when it comes to the presence and work of the Holy Spirit. The reasons for this refusal are several. First, canonical theists operate with a principle of over-determination when it comes to the gifts of the Spirit to the church. On this principle, the Holy Spirit is generous beyond our wildest imaginations, giving us more than we need for our restoration to God. Second, we affirm the fullness of the presence and transforming power of the Holy Spirit in each of the canonical materials, persons, and practices. Thus we reject the notion that, if a particular church does not acknowledge, say, the canon of saints, the Spirit is somehow less present or less at work in that church. Third, we hold that the Spirit is ever-creative and therefore capable of working through, say, images and saints, even in those churches that do not officially recognize a canon of images and saints. In short, the Spirit does not need our permission to be present and to work among us.

Finally, as pertains to the freedom of the Spirit, we want to stress that, just as churches that lack the fullness of the canonical heritage of the church do not automatically lack the presence of the Holy Spirit, churches that formally or officially possess and make use of the fullness of the canonical heritage of the church do not automatically enjoy the presence and work of the Spirit. Put simply, the gift of the Spirit that really matters is not the canonical heritage of the church per se, but the Spirit's continuing presence and work in the canonical heritage of the church today. Without the gift of the Spirit's inspiring, life-giving presence, the various elements of the canonical heritage of the church are dead leaders, museum pieces, cultural artifacts, and the like.

As a gift, the Spirit's inspiring, life-giving presence is something for which we must always wait upon in hope and in anticipation. The model for this is the Pentecost event itself. Like the disciples, we must give ourselves to the task of tarrying together while we wait upon the Spirit. To be sure, our tarrying is to be a tarrying in expectancy. Yet, there is a fine line between tarrying in expectancy and tarrying in presumption. The Spirit blows where it will.[27]

Conclusion

Canonical theists believe that a robust vision of the generosity, creativity, and freedom of the Holy Spirit has both profound ecumenical significance and striking potential for the renewal of both theology and the worldwide church. The chief thing to notice here is that canonical theism's vision of the presence and work of the Holy Spirit does not lead to division or disunity among the churches of the world. From the vantage point of canonical theism, there is no need to be miserly in our understanding of the presence and work of the Spirit among us. Rather, there are grounds for recognizing in all the churches of the world the presence and ongoing therapeutic and restorative activity of the Holy Spirit.[28] Thus, wherever persons find themselves being renewed in the image of God, caught up in the life of the Triune God, becoming partakers of the divine nature, knit together with one another in the body of Christ, or beholding the glory and grace of God, there the *ecclesial-constituting* presence and work of the Spirit is to be celebrated in a spirit of thanksgiving and praise.

27. John 3:8.

28. For an enticing essay on the unity of the church in the Spirit, see Dumitru Staniloae, *Theology and the Church* (Crestwood, NY: St. Vladimir's Theological Seminary Press, 1980), ch. 2.

Scripture and the *Regula Fidei:*
Two Interlocking Components
of the Canonical Heritage

Paul L. Gavrilyuk

Canonical theism, as it is conceived in our collection of essays, is not meant to replace all other versions of theism but rather to point out a significant dimension that is often missing from them, namely, that the true home of Christian theistic beliefs is the canonical heritage of the church. Most modern versions of theism propose to update classical theism in the light of new epistemic proposals, scientific discoveries, historical-critical methods, moral sensibilities, and political agendas. Canonical theism calls for something quite different; it announces a massive retrieval of the church's canonical heritage. According to William J. Abraham, the canonical heritage of the church is constituted by materials, practices, and persons that formally or informally have been adopted by the whole church as canonical.[1] The canonical heritage of the church includes the following items:[2]

Canons of faith	Confessional statements and creeds
Canons of scripture	Lists of sacred writings
Canons of liturgy	Guidelines for conducting worship services
Canons of bishops	Approved lists of episcopal authorities

---

1. William J. Abraham, *Canon and Criterion in Christian Theology: From the Fathers to Feminism* (Oxford: Clarendon, 1998), 29; Theses on Canonical Theism, thesis ix.

2. This table is constructed on the basis of the list in Abraham, *Canon and Criterion in Christian Theology,* ch. 2. I take into account historical developments and speak about canons (plural), whereas Abraham focuses on the final results of these developments and uses the singular.

Canons of saints	Lists of the saints venerated locally or universally
Canons of fathers and doctors	Lists of authoritative theologians
Canons of councils	Disciplinary and doctrinal guidelines imposed by the councils
Canons of iconography and architecture	General rules regulating the depiction of God and the saints; rules of church architecture

By distinguishing eight components of the canonical heritage of the church, canonical theists call for a reevaluation of the standard scripture/tradition taxonomy. The acceptance of the latter dichotomy often leads to reducing the canon properly so called to the Bible, which alone is then invested with (variously qualified) normative status within the tradition. While building upon the premise of scripture's normativity, various accounts of doctrinal development differ in their emphasis either upon continuity or discontinuity between scripture and tradition.

In contrast to this approach, canonical theists propose to view scripture as a canon among other canons, not as the canon *tout court*. According to our reading of early church history, scripture is a canon that developed alongside the canons of episcopacy, liturgy, and creed, interacting with them in a complex way. In our judgment, this fundamental point is often obscured and at times distorted by the standard dichotomy of scripture and tradition. The canonical heritage, we argue, is a diamond with at least eight distinct facets, not a two-dimensional plane.

In this chapter I will explore the interconnections between two components of the canonical heritage, namely, scripture and the creed. First, I will show that they developed gradually by influencing each other in a complex dialectical fashion. Second, I will argue that the creed is both less and more than a mere summary of scripture. Third, I will demonstrate that these two components of the canonical heritage perform distinct and irreducible, but interconnected and in some cases overlapping functions. Finally, I will assess select contemporary revisionist accounts of Christology and canon in light of my findings.

A Brief Survey of the Forms, Origins, Contexts, and Select Functions of the Earliest *Regulae fidei*

It is commonly agreed that already in the writings that later became the New Testament, one finds confessional formulae of three distinct types. Christological confessions, such as, "Jesus [Christ] is Lord" (1 Cor 12:3; Phil. 2:11) are predominant.[3] Some of these statements appeared in the context of apostolic preaching and teaching; others probably functioned as hymns sung or recited in worship. Less common are bipartite formulae, such as, "there is one God, the Father, from whom are all things and for whom we exist, and one Lord, Jesus Christ, through whom are all things and through whom we exist."[4] In contrast, the distinctly tripartite confessions appear only twice, in the baptismal context (Matt. 28:19) and as a benediction (2 Cor. 13:13).[5] In both cases the tripartite formulae amount to little more than the invocation of the three names of the Father, Son, and Holy Spirit. In the absence of any developed theology of the Trinity in the New Testament, it would be naive biblicism to suppose that the two quite rudimentary tripartite formulae, and not any other confessional form, were arbitrarily lifted out of scripture to serve as future creeds. Although Matthew 28:19 and 2 Corinthians 13:13 were not neglected in the later trinitarian controversies, it must be stressed that the conciliar creeds cannot be reduced to embellished quotations from scripture.

The immediate precursors of the tripartite conciliar creeds are not the specific scriptural texts, but rather the ancient *regulae fidei,* which are well-attested in the second century. These creed-like confessions appear with repetitious persistence in the writings of such early church fathers as Justin, Irenaeus, Tertullian, Hippolytus, Clement of Alexandria, Origen, and others. Some scholars question the genetic relationship between the second-century *regulae fidei* and the fourth-century conciliar creeds on the grounds that the *regulae fidei* referred more broadly to the oral sum-

3. See Mark 3:11; 5:7; 8:30; and par.; John 1:1-3; 1 Cor. 15:3-9; Rom. 1:3; 8:34; 10:9; 1 Thess. 4:14; 5:9; Col. 1:15-20; Heb. 1:3; 1 Tim. 3:16; 2 Tim. 2:8; 1 Pet. 3:18; 1 John 2:22; 4:15; 5:5. For a classical treatment of the subject see J. N. D. Kelly, *Early Christian Creeds,* 3rd ed. (New York: Longman, 1985), 14-19.

4. 1 Cor. 8:6; cf. 1 Tim. 2:5, 6:13; and doxologies: Rom. 1:7; 1 Cor. 1:3; 2 Cor. 1:2; Gal. 1:3; Eph. 1:2; Phil. 1:2; 2 Thess. 1:2. See Kelly, *Early Christian Creeds,* 19-21.

5. A variant reading of 1 John 5:7 that includes reference to the Father, the Word, and the Holy Spirit should most probably be regarded as a later gloss.

maries of the apostolic tradition, varied in wording, and allowed for both bipartite and tripartite structures; whereas the conciliar creeds were set in writing, their terminological precision was a subject of public debate, and their form was consistently trinitarian.[6] I would rejoin that the fourth century knew extensive creed-making and creed-changing, that the original form of the creed adopted by the council of Nicaea had a comparatively underdeveloped third article (as did some other local creeds), and that the local baptismal creeds continued to be used and transmitted orally in catechesis well after the Council of Constantinople (381). While it is obvious that there is a difference between, say, the *regulae fidei*, attested by Irenaeus, and more elaborate and precise trinitarian theology of the Constantinopolitan creed, it would be misleading to reject a complex genetic connection between these sources altogether. In what follows I will assume that the ancient *regulae fidei* are the proto-creeds.[7]

The primary context, or rather contexts within which the second-century proto-creeds emerged and developed is a tangled issue. We mentioned earlier that in the New Testament such confessions were often found in the context of preaching, exhortation, baptism, and worship. Likewise, the primary *Sitz im Leben* of the second-century proto-creeds is proclamation, baptismal initiation, and adoration.[8] For example, Irenaeus cites the tripartite rule of faith in the beginning of his catechetical work, emphasizing that the proto-creed is foundational for Christian beliefs and conduct.[9] The use of interrogatory creeds in baptism is attested in Rome and Alexandria in the beginning of the third century.[10] The custom of *traditio symboli*, i.e., of the initiate's recitation of the creed by heart in the presence of the church's leaders on the eve of or during baptism was so

---

6. See, for example, L. Wm. Countryman, "Tertullian and the Regula Fidei," *Second Century* 2 (1982): 214-16.

7. Similarly, Robert W. Wall, "Reading the Bible from within Our Traditions: The 'Rule of Faith' in Theological Hermeneutics," in *Between Two Horizons: Spanning New Testament Studies and Systematic Theology*, ed. Joel B. Green and Max Turner (Grand Rapids: Eerdmans, 2000), 88.

8. W. Kinzig and M. Vinzent, "Recent Research on the Origin of the Creed," *Journal of Theological Studies* 50 (1999): 535-59.

9. Irenaeus, *On the Apostolic Preaching* 6-7.

10. Hippolytus (?), *Apostolic Tradition* 21.11-18; cf. Irenaeus, *Adversus haereses* 1.4.4; hints in Justin, *Apologia* 1.61. For the discussion of Alexandrian evidence see Paul Bradshaw, "Baptismal Practice in the Alexandrian Tradition: Eastern or Western?" in *Essays in Early Eastern Initiation* (Bramcote: Grove Books, 1988), 5-30; Maxwell E. Johnson, *The Rites of Christian Initiation: Their Evolution and Interpretation* (Collegeville, MN: Liturgical Press, 1989), 58.

widespread in the fourth-century church as to make an earlier, perhaps late second-century origin of this practice probable.[11]

Although the proto-creeds emerged spontaneously and developed gradually in the contexts of proclamation, initiation, and adoration, the *regulae fidei* soon also came to be used for polemical purposes. A good example of such use is the bipartite confession from 1 Corinthians 8:6, cited earlier, which St. Paul invoked as a statement against polytheism and idolatry. The apologists followed the same strategy.[12] Other ante-Nicene theologians frequently appealed to the rule of faith in their debates with the Gnostics and other heretics.

For Irenaeus, the *regula fidei* provided a summary of orally transmitted apostolic tradition. The bishop of Lyons stressed that because of the adherence to the rule of faith the apostolic tradition enjoyed stability and unity among the churches known to him.[13] The rule of faith was guarded carefully. It was the responsibility of local church leaders to interpret the rule of faith correctly. According to Irenaeus, no bishop could expound the rule of faith in such a way as to diminish or add to it in any substantive way. The proto-creed stood for the unchangeable kernel of the gospel (Gal. 1:6-9).[14]

Similarly, for Tertullian, the rule of faith was "immovable and irreformable."[15] Arguing against the heretical misuse of philosophy Tertullian declared that "to know nothing against the rule [of faith] is to know everything."[16] What Tertullian seems to say (if we take into consideration his tendency toward rhetorical exaggerations) is that the rule of faith determines the acceptable boundaries of Christian belief and serves as an unshakable foundation of theology.

It is often missed that Origen and Tertullian, their obviously different attitudes toward the role of philosophy in theology notwithstanding,

---

11. Cyril of Jerusalem, *Catecheses* 5-18; John Chrysostom, *Baptismal Instructions* 1.19-24; Theodore of Mopsuestia, *Baptismal Instructions* 1-11; Augustine, *De fide et symbolo* 1.1. Irenaeus hints at it in *Adversus haereses* 1.9.4.

12. Athenagoras, *Apologia* 10; anonymous author, *Ad Diognetum* 11.

13. Irenaeus, *Adversus haereses* 1.10.1-2; 1.22.1. For the discussion see John Behr, *Formation of Christian Theology: The Way to Nicaea* (Crestwood, NY: St. Vladimir's Theological Seminary, 2001), 35.

14. William Farmer, "Galatians and the Second-Century Development of the Regula Fidei," *The Second Century* 4 (1984): 143-70.

15. *De virginibus velandis* 1.

16. *De praescriptione haereticorum* 13.

held strikingly similar positions vis-à-vis this particular function of the proto-creed. For the Alexandrian theologian the articles of the *regula fidei* comprised the indubitable first principles, which formed the indisputable foundation of the church's doctrine. Having briefly explained the meaning of the rule of faith in the preface to *De principiis,* Origen observed:

> Everyone therefore who is desirous of constructing out of the foregoing a connected body of doctrine must use points like these [i.e., the articles of the proto-creed] as elementary and foundational principles. . . . Thus by clear and cogent arguments he will discover the truth about each particular point and so will produce, as we have said, a single body of doctrine, with the aid of such illustrations and declarations as he shall find in the holy scriptures and of such conclusions as he shall ascertain to follow logically from them when rigidly understood.[17]

It is clear from this statement that in the face of controversy with those who misinterpret scripture, Origen takes the rule that encapsulates the apostolic tradition to be even more foundational than the words of scripture themselves.[18] Once the foundational principles are established, scripture then helps to elucidate the points left unclear in the apostolic tradition. Not unlike Tertullian, Origen treats the proto-creed as the foundation, while rational arguments and scripture function as the building blocks of the edifice of systematic theology. We may conclude that for Irenaeus, Tertullian, and Origen the rule of faith served as a list of non-negotiable Christian beliefs, determined the boundaries of acceptably Christian worldview, and served as the summary of the apostolic tradition.[19]

17. *De principiis* I. Praef. 10; trans. G. W. Butterworth, *Origen On First Principles* (Gloucester, MA: Peter Smith, 1973), 6.

18. *De principiis* I. Praef. 2.

19. Similarly, see C. G. González, "The Rule of Faith: The Early Church's Source of Unity and Diversity," in *Many Voices, One God,* ed. W. Brueggemann and G. W. Stroup (Louisville: Westminster John Knox, 1998), 98; Joseph F. Mitros, "The Norm of Faith in the Patristic Age," in *Orthodoxy, Heresy, and Schism in Early Christianity,* ed. Everett Ferguson (New York: Garland Publishing Company, 1993), 445-46, 448. Mitros's claim that Christ himself was the norm of faith for early Christians fails to take into account the fact that Christ's identity was itself the subject of a bitter controversy. The revelation of God through Christ cannot serve as a meaningful norm if it is abstracted from the summaries of faith.

The *Regula fidei* and the Problem of the Bible's Unity and Diversity

It is commonplace among the scholars of Christian origins to emphasize the diversity of Christianity in the first three centuries. It is certainly true that the contours of acceptable belief and practice became more definite in the post-Constantinian era. However, it is not sufficiently emphasized that the diversity of early Christianity was substantially different from that of pagan religions and early Judaism. The concern for the unity of the kerygma, for the right teaching and practice was dominant in Christianity from the very beginning.[20] The pagan cults, in contrast, exhibited no tendency toward the unification of beliefs. While some syncretism and blending was inevitable, the cultic leaders showed no interest in reconciling divergent mythological accounts or providing one confessional statement.[21]

According to Irenaeus, the rule of faith was a confessional statement which secured the doctrinal unity and Christian identity of the churches separated geographically, culturally, and linguistically. Referring to the tripartite rule of faith, which he cites (with variations) several times in *Adversus haereses,* Irenaeus writes:

> Even if the apostles had not left their Writings to us, ought we not to follow the rule of the tradition which they handed down to those to whom they committed their churches? Many barbarian peoples who believe in Christ follow this rule, having [the message of their] salvation written in their hearts by the Spirit without paper and ink. [The rule of faith follows.][22]

It was primarily the adherence to the oral apostolic tradition summarized in the rule of faith, not to the sacred writings, that defined the Christian character of Irenaeus's community. The Christianity of the great church emerged and differentiated itself from all religions of the Roman Empire, as well as from most of its heterodox rivals, as a confessional faith, as a religion uniquely committed to the rule of faith.[23]

---

20. Gal. 1:6-9; 5:20; 1 Cor. 11:18-20; 1 Tim. 1:3; Heb. 2:1; Acts 18:26; 1 John 2:24; 4:2-3; Ignatius, *Trallians* 6.1; *Philadelphians* 2.1; *Polycarp* 3.1.

21. Athenagoras, *Legatio* 1.5.14.

22. *Adversus haereses* 3.4.1-2; trans. C. Richardson, *Early Christian Fathers* (New York: Touchstone, 1996), 374-75.

23. Similarly, Francis Young observes: "Christianity in the only major religion to set

I have shown earlier that the *regula fidei* cannot be derived from any part of scripture. It is equally easy to show that the rule of faith, no matter how elaborate its form, is not a summary of scripture.[24] The *regulae fidei* do not qualify as summaries of scripture because they completely leave out, for example, scripture's moral teaching. Most creeds provide highly condensed and fairly selective summaries of the history of salvation that dwell at comparatively greater length upon the earthly ministry of Jesus. Furthermore, unlike scripture, the rules of faith are not organized historically, but rather thematically, often following a tripartite pattern.[25] The fact that, for example, the Nicene Creed starts with the activity of God the Father in creation and ends with the hope of the life of the age to come does not undermine my basic contention that the creed is not structured historically.[26]

If the *regula fidei* is not a précis of scripture, then what is it? It should be noted that toward the end of the second century the proto-orthodox church achieved a broad agreement upon the content of the *regula fidei,* while it was still in the process of selecting the biblical canon, especially its New Testament part. In other words, the church possessed the rule of faith long before it came to possess the closed biblical canon. In the fourth century the church finalized its biblical canon as its leaders were discussing the precise wording of the creed.

The *regula fidei* functioned as one of the informal selection criteria for accepting a given writing as scripture. Additionally, the early fathers considered such matters as the writing's apostolic origin and its wide-

---

such store by creeds and doctrines. Other religions have Scriptures, others have their characteristic ways of worship, others have their own peculiar ethics and lifestyle. . . . But except in response to Christianity, they have not developed creeds, statements of standard belief to which the orthodox are supposed to adhere" (*The Making of the Creeds* [London: SCM Press, 1991], 1). See also Abraham, *Canon and Criterion in Christian Theology,* 35.

24. *Pace* Eric Osborn, *Tertullian, First Theologian of the West* (Cambridge: Cambridge University Press, 1997), 46.

25. "Story" does not strike me as an apt category for conceptualizing the function of the creed. *Pace* Paul M. Blowers, "The *Regula Fidei* and the Narrative Character of Early Christian Faith," *Pro Ecclesia* 6 (1997): 199-228.

26. This becomes especially clear if one compares the ancient catechisms based upon the history of salvation, such as Irenaeus's *Exposition of the Apostolic Teaching* and *The Teaching of St Gregory: An Early Armenian Catechism* (Cambridge, MA: Harvard University Press, 1970) with those based upon the articles of the creed, such as Cyril of Jerusalem's *Catecheses* and Theodore of Mopsuestia's *Baptismal Instrustion.* See my *Istoriia katekhizatsii v drevnei tserkvi* (Moskva: Sviato-Filaretovskaia Shkola, 2001). See also Francis Young, *Virtuoso Theology: The Bible and Interpretation* (Cleveland: Pilgrim Press, 1993), 48-53.

spread ecclesiastical use.[27] It should be stressed that the latter two criteria were comparatively more flexible, especially if we take into account the pervasiveness of pseudepigrapha and the absence of fixed lectionaries in the second century. Although the process of scripture's canonization was largely informal, it was the agreement with the rule of faith that proved to be decisive for shaping the contours of the biblical canon.

It was the great church's firm commitment to the rule of faith that protected its endorsement of the Old Testament as scripture in the face of Marcion's attempt to devalue the Old Testament as a message of an alien God.[28] Pushing Paul's antinomian statements to their logical limits, Marcion ignored the rule of faith and read the two parts of scripture antithetically. Other ancient teachers, including some Gnostics and the Manicheans, found Marcion's reading convincing and plausible. In response to such a reading, Clement of Alexandria emphasized the unitive function of the rule of faith, which provided "the concord and harmony of the law and the prophets with the covenant delivered at the coming of the Lord."[29] Commenting on this passage, William Farmer observes: "It is a truism that one can read the Law and the Prophets and come to very divergent conclusions. It is also probably true that one could read the Law and the Prophets and, considering the ministry of Jesus of Nazareth, conclude that the lack of correspondence between the two realities precluded a belief in Jesus as Messiah."[30] Farmer emphasizes that the extrascriptural rule of faith supplied precisely "the concord and harmony" of the two testaments, the vital connection between the Old Testament promise and the New Testament fulfillment that was not sufficiently evident (at least to the likes of Marcion) in the biblical text itself.

One could object that the pattern of promise and fulfillment is deeply ingrained in the Gospels and the other New Testament writings,

---

27. Following Bruce Metzger, *The Canon of the New Testament: Its Origin, Development, and Significance* (Oxford: Clarendon, 1997), 251-54. In a survey article Lee Martin McDonald adds the fourth criterion, antiquity, to apostolicity, orthodoxy, and use. "Identifying Scripture and Canon in the Early Church: The Criteria Question," in *The Canon Debate* (Peabody, MA: Hendrickson Publishers, 2002), 424-39; cf. Geoffrey Wainwright, "The New Testament as Canon," *Scottish Journal of Theology* 28 (1975): 555.

28. As reported by Irenaeus, *Adversus haereses* 1.27.2-4.

29. *Stromata* 6.15.125. 3; cf. Irenaeus, *Adversus haereses* 2.9.1; Tertullian, *De praescriptione haereticorum* 13.

30. William R. Farmer, "Galatians and the Second-Century Development of the *Regula Fidei*," *The Second Century* 4 (1984): 153.

which represent Jesus as the Christ "according to the scriptures." Furthermore, the Marcionite portrayal of an angry and incompetent creator God is refutable by the material in the Old Testament that speaks of God's goodness, mercy, longsuffering, kindness, and the like. Marcion was simply mistaken. It would seem that one does not need to have recourse to some extra-scriptural theological foundation, such as the rule of faith, to show that scripture possesses an underlying unity.[31]

As I see it, there are two main problems with this objection. First, it provides no way for adjudicating between the two competing visions of scripture, which we may call "antithetical" and "harmonizing" respectively. Marcionites would appeal to their set of proof-texts, and the opposition would produce theirs. Both, it seems, have a plausible case to defend. The strange persistence of Marcionism both on the popular level in the contemporary church and in some versions of modern biblical theology attests to the fact that the abandonment of the creedal pattern often leads to the disintegration of scripture's unity.[32] This point is brought up by Irenaeus in his critique of the misuse of scripture by the Valentinian Gnostics:

> Their manner of acting is just as if one, when a beautiful image of a king has been constructed by some skilful artist out of precious jewels, should then take this likeness of the man all to pieces, should rearrange the gems, and so fit them together as to make them into the form of a dog or of a fox, and even that but poorly executed; and should then maintain and declare that this was the beautiful image of the king which the skilful artist constructed, pointing to the jewels which had been admirably fitted together by the first artist to form the image of the king, but have been with bad effect transferred by the latter one to the shape of a dog, and by thus exhibiting the jewels, should deceive the ignorant who had no conception what a king's form was like, and persuade them that that miserable likeness of the fox was, in fact, the beautiful image of the king. In like manner do these persons patch together old wives' fables, and then endeavour, by violently drawing away from their proper connection, words, expres-

---

31. For an influential articulation of this position see James Dunn, *Unity and Diversity in the New Testament* (Philadelphia: Westminster, 1992).

32. For one example of a Marcionite reading of the New Testament by a contemporary theologian see Jack Nelson-Pallmeyer, *Jesus against Christianity: Reclaiming the Missing Jesus* (Harrisburg, PA: Trinity Press International, 2001).

sions, and parables whenever found, to adapt the oracles of God to their baseless fictions.[33]

Irenaeus compares scripture to a mosaic. The creed provides the pattern according to which various tessarae fit together to form a harmonious whole. Since the Valentinians do not accept the rule of faith, they "disregard the order and the connection of the Scriptures," says Irenaeus.[34] In the absence of the rule of faith, the verses of scripture could be rearranged to fit other patterns. As a result, scripture's integrity is ruined and its overarching purpose is distorted. Specifically, polytheistic Valentinian and dualistic Marcionite deconstructions become as plausible as the reading which endorses trinitarian monotheism.

On a micro-level of specific texts, the narratives of Jesus' baptism may be read and have been read as adoptionist;[35] the stories of Jesus' sudden disappearances in crowded places as well as the story of his transfiguration may, with some imagination, be interpreted Doceticly;[36] Jesus' acknowledgment of the Father's greatness and perfection as well as his manifestly human qualities allow for subordinationism as a major hermeneutical trajectory.[37] However, a reader equipped with the rule of faith as a guiding hermeneutical principle will be able to avoid the above-mentioned interpretive pitfalls.[38]

Second, one could respond to the objection that scripture's inherent unity is quite independent from the rule of faith by reemphasizing the point made earlier in this essay that the New Testament acquired its particular shape largely due to the church's commitment to the rule of faith. For

---

33. *Adversus haereses* 1.8.1; trans. A. Roberts, in *The Ante-Nicene Fathers,* vol. 1: The Apostolic Fathers, Justin Martyr, Irenaeus (Grand Rapids: Eerdmans, 1993), 326.

34. *Adversus haereses* 1.8.1; cf. 1.9.4-5.

35. Cerinthus's teaching had adoptionist motifs, if Irenaeus's report in *Adversus haereses* 1.26.1 is reliable. On adoptionist interpretations of scripture see Bart D. Ehrman, *The Orthodox Corruption of Scripture* (Oxford: Oxford University Press, 1993), 47-118.

36. See John A. McGuckinn, "The Changing Forms of Jesus," in *Origeniana Quarta,* ed. H. L. Lies (Wien: Innsbruck, 1987), 215-22.

37. This point is emphasized by Maurice Wiles, "In Defense of Arius," *Journal of Theological Studies* 13 (1962): 339-47, and *Archetypal Heresy: Arianism Through the Centuries* (Oxford: Clarendon, 1996).

38. See Wall, "Reading the Bible from within Our Traditions," 100. Similarly, G. R. Sumner and E. Radner see scripture and creed as "mutually informing rules." See "Introduction," in *The Rule of Faith: Scripture, Canon, and Creed in a Critical Age* (Harrisburg, PA: Morehouse Publishing, 1998), xiv.

example, Bishop Serapion of Rhossus (ca. 200) prohibited the use of the *Gospel of Peter* in worship on the grounds that the book did not agree with the rule of faith.[39] Without the *regula fidei*, the church could have ended up canonizing only one Gospel, as the Ebionites and Marcionites did, or the church could more liberally endorse as many as thirty-four gospels along with numerous pseudepigraphic acts, epistles, apocalypses, and so on.[40] The New Testament would have been substantially different if it did not have its point of doctrinal reference in the rule of faith. The reason why the New Testament Jesus is portrayed as the Christ "according to the Scriptures" is because those writings, which conflicted with the creedal pattern of the Old Testament promise and the New Testament fulfillment, have been excluded from the New Testament canon. The doctrinal and canonical chaos of the Gnostics would have been the fate of the great church if the latter had not been adamant about the importance of imparting the creed to its new members and using the rule of faith as a guiding hermeneutical principle.[41]

Select Modern Attempts to Read the Bible
etsi regula fidei non daretur

It is a commonplace among liberal Protestant and secular scholars to denounce the shift from doctrinal diversity allegedly found in scripture to what (in their judgment) became suffocating conformity and arbitrary doctrinal rigidity imposed by the creeds. In the previous two centuries historians of a liberal bent embarked upon the liberation of the gospel from the shackles of the church's dogma. The church fathers, thought Harnack, made a mistake of translating the gospel into the alien idiom of Hellenistic philosophy. For the prominent German historian, the study of church history became an emancipatory discipline. Specifically, the goal was "to set forth the origin and development of dogma, to offer the best means of

---

39. Eusebius, *Historia ecclesiae* 6.12.4. On this see McDonald, "Identifying Scripture and Canon," in *The Canon Debate*, 428.

40. Charles W. Hedrick, "The Thirty-Four Gospels: Diversity and Division among the Earliest Christians," *Bible Review* 18 (2002): 20-31, 46-47.

41. Similarly, Georges Florovsky, "The Function of Tradition in the Ancient Church," in *Bible, Church, Tradition: An Eastern Orthodox View* (Belmont, MA: Nordland Publishing Company, 1972), 79-83; Justo L. González, "How the Bible Has Been Interpreted in Christian Tradition," in *The New Interpreter's Bible* (Nashville: Abingdon Press, 1994), 1:90.

freeing the Church from dogmatic Chrsitianity."[42] As Harnack famously declared, the essence of the gospel was "the Fatherhood of God and the brotherhood of men," not some creed packed with outdated metaphysical notions.[43] Other scholars modify Harnack's version of *Verfallstheorie* and view the rule of faith as a product of the power struggle rather than philosophical reflection. They dismiss the appeal to the rule of faith as the bishops' attempt to domesticate scripture and to retain control and power over the churches.[44]

One may also recall that the first quest for the historical Jesus was predicated upon the central polemical contention that the central figure of the Gospels had to be distanced from the Christ of later Christian confessions. In his classic *The Quest of the Historical Jesus*, Albert Schweitzer succinctly summed up this common assumption: "That the historic Jesus is something different from the Jesus Christ of the doctrine of Two Natures seems to us now self-evident."[45] Equipped with naturalist presuppositions, the scholars who follow this trajectory commonly draw a picture of a purely human Jesus who turns out to be very different from the consubstantial deity of the Nicene creed.[46] Strauss's *Life of Jesus* remains a classical statement of this position.

Other biblical scholars standing in this tradition, while acknowledging that the New Testament christological material has a common theological core, take pains to show the dissimilarity of the apostolic kerygma from the fully divine and fully human person confessed in the Chalcedonian definition. Accordingly, for the scholars whose views fall into these categories, both Jesus historically reconstructed and the Christ of the apostolic kerygma have very little to do with the God incarnate of the church's dogma. Others, more radically, deny the unity of the kerygma altogether and argue that the New Testament presents several irreconcilable portraits

42. A. Harnack, *Outlines of the History of Dogma,* trans. E. K. Mitchell (Boston: Beacon Press, 1957), 7-8.

43. A. Harnack, *What Is Christianity?* (Philadelphia: Fortress Press, 1986), 207, 211-12; *History of Dogma* (New York: Dover Publications, 1961), 1:227-28.

44. This view is advanced, for example, by Elaine Pagels, *The Gnostic Gospels* (New York: Random House, 1979), 34-47.

45. Albert Schweitzer, *The Quest of the Historical Jesus,* trans. W. Montgomery (New York: Macmillan Co., 1968), 3.

46. This point was brought out most vividly in a debate between William Lane Craig and John Dominic Crossan, *Will the Real Jesus Please Stand Up?* ed. Paul Copan (Grand Rapids: Baker Books, 1998).

of Jesus which cannot all fit into the procrustean bed of the creed.[47] All agree that it is uncritical and anachronistic to read the theology of the creed back into the scriptural text.

While canonical theists would be prepared to challenge many of the assumptions of the historical Jesus researchers, ironically, some of their seemingly radical conclusions play into our hands. It is true that, for example, the creed cannot be read out of scripture. It is also true that, if one withdraws the unifying pattern of the creed, then the harmony of scripture can be easily destroyed. Someone who is not attuned to the melody of the creed will soon find a cacophony of christologies in scripture.

To use Irenaeus's analogy, without the rule of faith, various parts of scripture become like pieces of dismembered mosaic. One can make all sorts of theological animals out of those pieces, either Gnostic foxes and dogs, or, more fashionable in modernity, historically reconstructed Jesuses. All of them will bear little resemblance to the king, if the pattern of the creed is distorted or abandoned. The iconic Christ of canonical theism will disintegrate into cubistic Jesuses critically deconstructed.

The creed is integral to scripture as a properly functioning nervous system is integral to the health of a human organism. Those who undercut a vital connection between scripture and the creed, usually end up discarding for a variety of historical, philosophical, theological, political, and ideological reasons significant portions of scripture. Such a scholar is like a person who stumbles upon a beautiful garden of canonical heritage, tears out all the flowers but one — scripture — and then proceeds to peel off the petals of that flower until she is left with a bare stem or nothing at all in her hands. She then looks at the remains and marvels at the fact that they bear no resemblance to the garden in front of her!

Canonical theism is an invitation to cultivate the garden, not to pluck out the flowers. Canonical theism is a proposal to undo the damage made by canonical minimalists who reduce the canonical heritage to one normative principle and then proceed to create even narrower canons within the remaining canon.

The abandonment of the framework of the canonical heritage has created and will continue to give birth to the modern Marcionites, who

---

47. Oft-quoted words of Ernst Käsemann come to mind: "The New Testament does not, as such, constitute the foundation of the unity of the Church; on the contrary, as such it provides the basis for the multiplicity of the confessions" ("The New Testament Canon and the Unity of the Church," in *Essays on New Testament Themes* [London: SCM Press, 1964], 103).

would propose to abbreviate and edit the canon, as well as the modern Gnostics, who would presume to expand it. Recently, Robert Funk, the mastermind of the Jesus Seminar, managed to do both. With characteristic defiance, he put forward the following manifesto:

> We require a new New Testament, indeed, a new Bible, that will find its way into bookstores and on the internet in a section clearly marked "Bibles." There readers will stumble across it and be surprised at its contents. They will make use of copies in private study and in discussion groups, and carry those copies into their churches, where pastors and teachers will finally have room and warrant to respond to the issues being raised by biblical scholars, theologians, and secular critics. The effect will be electric. Let me amend the statement just made. We need not one new New Testament but several new New Testaments. First of all, we need one smaller than the current twenty-seven books to indicate that the quest is always searching for a canon within the canon. In the second place, we need at least one larger than the current New Testament because the church fathers unduly narrowed the scope of the founding documents in order to preserve their own definition of the faith and secure the foundation of their power. In the third place, we need a new New Testament that is differently ordered than the traditional canon, which after all reflects many mistaken judgments about the rise of tradition, both chronologically and theologically. In any case, our ingenuity in revising and redefining the function of canon will probably determine the future, if any, of the Christian tradition.[48]

Funk's proposal is not original. In the twentieth century the suggestions to shorten or expand the list of the New Testament books were even more numerous than in the second. To name only two well-known cases, Harnack thought that the church was now ready to dispense with the Old Testament altogether; Kurt Aland appealed to the international community of biblical scholars to abbreviate the New Testament with the hope of bringing about church unity.[49]

What is new is Funk's revolutionary rhetoric. It is akin to that of the Dada artists marching on the streets of Paris in the second decade of the

---

48. Robert Funk, "The Once and Future New Testament," in *The Canon Debate*, 555.

49. Kurt Aland, *The Problem of the New Testament Canon* (London: Λ. R. Mowbray, 1962), 28-33.

twentieth century with the goal to burn the Louvre and to redefine the meaning of art. When the police intercepted their original plan, the Dadaists organized their exhibitions in the public toilets.[50] Dadaism, although it now forms an obscure chapter of art history, managed to get the attention of art critics and historians because of the treasures it threatened to destroy. Funk's strategy is the same. His proposal goes far beyond the cool-headed historical scholarship that he professes to represent and becomes an attack upon one of Christianity's foundations, its biblical canon. Funk dreams of the modern-day Gnostics gradually infiltrating the church in a sectarian fashion, each with his own version of the Bible in hand, armed with the tools of critical scholarship. Funk's bold revisionist utopia is catered toward those who have imbibed extreme forms of modern individualism. His project is entirely parasitic upon the traditional Christianity that he promises to debunk. Ancient Gnostics had a similar strategy. Only they chose popular dualistic tendencies and murky mysticism, not individualism and Enlightenment naturalism, as their framework and then proceeded to take a well-known story about Jesus apart and to remake it according to their theological tastes.

Prominent biblical scholars such as Luke Timothy Johnson have already provided a first-rate rebuttal of the Jesus Seminar project.[51] I will not repeat their arguments here. I would like to suggest instead that canonical theism offers to change the rules of engagement. We ask, what is a deeper cause of the radical revisionism à la Funk? Our answer is that it is the loss of the canonical heritage. The overall message and the integrity of scripture are lost because the rest of the canons have been abandoned. Scripture will regain its voice when the canons of faith, worship, sacraments, episcopate, saints, and iconography are returned to their proper places. The remaining components of the canonical heritage will be considered in the chapters that follow.

---

50. See Herschel B. Chipp, *Theories of Modern Art: A Source Book by Artists and Critics* (Berkeley: University of California Press, 1968), 366-82.

51. See Luke Timothy Johnson, *The Real Jesus: The Misguided Quest for the Historical Jesus & the Truth of the Traditional Gospels* (San Francisco: Harper & Row Publishers, 1997).

Handing on the Teaching of the Apostles: Canonical Episcopacy

WILLIAM J. ABRAHAM

The quests for the historical church and the historic episcopacy are as tangled and self-involving as the quest for the historical Jesus. Indeed a position on one of these contested realities correlates with positions on the others.[1] Hence it is quite impossible to take a stand on the historical Jesus without at the same time showing one's hand on the nature of the historical church. The polemical and adversarial tone of much work in this domain is only natural once one realizes what is at stake. Historical judgments do not just reflect contemporary commitments; they are a means (and often a concealed means) of fostering and defending contemporary commitments. To take an obvious example, one's position on the status of the bishop of Rome depends on crucial historical judgments that reach right back to Jesus of Nazareth, to the historical church in its infancy, and to the historic episcopate. Ecclesiological claims about the status of the bishop of Rome are clearly falsifiable in principle by historical investigation. Hence historical investigation is invested with enormous theological freight.

There are no surprises here, for the same holds with respect to christological claims advanced about Jesus of Nazareth. To look upon Jesus of Nazareth as the incarnate Son of God, fully human and fully divine, is to commit oneself also to a network of historical claims about his life and ministry, not least his resurrection from the dead. Historical and theological work is simply shot through on all sides with rival possibilities that hang together. Efforts to clear a space for "historical criticism" that can

---

1. This was the deep insight of Gerald Downing's much-neglected book *The Church and Jesus* (London: SCM Press, 1968).

somehow act as a neutral criterion of success and failure have turned out to be illusory. Historical critics have their own theological and atheological commitments (if not agendas) that bear more or less on their critical judgments.

The drive to move to "critical historical investigation" coincided with a resolute dissatisfaction with "dogmatic" accounts of early church history. Influential Christian intellectuals discovered a massive gap between what their churches claimed and what they saw in their reading of the historical sources. The very notion of the historical Jesus is predicated on the view that the church got it wrong when it developed its vision of the canonical Christ of faith, whether of scripture or of the ecumenical councils. The various quests for the historical Jesus are essentially exercises in setting the record straight. The same dialectic of argument informs the polemic against the church's own self-consciousness, say, as the bearer of "orthodoxy" over against "heresy." Current efforts to trace the true trajectories to be found in early Christianity across the first four centuries clearly reflect the worry that later debates are projected into earlier disputes.[2] The quest for the historical church in all its teeming diversity and variety is meant to replace a normative and harmful theological vision of the church that cannot be sustained by the historical sources. Thus the contrast, or rather the sharp conflict, between history and theology continues to be the heartbeat of much contemporary scholarship.

It is clear that the vision of canon that became standard in the West over time aided and abetted this strife within the theological faculties. The canon of scripture was seen first and foremost as a norm of truth. Hence exegetical study of scripture became not just the first step in theology; it became the foundational and normative step that controlled virtually everything else.[3] Given this background, it was natural in the West after the

2. For some of the fruit of such work see Karen L. King, *What Is Gnosticism?* (Cambridge, MA: Harvard University Press, 2003).

3. This is very clear in the work of the great Philip Schaff: "The Bible being the storehouse of Divine revelation, and the infallible rule of faith and practice for the church, this exegetical department may be styled *fundamental* theology. . . . Where exegesis stops, church history begins — the two coming in contact, however, in the apostolic age. . . . Exegesis, therefore, has to do with the *regulative charter,* with which the revelation begins; church history, with the continuation of the revelation in time *past;* speculative theology, with the *present* scientific posture of the church; and practical theology looks to the *future*" (in Charles Yrigoyen Jr. and George M. Bricker, eds., *Reformed and Catholic: Selected Historical and Theological Writings of Philip Schaff* [Pittsburgh: Pickwick, 1979], 178-79; emphasis original).

Reformation for the various Christian groupings to make a straight appeal to scripture to validate their competing visions of church structure and polity. Roman Catholics, Anglicans, Presbyterians, Congregationalists, and the whole array of denominations that ensued insisted that they were the truly scriptural church.[4] This in turn naturally entailed that they were also either the continuation or the recovery of the embodiment of the earliest church. So the vision of canon as criterion was absolutely pivotal in reaching judgments both about historical matters of fact and about normative visions of the church for all space and time.

Even after the rise of critical theories of scripture, this correlation still holds. Thus Ernest Käsemann in a dramatic essay argued that the obvious diversity in the New Testament church mandated diversity in the church today rather than the kind of unity that was pursued in the ecumenical circles of his day.[5] We can see in this instance how the idea of canon as a criterion dies very hard indeed even in those circles that would have found earlier deployments of the canon as a criterion theologically otiose, dangerous, and nonsensical.[6] Critical historical investigation has relocated rather than removed the boundaries of debate.

The canonical theist finds much in these debates passé. This evaluation does not stem from capitulation to a particular vision of historical criticism or its current material options but because the theological vision of canon against which so many historians have protested is intellectually and spiritually barren. Once one has made the shift into canonical theism, one is free to look again at the historical developments that run from Jesus of Nazareth, through the apostolic period, and up into the

---

4. This development reached something of a crescendo in North America in the nineteenth century when Christians were set free from political constraint and let loose to go their own way. For a devastating (if intemperate) analysis of this development see John Williamson Nevin, "The Sect System," in *Catholic and Reformed: Selected Writings of John Williamson Nevin*, ed. Charles Ygriven Jr. and Geroge H. Bricker (Pittsburgh: Pickwick, 1978), 128-74.

5. Ernest Käsemann, "The Canon of the New Testament and the Unity of the Church," in *Essays on New Testament Themes* (London: SCM Press, 1964), 95-107. A similar position is developed by J. D. G. Dunn in *Unity and Diversity in the New Testament* (Philadelphia: Westminster, 1977).

6. The usual way to signal the continued use of the canon as a criterion takes the form of conceiving the scriptures as "authoritative" in some sense or other. The quest to find a way to make the canon of scripture an "authority" is insatiable even when the concept of authority has disintegrated and lost its usefulness. Authority has become a mere shadow or shell of its former self.

early centuries. Indeed, canonical theism as a program of research expects a fresh and fruitful yield that goes beyond the current options in historical investigation.[7]

The general conviction to be explored is that the church developed its canonical treasures and practices over time under the guidance of the Holy Spirit for broadly soteriological purposes. Exactly how this happened cannot be determined in advance; we are crucially dependent on sensitive historical investigation where there will be a variety of possibilities on offer. More specifically, the canonical theist will be on the lookout for efforts to push various elements in the canonical heritage into an epistemic role that goes beyond the available evidence. If we find that our historical investigation supports a more modest and less inflated vision of the various components of the canonical heritage, then one of the central claims of canonical theism will have been vindicated. In this essay I shall take up this nest of issues as they apply to the issue of episcopacy. I offer a preliminary narrative and a concluding commentary.

One of the explosive effects of Jesus of Nazareth was to leave behind a network of followers who formed a community of disciples and believers. Outsiders had their own way of making sense of this development, assimilating them to whatever linguistic and explanatory categories were to hand. Thus the main population at Lystra thought that Barnabas and Paul were appearances of Zeus and Hermes.[8] Insiders developed their own self-descriptions, deploying a wealth of metaphors to explore their identity and continuity. Beginning with the twelve apostles the early church also developed varied structures to meet the host of needs that contingently arose. Thus when a dispute arose about the distribution of food, seven deacons were appointed to create space for the more kerygmatic and pastoral work of the initial apostles.[9] Clearly the early Christians in Jerusalem felt entirely free

---

7. One critical area in need of work involves a revisiting of epistemological developments as these emerged in the history of the church. The standard accounts are far too overdetermined by epistemological commitments or far too underinformed by epistemological sensitivity to warrant too much trust at this point.

8. Acts 14:11-18.

9. Acts 6:1-6. I use here the language that becomes familiar later. Strictly speaking there is no mention of deacons as an office in the church. But we can detect here the seed from which the later usage develops. The Synod of Neocaesarea in 315 went so far as to insist that there could only be seven deacons in a local church: "Deacons must only be seven in number, according to law. This may be proved from the Acts of the Apostles." See John N. Collins, *Deacons in the Church* (Harrisburg, PA: Morehouse Publishing, 2002), 108. Some have argued that Acts 6 supplies evidence not of deacons but of elders. See A. M. Farrer,

to develop the institutional organs or mechanisms that were appropriate. Moreover, they insisted on the guiding hand of the Holy Spirit in their decisions and practices. This applies as much to the decisions of a council by the mother church in Jerusalem as it does to the appointing of a diaconate.

Once we go beyond this initial account as supplied by Luke, the history becomes murky. Between the deaths of the leading apostles and the beginning of the second century we hit a tunnel period where we have to do what we can to fill in what happened across a sprawling array of congregations started in ways that are often obscure and unknown. We know on the other end of the tunnel that there emerges a threefold order of deacons, presbyters, and bishops that eventually becomes the agreed practice of the church as a whole. The undermining of later dogmatic attempts to cook the historical books was a critical breakthrough in coming to terms with what actually happened. The work of Rothe, Lightfoot, Hatch, Harnack, Bauer, Kirk, Telfer, Collins, Sullivan, Brown, Nichols, and many others have exposed a rich if contested narrative.[10] The historical consensus that has emerged is remarkable, even though any story we tell remains fragile.

Three features of what happened bear mention at this point. First, the early Christians clearly saw themselves as constituting one people. Thus there was a deep interconnection that cut across the whole Christian community.[11] This is conspicuously revealed as much by disputes about identity as it is by the search for unity. Hence the move to include Gentiles without their first becoming Jews bespeaks a deep commitment to unity; the issue was engaged precisely because the protagonists cared about an identity that went beyond local options. Second, the initial institutional structures were simply taken over and adapted from the Jewish heritage. This was entirely natural given that the first Christian communities emerged from within Jewish synagogues and appropriated, for example,

---

"Ministry in the New Testament," in *The Apostolic Ministry,* ed. Kenneth E. Kirk (London: Hodder and Stoughton, 1946), 138.

10. Raymond E. Brown, *The Churches the Apostles Left Behind* (New York: Paulist Press, 1984), provides an excellent point of entry into recent historical investigation of what emerged after the apostles in various ancient Christian communities. Terence L. Nichols, *That All May Be One: Hierarchy and Participation in the Church* (Collegeville, MN: Liturgical Press, 1997), and Francis A. Sullivan, S.J., *From Apostles to Bishops: The Development of Episcopacy in the Early Church* (New York: Newman Press, 2001), are also exceptionally illuminating.

11. Karl Baus brings out that this sense of unity was in sharp contrast to the Judaism of the Diaspora in the first century. See Hubert Jedin and John Nolan, eds., *History of the Church* (New York: Crossroad, 1982), 1:146.

the practice of eldership already available to them. Third, it is clear that Christians through the Holy Spirit added new gifts to the body that went beyond the office of elder,[12] and that local communities experimented with various ways of internal organization. This was especially the case where the gospel spread into new communities that were outside the confines of the Jewish heritage. In this instance, one link to the wider body was supplied through apostles, most especially Paul and his assistants.

The tunnel period begins with the deaths of the leading apostles and with the destruction of Jerusalem. This double crisis that removed the initial leadership and virtually destroyed the model of the mother church in Jerusalem clearly created space for improvisation and development. Without losing a sense of deep bonding and unity, the scattered Christian congregations continued in the faith and used what lay to hand to preserve the gospel, to nurture new converts, and to hand over their treasures to new generations. Within this horizon, there is no need to underestimate the difficulties, disputes, and tensions that were bound to arise. These are patently obvious in the New Testament materials that pertain to the time both before and after the life of Jesus. We need only mention the standoff between Paul and Peter to make the point. The current attempt to track various competing trajectories, while fraught with risks, should surprise no one with a robust sense of history and human nature. What is astonishing is that the Christian movement as a whole developed and then appropriated over time a single vision of institutional structures centering in the office of bishop aided by deacons and presbyters.

Prior to this development there is common agreement that a combination of presbyter-bishops and deacons was one way of solving the problem of oversight and ministry.[13] The presbyter-bishops were probably cho-

---

12. Telfer points out that new titles (presbyter, bishop, deacon) were chosen so as to capture the specifically Christian functions that arose in Christian congregations. He adds: "But the fluctuating use of titles, side by side with another set of titles, apostle, prophet, teacher expressive of another set of functions in the Christian society, and different from those designating general functionaries in the society of Israel, suggests that it was the life of the community that was shaping functions and producing appropriate offices, and not a preconceived hierarchy of offices that was moulding the life of the community" (W. Telfer, *The Office of a Bishop* [London: Darton, Longman & Todd, 1962], 27).

13. It is far from easy to find a felicitous way to name the office of elder in the early history of the church. As is common, I use the term *presbyter-bishop* to designate one office that is described functionally in a variety of ways as elder, presbyter, and bishop. The crucial historical point is that there is a shift to a threefold office from a twofold office. The twofold office is clearly assumed in the Pastoral Epistles.

sen initially because of their age and, presumably, wisdom. In function they may well represent a fusion of two traditions within Judaism. Brown suggests persuasively:

> I think it plausible that from the synagogue Christians borrowed a pattern of groups of presbyters for each church, while the pastoral-supervisor (episkopos) role given to all or many of the presbyters came from the organizational model of close-knit Jewish sectarian groups such as the Dead Sea Essenes.[14]

The Pastoral Epistles, supplemented by Acts and 1 Peter, provide an important window into the ideal requirements of the offices of presbyter-bishops and deacons. Limiting ourselves to the presbyter-bishops, they clearly have a role in holding to the sound doctrine they have received.[15] The virtues sought in the office are of the kind needed in an organization that is moving into a second or third generation and that fit with the respectable mores of society as a whole. Thus stress is laid on self-control, family life, a responsible attitude to money, maturity in the faith, and absence of drunkenness. "Rough vitality and a willingness to fight bare-knuckled for the Gospel were part of what made Paul a great missionary, but such characteristics might have made him a poor residential supervisor."[16] The contextual and pastoral adjustments visible in this contrast are surely entirely natural and praiseworthy.

We can say without risk of censure that the move to a system of deacons, presbyters, and bishops arose out of the original Jewish model that was put in place in Jewish congregations but transposed to meet Christian needs. We can readily surmise why bishops emerged out of the order of presbyter-bishops. To begin, they filled a space in the system as a whole that had been vacated by the deaths of the apostles. Further, while presbyter-bishops were critical in overseeing the care of local congregations, unity across congregations required trans-congregational, connectional ties that could be supplied by bishops. Moreover, within the system of presbyter-bishops it was natural that there be a presiding elder who coordinated the work of the ruling council so that upgrading such a function would be relatively easy. Finally, it was natural that one group that operated as an instrument of unity for the whole have responsibility to carry apostolic teaching,

---

14. Brown, *The Churches the Apostles Left Behind,* 33.
15. Tit. 1:9–2:1; 1 Tim. 4:1-11; 5:17.
16. Brown, *The Churches the Apostles Left Behind,* 35.

practice, and identity across space and time. Lightfoot's temperate summary of what happened states the outcome accurately:

> They [the indirect evidences] indicate that the solution suggested by the history of the word "bishop" and its transference from the lower to the higher office, is the true solution, and that the episcopate was created out of the presbytery. They show that this creation was not so much an isolated act as a progressive development, not advancing everywhere at a uniform rate, but exhibiting at one and the same time different stages of growth in different churches. They seem to hint also that, so far as this development was affected at all by national temper and characteristics, it was slower where the prevailing influences were purely Greek, as at Corinth and Philippi and Rome; and more rapid where an Oriental spirit predominated, as at Jerusalem and Antioch and Ephesus. Above all, they establish this result clearly, that its maturer forms are seen first in those regions where the last surviving apostles (more especially St. John) fixed their abode, and at a time when its prevalence cannot be dissociated from their influence or sanction.[17]

Perhaps the most interesting experiment outside the Jewish model and its adaptation is that Paul experiments with a structure where there are no elders but where there are various charismatic offices and gifts.[18] As the Corinthian correspondence shows, this option, if it existed, proved disastrous when Christians went to court to settle disputes because they had no internal mechanism in place for resolving them. Contemporary attempts to recover this kind of model appear to fail as miserably as this one did. Yet we can understand why it was initially a lively possibility and lasted as long as it worked; in time it was simply superseded by neighboring improvements.

It is also interesting to note that both James operating in Jerusalem and John in Ephesus may have been profoundly influential in leading the church to adopt a single set of offices. Certainly, if they are behind the development in which a single presbyter was upgraded to the position of single bishop, one can understand why the church as a whole bought into this

---

17. J. B. Lightfoot, *Saint Paul's Epistles to the Philippians* (London: Macmillan and Co., 1883), 227-28. The other main option is to see episcopacy arising from imitation of the leadership structures of pagan clubs and societies.

18. There could well have been a gap between the establishing of local Christian groupings and later leadership development in the Pauline tradition.

option. This kind of backing strikes one as well nigh irresistible.[19] As the vision of monarchical episcopacy won support, the enthusiasm for it that emerged in figures like Ignatius of Antioch and Clement of Rome by the beginning of the second century was intense. One can detect a snowball effect that is well stated by Lightfoot:

> Though something must be attributed to the frailty of human pride and love of power, it will nevertheless appear that the pressing needs of the Church were mainly instrumental in bringing about the result, and that this development of the episcopal office was a providential safeguard amid the confusion of speculative opinion, the distracting effects of persecution, and the growing anarchy of social life, which threatened not only the extension but the very existence of the Church of Christ.[20]

Once established, there was still plenty of room for local diversity in the practice of episcopacy. Itinerant prophets, once tested, clearly were free to hold the eucharist as they willed.[21] Especially noteworthy at a later stage in developments is the fact that in Alexandria bishops were elected and ordained by a ruling council of elders. Massy H. Shepherd Jr., among several scholars, holds that "the bishops of Alexandria down to 328 were elected by the twelve presbyters of the city from among their number and were ordained by them. Athanasius was the first to be chosen and ordained to the episcopate in the customary way — perhaps as a result of the fourth canon of Nicaea, 325."[22] Moreover there was plenty of

---

19. Raymond E. Brown argues for a very different outcome initially in the Johannine communities in *The Churches the Apostles Left Behind*, chs. 6 and 7. Brown stresses the importance of the guidance of the Holy Spirit to individuals in the Johannine materials, but suggests that in the end one of the Johannine communities came around to see the critical importance of human shepherds: "[O]ne branch of the Johannine community had to come to grips with the ecclesiology of the pastorals, stodgy and formal as it is, in order to become part of a non-gnostic Christianity" (123).

20. Lightfoot, *Philippians*, 234.

21. This is clearly attested in the *Didache* 10.7.

22. Massy H. Shepherd Jr., "Response to Henry Chadwick," in *The Role of the Bishop in Ancient Society*, ed. Edward C. Hobbs and Wilhelm Wuellner (Berkeley, CA: Center for Hermeneutical Studies, 1980), 32. The early evidence for this claim comes from Jerome, Severus of Antioch, and Eutychius of Alexandria. See Everett Ferguson, "Origen and the Election of Bishops," *Church History* 43 (1974): 26-33. The appeal to developments in Alexandria became famous later at least once in church history when it was seized upon by John Wesley, following Peter King's *Inquiry into the Constitution of the Primitive Church* and Ed-

room for adaptation both to the singular personalities of the office holders and to political circumstances. These features are visible in the life and work of Cyprian. What had been a grand title annexed to vague assumption became "a substantial and patent and worldwide fact."[23] The complications that came with acceptance by the political powers that be in the fourth century are all too well known to bear repetition here. Suffice it to say that the added responsibilities posed a terrible burden for the spiritually sensitive and afforded a nifty opportunity for the arrogantly self-serving. Overall what we see is a church order that is stable in its basic elements, but where there is lots of room for adjustments and for local variations of style.

What did bishops do and what function did they serve? It is at this stage that critical issues about the nature of canon are joined.

There is no dispute that the work of bishops was varied. In broad terms it is clear that they engaged in evangelistic, catechetical, pastoral, and administrative work. They presided at the eucharist and ensured that the sacraments were properly administered.[24] They exercised leadership and in time joined with other bishops in resolving contested disputes. They had a critical (if not exclusive role) in ordinations to the ministries of the church. They taught the faithful. They were in charge of extensive charitable care. They suffered and died for the gospel. They defended the faith of the church against attack from within and from without. They contested their own authority against that of others, as we see in the dispute between Cyprian of Carthage and Stephen of Rome. They were critical agents and instruments of unity in the church as a whole. They helped to articulate the developing theology of the church as a whole, most notably in the case of Athanasius in the great dispute with Arias. They had a hand in working through to informal agreements that emerged on the

---

ward Stillingfleet's *Irenicum*, as a justification for his ordinations for the work in Scotland and North America. The developments in Alexandria constitute an enduring stone in the shoe for those who insist that there was a uniform vision and practice of episcopacy from the beginning. The situation in Gaul may well have been the same for a period. "Earlier evidence indicates that a bishop was made after being chosen by the clergy and the people and recognized by neighbouring bishops" (Telfer, *The Office of a Bishop*, 98).

23. Lightfoot, *Philippians*, 240.

24. The move to allow presbyters to preside at the eucharist is a significant shift in the fourth century and involves interesting changes in the ordination liturgies. John Zizioulas, *Eucharist, Bishop, Church: The Unity of the Church in the Divine Eucharist and the Bishop During the First Three Centuries* (Brookline, MA: Holy Cross Orthodox Press, 2001) is indispensable reading on issues related to this topic. See especially Part III.

canon of scripture.[25] They sought to preserve the manifold treasures of the faith delivered from of old. In and through all of this work it was assumed that the activity of the Holy Spirit was indispensable to the proper functioning of their ministry and office. We might capture this by insisting that the ministries of bishops, presbyters, and deacons were charismatic gifts and offices in the life of the church.[26] As such they operated soteriologically. They provided an indispensable function in preserving the life of the church across the generations. In this respect their work was absolutely pivotal and salutary.[27]

In time the names of bishops were informally listed so that there emerged a canon of bishops that was accepted across the face of the church. It is precisely at this point that we encounter the famous comment of Irenaeus that emerged in his dispute with the Gnostics of his region and that deserves to be quoted at length:

> It is within the power of all, therefore, in every Church, who may wish to see the truth, to contemplate clearly the tradition of the apostles manifested throughout the world; and we are in a position to reckon up those who were by the apostles instituted bishops in the Churches, and to [demonstrate] the succession of these men to our own times;

25. The role of Athanasius's Easter letter of 367 in providing a list of New Testament texts is well known to students of the canon of scripture.

26. They represent diachronic as opposed to synchronic charismatic gifts in the life of the church in that they operated across space and time rather than immediately in the life of the congregation, as would be the case, say, in the instance of the prophet. With this distinction in hand we can refuse the common move to set charismatic gifts against institutional gifts in the church.

27. It is sometimes claimed that the office of bishop arises from above rather than from below, but this is an unfortunate contrast. Kirk poses the central theological issue as follows: "Is the ministry 'from above' or 'from below'? Is it a gift to the Church from her Founder and Saviour, or an expedient evolved by the Church to meet the exigencies of her daily life? Has it a commission transmitted in orderly sequence from the Lord Himself, or is it commissioned simply and solely by the congregation of believers among whom the minister is to serve?" (Kirk, ed., *The Apostolic Ministry*, v). This is a false set of contrasts. The office arises both from above and from below. Thus the order of ministry should be seen as a gift of the Holy Spirit emerging in the vicissitudes of history. Adolf von Harnack makes a similar mistake when he sets up a very different set of false alternatives between the primitive Spirit-inspired ministry of apostles, prophets, and teachers who are succeeded by the routine ministry of the executive officers of the local churches. In both cases what is missing is an adequate pneumatology. This principle applies across the board in the development of the canonical heritage of the early church.

those who neither taught nor knew of anything like what these [heretics] rave about. For if the apostles had known hidden mysteries, which they were in the habit of imparting to the "perfect" apart and prively from the rest, they would have delivered them especially to those to whom they were also committing the Churches themselves. For they were desirous that these men should be perfect and blameless in all things, whom also they were leaving behind as their successors, delivering up their own place of government to these men; which men, if they discharged their functions honestly, would be a great boon [to the Church], but if they should fall away, the direst calamity.

Since, however, it would be very tedious, in such a volume as this, to reckon up the successions of all the Churches, we do put to confusion all those who, in whatever manner, whether by an evil-pleasing, by vain-glory, or by blindness and perverse opinion, assemble in unauthorized meetings; [we do this, I say,] by indicating that tradition derived from the apostles, Peter and Paul; as also [by pointing out] the faith preached to men, which comes down to our time by means of the succession of bishops. For it is a matter of necessity that every Church should agree with this Church, on account of its preeminent authority, that is, the faithful everywhere, inasmuch as the apostolical tradition has been preserved continuously by those [faithful men] who exist everywhere.[28]

This familiar passage has been the charter for an epistemic reading of episcopacy in the life of the church. It is not difficult to see why. Irenaeus appears here to be appealing to the canon of bishops as a norm or criterion of apostolic truth. Hence the canon of bishops is much more than a gift of the Holy Spirit that operates soteriologically within the church as a whole; the canon of bishops is a reliable mechanism for ascertaining the truth of scripture. More particularly, the church in Rome is a preeminent criterion of truth in theology.

In rejecting this inflated epistemic reading of Irenaeus I leave aside the obvious historical difficulties in his claims, that is, the claims about apostolic succession for every local congregation and the special succession in Rome connected to Peter and Paul. There were in fact Christian congregations in Rome before Paul got there. The picture is far more murky than Irenaeus allows. However, there is no need to doubt the sincerity of Irenaeus's claims; while the details are insecure, the wider argument in

28. Irenaeus, *Against Heresies* 3.3, in *Ante-Nicene Fathers*, 1:425.

context is convincing. Irenaeus is simply insisting that the Gnostic claim to have a special testimonial pipeline back to the apostles is false. And it can be shown to be false by consulting the chain of witnesses back to the churches that exists in Rome, Smyrna, the Asiatic churches, and Ephesus. This is more than enough to confound his theological opponents.

What we have here first and foremost is a reason for rejecting the Gnostic claim. However, a reason in itself does not constitute a canon or criterion of theological truth. Nor does it need to be inflated to this grand level to work effectively in Irenaeus's situation. Irenaeus's argument is a contingent apologetic strategy that works effectively. To be sure, we can then go on to construct an epistemic theory that builds on this argument. This, however, is another matter entirely. To pull this off successfully we will then need a full-scale epistemological vision of divine revelation, apostolic witness, transfer of truth across generations, the special epistemic status of the Roman episcopate, the location of the Holy Spirit in the church, and the like. To be sure, such arguments are indeed developed over time. But they cannot be constructed from this isolated argument in Irenaeus. As we can see in the case of Cyprian later, this kind of development was clearly rejected in the dispute with Pope Stephen over the issue of rebaptism.[29] It is not in itself constitutive of the Irenaean tradition; one can fully agree with Irenaeus and reject the full-scale epistemology of theology in which it is later embedded in the West.[30]

29. Cyprian called a council to discuss the issue in September 256. His comments are significant in rejecting an epistemic construal of Roman episcopacy. "For neither does any of us set himself up as a bishop or bishops nor by a tyrannical terror force his colleagues to a necessity of obeying; inasmuch as every bishop, in his free use of his liberty and power, has the right of forming his own judgment, and can no more be judged by another than he himself can judge another. But we must all await the judgment of Our Lord Jesus Christ, who alone has the power both of setting us in the government of his church, and of judging our actions therein" (quoted in Nichols, *That All May Be One*, 111).

30. There is, of course, an additional claim in Irenaeus that also bears on our topic. "Wherefore it is incumbent to obey the presbyters who are in the Church, — those who, as I have shown, possess the succession from the apostles; those who together with the succession of the episcopate, have received the certain gift of truth, according to the good pleasure of the Father. But [it is also incumbent] to hold in suspicion others who depart from the primitive succession, and assemble themselves together in any place whatsoever, [looking upon them] either as heretics of perverse mind, or as schismatics puffed up and self-pleasing, or again as hypocrites, acting thus for the sake of lucre and vainglory. For all these have fallen from the truth" (*Against Heresies* 4.26.2). The obvious problem with this move is that it proves too much, for the succession is now stated as coming through the presbyters rather than through the bishops, even though bishops have a necessary role in the epistemic

We can, of course, mount a more general argument about the work of the Holy Spirit guiding the church into the truth. Clearly, we can argue that Irenaeus provides one way of trying to spell out this argument. This more general argument strikes me as correct. It is surely odd to claim that the Holy Spirit breathes through the whole life of the church and then say that it is likely that the church goes off course where the essential truths about God and salvation are concerned. What this claim does is give us a reason for thinking that the church gets fundamental matters right; it does not supply us with a canon or criterion of truth. Nor does it begin to specify how we are to discern the truth in the church. It is enough that the church declares and teaches its faith in a host of appropriate ways in and through its canonical materials and practices. There is more than enough there to save our souls and to set us reliably on the path to holiness and heaven.

If we are dissatisfied with these arrangements, then so be it. We may want more. We may want an exact theory of epistemic reliability lodged in the bishop of Rome, or bishops more generally, or bishops in council, or the church as a whole, or the faithful within the church, or whatever. We may crave a detailed theory of faith and reason or of revelation and tradition. In time this is exactly what many Christians in the West came to crave. Epistemic desiderata were invented and then imposed as conditions of success that even God had to fulfill before we would accept the faith of the church as true. New believers were required to sign on to elaborate epistemic theories on pain of rejection. But to take this route is to work backwards from our epistemic desiderata to a theory of what must have been the case. God is told (albeit piously) what must be the case in the church. Against this the canonical theist is content to start from the bottom up, allowing the Holy Spirit freedom to use whatever mechanisms are thought appropriate.

---

system as a whole. Thus those who appeal to this text quietly drop the reference to the presbyters and limit the "certain gift of truth" to the episcopate. Moreover, Irenaeus introduces an element of virtue epistemology into this proposal that would need to be incorporated into any full-dress epistemology derived from this text. This virtue component is not a secondary element in Irenaeus's claim as the rest of the chapter makes all too clear. The crucial issue in the end, however, is simply that this text represents *one* effort on the part of *one* theologian to try out *one* apologetic move to support his claim that the church possesses the truth. This move (while it was picked up over time and made to serve wider ends) was not endorsed by the church as a whole. Nor does this move begin to supply what is needed if the epistemological issues in and around it are to be pursued with thoroughness.

If one follows this route then one will look not to an isolated element in the canonical heritage to carry the load but to the heritage as a whole. Bishops have been, to put it mildly, a mixed bunch. They have their own distinctive vices; and they can fall into error and sin like the rest of the church.[31] Kenneth E. Kirk, a bishop of great distinction and spirit, speaks volumes when he says of his own tradition: "when we consider the Anglican episcopate as it has impinged on the life and thought of the Church in history, we cannot but experience a certain lowering of spirits. English bishops . . . have been in turn feudal barons, Tudor civil servants, Whig landed proprietors, Victorian parliamentarians."[32] When bishops fail, it is surely a happy arrangement that other elements in the tradition as a whole can more than make up for the defect. Indeed, bishops, like Saul of old, are accountable to the law and life of the church. Providence has secured more than one way for the faith to be kept alive across the generations. Truth be told, there have been times when the lives and actions of bishops in the canon have been a grave danger to the life of the church. We need not have recourse at this stage to some of the more egregious examples of failure that have been the delight of Protestant triumphalists to make the case. The problem was there from the very beginning, starting from Judas, and it reappeared regularly thereafter. The wheat and the chaff reached right into the bosom of the church and its leadership. The provisions supplied by the Holy Spirit in the canonical heritage are more than enough to supply what is needed in the eventuality of lapses, mistakes, and even corruption. Providence works even through tainted hands and tongues; and in time the Holy Spirit repairs the diseases that beset the church across the generations.

Yet we can surely see how important bishops came to be and why we cannot dispense with them without great loss. There can be no community without responsible leadership and oversight. Current worries about abu-

---

31. For a sensitive discussion of this topic as it applies in the famous cases of Pope Vigilius (537-555) and Pope Honorius I (625-638) see Nichols, *That All May Be One*, 119-21. Nichols draws attention to the following fascinating material from the Second Council of Constantinople: "The holy fathers, who have gathered at intervals in the four holy councils, have followed the examples of antiquity [i.e., the apostles at the Council of Jerusalem]. They dealt with heresies and current problems by debate in common, since it was established as certain that when the disputed question is set out by each side in communal discussion, the light of truth drives out the shadow of lying. The truth cannot be made clear in any other way when there are debates about questions of faith, since everyone requires the assistance of his neighbor" (120). The epistemic suggestions of this passage are well worth pondering.

32. Kenneth E. Kirk, "The Apostolic Ministry," in Kirk, ed., *The Apostolic Ministry*, 47.

sive hierarchies tend to ignore this principle. In practice new hierarchies of concealed power and domination often upend hierarchies of responsibility and gifts. Moreover, turning to a book, say, the Bible, simply fails as an alternative. Books cannot provide the discipline that is needed in the face of the challenges that crop up in the life of the church. The church needs holy overseers who will give themselves body and soul to the care of the faithful across space and time. We need living, breathing agents of the Spirit who humbly and firmly exercise their ministry as a gift to the church as a whole. The same network of considerations applies to presbyters and deacons. If we abandon bishops, presbyters, and deacons then we simply have to find functional equivalents in other offices and committees. We can surely trust that when Christians have done so in faith, inviting the Holy Spirit to work, that their prayers are answered. Hence this whole matter is best approached with a hermeneutic of generosity rather than a hermeneutic of hostility and suspicion. Once we get beyond the kind of exclusionary vision that all too often rides on epistemic conceptions of episcopacy, receiving and sustaining the ministry of canonical episcopacy as it reaches back in space and time can be an occasion not for one-upmanship and hubris but for celebration on all sides in the church of the future.[33]

One reason for celebration would surely be the critical role that episcopacy has in sustaining the canonical treasures of the church. This is easily missed if we construe episcopacy in terms of our current experience of episcopacy. Where the threefold order exists today, bishops operate in a world that is far removed from the workaday world of local congregational life. They are systematically cut off from the grass roots, often work surrounded by assistants who are afraid to speak the truth, and spend countless hours in administrative and legal labor that saps their energies. They all too readily operate in an isolated fashion, trusting merely in their office to protect them from mistakes; it is relatively easy for them to gather their skirts around them and piously believe that they are above the church and the vicissitudes of history. Precisely because of this, many people resist the work of bishops and would be terrified if there were more of them. The solution to this dilemma is quite simple: we need more and less powerful bishops, not less and more powerful bishops.[34] Bishops should be close to

33. This claim has important ecumenical implications, but sufficient unto the day are the questions thereof.

34. None other than the contentious John Knox supported this move when he was confronted with the situation in England while the Elizabethan settlement was in process. Like many of the Reformers he was not an unqualified opponent of bishops; indeed, he sug-

the ground, should be deeply involved in local congregations, and should know their local environments intimately. They should be elected as fitting agents of the Holy Spirit; and they should fulfill their ministry in fear and trembling and in humble dependence on the Holy Spirit.

This separation of bishops from the life of the church was not the case when canonical episcopacy was instituted and developed. Oversight required close contact with the life and work of the church on the ground, as we can see from great figures like Cyprian, Athanasius, Ambrose, Augustine, John Chrysostom, and the like. In this situation ecumenical councils of bishops were appropriately representative; and bishops could know the persons for whom they exercised spiritual responsibility. Moreover, having more bishops would mean that episcopal authority is shared over a much larger network of leaders so that power would be radically dispersed rather than concentrated in the hands of the few. Given more bishops more closely connected to the ongoing ministry of the church, we would have more leaders set apart for teaching and sustaining the great treasures of the gospel.[35]

The sustaining of the canonical treasures of the church is pivotal for the welfare of the church. Such critical elements of the canonical heritage as the scriptures, the creed, the sacraments, proper worship, the canon of saints and teachers, and the like have to be in place if they are to serve the soteriological purposes for which they were developed. This is precisely one of the crucial responsibilities of the episcopate. If bishops fail to mind the store, then we can be sure that the materials, practices, and persons of the canonical heritage will fall by the wayside. In time the gospel that is mediated so richly through the canonical heritage will slip from its central place in the life of the church, and false substitutes will readily fill the vacuum. Of course, initially this will not be visible; churches can live off the capital of the canonical heritage for a long time before they wake up and discover that the vault has been looted. On the other side of the loss of the gospel, the church will splinter into a hundred pieces as rival networks of doctrine, practice, liturgy, teachers, and the like will spring up to offer their various brands of salvation. As these rivals enter the bloodstream, their adherents reach for epistemological strategies to defend their proposals; in turn these epistemological strategies give birth to a whole new network of

---

gested that they be multiplied tenfold. See John T. McNeill, "The Doctrine of the Ministry in Reformed Theology," *Church History* 12 (1943): 92.

35. All the faithful by virtue of their faith and baptism are, of course, responsible for the life of the church. Bishops simply bear a heavier burden and responsibility.

rivals; and so the merry-go-round continues from one generation to another until the faithful look up and are given stones when they look for bread.

The work of sustaining the treasures of the canonical heritage of the church is so demanding that it can be done only through the wisdom and power supplied by the Holy Spirit. Bishops who ignore this and turn the office into a secular profession are destined in the end to a life of incompetence and misery. Worse still, bishops who turn the office into an opportunity to impose their idiosyncratic vision of the faith on the church at large are a menace. We can hope and trust that they will fall into the hands of the living God. Hence we are not looking to the bishops as some sort of foolproof system against corruption, deviation, and apostasy. The bishops themselves belong in a network of materials, practices, and persons that can operate effectively only as a gift of the Holy Spirit in the church. There are no surefire ways of securing such faithfulness on the part of bishops. What we can depend on is the promise of God to sustain the church through hell and high water. In this context we note again that when this or that bishop fails, the Holy Spirit supplies sufficient resources elsewhere in the canonical heritage of the church to preserve the faith across space and time.

Canonical Liturgies:
The Dialectic of *Lex Orandi* and *Lex Credendi*

PAUL L. GAVRILYUK

Along with the canons of scripture and creed, the church over time developed canonical patterns of worship. The liturgical scholarship of the last century has made considerable advances in mapping the development of liturgies in the patristic period.[1] While the details remain contested, there is a general consensus that early Christian worship exhibited a broad variety of forms. Thus, Paul Bradshaw argued conclusively that no one common liturgical core from which later local traditions had subsequently sprung could any longer be assumed.[2] Toward the fourth century some of these forms died out, while others acquired more universal character. The post-Constantinian church, due to its better organization and more centralized structure, accelerated the process of the standardization of the major liturgical forms.

The development of the canonical liturgies, from greater diversity in the first three centuries to increasing uniformity in later times, parallels the process of canonization of the scriptures and creeds. The second century, as we may recall, was a time of remarkable proliferation of pseudepigraphic literature. Concurrently, the informal process of sorting out which scriptures represented the apostolic tradition and which did not was going on in the church. Toward the middle of the fourth century, the major contours of the biblical canon had been defined, although some gray areas still

---

1. Recent studies include Paul Bradshaw, *Eucharistic Origins* (Oxford: Oxford University Press, 2005); Enrico Mazza, *The Origins of the Eucharistic Prayer* (Collegeville, MN: Liturgical Press, 1995); Enrico Mazza, *The Celebration of the Eucharist: The Origin of the Rite and the Development of Its Interpretation* (Collegeville, MN: Liturgical Press, 1999).

2. Paul Bradshaw, *The Search for the Origins of Christian Worship* (Oxford: Oxford University Press, 1992), 56-64.

remained. The same century was also a period of extensive creed-making. The language of the creeds was refined with increasing precision in theological debates. The creeds of Nicaea and Constantinople over time were endorsed as the standards of doctrine. It should be noted, however, that in the dioceses outside of the immediate sphere of Constantinople's influence the local confessions of faith, not conciliar creeds, continued to be used in catechesis and baptism long after the Second Ecumenical Council (381).

One point of clarification is in order from the very beginning. When we speak of the liturgy as canonical, we mean primarily the shape and order of the liturgy, not the exact wording of prayers. We insist that despite the local variations it is still meaningful to speak of the canonical liturgies. To continue my parallels with the canons of the scriptures and creeds further, the canonization of four Gospels does not prevent one from speaking of the scriptures as canonical. In the same way, one could speak of at least three creeds — Apostles', Athanasian, and Constantinopolitan — as enjoying canonical status in the West. Similarly, in the Byzantine Orthodox tradition the three liturgies of St. John Chrysostom, St. Basil of Caesarea, and St. Gregory the Dialogus could be regarded as canonical.

In what follows I will argue that it is a mistake to postulate a one-way causal connection between *lex orandi*[3] and *lex credendi,* and that instead, there is a constant dialogue between these two parts of the canonical heritage. I will then discuss particular ways in which liturgy and scripture influenced each other. In conclusion I will consider three developments that have led to the destruction of the canonical liturgy.

The Interdependence of the Rule of Prayer and the Rule of Faith

In the history of most religions the acts of worship preceded well-articulated belief. Most polytheistic cults throughout history, while they had sophisticated forms of worship, possessed neither an equivalent of the creed nor that of scripture. To consider an example closer to Christianity, sacrificial activity in ancient Israel was in place well before the majority of the Jews came to profess monotheism. Similarly, the Hebrew scriptures began to be written, collected, and edited several centuries after the earliest archeologically attested Israelite worship.

---

3. The expression was most probably coined by Cyprian of Carthage, *De unitate catholicae ecclesiae* 13, with reference to Jesus' words in Mark 11:25.

Likewise, the early Christians had been singing hymns to the crucified and risen Christ "as if to God"[4] before they consciously adopted *regulae fidei.* As we may recall, the earliest creedal formulae, such as "Jesus is Lord," possibly emerged within the context of baptismal instruction and worship. Given the relative temporal priority of the earliest forms of Christian worship over the well-defined canons of scripture and creed, it is tempting to conclude that *lex orandi legem statuat credendi,* i.e., that the rule of prayer establishes the rule of faith.[5]

The fathers, it should be noted, frequently appealed to the liturgical practices of their time to buttress their doctrinal views. For example, Ignatius of Antioch pointed out that since in the eucharist baptized Christians partook of the real body and blood of Christ, they could not at the same time consistently hold the Docetic belief that Jesus' body was a phantom.[6] Ignatius was the first to establish a correlation between the reality of the incarnation on the one hand and the reaffirmation of the same truth in the eucharist.

In the context of the Arian controversy, Athanasius and other patristic authorities argued from the practice of triple baptismal immersion that these ritual actions assumed the equality, not the subordination, of the three persons of the Trinity. Athanasius wrote: "It was His will that the summary of our faith should have the same bearing, in bidding us be baptized, not into the name of Unoriginate and originate, nor into the name of Creator and creature, but into the Name of the Father, Son, and Holy Ghost."[7] It is noteworthy that the Constantinopolitan creed establishes the full divinity of the third person of the Trinity not by explicitly proclaiming his consubstantiality with the other two persons, but rather by stating that the Spirit "is worshipped and glorified together with the Father and the

---

4. Pliny the Younger, *Ep.* 10.96.

5. See Georges Florovsky, "The Function of Tradition in the Ancient Church," in *Bible, Church, Tradition: An Eastern Orthodox View* (Belmont, MA: Nordland Publishing Co., 1972), 84.

6. Ignatius, *Trallians* 8-10.

7. Athanasius, *Orationes adversus Arianos* 1.9.34, trans. A. Robertson, *Nicene and Post-Nicene Fathers,* 2nd ser., vol. 4 (Grand Rapids: Eerdmans, 1991), 326. See R. Williams, "Baptism and the Arian Controversy," in *Arianism after Arius,* ed. M. R. Barnes and D. H. Williams (Edinburgh: T&T Clark, 1993), 149-80. Cf. Gregory of Nyssa, *In diem Luminum sive in baptismum Christi;* Basil of Caesarea, *De spiritu sancto* 10.26; 12.28; 17.43; 27.67; Theodore of Mopsuestia, *Baptismal Instructions* 3.20; Nicetas of Remesiana, *De spiritu sancti potentia* 5, 7. On Basil see Andrew M. Manis, "The Principle of *Lex Orandi Lex Credendi* in Basil's Anti-Arian Struggle," *Patristic and Byzantine Review* 5 (1986): 33-47.

Son." Therefore, the creed makes use of the doxological practice as the ground for affirming the ontological equality of the third person with the other two.

Along similar lines, Basil of Caesarea pointed out that the tacit assumption behind the *epiclesis* was that it was the agency of the Holy Spirit that turned the eucharistic gifts into the body and blood of the second person of the Trinity. As an agent of sanctification of the gifts and deification of believers the Holy Spirit had himself to be divine.[8] A generation later Cyril of Alexandria explored a different theological dimension of the same sacrament when he argued against Nestorius that it was not enough to partake of the merely human body and blood of Christ in the eucharist in order to enter into the life of God. To Nestorius's charge that Cyril's explanation presupposed consuming and breaking into pieces God himself, the patriarch of Alexandria responded: "When we eat, we are not consuming the Godhead — perish the awful thought — but the Word's own flesh, which has been made life-giving because it is the flesh of him who lives because of the Father."[9] According to Cyril, it is precisely because God made human nature his own in the incarnation that the eucharist could become a point of entry into eternal life.

In the eighth century, John of Damascus argued against the iconoclasts that since the use of material substances of bread and wine was inescapable in the eucharist, it was both legitimate and fitting to acknowledge the mystery of incarnation through the veneration of other material objects, the icons.[10]

Since anti-Docetic, anti-Arian, anti-Pneumatomachian, anti-Nestorian, and anti-iconoclastic arguments briefly surveyed above rely upon liturgical practices in order to establish a controversial theological point, such considerations seem to give additional weight to the slogan *lex orandi legem statuat credendi*. Some liturgical theologians have taken this

---

8. Basil of Caesarea, *De spiritu sancto* 15.36–16.37.

9. Cyril, *Contra Nestorium* 4.5 (ACO 1.1.6.85); trans. Norman Russell, *Cyril of Alexandria* (New York: Routledge, 2000), 169. For the discussion see Daniel A. Keating, *The Appropriation of Divine Life in Cyril of Alexandria* (Oxford: Oxford University Press, 2004); Ezra Gebremedhin, *Life-Giving Blessing: An Inquiry into the Eucharistic Doctrine of Cyril of Alexandria* (Uppsala: University of Uppsala, 1977); Paul Gavrilyuk, *The Suffering of the Impassible God* (Oxford: Oxford University Press, 2004), 165-66; H. Chadwick, "Eucharist and Christology in the Nestorian Controversy," *Journal of Theological Studies* 2 (1951): 145-64.

10. John of Damascus, *On the Holy Images* 1.16; 2.14.

idea to its logical extreme and proposed that liturgy is *theologia prima,* that the rule of prayer is indeed the foundation of the rule of faith.[11]

Let us label the position that establishes a one-way causal relationship between the rule of prayer and the rule of faith "strict liturgical empiricism." A closer look at the history of doctrine will show that strict liturgical empiricism is one-sided, if not altogether false. We know, for example, that in Justin's Christian school in mid-second-century Rome, the converts were immersed three times in the name of the Father, Son, and Holy Spirit.[12] The baptismal practice, however, did not prevent Justin from giving his account of the Godhead a subordinationist cast.

It is also clear that Arius and Alexander of Alexandria attended services that did not differ considerably from one another. However, Arius's conclusions regarding the divinity of the Son were substantially different from those of his bishop.[13] Later Arians, for example, could appeal to the fact that the main addressee of the eucharistic prayers was God the Father alone. For the anonymous neo-Arian editor of the *Apostolic Constitutions* the accentuation of the higher status of God the Father became a dominant liturgical concern.[14] It follows that liturgical practices are fraught with theological ambiguities and often cannot resolve even the most fundamental doctrinal disputes conclusively.

What is more important, in many cases it was the *lex credendi* that influenced and even brought about changes and innovations in the *lex orandi.* To draw upon our last example, some fourth-century eucharistic prayers underwent editorial changes in the hands of pro-Nicene liturgists and became more explicitly trinitarian.[15] For instance, in the liturgy of St. John Chrysostom the prayers addressed exclusively to God the Father with time came to be addressed to all three persons of the Trinity.

---

11. Aidan Kavanagh, *On Liturgical Theology* (New York: Pueblo, 1984), 74-75, 89; Gordon W. Lathrop, *Holy Things: A Liturgical Theology* (Minneapolis: Fortress, 1993).

12. Justin, *Apologia* 1.61: "for they are washed in the water in the name of God the Father and Master of All, and of our Savior Jesus Christ, and of the Holy Spirit."

13. I owe the insight expressed in the last two sentences to a comment made by Professor William Babcock at one of the canonical theism conferences.

14. *Apostolic Constitutions* 8.12. On the neo-Arian character of this work see Georges Wagner, "Une Liturgie Anoméenne," in *Trinité et liturgie,* ed. A. M. Triacca and A. Pistoia (Rome: Edizioni Liturgiche, 1984), 385-93; Tomáš Kopeček, "Neo-Arian Religion: The Evidence of the *Apostolic Constitutions*," in *Arianism: Historical and Theological Reassessments* (Cambridge, MA: Philadelphia Patristic Foundation, 1985), 153-79.

15. Robert Taft, "On Eastern and Western Liturgy," 9, at http://www.praiseofglory.com/taftliturgy.htm.

As for the appeals to the rite of baptism, the meaning of the rite, when applied to different groups of people, was far from transparent. At the turn of the second century Tertullian could challenge the practice of infant baptism on the grounds that infants and small children were innocent and did not require the washing of sins.[16] Two centuries later Augustine had recourse to the (by his time fairly common) practice of infant baptism to support the position diametrically opposite to that of Tertullian, i.e., that it was expedient for infants to be baptized since they too had to be washed of the stain and guilt of original sin.[17] It is clear from this example that the same ritual action, depending upon its application, could justify two very different theological anthropologies.

In later Arianism it was precisely the *lex credendi* that brought about significant changes in the *lex orandi*, when the triple immersion was reinterpreted to symbolize Christ's three-day burial in the tomb. The pro-Nicenes were quick to point out that, strictly speaking, Christ did not spend three full days in the tomb, but only a day and a half from Friday afternoon to Sunday morning. Partly in response to this objection and partly following the logic of their subordinationist doctrine, some Eunomians reduced the number of immersions to just one.[18] The heretics were not the only ones to initiate such bold innovations. According to his opponents, Basil the Great was innovating when he endorsed the doxology "glory to the Father with the Son together with the Holy Spirit" in Caesarea side by side with an older one: "glory to the Father through the Son in the Holy Spirit."[19] In Basil's mind the change of conjunctions reinforced the idea of equality of the three divine persons by making all of them, not God the Father alone, the objects of praise.

It goes without saying that theologically sophisticated Byzantine hymnography was more a fruit of a sustained theological reflection than an expression of spontaneous religious feeling. Byzantine hymnography is didactic in character. It was for the purpose of instructing the faithful that the Constantinopolitan creed (with local variations), previously reserved for baptismal initiation alone, was introduced for public recitation in the liturgies of the East and West in the sixth century.[20] The primal experience

16. Tertullian, *De baptismo* 18.
17. Augustine, *De gratia Christi et de peccato originali* 32.35.
18. Didymus the Blind, *De trinitate* 2.15 (PG 39:720).
19. Basil of Caesarea, *De spiritu sancto* 1.3.
20. Bernard Capelle, "L'introduction du symbole à la messe," in *Mélanges Joseph de*

of God in prayer is transformed by engagement with other theological resources available in the canonical heritage. It is true that the *lex orandi* in some cases established the *lex credendi*. As Irenaeus put it, "our opinion is in accordance with the Eucharist, and the Eucharist in turn establishes our opinion."[21] But it is equally indisputable that the *lex credendi* likewise informed and shaped the *lex orandi*. In the words attributed to Prosper of Aquitaine, *lex credendi legem statuat supplicandi*. What we believe influences how we pray, and vice versa. Therefore, in the Christian tradition of the first millennium one finds a complex dialogue between the rule of prayer and the rule of faith.

The Interdependence of the Canon of Scripture and the Rule of Prayer

The interconnections between scripture and liturgy are equally intricate and multifaceted. The canon of the New Testament, as it is often recognized, owes much of its present shape and content to the early forms of Christian worship. While the original use of some texts remains debatable, modern form critics have shown that the New Testament authors often cite hymnographic and liturgical material.[22] The reader may recall that this situation parallels the earliest Christian confessions or proto-creeds that could similarly be found in the New Testament.[23] The so-called pan-liturgists hold a stronger view that *all* New Testament material was liturgically molded to various degrees.[24] While this is less likely, it is certain that some biblical narratives do echo early liturgy. To mention just two well-known examples, both the miracle of multiplication of bread and fish and the story of Jesus' appearance before his disciples on the road to Emmaus

---

Ghellinck, S.J. (Gembloux: J. Duculot, 1951), 1003-27; Paul Gavrilyuk, *Istoriia katekhizatsii v drevnei tserkvi* (Moskva: Sviato-Filaretovskaia shkola, 2001), 208, 245.

21. Irenaeus, *Adversus haereses* 4.18.4.

22. Mark 11:9-10; Matt. 21:9; Luke 1:46-55, 68-79; 2:10-14, 29-32; 19:38; John 1:1-18; Phil. 2:6-11; 1 Cor. 8:6; 13:1-13; Rom. 8:35-39; 13:11-12; 16:25-27; Col. 1:1-15; Eph. 4:3-6; 5:14; Heb. 12:22-24; 1 Pet. 3:18-22; 3:22-25; 4:11; 5:10-11; 1 Tim. 1:17; 3:16; Rev. 1:5-8; 4:11; 5:12-13; 11:17-18; 15:3-4; 18:2-23; 19:1-9; 22:16-17, 20. List taken from F. Forrester Church and Terrence J. Mulry, *The Macmillan Book of Earliest Christian Hymns* (New York: Macmillan Publishing Co., 1988), 1-28.

23. See p. 29 above.

24. For an excellent survey and criticism of pan-liturgism see Bradshaw, *The Search for the Origins of Early Christian Worship*, 30-36.

have strong eucharistic overtones reflected in their resemblances to the Last Supper narratives.

The New Testament is a liturgical book in a broader sense, inasmuch as liturgical use proved to be such an important informal criterion for determining the boundaries of the biblical canon. In fact, it was precisely the proclamation and homiletic exposition of the "memoirs of the apostles"[25] during communal worship that gave to some writings associated with the apostolic times the status of scripture. Conversely, Irenaeus held that since the Gnostic gospels were not in use in the catholic churches these writings could not be regarded as representing the apostolic teaching.[26] Early Christian worship not only defined the final form of certain New Testament passages, but was also integral to the process of the canonization of scripture.

The impact of scripture upon early worship was equally profound. For the apostles, it was the Law and the Prophets that functioned as scripture. Although the exact contours of the Writings were defined only toward the end of the first century or even later,[27] the Psalms were widely used by the early Christians in communal prayer and private devotion. Christian worship grew out of the practices of the synagogue, the Temple, daily Jewish prayer, and specific traditions, like the Last Supper, associated with the recorded memory of Jesus. It should be emphasized, however, that the narrative of the Last Supper found in the Synoptics and alluded to in Johannine and Pauline writings had already been molded by liturgical use of local communities.

The Synoptic account of the Last Supper did not enjoy equally strong influence upon all early Christian communities. For example, the blessings over bread and wine in the eucharistic meal described in *Didache* 9–10 do not include the words of institution.[28] Some other early Syrian *anaphorae*, such as that of the apostles Addai and Mari, equally lack this key component of the New Testament account of the Last Supper.[29] It follows that

---

25. Justin, *Apologia* 1.67.

26. Irenaeus, *Adversus haereses* 3.11.9.

27. See Jack P. Lewis, "Jamnia Revisited," in *The Canon Debate,* ed. Lee Martin McDonald and James A. Sanders (Peabody, MA: Hendrickson, 2002), 126-62.

28. I take the majority view that the *Didache* describes a eucharistic meal, not a non-eucharistic agape. See Willi Rordorf, "The Didache," in *The Eucharist of the Early Christians* (New York: Pueblo, 1978), 3-9.

29. See Enrico Mazza, *The Celebration of the Eucharist: The Origin of the Rite and the Development of Its Interpretation* (Collegeville, MN: Liturgical Press, 1999), 72-73, with an excellent bibliography. This issue has recently become an ecumenical problem in Syria in the

these ancient eucharistic canons show a high degree of independence from the relevant New Testament accounts. An *anaphora* without the words of institution could not possibly be based upon the practice described in the New Testament in any direct way.

Toward the end of the second century[30] some *anaphorae* came to include the *epiclesis*, i.e., the invocation of the Holy Spirit upon the celebrant, those present, and the bread and wine. Basil of Caesarea considered this development to be a part of the church's unwritten tradition, not contained in Scripture:

> Concerning the teachings of the Church, whether publicly proclaimed *(kerygma)*, or reserved to members of the household of faith *(dogmata)*, we have received some from written sources, while others have been given to us secretly, through apostolic tradition. Both sources have equal force in true religion. No one would deny either source — no one, at any rate, who is even slightly familiar with the ordinances of the Church. If we attacked unwritten customs, claiming them to be of little importance, we would fatally mutilate the Gospel, no matter what our intentions — or rather we would reduce the Gospel teachings to bare words. For instance (to take the first and most common example), where is the written teaching that we should sign with the sign of the cross those who, trusting in the Name of Our Lord Jesus Christ, are to be enrolled as catechumens? Which book teaches us to pray facing the East? Have any saints left for us in writing the words used in the invocation *(epiklesis)* over the Eucharistic bread and the cup of blessing? As everyone knows, we are not content in the liturgy simply to recite the words recorded by St Paul or the Gospels, but we add other words both before and after, words of great importance for this mystery. We have received these words from unwritten teaching.[31]

Basil proceeds to enumerate other unwritten customs not mentioned in scripture: the blessing of baptismal water, chrismation, triple immersion, renunciation of Satan, standing for prayer on Sunday and during

---

intercommunion of the Chaldean Christians who use the East Syrian liturgy of the apostles Addai and Mari, which has no words of institution, and the Eastern Rite Catholics for whom the words of institution are a necessary part of the eucharistic canon.

30. The earliest example is recorded by Hippolytus(?), *Apostolic Tradition* 4.12.

31. Basil of Caesarea, *De spiritu sancto* 27.66; trans. David Anderson, *On the Holy Spirit* (Crestwood, NY: St. Vladimir's Theological Seminary Press), 98-99.

the season of Pentecost, and, finally, the wording of the trinitarian doxology.[32] According to Basil, Christian worship cannot be derived from scripture alone. It is rooted in an equally authoritative unwritten component of the apostolic tradition. It would be wrong to reduce this vital component to secondary local customs and to insignificant ritual elements. In the Cappadocian bishop's mind, the unwritten tradition is much more than that. To attack the unwritten tradition is to mutilate the gospel, to reduce scripture's teaching to bare words. Elsewhere Basil identifies this tradition with the "unwritten testimony of the Fathers," which functions as a "standard of teaching" in baptismal catechesis.[33] This liturgical tradition provided a framework for discerning the mind of scripture.

We are now in a better position to discuss the main components of the canonical liturgies. To reiterate my earlier observation, the canon of the liturgy must not be identified with any particular liturgical text frozen in time. There are certainly many important historical instantiations of the canonical liturgies, such as the ancient Roman Mass or the liturgy of St. John Chrysostom.

The canonical liturgy is divided into the two major parts (excluding the preparation of the gifts): the liturgy of the catechumens and the liturgy of the faithful. The first part includes prayers, hymns, litanies, scripture readings, and a homily. The core of the second part is the *anaphora*. The major elements of the *anaphora*, as it developed toward the end of the fourth century, include entrance with the gifts, introductory dialogue, preface, *sanctus*, post-*sanctus*, words of institution, *anamnesis, epiclesis,* litanies, Lord's Prayer, offertory, communion with post-communion prayers, and dismissal. While I am reproducing these elements in their traditional order, some ancient liturgies depart from this plan by incorporating other elements. With time the liturgical *ordo* became more complex and came to include, for example, the recitation of the creed.

It is not my task here to elaborate on the function of each of these elements or to offer a theological account of how they function within the liturgy.[34] Clearly, all of these elements are not of equal value. Litanies, for example, represent an element of lesser significance than, say, the words of institution, or *epiclesis,* or communion itself. What is important, however,

---

32. Basil of Caesarea, *De spiritu sancto* 27.66.

33. Basil of Caesarea, *De spiritu sancto* 10.25-26.

34. On this see, e.g., Alexander Schmemann, *The Eucharist* (Crestwood, NY: St. Vladimir's Theological Seminary Press, 1988).

is that all these elements form a coherent and organic whole. The *anaphora*, clearly, is not a mere reproduction of the Last Supper in its historical details. The pattern of the liturgy developed to a great extent independently from the New Testament accounts of early Christian worship. At the same time, it is the law of liturgical studies that with time the church's prayers absorbed more and more quotations and allusions to biblical material. Thus, there is a subtle interpenetration, a *perichoresis,* between the canon of scripture and the canon of liturgy. In prayer both canons are united, and yet distinct; both feed into each other, but one canon cannot be reduced to the other.

Conclusion

As I have shown, there is a continuous dialogue between the canons of scripture, creed, and liturgy throughout Christian history. There are various ways in which the integrity of each of the canons and the harmonious balance between them could be violated. To illustrate this observation, in what follows I will consider three cases of such violations.

In the Dark Ages, due to the general decay of learning and the demise of adult catechumenate, the link between the ritual actions and baptismal initiation vital for understanding the ritual was severed. The language of the liturgy became less and less comprehensible to ordinary believers. The voice of the Bible within the liturgy was muted due to the dearth of competent preachers. Centuries later scholastic theology broke down the unity of the liturgy by focusing on specific elements, such as the precise function of the words of institution. The result was the drifting apart of liturgical theology from the theology of the schoolmen, the silencing of the proclamation of the Word for the sake of the adoration of the sacrament. Such damaging dichotomies could not but break the unity of the canonical heritage.

Another way to destroy the harmony of the exchange between the canons was to convert one of them into the norm regulating the rest of the canons.[35] John Calvin, for example, appealed to the principle of *sola scriptura* in order to purify worship of all non-scriptural elements. When scripture was superimposed upon late medieval Mass in this way, the result was not only a justifiable elimination of certain abuses, but also a con-

---

35. On this issue, see William Abraham, *Canon and Criterion in Christian Theology: From the Fathers to Feminism* (Oxford: Clarendon, 1998).

siderable impoverishment of the liturgy. When the Bible was turned into the norm of liturgy, the logic of canon development was violated. To claim that only scriptural elements had the right to be retained in worship was to misunderstand how the two components of the canonical heritage functioned. In the end, the conversion of scripture into a liturgical norm was to cause a potent wave of iconoclasm that proved to be detrimental to the eucharistic life of the church.

The third and final way to disrupt the harmony of the liturgy is by orchestrating liturgical revolutions in the name of returning to the ancient sources. Repetition is at the very core of liturgical action. It is healthier for liturgical life to develop by gradual evolution, not by revolution. As Robert Taft rightly emphasized,[36] liturgies should not be artificially constructed by liturgists, no matter how erudite and well-wishing, but rather should gradually evolve in accordance with the changing modes of piety of the people of God. Liturgical materials attested in the patristic period must not be frozen in time and imposed as norms upon contemporary developments. Canonical theists are as far from liturgical fundamentalism of this kind as they are from its biblical twin brother. The liturgies of the patristic period as well as patristic liturgical theology are informative, not normative, today. Canonical liturgy is first and foremost the sacrament of participation in the kingdom of God and the medicine of immortality. While it plays a distinct and prominent role in the canonical heritage of the church, it is also inextricably connected to other means of grace, such as scripture and creeds.

36. Robert Taft, "On Eastern and Western Liturgy," at http://www.praiseofglory.com/taftliturgy.htm.

Christ Present in the Moment:
The Canon of Sacraments

NATALIE B. VAN KIRK

Mysteries, Signs, and Types

Clearly, sacraments — ritual acts, practices, or things,[1] which somehow mediate the grace of God given through Jesus Christ — were an essential part of early Christian life even before Paul began to write his letters to the fledgling churches scattered around the eastern Mediterranean. In 1 Corinthians, Paul speaks of *what was handed down to him* about the eucharist and speaks of the incorporation of the individual into the body of Christ through the body and blood of the communion. In Romans, he spells out a fairly detailed theology of a baptism marked by repentance and regeneration. The setting apart by the laying on hands of *diakonoi, presbyteroi,* and *episcopoi* is recognized in Acts, the letters to Timothy, Ephesians, and Colossians, and the pastoral letters. Confession, anointing of the sick, distinctly Christian interpretations of the purposes and place of marriage in the Christian life, and even confirmation (or anointing) are all found in the epistles of the New Testament canon.[2]

The mysteries given by Christ to the church were sign and symbol,

---

1. The word "things" is intentional as a way of avoiding confusion with the normal use of the word "materials" in this volume to refer to specific canons in the heritage of the church. Further, it is the position of this essay that sacraments are about far more than these materials and what happens to them in the prayers and rituals of the church.

2. There are Old Testament as well as New Testament types and sources for understanding these rites in the community of the church. Notable New Testament texts include the following: on confession: James 5:16; Matt. 16:19 and 18:18; on anointing the sick: James 5:14-15; on marriage: Matt. 5:42 and other Synoptic accounts of Jesus' teaching on divorce; Heb. 13:14; and Paul's teaching in Rom. 7:1; 1 Cor. 7; Eph. 5; on anointing: 1 Pet. 2:5-9.

type and antitype of the promises of God to God's people. They were understood by the church to be essential markers in its life together.[3] There were three sacred mysteries that were generally held to be constitutive of the church itself — baptism, unction or anointing, and the mystery of the Lord's body and blood. There was also a rather less formal list of others that included scripture, confession, funerals, holy orders, monastic vows, anointing of the sick and dying, marriage, the creeds, and even the church itself.

Our concern for this chapter will not be with relating each of these sacraments to one another or relating them to the prototype of the eucharist. Our concerns here are not the concerns of medieval and Reformation era theologians like Hugh of St. Victor, Aquinas, Bradwardine, Staupitz, Luther, or Calvin regarding *how* the sacraments worked, what the material element of each sacrament was, or how the Holy Spirit worked through them. Rather, as is true with the canonical theism project as a whole, our focus here is on *what* these mysteries were perceived to be doing and making available to the church in the first millennium of Christianity. In *what ways*, in other words, were the mysteries forming Christians and the church?

The remainder of this chapter will be focused on the ways in which the mysteries[4] served as soteriological, anthropological, and eschatological signs of God's engagement with the church: most particularly in the three constitutive mysteries of baptism, anointing, and eucharist. Gregory Palamas proclaims that "in these two [sacraments (baptism and eucharist)], our whole salvation is rooted, *since* the entire economy of the God-man is recapitulated in them."[5] Gregory lived nearly seven hundred years later than the writers that we are examining here, but his comment still serves as a good summary of the theological position from which the early church regarded the work of the mysteries. This chapter takes the view that sacraments are, in the writings of the early fathers, a recapitulation and revelation of the entire economy of the God-man. It is a view of the sacraments that sees them as expressions of the mystery of salvation and the means by which the church is established as the *koinonia* of the body of Christ and incorporated into the *koinonia* of the Triune God.

3. For this discussion we will focus on the first six centuries of the church: the period of the seven Ecumenical Councils and a time when the divisions between East and West were not deemed unbridgeable.

4. In keeping with the practice of the church fathers, this chapter will refer to the sacraments as "mysteries" rather than by the equivalent Latin term "sacraments."

5. Gregory Palamas, *Hom.* 60, quoted in John Meyendorff, *Byzantine Theology* (New York: Fordham Press, 1974, 1979), 192; emphasis added.

Mystery is the appropriate word to be applied to salvation and to the sacraments. *Mystery* is not used here in the sense of something for which the natural explanation has yet to be found, or for which we just do not have all the pieces needed for clarity. Rather, *mystery* is used to express such a superfluity of meaning in the work of the divine that it cannot be grasped cognitively *in toto,* no matter how many pieces we might understand. While it is easy to recite, who fully comprehends the implications of John 3:16? The great mystery was, for the fathers, the mystery of salvation. The "mysteries" were smaller pieces or types of the greater mystery of salvation in and through the God-man.

Seeing the Enigma

The most important thing to understand about the use of the language of type and sign is that it was not seen as tying two unrelated things together. The Aristotelan definitions that were revived during the Middle Ages had not always obtained in the ways that late antique and early medieval writers used the language of sign and type.[6] A "sign" or "type," for example, did not point beyond itself to something completely unrelated to it.[7] Rather,

6. There is a substantial body of literature in philosophy and literary criticism on modern, medieval, and ancient sign theory that we have neither time nor space to reprise, though this literature remains a significant opportunity to examine the ways in which Christian theologians intended to employ this language.

7. Much Protestant sacramental theology is built upon a modern understanding of St. Augustine's use of the language of sign and symbol in *De doctrina Christiana* and *De magistro.* This may, however, simply be a misinterpretation of the meaning of the word as used by a fourth-century bishop. In his very helpful article on sacraments in Augustine's theology, E. Cutrone notes that three Pauline texts — 1 Cor. 13:2, Eph. 5:32, and 1 Cor. 4:1 — "provide a specific connection between sacrament and mystery for Augustine. In each passage the African version of Scripture used by Augustine translated the mystery in question with the word *sacramentum,* and his exegesis of these passages brings together sacrament, mystery, symbol, and ritual. *Sacramentum* emerges as the term which identifies the mystery of Christ, and when used in this manner, *sacramentum* is identical with *mysterium* in Augustine's work. The visible manifestation of God's saving present in the historical Christ and within the church is the *sacramenta* whereby one comes to understand and participate in the divine mystery" (in Allan D. Fitzgerald, O.S.A., ed., *Augustine through the Ages* [Grand Rapids: Eerdmans, 1999], 742). Further analysis of the use of the language of *figura* in Tertullian and Ambrose can be found in St. Ambrose, *On the Sacraments and On the Mysteries,* trans. T. Thompson, ed. and with an introduction and notes by J. H. Srawley (London: SPCK, 1950), 36ff.; and on general use of the language of type and figure in the fathers see

the sign or the type held an almost prophetic revelatory role, adumbrating in some greater or lesser manner God's revelation in a later event. Late antique and medieval writers were not bound by the rules of historical criticism or modern concepts of the role of prophecy. Events a thousand years earlier were seen to have revelatory bearing on events in the present.

Further, the fathers operated with a deep theological conviction that God is not bound by time. Thus, when one speaks of or deals with the things of God, past, present, and future are all visible. It is as the αἴνιγμα (enigma) of which Paul speaks in 1 Corinthians 13. We stand in the midst of mirrors endlessly reflecting one another, but our current sinful state means that we see those reflections of God's work only dimly. Nevertheless, they are there, promises of the day when we shall see face to face.[8]

The language of sign and type in premodern texts might be likened instead to the practices of intertextual reading that were so dominant in the rhetorical forms of late antiquity and the Middle Ages.[9] An intertextual reading would use cross references and allusions to older authoritative texts to build authority in a new work and simultaneously to demonstrate that the new text had built on old authority to reach beyond it to a new truth. Any of the books in the New Testament canon are replete with such intertextual readings. Matthew, for example, looks to Moses as a type for Jesus and then goes on to "prove" that Jesus is not simply like Moses, but greater than Moses. Moses was God's intimate friend,[10] but Jesus was and is Emmanuel, God with us. Moses led the people God formed and called out of Egypt, but Emmanuel calls all the nations to himself. For the writer of the Gospel, Moses is a type for Jesus, and the relationship is clearly far too important to Matthew for there to be no real relationship between the two. Here the concept of type (or sign, symbol, or allegory) does not mean one thing standing in for something to which it has no relationship, as it will begin to mean in the sixth century. Rather, Moses reveals one way that God worked in the world, and he adumbrates the way in which God will work in the world when God himself takes on flesh.

A less historical and more symbolic example of this matter of type re-

---

Daniel J. Sheerin, *The Eucharist,* Message of the Fathers of the Church, vol. 7 (Wilmington, DE: Michael Glazier, 1986), 17-19.

8. 1 Cor. 13:12.

9. For an excellent summary of the uses and meanings of intertextuality in late antiquity see Frances Young, *Biblical Exegesis and the Formation of Christian Culture* (Peabody, MA: Hendrickson Publishers, 2002).

10. Exod. 33:12, NAB.

vealing something but not all of what will be, of being related but not exactly alike, can be seen in the patristic association of Mary and the burning bush in Exodus 3. In modern ways of doing taxonomy, there are no congruent or coherent categories in which a human woman and a desert shrub can be considered similar. We, however, start with a much different question than was asked 1,700 or 1,800 years ago. The question then might well have been phrased rather like this: "How could this woman have survived carrying God within her when Scripture says, 'God is a consuming fire'? [Deut. 4:24 NAB]." And here, then, one finds the connection with the burning bush. Mary and the burning bush both contained God and were not consumed.

Above all, the concern for the writer of Matthew and for those who saw connections between the Virgin Mary and the burning bush was to show that the God who created the world was the same God who became Emmanuel, and the events of the past both foreshadow and find their fulfillment in the gospel of Jesus Christ. In biblical intertextuality, signs and types always begin by looking back from the New Testament texts to see which ways God, in past dealings with God's people, has adumbrated or foreshadowed dealings with the new people the Incarnate Word has called to himself.

This same sort of "intertextual" and timeless reading is applied to the mysteries of the sacraments. They are foreshadowed, if darkly, in the events of the Old Testament (for example, by the association of manna and the bread of the eucharist) and simultaneously foreshadow that which is to come — the banquet table of the kingdom of God. In the mystery of the Lord's body and blood, bread, like the bread shared by Melchizedek and Abraham, is brought to the fullness of its "breadness," the food of the banquet table of God's kingdom. In the eucharist, in Christ, bread becomes all that it was ever intended to be in God's creation — so that human beings can, by being nourished by that bread, be brought to the fullness of their humanity and united with the divine. Thus, the mystery becomes both type and antitype: *mimesis* of what was and of what will be. The mysteries are, at one level, ways in which the church remembers its future.[11]

Despite all the language of sign and type in the fathers, it is important to see the existential realism of the interpretation of the sacraments. Bread still nourishes, wine still inebriates, water still washes, and oil still

11. A phrase borrowed from Mary Carruthers, *The Craft of Thought: Meditation, Rhetoric, and the Making of Images, 400-1200*, Cambridge Studies in Medieval Literature, vol. 34 (Cambridge: Cambridge University Press, 2000). Carruthers applies the concept of "remembering the future" to the purposes of contemplative prayer.

heals and anoints priests. There is no pretense that these things *magically* become something other than what they are. God's grace employs very ordinary things and means to constitute God's people, and in Christ and the work of the Holy Spirit they are brought into their fullness by serving the highest and best purposes that bread, wine, water, and oil could ever serve. For the fathers, the sacraments never become so spiritualized that God works with material things only from a great distance, rather than actually being present in and through them.

There are four important theological reasons for this. First, as we will see below, God's grace works an ontological change in the recipient of the three great sacraments of initiation. If the mysteries were only spiritual signs, then there would be a question about what part of a human being was affected by them. In a world where "What is not assumed is not redeemed" (coined by Gregory of Nazianzus in his letter to Cledonius) was a maxim of orthodoxy, spiritualized sacraments would have fed the prevailing Hellenistic dualism and its conviction that the material world was beneath God's involvement. Second, a highly spiritualized and allegorized sacrament smacks of magic — an incantation with no grounding in reality. Third, to deny that God could work in and with material things would be, essentially, to deny the Incarnation. Lastly, spiritualized sacraments would deny the continuity between creation and redemption.

If the Holy Spirit could not work in the water of baptism, if Christ was not present in bread and wine, then how and why would one think the divine Logos had assumed human flesh and nature? What is more, without the presence of the Trinity in the materiality of the sacraments, there can be no union of God and humankind in the person of Christ. In other words, we cannot share or participate in the union of divinity and human nature effected by Christ Jesus. Thus, we are cast back upon the same problems that faced the orthodox party in the Arian controversy. What is not assumed (or in this case, consumed) is not redeemed, and the church is open to becoming dualist, privileging spirit over matter. *Hocus pocus,* indeed.

What Grace for What Purpose?

Among Christians who observe a sacramental tradition there is agreement on at least this much: sacraments have something to do with God's grace and human beings as recipients of that grace; the grace of the sacraments is meant for the body of Christ in the church and somehow binds that body together.

All sacraments then require this much, God's gracious action and individual human beings gathered together in the body of Christ that is the church.

A doctrine of the church is thus implicit in every understanding of the sacraments. What is believed to be true about the nature and purposes of the church will govern what is believed to be true about the sacraments and vice versa. As the fathers understood them, the mysteries are types, recapitulations of the great mystery of salvation for the church. The mystery of salvation, like the church and like the sacraments, functions on soteriological, anthropological, and eschatological planes. Further, it is clear from the writing of the early fathers that baptism, anointing, and eucharist were simultaneously initiatory and constitutive rights of the church. Thus, the mystery of the church did not, could not, come into being without sacraments, and the mysteries of the sacraments could not, did not, have a purpose separated from the church.

The *koinonia* expressed in the patristic conception of the church was a much thicker understanding of community than one expressed by tolerance and diversity. Church was much grander than an institutional association — something more concrete than an invisible reality, more historical than a church that would exist in reality only after the eschaton, something far more formative than a club or association of like-minded individuals who gathered together to serve God and worship in a particular way.

This thicker, richer *koinonia* is itself a gift of the Spirit that enables the church to be a unity of individuals merged into one body headed by Christ Jesus and yet still retaining individual identities. It is an ecclesiology lodged explicitly in the Triune God. As John Meyendorff helpfully explains it, "the Church is not simply a society of human beings, associated with each other by common beliefs and goals; it is a *koinonia* in God and with God. And if God Himself were not a Trinitarian *koinonia*, if He were not three Persons, the Church could never be an association of persons, irreducible to each other in their personal identity. Participation in the divine life would be nothing more than a Neoplatonic or Buddhist integration into an impersonal 'One.'"[12]

It would be hard to underestimate the organic vitality of this view of the church. Such a view takes quite literally the unity of the body referred to in texts like Ephesians 4:1-6, Colossians 3:15, or 1 Corinthians 12:12. In Greek and in Latin this body was referred to as σῶμα (*sōma*) and *corpus*. This is not flesh, raw and bloody, but a material living body, a substantive

---

12. Meyendorff, *Byzantine Theology*, 174.

thing, that could be depicted with some accuracy in the metaphors Paul uses in 1 Corinthians 12 and 14.

The eschatological promise that the church reflects in some way the kingdom of God reinforces the language of type and symbol used for the mysteries. The mysteries are the mirrors through which we dimly perceive the reality of the kingdom that will come. What we see in those mirrors is real enough in its way, but its full reality is obscured to us because of our as yet unrestored nature. As type and symbol the mysteries are closely related to what they profess to be; they are not stand-ins. They are mysteries because the fullness of that connection is not clear to us.

Ecclesiology cannot be an afterthought or add-on to sacramentology. When one focuses the questions of sacramentology on what the sacraments do in or for the church, ecclesiology is essentially tied to the topic. We must begin with Cyril of Alexandria's admonition to "think carefully about the way in which we too are one in body and spirit in relation to one another and also to God."[13]

> And so the Church is also called body of Christ and we individually are limbs, as Paul teaches [see 1 Cor. 12–27]. For we are all united to the one Christ through the holy body, since *we receive him who is one and indivisible in our own bodies. Our obligation then as limbs of his is to him rather than to ourselves.* The Saviour's role is that of head and the Church is the remainder of the body, made up of the various limbs.[14]

Note how much of this somatic image of the church is ontological. Adoption was considered an ontological change, literally remaking the adoptee into a member of a new bloodline in the first century. Thus, incorporation into the body of Christ was, in fact, a change in being; immortality instilled in us, as well as a change in status vis-à-vis the world.

The church becomes the nexus of the union between the divine and the human. What is wrought in individuals is made effective in the corporate body of the church.

What is offered here is in no way a fully developed ecclesiological statement, but only the barest outline of the way in which the fathers con-

13. Cyril of Alexandria, *Commentary on John XI,* in *Documents in Early Christian Thought,* ed. Maurice Wiles and Mark Santer (Cambridge: Cambridge University Press, 1975, 1996), 169.

14. Cyril of Alexandria, *Commentary on John XI,* in Wiles and Santer, eds., *Documents in Early Christian Thought,* 170; emphasis added.

strued church and therefore construed sacraments. The bits and pieces of Scripture and the early teaching presented here could be roughly sorted into the categories of soteriology, anthropology, and eschatology, but to do so rigidly would ignore the deep inner connections between those three concerns in the theology of the mysteries.

It is best to once again turn to Gregory Palamas's observation about the sacraments and apply it analogously to the church. In the church, the whole economy of the God-man is recapitulated; and, I would add, in the church the Triune God is present in the world. In the church, God has called those who once were no people, with no relationship of ethnicity, tribe, language, family, or citizenship, and made them into a new people. The church would not exist without divine initiative, and it is in and through the grace of God at work in the sacraments that the church is constituted and becomes the body of Christ.

Mysteries of Admission, Confecting the Church

In Romans, Paul gives us the earliest known Christian account of the purposes and grace of baptism:

> How can we who died to sin yet live in it? Or are you unaware that we who were baptized into Christ Jesus were baptized into his death? We were indeed buried with him through baptism into death, so that, just as Christ was raised from the dead by the glory of the Father, we too might live in newness of life. For if we have grown into union with him through a death like his, we shall also be united with him in the resurrection. We know that our old self was crucified with him, so that our sinful body might be done away with, that we might no longer be in slavery to sin. For a dead person has been absolved from sin. If, then, we have died with Christ, we believe that we shall also live with him. We know that Christ, raised from the dead, dies no more; death no longer has power over him. As to his death, he died to sin once and for all; as to his life, he lives for God.[15]

This passage, along with the earlier teachings in 1 Corinthians and Galatians, were the first texts in the church to spell out the meanings and purposes of the mystery of baptism. Paul does not give us any details of

15. Rom. 6:2-10.

the rite, or tell us which part of the rite confers the Holy Spirit, but he does set down the theological premises for a Christian understanding of the rite.

Baptism is a union of the believer with Christ Jesus in his death and resurrection. The newness of life conferred upon Christians in baptism involves a freedom from the ordinary human condition of enslavement to sin, absolution for the sins of the past, and new reality that just as Christ was resurrected from the dead, so too shall the Christian believer be resurrected. Eternal life is the new reality and the context for all Christians, and only, according to Paul, for Christians. It is a whole new sort of existence, which begins in the mystery of our conformity to the death and resurrection of Christ in baptism.

The lengthy discussion of the relationships between sin, the law, grace, the body (more properly worldly existence), and freedom in Christ in the following two chapters of Romans often obscures what Paul says, and does not say, about baptism. First, he simply presumes that the Romans are familiar with the rite and that it is the means by which one enters the community of the saved. Paul presumes that much about this rite is understood by his audience.[16] Second, this deeply eschatological understanding of baptism is built on the conviction that union with Christ in his death also brings the believer into union with Christ in resurrection. The current and visible manifestation of that union ought to be the rejection of sin and one's attachments to the world that encourages sinful behaviors.

In 1 Corinthians Paul has already said that Christians are individually temples of the Holy Spirit, and he insists elsewhere that believers are indwelt by Christ or by the Spirit of Christ. The union is therefore something more than a figure of speech to Paul. The divine presence indeed is united to the believer, in a way which is analogous though less complete than it was in Christ Jesus. Further, as a corollary, Paul has also taught in 1 Corinthians and Galatians that baptism has united the individual members of the church into one body: a single unity guided by the Spirit. Thus, the union with Christ that takes place in baptism is both individual and corporate. The transformation from one sort of being into a new sort of being is for the church and for the individual, and neither happens independently of the other.

The entire pattern of salvation, incarnation, death, and resurrection

16. See, for example, Brendan Byrne, S.J., *Romans,* ed. Daniel J. Harrington, S.J., Sacra Pagina, vol. 6 (Collegeville, MN: Liturgical Press, 1996), 189ff.

is made real for the believer in the small mystery of baptism. And, as is always the case for the already–not yet eschatology of the New Testament, it is not the past, nor the ultimate future, with which believers and the church must struggle, but the incomplete nature of the transformation of the present moment.

In debates with the Gnostics and the later trinitarian and christological controversies, the great teachers of the church were forced to answer deeper questions about how God's grace worked through the mystery of baptism. According to Tertullian, whose treatise on baptism is the earliest to have come down to us, part of the Gnostic complaint was that baptism was too simple. God, it seemed to the Gnostics, would need something fancier than plain old water. There ought, at a minimum, to be an elaborate rite, and a fee for the privilege of receiving it. Apparently many of Tertullian's flock wondered about this, too. In response, Tertullian says to his people, "What wretched unbelief to deny God his distinctive attributes — simplicity and power! Is it not a marvel that death is washed away by bathing? It is indeed a marvel; but is that is that a reason for not believing in it?"[17]

Tertullian then goes on to explain that in baptism the spirit of human beings receives a "bodily washing" (immersion in water) and the body a "spiritual cleansing" (release from sin). It is in baptism that "man is being restored to God; he who was originally in God's image is being reinstated in his likeness (the image is to be found in man as created; the likeness in man as eternal); he receives again that spirit of God which he had earlier been given by God's breathing on him, but which he had subsequently lost through sin."[18] Here, too, baptism involves an ontological change.

Tertullian's treatise also contains a full exposition of the links of the waters of baptism to the economy of creation and salvation, seeing stories like that of Noah, or the crossing of the Red Sea, as types of what is fulfilled and made whole in baptism. Tertullian understands that the Holy Spirit descends upon the waters of baptism and "rests upon them, and sanctifies them within himself. By being thus sanctified, they absorb the powers of sanctifying."[19] The efficacy of the cleansing depends upon the

17. Tertullian, *On Baptism,* in Wiles and Santer, eds., *Documents in Early Christian Thought,* 174.

18. Tertullian, *On Baptism,* in Wiles and Santer, eds., *Documents in Early Christian Thought,* 178.

19. Tertullian, *On Baptism,* in Wiles and Santer, eds., *Documents in Early Christian Thought,* 176.

Holy Spirit's resting on the waters of baptism. The descent of the Holy Spirit upon the waters of baptism is not the same as the descent of the Spirit upon the baptizand. To the extent that Tertullian defines the ritual location of the baptism of the Spirit, it apparently comes with unction and laying on of hands in following the cleansing of the baptismal waters. What Tertullian most wanted his congregation to understand was that the rite of baptism involved renunciation of evil and the past way of life, forgiveness of past sins, ontological change that freed the believer from captivity to sin and made him or her a child of God, unity with Christ, and the promise of eternal life.

In the fourth century, Ambrose and Cyril of Jerusalem offer clearer statements of the theological implications of the mysteries of baptism and unction (or anointing), as well as more complete descriptions of the rites. Tertullian's importance to this conversation is, however, critical. While he expands upon the theological hints given by Paul, he never contradicts the ontological and eschatological understanding of the mystery. In Tertullian's treatise, and in the works of the church fathers after him, baptism is indeed presented as a recapitulation of the entire mystery of salvation through which God's grace incorporated the believer into the community of the church.

Further, for Tertullian, and Ambrose and Cyril after him, baptism was separate from the rite of anointing that followed it. The anointing was related to baptism, but more than a seal of the grace of baptism. It was a separate manifestation of God's grace, which on its own brought the believer into a new relationship with the body of Christ. And, so, it is to anointing that our discussion now turns.

Ambrose, in the fourth-century treatise *De mysteria,* gives a detailed account of the sacraments of baptism, anointing, and eucharist in his instruction to catechumens who will receive all three sacraments at the upcoming Easter Vigil. The anointing is related to the anointing of Aaron and an initiation of the baptizand into the priesthood of all believers.[20]

The connection to the anointing of Aaron and the Aaronic priest-

---

20. In the past, there has been considerable doubt about whether or not *De mysteria* could actually have been written by Ambrose. Current scholarship tends to credit the treatise to Ambrose. The objections to Ambrosian authorship were originally raised by Protestant Reformers, who were quite sure that a church father whom they regarded as orthodox could never have authored documents that insisted on the physical presence of Christ in the eucharist, the regenerative nature of baptism, or a host of other "popish" accretions to what they believed was the pure doctrine of the early church.

hood was not unique to Ambrose or the Latin church. Cyril of Jerusalem also connects the anointing to Aaron:

> For what time Moses imparted to his brother the command of God, and made him High-priest, after bathing in water, he anointed him; and Aaron was called Christ or Anointed, evidently from the typical Chrism. . . . To them however these things happened in a figure, but to you not in a figure, but in truth; because ye were truly anointed by the Holy Ghost. Christ is the beginning of your salvation; for He is truly the First-fruit, and ye the mass; but if the First-fruit be holy, it is manifest that Its holiness will pass to the mass also.[21]

Cyril cautions his hearers not to form too low an opinion of the chrism used in the anointing. It is indeed a holy thing, a means of grace.

> But beware of supposing this to be plain ointment. For as the Bread of the Eucharist, after the invocation of the Holy Ghost, is mere bread no longer but the Body of Christ, so also the holy ointment is no more simple ointment . . . after invocation, but it is Christ's gift of grace, and by the advent of the Holy Ghost, is made fit to impart his Divine Nature.[22]

With the chrism of the anointing, Cyril insists that believers, "having been made partakers and fellows of Christ" by being "crucified, buried, and raised together with Him" in the likeness of baptism, are anointed with the "oil of gladness, that is, with the Holy Ghost, called the oil of gladness, because He is the author of spiritual gladness."[23] Thus, like Christ, the believer is anointed by the Holy Spirit following baptism, at the beginning of his or her ministry in the church.

Cyril and Ambrose are not alone in this understanding of anointing as a fulfillment of the priesthood of all believers. The epiclesis of the Syriac liturgy of Antioch asks that the Father send the Holy Spirit to consecrate the sacred chrism "so that it may be for all who are anointed and marked with it holy myron, *priestly* myron, royal myron."[24] The chrism used at the

---

21. Cyril of Jerusalem, *On the Mysteries III: On Chrism*, 6, from an electronic version of *The Nicene and Post-Nicene Fathers*, series II, volume VII, ed. Phillip Schaff, http://www.ccel.org/fathers2/NPNF2-07/Npnf2-07-27.htm#P2800_800487.

22. Cyril of Jerusalem, *On the Mysteries III*, 3.

23. Cyril of Jerusalem, *On the Mysteries III*, 2.

24. *The Catechism of the Catholic Church*, ¶1297 (Ligouri, MO: Ligouri Publications, 1994), 329; emphasis added.

anointing is the same chrism used for anointing priests and royalty. For Christians, priests were those called out of the priesthood of all believers for a further deepening of their ministry.

In the late antique world, oil had specific, clearly understood religious and medicinal uses. It was used for cleansing the body, for healing wounds, and for anointing priests and rulers: for making christs (anointed ones), as Cyril of Jerusalem called the new believers. Cyril and Ambrose make a pointed distinction between oil used for cleansing and healing prior to the baptismal liturgy itself and this oil that is used for anointing afterward. This oil of anointing confers the Holy Spirit upon the believer in a particular manner, a manner that the early fathers seemed to understand made the baptized Christian a member of the royal priesthood of all believers. The reminder in 1 Peter 2:9-10 that the beloved are now a chosen race, a royal priesthood, a new people where there was once no people makes scriptural sense of the relationship of baptism and anointing in the early church. Ambrose explained the connection by likening the newly baptized to the rod of Aaron, which was dry and without blossom:

> You too were dry, and you began to flower by the watering of the font. You had become dry by sins, you have become dry by errors and transgressions, but now you have begun to bear fruit, "planted by the courses of water" (Ps. 1:3). But perhaps you may say: "What had this to do with the people, if the rod of the priest became dry and blossomed again?" What is the people itself if not priestly? To them was said "But you are a chosen race, a royal priesthood, a holy nation," as the Apostle Peter says (1 Pet. 2:9). *Each one is anointed into priesthood, each is anointed into the kingdom, but it is a spiritual kingdom and a spiritual priesthood.*[25]

In baptism the Holy Spirit regenerates human beings and unites them to Christ in Christ's crucifixion, burial, and resurrection. The "finishing" of the mystery comes in anointing or confirmation, actual incorporation of the body of believers, the church, into a new people — a people free of all past relationships and divisions of family ethnicity, tribe, language, family, or citizenship as priests of the Most High God. Believers are not priests in the sense that all were ordained to teach and preach and be stewards of the mysteries of God,[26] but priests in that all were made holy so that "with un-

---

25. Ambrose, *On the Sacraments* IV.2-3, in Sheerin, *The Eucharist*, 75; emphasis added.
26. 1 Cor. 4:1.

veiled face ye might reflect as a mirror the glory of the Lord," and at the last day drink the wine of gladness in the presence of the Lord.[27] This is the eschatological promise of the priesthood of all believers: that when the kingdom is fulfilled all believers will go beyond the veil and see the Holy of Holies face to face. It is through anointing that the believer is united with the ministry of Christ, and that Christ, through the Holy Spirit, enables the church to live out the unity with him into which believers are baptized.[28]

Baptism and anointing are among the indelible mysteries of the church, the ones which cannot be repeated, and thus their initiatory and constitutive character is more readily apparent, though it can be more difficult to see how they recapitulate the greater mystery of salvation. With eucharist, the situation is reversed. It is obvious that the eucharist recapitulates the mystery of salvation. In all traditions that retain sacraments, the *anaphora,* or prayers of the Great Thanksgiving, retell the story of salvation in Christ Jesus and of the institution of the Lord's Supper. It is the unity of the individual believers in the church, and the unity of the church with Christ, that is often less obvious. This is especially true in the West, where we are inclined to focus on the individual's experience of communion with the Lord in the Lord's Supper.

Once again we must begin with Paul for the discussion of the eucharist. In 1 Corinthians 11:23-28[29] we are given the first account of the words of institution for the mystery of the Lord's body and blood. Once again Paul presumes familiarity with and understanding of the practice. What is

---

27. Cyril of Jerusalem, *On the Mysteries III,* 4.7.

28. This is, in fact, a theological point very closely aligned to the theology of the Eastern churches regarding chrismation. See, for example, *The Living God: A Catechism for the Christian Faith,* vol. 2, trans. Olga Dunlop (Crestwood, NY: St. Vladimir's Theological Seminary Press, 1989), 302-4. In the West, the debates about confirmation have often centered around when the Holy Spirit is conferred and to what purpose, and how confirmation "completes" baptism; whether or not one could be baptized and not receive the Holy Spirit; or whether confirmation really amounts to little more than a reaffirmation of baptismal vows and induction into the adult membership of the church. Many Protestant denominations dropped the practice, which seemed pointless and without scriptural relationship. All of this, it seems to me, misses the point. If we take the fathers seriously, then it seems clear that they understood this as a type of priestly anointing that brought the believer into fullness of unity with Christ's life, death, and resurrection through the Holy Spirit, and which brought together those who were no people and made them into God's people. Scriptural warrant for the practice, if not dominical command, can be found in 1 Peter and Hebrews. For those who have placed a high value on the concept of the priesthood of all believers, confirmation/unction/anointing seems to be an essential means of grace for the church.

29. 1 Cor. 11:23-28.

at issue throughout the tenth and eleventh chapters of 1 Corinthians is the community's response to the grace given them in the sacrament. In chapter 10 Paul explains at least one way in which God's grace works in the sacrament.[30] Sharing one loaf and one cup enables believers to participate in the body and blood of Christ Jesus and to become one with one another.

Paul tells the Corinthians in chapter 10 that all of the community participates in the Lord when it shares the cup of blessing and breaks the bread. The community is made into one body that participates in the body of Christ by virtue of its partaking of one loaf together. This is not just a symbolic act. It is an ontological change. This is why St. Paul enjoins the community not to knowingly participate in sacrifices to the gods: it unites them with demons. Those who continue to go to the sacrifices attempt that which is ontologically impossible: to unite their bodies, which have become temples (dwellings) of the Lord, with demons. God will not reside with demons.

Making one out of many by participation in the body and blood of Christ is a dominant theme of Pauline and patristic theological reflection on the eucharist but far from the only one presented. The nutritional metaphors for the mystery of the Lord's body and blood, and the corollary metaphor of eucharist as the medicine of immortality, predominate in much of the patristic literature. The fathers were convinced that Christians did indeed become what they ate. These nutritional metaphors are highly dependent upon an understanding of the eucharistic elements that sees them as materially as well as spiritually effective. Consumption of the elements of the eucharist made body and soul more like Christ, transforming Christians into the little christs that Paul called them to become.

What is notable in the first accounts of eucharistic practice is the frank realism with which the elements are regarded as the body and blood of the Lord. In the *First Apology,* Justin Martyr says simply that bread and wine become flesh and blood in the prayers:

> Not as common bread or as common drink do we receive these, but just as through the word of God, Jesus Christ, our Saviour, became incarnate and took on flesh and blood for our salvation, so, we have been taught, the food over which thanks has been given by the prayer of His word, and which nourishes our flesh and blood by assimilation, is both the flesh and blood of that incarnate Jesus.[31]

---

30. 1 Cor. 10:15-22.
31. Justin Martyr, *First Apology* 66, in Sheerin, *The Eucharist,* 34.

Justin wrote to defend Christians from the charge of cannibalism, which he did by setting down in plain language an account of Christian practice. What he does not do is distance himself from the realism of the tradition he has apparently received. Through prayer, though the mechanics or metaphysics of the change are not explained, bread and wine become body and blood and so assimilate the believer to Christ Jesus.

There have always been those within and without the church who concerned themselves with the "how" of the mystery. How could such a thing happen to bread and wine? How could one believe such a thing? With the sharpness of a teacher used to addressing a question that he sees as a dangerous red herring, Cyril of Jerusalem told his catechumens to leave the question alone.

> These words of the blessed Paul [1 Cor. 11:23-25] are in themselves sufficient to give you full assurance about the divine mysteries to which you have been admitted and by which you have been made of one body and one blood with Christ. Paul was there affirming "that on the night that he was betrayed our Lord Jesus Christ took bread. . . ." As therefore he himself expressly said, "This is my body," who will dare to doubt it any longer? As he has specifically stated, "This is my blood," who will even voice a suspicion that it may not be his blood? He once changed water into wine by a word of command at Cana of Galilee. Should we not believe him in his changing wine into blood? . . . So, let us have full assurance that we are partaking of Christ's body and blood.[32]

In the battle against Arianism and Hellenistic dualism, against the temptation to privilege the spiritual over the material and to denigrate the goodness of God's creation, the reality of the body and blood was an important theological issue. Because bread and wine were body and blood, Christians became "Christ-bearers, since his body and his blood are spread throughout our limbs. In the words of the blessed Peter 'we are made sharers in the divine nature' [2 Pet 1:4]."[33] If the union with Christ was purely spiritual, then one half of that which made human beings distinctively human, namely the body, would not share in the nature of Christ and would

32. Cyril of Jerusalem, *On the Mysteries* 4.1-3, in Wiles and Santer, eds., *Documents in Early Christian Thought*, 188.

33. Cyril of Jerusalem, *On the Mysteries* 4.3, in Wiles and Santer, eds., *Documents in Early Christian Thought*, 188.

therefore not be redeemed. If that were the case, then the heretics were right. It was a truth vigorously defended by orthodox Christianity as early as the second century.

> But vain in every respect are they who despise the entire dispensation of God, and disallow the salvation of the flesh, and treat with contempt its regeneration, maintaining that it is not capable of incorruption. But if this indeed does not attain salvation, then neither did the Lord redeem us with His blood, nor is the cup of the Eucharist the communion of His blood, nor the bread which we break the communion of His body. . . . He has acknowledged the cup (which is a part of the creation) as His own blood, from which He bedews our blood; and the bread (also a part of the creation) He has established as His own body, from which He gives increase to our bodies.
>
> When, therefore, the mingled cup and the manufactured bread receives the Word of God, and the Eucharist of the blood and the body of Christ is made, from which things the substance of our flesh is increased and supported, how can they affirm that the flesh is incapable of receiving the gift of God, which is life eternal, which [flesh] is nourished from the body and blood of the Lord, and is a member of Him? — even as the blessed Paul declares in his Epistle to the Ephesians, that "we are members of His body, of His flesh, and of His bones." He does not speak these words of some spiritual and invisible man, for a spirit has not bones nor flesh; but [he refers to] that dispensation [by which the Lord became] an actual man, consisting of flesh, and nerves, and bones.[34]

Neither Irenaeus's nor Cyril's answer to the doubters is a peculiarly Eastern notion. Augustine and Ambrose say much the same thing.[35]

---

34. Irenaeus of Lyons, *Against Heresies* 5.2.2-3; from the Ante-Nicene Fathers, vol. 1, ed. Phillip Schaff. Electronic resource: http://www.ccel.org/fathers2/ANF-01/anf01-55.htm #P6120_1360484.

35. In Western theological debate there is often a divide posited between an "Ambrosian" approach to sacraments and an "Augustinian" approach to sacraments. In part, the division is understood to be a function of Augustine's preaching in his eucharistic catechesis. In Sermon 272 he raises the question of how bread and wine are body and blood. Christ Jesus took flesh from the Virgin Mary, was born, lived, died, and ascended into heaven, and now sits, "enthroned at the right hand of the Father. How is the bread His body? And the cup, or what is in the cup, how is that His blood?" (Augustine, *Sermon 272*, in Sheerin, *The Eucharist*, 94-95). Augustine's emphasis in the sermon is the unity of the church within itself and with Christ, which is made possible through participation in the sacra-

The corporate unity of the church granted through one loaf and one cup is crucial for the church's understanding of itself as a unified people. The church's understanding of itself *qua* church, as the people called out and made into one body with Christ at its head, is not, however, grounded primarily in the participation in one loaf and one cup. It is not through unity of action that this body is created. Rather, it is the participation in Christ granted the faithful in the mystery of the Lord's body and blood, the new character and being that each is given and in which all share, that makes the *ecclesia* the body of Christ.

"He mingles Himself with each one of the faithful through the mysteries. He feeds with Himself those whom He has begotten."[36] And so, by feeding believers with himself, Christ our Passover makes eucharist a Passover. Bread and wine, as they unite with the body and nourish it, become the medicine of immortality, building up, bit by bit, the immortal nature in each recipient — driving out corruption and replacing it with incorruption, sin with sinlessness, fear with freedom, slavery with the power to be the children of God. It is in eucharist that the body comes to participate in its Savior, and so join the soul in salvation.

Gregory of Nyssa says, "we had eaten something that was disintegrating our nature [the effects of sin, including the penalty of death, upon the body]. It follows, therefore, we needed an antidote. . . . And what is this remedy? It is that body which proved mightier than death and became the course of our life . . . the entry of the immortal body into the body that receives it transforms it in its entirety into its own immortal nature."[37] "If you were incorporeal," says John Chrysostom, "He would have given you the incorporeal gifts unclothed, but because the

---

ment. He does not actually answer the objection to the presence of body and blood. "These things, my brothers, are called sacraments for the reason that in them one thing is seen, but another is understood. That which is seen has a physical appearance, that which is understood has spiritual fruit" ([Augustine, *Sermon 272*, in Sheerin, *The Eucharist*, 94-95). It is a stretch, however, to assert on the basis of two sentences that Augustine meant to deny the reality of physical presence in the elements of the mystery. In the treatise *On the Merits and Remission of Sins* it is quite clear that Augustine accepts the presence of body and blood in bread and wine (in Sheerin, *The Eucharist*, 274-75). It is the spiritual unity of the church, however, that is Augustine's greatest concern in this sermon, as it is in Sermon 272 and Sermon Wolfenbüttel 7 on the same topic. The bulk of the sermon expounds on the metaphor of many grains of wheat becoming one loaf, and many participants sharing in that loaf becoming one body.

36. John Chrysostom, *Homily on Matthew* 82.4-6, in Sheerin, *The Eucharist*, 290.

37. Gregory of Nyssa, *Catechetical Oration* 37, in Sheerin, *The Eucharist*, 194.

soul has been mingled with the body, He gives you spiritual things in things sensible."[38]

There remains, of course, an aspect of the mystery of eucharist that is woven through all of the discussions but must be dealt with on its own terms, and that is the issue of the ways in which the ritual of the eucharist remembers, re-presents, and reenacts the sacrifice of Christ. Once again the place to begin the discussion is with scripture, in this case with chapter 7 of Hebrews and chapter 10 of 1 Corinthians.

In *Against Heresies,* Irenaeus presents the eucharist as "a pure sacrifice" offered to God by the church through the agency of Christ. "This oblation was handed on to the Church by the apostles, and she offers it throughout the world to the God who gives our sustenance, as the first-fruits of his gifts under the new covenant."[39] It is a pure sacrifice, says Irenaeus, because, in fact, we offer nothing of our own (which may be corrupted), but we make offering to God of what it already his, namely bread and wine to be flesh and blood, and these are incorruptible. "This offering, this pure offering, is presented to the Creator by the church alone, as she offers him with thanksgiving a portion of his own creation."[40] The eucharistized[41] bread and wine become the body and blood of Christ, and because Christ is the Creator of the universe, the church finds herself offering to God what is God's already. She makes this offering for no other reason than that the church (the people of God) needs to make offerings to God.

Irenaeus uses the language of sacrifice with relation to Christ and the language of offering with respect to the church, but that does not necessarily mean he finds Christ's sacrifice and the ritual of the mystery of eucharist as completely distinct. First, he is clear that bread and wine are truly flesh and blood consumed and saving all of human nature. Second, his real concern in this passage is with the Valentinians who insisted that the bread and wine were body and blood, but denied Christ's creative agency. For

38. John Chrysostom, *Homily on Matthew* 82.4-6, in Sheerin, *The Eucharist,* 289.

39. Irenaeus, *Against Heresies IV,* 17.5, in Wiles and Santer, eds., *Documents in Early Christian Thought,* 184.

40. Irenaeus, *Against Heresies IV,* 18.4, in Wiles and Santer, eds., *Documents in Early Christian Thought,* 187.

41. Irenaeus uses the verbal form. To use a verbal form here implies a change; something happens to bread and wine. These are not dry signs or memorials but very reality. By giving God's gifts back to God the church mirrors the gift of the Son, Creator of the universe and Divine Logos, giving back his own being to free humankind from sin and death.

Irenaeus it was of vital importance to establish the Christian understanding that the God who created the cosmos is the God who saves. Thus, it would be a mistake to read his argument as primarily an effort to clarify offering and sacrifice. Rather, his argument was quite properly trying to draw the connection between the mystery of salvation and the mystery of eucharist.

In his homily on 1 Corinthians 10:15-16, Chrysostom makes it clear that he believes that Christ is actually present in the elements in something much more than a symbolic sense, that the eucharist is a recapitulation of the sacrifice made on the cross to free us from error.

> In the days of the old covenant, since men were at a much more imperfect stage, he was prepared to accept the blood which they offered to idols — with the aim of drawing them away from such things; and that is yet another example of his unspeakable love. But now he has provided in its place a far more awesome and glorious way of worship. *He has changed the very sacrifice itself, and in place of the slaughter of irrational beasts, he has commanded us to offer up himself.*[42]

The interesting part of Chrysostom's argument in these homilies is that he grounds his argument in the reality of the unity created by participation in the body and blood of Christ preached by St. Paul in 1 Corinthians. It is the reality of the blood in the cup of blessing and the body created by participation in a single loaf which is Christ's flesh that leads St. John to see the mystery as a recapitulation of Christ's sacrifice.[43] It is as if, he tells us, Christ has said to the faithful, "If you want blood, do not make an altar of idols red with the blood of irrational beasts; let it be my altar with my blood."[44] That this is not strictly metaphorical language is made clear by the emphasis placed on the reality of the word "participation." It is, in fact, the unity found in participation that is St. John's larger point in the sermon, but he clearly sees the presumption of the sacrifice on the altar as necessary to his argument. Nor should it be ignored that, as Chrysostom

---

42. John Chrysostom, *Homilies on 1 Corinthians* 24.1-2 (on 1 Cor. 10:16-17), in Wiles and Santer, eds., *Documents in Early Christian Thought*, 198.

43. This language of participation is Neo-platonic in origin and can be seen in St. Augustine as well as Chrysostom. Augustine's conception of sacramental realism was developed from within Neo-platonic culture and is therefore based on participation. See Mazza, *Celebration of Eucharist*, p. 156.

44. John Chrysostom, *Homilies on 1 Corinthians* 24.1-2 (on 1 Cor. 10:16-17), in Wiles and Santer, eds., *Documents in Early Christian Thought*, 197.

sees it, we, the church, are indeed offering Christ up to himself on the altar. It is, to be sure, the church's sacrifice of praise and thanksgiving, but it is *also* the church's offering of Christ to Christ.

All through the fathers, the discussion of the eucharist is wrapped with the language of altar and sacrifice. This language is not accidental, nor is it disposable. It is not, however, the language of reenactment. Neither can it be read simply as the language of remembrance. The eucharist is not *mneia;* rather, it is *mimesis.* In the offering and sacrifice of bread and wine on the altar, the church imitates and is thus drawn into the mystery of Christ's own sacrifice, and called to participate in the body and blood of Christ. This is all Christ's work as the eucharistic sacrifice reveals the great mystery of salvation.

St. Ambrose makes a distinction in his teaching on the sacraments that is helpful for understanding the nature of the sacrifice that the fathers were inclined to believe was taking place on the altar of Christ's church. The visible elements of the sacrament are *species,* but the word that he uses to designate the essential connection between the mystery of salvation and the sacrament is *similitudo* ("likeness" or "symbol"). It is what Mazza calls the "invisible aspect" of the eucharist; it can be known only through learning, not observation, and is thus the proper concern of eucharistic catechesis.[45] So, it is in the nature of the *similitudo* that the sacrifice takes place on the altar. The truth of the sacrifice can be known only by learning and instruction, not by examination of or focus on the *species.*

This does not mean that the sacrifice is any less real than if it were the sacrifice of a ram or bull on the altar. It is the very likeness of the bloodless sacrifice of Christ secured by the reality that, when the *species* are consumed, one consumes the body and blood of Christ and so participates in a vital way in him and in the salvation he wrought. Borrowing from the words of Christ at the Last Supper, and from the theology of Hebrews, it is plain to the teachers of the early church that the eucharist is *mimesis* of Christ as Passover lamb: the Passover sacrifice made by Christ himself for the creation, salvation, and feeding of the people of God.

The fathers never go so far as to define how the bread and wine become body and blood. But their existential realism, and their conviction that the Word became incarnate in order to save all of human nature, leads them to take the Word at his word: bread is his body, and wine is his blood, the same body and blood that were given for them and for all for their sal-

45. Mazza, *Celebration of Eucharist,* 152.

vation. In Christ's willingness to unite himself with humanity in the mystery of the eucharist, all of those who are anointed and made little christs will be fulfilled in their Christlikeness, sharing in his unity of human and divine.

Partaking in the Mystery of God

The three mysteries discussed here appear together in the majority of the fathers' writings and are seen as the constitutive mysteries of the church. There are, as was noted in the introduction, many others that are often listed, most notably holy orders, anointing of the sick, penance, marriage, scripture, creeds, and the church itself. Space does not allow for treatment of all sacramental possibilities, but I hope that careful listening to how the fathers talk and think about these constitutive smaller mysteries and the ways in which the mysteries reveal the truths of the great mystery of salvation will generate some fruitful consideration.

Often a discussion of the mysteries starts with the question of how the sacraments work, what the elements are, and how God gets into those elements. Mechanics and metaphysics were not the fathers' primary concerns. To start with the question of how is rather like asking in which ways a human woman and a burning bush are similar. Both questions presume the wrong categories. The question of the mysteries is always about what God is revealing and remaking through these signs, these little types of the great mystery of salvation. How do the mysteries we call sacraments recapitulate and *make real in believers* the work of God — the grace — given to the church in them? What effect do the mysteries have on the church and on the souls that are united in the body of Christ?

Germanus I, in his mid-eighth-century commentary on the divine liturgy, explains that in liturgy even earthly things imitate the spiritual, heavenly, and transcendent order. In the end, that is also most likely the best way to think of the canon of the mysteries in the first half of the life of the church. The mysteries are expressions of God's grace — God's work — through earthly and material things to bring earthly and material things, specifically human beings, into alignment with the spiritual, heavenly, and transcendent order. The mysteries are only secondarily about the individual recipients, and it is hubris to put concern with human recipients first. The mysteries are about God's longing and desire for his creation and his creatures to be restored to his original plan. They are expressions of a longing so great that the Word of God took on flesh, suffered death, and was resurrected in order to make that restoration possible.

God's grace in the mysteries is not adequately defined as pills to strengthen us, vitamins for virtue, or patches for the tears in our relationship with God. While it is all those things, we emphasize the gift at the risk of making the recipient the most important part of the equation. Neither would the fathers have been content to define grace simply as God's unmerited favor: a strange willingness to forgive human beings for their inherent and actual sinfulness when they deserve all the punishment and death God could rightly rain down on them.

In the patristic tradition God's grace given in the mysteries is not, in the end, primarily something dispensed in little packets of ritual, nor is it primarily transactional and account balancing. Rather, grace takes on the character of the love of a bridegroom for his beloved — in fact, the Song of Songs is frequently used to explain some effect of a mystery. Eucharist, for example, is explained as the kiss of the Bridegroom on the lips of the Bride.

> You have come to the altar. The Lord Jesus calls you — or your soul, or the church — and He says, "Let him kiss me with the kiss of his mouth" (Sg. 1:1). Do you wish to apply it to Christ? There is nothing more welcome. Do you wish to apply it to your soul? There is nothing more pleasant. "Let him kiss me." He sees that you are clean of every sin, because transgressions have been washed away. On that account he judges you worthy of the heavenly sacraments, and therefore invites you to the heavenly banquet, "Let him kiss me with the kiss of his mouth."[46]

God's grace in the mysteries is passion and longing, and the most intimate of unions. It is the Lord preparing his Bride for his own pleasure and delight, and then wooing and working to draw her ever closer, to make her more like himself. God's grace as revealed in the mysteries we call sacraments is, as I read the fathers, about what God does rather than about what God gives. The grace of the mysteries is a revelation of the engagement of the Triune God with human beings — God's work for God's delight and the benefit of those whom he loves.

---

46. Ambrose, *On the Sacraments*, 5.5-6, in Sheerin, *The Eucharist*, 82.

Saints and Teachers:
Canons of Persons

HORACE SIX-MEANS

His beloved teacher and spiritual father Pamphilus had been imprisoned and martyred in 310.[1] In response, Eusebius of Caesarea fled to the Egyptian desert. He was eventually caught and imprisoned, only to be spared the fate of his teacher by the Emperor Galerius's Edict of Toleration in 311. Eusebius had seen the peace of the Christian community of the last decade of the third century shattered by persecution only to have peace return in the second decade of the fourth century, but this time with increasing favor from the Emperor Constantine. In the midst of these transitions Eusebius's *Ecclesiastical History* developed through a number of editions. For questioning Christians trying to find a way forward into the future in these turbulent times, Eusebius developed answers by looking back into the past and writing the first history of Christianity to establish a tradition that would guide Christians into the future. For Eusebius, distinguishing canons, or lists, of persons who were saints, teachers, and transmitters of the true faith was crucial to the healthy existence of the Christians of his time and for the future. Consider Eusebius's description of the importance of these lists in his work:

> 1 It is my purpose to write an account of the successions of the holy apostles, as well as of the times which have elapsed from the days of our Saviour to our own; and to relate the many important events which are said to have occurred in the history of the Church; and to mention those who have governed and presided over the Church in

1. Eusebius of Caesarea even took the name Pamphilii (son of Pamphilus) to show the importance of the relationship. See Rebecca Lyman, "Eusebius of Caesarea," in *Encyclopedia of Early Christianity* (New York: Garland, 1990).

97

the most prominent parishes, and those who in each generation have proclaimed the divine word either orally or in writing.

2 It is my purpose also to give the names and number and times of those who through love of innovation have run into the greatest errors, and, proclaiming themselves discoverers of knowledge falsely so-called have like fierce wolves unmercifully devastated the flock of Christ.

3 It is my intention, moreover, to recount the misfortunes which immediately came upon the whole Jewish nation in consequence of their plots against our Saviour, and to record the ways and the times in which the divine word has been attacked by the Gentiles, and to describe the character of those who at various periods have contended for it in the face of blood and of tortures, as well as the confessions which have been made in our own days, and finally the gracious and kindly succor which our Saviour has afforded them all. Since I propose to write of all these things I shall commence my work with the beginning of the dispensation of our Saviour and Lord Jesus Christ.[2]

In the passage above, the opening to his *Ecclesiastical History,* Eusebius states his intention to give four lists, or canons, of persons. First, there is a list of those who "govern" (bishops) or "proclaim" (teachers). Second, he gives a list that is the antithesis to the first; these by their leadership and teaching have "devastated the flock of Christ." Third, Jews and Gentiles who plotted against the "saviour" and who persecuted Christians are remembered.[3] Last, he lists those who were persecuted and became martyrs or confessors. The four lists can be put into two groups. On the one hand there are the good persons who promote faithful Christianity, and on the other hand there are the bad persons, who oppose the Christianity of the good. Of the good list he later says: "From afar they raise their voices like torches, and they cry out, as from some lofty and conspicuous watch-tower, admonishing us where to walk and how to direct the course of our work steadily and safely."[4]

For Eusebius the good are "torches" or beacons who shed light on the

2. Eusebius, *Ecclesiastical History (EH)* 1.1.1-3, in the *Nicene and Post-Nicene Fathers,* ed. Phillip Schaff, Second Series (New York: Christian Literature Publishing, 1890), vol. 1.

3. Inordinate fear of this triple threat has unfortunately led to breaks in communities' bonds of fellowship and love and has also contributed to the rise in attitudes and actions of hate and violence directed toward non-Christians, "unorthodox" Christians, and Jews.

4. Eusebius, *EH* 1.1.4.

dimming past assuring a connection with Jesus and the apostles. They also illumine the present and show the faithful a way forward. His opinion of the bad is plain from the above passage. From within the Christian community the bad are those persons whose "love of innovation" led them to be "like fierce wolves [who] unmercifully devastated the flock of Christ." Outside of the Christian community on the one hand there are Jews who had "plots against our Saviour," and on the other hand Gentiles who "attacked" the divine word and produced martyrs.

Awareness of dangers is important for Christian communities, but too much control given over to the fear of threats is damaging to the health of the community as a whole. The more valuable purpose in identifying particular persons as beacons is to show other present and future Christians how to fulfill the commandment to love God and love neighbor.[5] This priority of love can be lost, however, as a misplaced emphasis on combating threats develops in the community. This feeds into what canonical theism sees as reducing canons of persons, materials, and practices into mere epistemic criteria for use in disputes over orthodoxy. This tends to allow memory to be dominated by fear rather than letting it be liberated by love.

In what follows I shall describe some of the ways Christian memory has developed over the centuries with respect to canons of persons generally and canons of saints and teachers in particular. The influential role of Eusebius on the writing of later historical memory will be emphasized, but other forms of remembering Christian beacons will also be touched on. I will note, but not exhaustively discuss, canons of persons associated with the yearly liturgical calendar, canons associated with the eucharistic prayer,[6] and variations according to time, place, and tradition, in light of major points of conflict among Christians. I will also note some of the effects that the reform impulses of the sixteenth century had on understandings of canons of saints and teachers. These reform impulses were diverse. Some expressed themselves within the institution of the Roman Catholic Church in Western Christendom. Others led to the establishment of a variety of institutions independent of the Roman Church. Considering this variety, it will be argued that, in spite of demonstrable epistemic uses of canons of persons, these canons ought to be embraced primarily for their

5. Matt. 22:37-40; Mark 12:29-31. See also the framing of these commands with the "Good Samaritan" story in Luke 10:25-42.

6. Also known as the *anaphora* or canon of the Mass. "Canon" with "Mass" in this instance primarily means "rule" with an implication of referring to a list of elements that make up the standard part of the liturgy at a certain point in the eucharistic service.

soteriological function.[7] The complexity of the uses of various lists of materials, practices, and persons, as standards for orthodoxy is recognized by canonical theism, but it is asserted that these lists or canons should aid the maintenance of Christian memory for the sake of leading people to God or, as said earlier, canons ought to guide us in loving God and loving our neighbor. We ought not to lose sight of Eusebius's reasons for making lists of bishops, teachers, and those known for their sanctity and commitment to Christ.

Eusebius and Christian Memory

According to Glenn Chestnut, Eusebius wrote his *Ecclesiastical History* with the intention of preserving and promoting what he saw as "orthodox," "ecclesial," or "catholic."[8] In his earliest version of the *Ecclesiastical History* and in subsequent editions, Eusebius gave a narrative account of the spread of Christianity from Jesus and the apostles to the early fourth century with adjustments to account for the outbreak of persecution led chiefly by the emperors Diocletian and Galerius and for the change in political alignment to favor first Licinius and then Constantine.[9]

Eusebius collected or created canons from around the Mediterranean that listed bishops, martyrs, and teachers with the aim of enhancing and defining an emerging sense of cohesion among Christian communities. Focusing on a few major centers, Rome, Alexandria, and Antioch, in particular, Eusebius presents lists that show which bishops,

7. See Thesis XI: "The canonical heritage of the Church functions first and foremost soteriologically. It operates as a complex means of grace that restores the image of God in human beings and brings them into communion with God and with each other in the Church. Each component is primarily a tool to be used in spiritual direction and formation."

8. This was equivalent to, or at least entailed an understanding of, catholicity. For example, Chestnut shows this link in Eusebius's *History* in a section where Eusebius is speaking of authoritative texts. With respect to the Acts, Gospel, and Revelation of Peter, Eusebius says "we have no knowledge of it at all in Catholic tradition, for no orthodox writer in ancient time or our own has used their testimonies." Clearly in this passage for Eusebius catholicity and orthodoxy are interchangeable terms. This passage of Eusebius's *History* dealt with canons of texts, but his primary focus was on canons of persons.

EH 3.3.2. See discussion in Glenn Chestnut, *The First Christian Historians: Eusebius, Socrates, Sozomen, Theodoret, and Evagrius*, 2nd ed. (Macon, GA: Mercer University Press, 1986), 127.

9. Chestnut, *The First Christian Historians*, 111-36.

teachers, saints, and martyrs stood within his understanding of orthodoxy. These lists, as Chestnut shows, are contrasted with lists developed
by heretics.[10]

Through the later editions of the work and through Eusebius's later
life and work[11] his understanding of orthodoxy would develop and take
account of the major controversy that enveloped Christian communities
after the Great Persecution, that is, the Arian/trinitarian controversy before, during, and after the Council of Nicaea.[12] Eusebius, although initially associated with the party of Arius,[13] sufficiently distanced himself
from Arius and his theology so as to be able to claim orthodox status.[14]
Going forward, Eusebius's history became the indispensable resource for
knowledge of Christianity's first three centuries. He greatly influenced the
historians who came after him. Successors like Rufinus translated and
built on his work. Socrates Scholasticus, Sozomen, Theodoret, and
Evagrius Scholasticus[15] built on his work but also extended Eusebius's
narrative to their own times. The framework for understanding the first
three centuries went largely unchallenged until the last two hundred
years. Perhaps the most influential reinterpretation is Walter Bauer's.[16]
We shall give greater attention to the work of Bauer shortly; for now let us
consider what Eusebius gave to succeeding generations in terms of canons
of persons.

---

10. Chestnut, *The First Christian Historians,* 127. See his note 39 where he points the
reader to *EH* 5.27.1, 6.18.1, and 7.27.2.

11. These other surviving works notably include his *Life of Constantine, Preparation of
the Gospel,* and *Demonstration of the Gospel.*

12. A most readable account that integrates the history of the councils with the socio-
political history in general is William Frend, *The Rise of Christianity* (Philadelphia: Fortress
Press, 1984), particularly 498-650. For background on Arius and his writings see Johannes
Quasten, *Patrology,* 4 vols. (Utrecht: Spectrum, 1950-), 3:7-13.

13. In Arius's letter to Eusebius of Nicomedia, preserved in Theodoret of Cyprus's *Ecclesiastical History* 1.4, *NPNF,* Second Series, vol. 3, Arius mentions Eusebius of Caesaria as
one of the bishops condemned for saying that "God had an existence prior to that of his
Son."

14. See Socrates, *Ecclesiastical History* 1.23, *NPNF,* Second Series, vol. 2. Eusebius's political and theological shrewdness during those times possibly contributed to the survival of
his works.

15. For discussion of these authors see Chestnut, *The First Christian Historians.*

16. Walter Bauer, *Orthodoxy and Heresy in Earliest Christianity* (Mifflintown, PA:
Sigler Press, 1996).

Eusebius and Various Canons of Persons

By the end of his life Eusebius had developed a vision of the Roman Empire as the providential matrix for the spread of an orthodox/catholic Christianity that would reach and unite all civilized people.[17] The unity would be elusive. Theological and political fractures were frequent. As soon as one breach would be closed another would open.[18] For more than a century in the wake of Constantine and his sons, the rule rather than the exception was an empire formally divided into Eastern and Western halves with two, often rival, emperors. Theologically, major divisions associated with the varying degrees of acceptance and rejection of the Nicene Creed and the fifth-century definition of Chalcedon continued on for centuries.[19]

As noted at the beginning of this essay, Eusebius was concerned with the importance of the tradition preserved in canons of persons for the sake of being guided by "torches" or beacons. His history gives canons of bishops, martyrs, and teachers. With respect to episcopacies, Eusebius was particularly concerned with bishops in Rome, Alexandria, Jerusalem, and Antioch, but he also names bishops in more than fifty cities in twenty-three regions of the empire.[20] Eusebius's canons of martyrs begin

17. The idea of this providential matrix is clearly found in Eusebius's two works *Preparation of the Gospel* and *Demonstration of the Gospel.*

18. For treatment of the details of theology in historical context from Nicaea (325) through Constantinople II (558) see Frend, *The Rise of Christianity,* 498-876. For more on the politics see A. H. M. Jones, *The Later Roman Empire, 284-602: A Social, Economic and Administrative Survey,* 2 vols. (Baltimore: Johns Hopkins University Press, 1992).

Politically, although Diocletian's plan of dividing the empire to give greater cohesion made good sense, its life was short. It was in fact Constantine, the Christian, who doomed it. He eventually brought about unity under his sole rule. His legacy, however, was one of political division between three rival sons: Constantine II, Constans, and Constantius.

19. After Chalcedon's definition resulted in three distinct traditions — Nestorians, Chalcedonians, and Monophysites — in 482 the Emperor Zeno tried to bring about unity with his *Henotikon,* which sought to circumvent Chalcedon and ground consensus in the tradition of "the 318 Fathers" of Nicea. This failed. Justinian and Theodora also tried a centrist move for broader consensus with the Council of Constantinople II, which produced the Three Chapters Controversy, an attempt to condemn extremists of Nestorian and Monophysite persuasion. This too failed to bring broader consensus. Constantine III condemned monethelitism, a pope who supported it, and monoergism. For discussion of the intricacies see Jaroslav Pelikan, *The Christian Tradition: A History of the Development of Doctrine,* vol. 1: *The Emergence of the Catholic Tradition, 100-600* (Chicago: University of Chicago Press, 1971), 226-77.

20. Canons of bishops are dealt with in greater detail in William Abraham's essay on

with Stephen[21] in Jerusalem and continue throughout the work to include martyrs from various regions according to the reigning emperor up to through the great persecution under Diocletian, Maximinus, and Galerius and its aftermath.[22] With respect to teachers, Eusebius provides two kinds of canons. He lists the orthodox, ecclesial, or catholic teachers, but these are contrasted with the lists of heretical and schismatic teachers. In the wake of the Council of Nicaea those historians that followed Eusebius also took care to distinguish between orthodox and heterodox canons of persons.

The Bauer Critique

Walter Bauer's *Orthodoxy and Heresy,* originally published in 1934, was a revolutionary critique of Eusebius and the prevailing views of early Christianity. Bauer set his arguments against three assumptions shared by many modern Christians but which he argues began in the second century. (1) Jesus gave the apostles "the pure doctrine." (2) The apostles then took "the unadulterated gospel" to their designated part of the world mission field. (3) Heresy came later as a perversion of, or encroachment on, the true gospel, such that the model of development is "unbelief, right belief, wrong belief."[23] Bauer claimed that too often those who would understand early Christianity have been too reliant on the testimony of "anti-heretical fathers."[24] Instead Bauer asserted that the historian should be like a judge that tries to assure the fair presentation of evidence from both sides. Bauer's study focused on sources for traditions in the early Christian centers of Edessa, Egypt, Antioch, and Rome. The received orthodox tradition was examined for inconsistencies, silences, and omissions. When these were found Bauer supplied reconstructions that took into account other available evidence and that gave voice to non-orthodox possibilities that, for Bauer, made more consistent stories.

Eusebius suffers vigorous cross-examination from Bauer, and he is

---

the episcopacy in this volume; my concern here is to speak to canons of teachers and saints. Thus there is some understandable overlap.

21. Eusebius, *EH* 2.1.

22. Concern to include the martyrdoms under Diocletian, Galerius, and Maximinus in his day led Eusebius to revise and expand his work. Eusebius, *EH* 8-10.

23. Bauer, *Orthodoxy and Heresy in Earliest Christianity,* 42.

24. Bauer, *Orthodoxy and Heresy in Earliest Christianity,* 42.

shown to be problematic on a number of points. For example, on Eusebius's treatment of the development of Christianity in Egypt, Bauer wrote:

> Eusebius, who found nothing in his sources about the primitive history of Christianity in Alexandria, had in any event searched very diligently in them. He repeats various items from pagan reporters concerning the Jewish revolt in Egypt under Trajan (*EH* 4.2), quotes excerpts from Philo and in his desperation even allows Philo's *Therapeutae* . . . to appear as the oldest Christians of Egypt and to be converted by Mark, the first bishop of Alexandria, after Philo previously had been in touch with Peter in Rome (*EH* 2.16-17). He traces a succession of ten bishops from Mark down to the reign of the Emperor Commodus (180-192). But this list, which he owes to Sextus Julius Africanus, serves only to make the profound silence that hangs over the origins even more disconcerting. There is absolutely no accompanying tradition — since this is so, what may be gathered at best is still almost less than nothing. And the timid notation of that copyist of the *Ecclesiastical History of Eusebius* who calls Annianus, the immediate successor of Mark, "a man beloved by God and admirable in all things," does not raise the tradition above the zero point. The first ten names (after Mark, the companion of the apostles) are and remain for us a mere echo and a puff of smoke; and they scarcely could ever have been anything but that. At least, here and there, the Roman succession list to the time of the Emperor Commodus offers us a living personality. And even in the defective catalogue of Antioch . . . , with its half dozen names for the same span of time, we already meet a familiar face in Ignatius, quite apart from the sixth figure, Theophilus. There is simply nothing comparable that can be established for Alexandria. Yet we can hardly suppose that some inexplicable misfortune overtook the account of the earliest period of Egyptian church history, and in this way explain the deathly silence.[25]

For Bauer, the silence suggests a cover-up, especially in light of the *Gospel of the Hebrews* and the *Gospel of the Egyptians,* texts which date to this early period in the Egyptian milieu but which were determined by the fourth century to be outside the orthodox theological mainstream. Consequently they are not part of the New Testament canon that is seen in

25. Bauer, *Orthodoxy and Heresy in Earliest Christianity,* 45.

Athanasius of Alexandria's famous Letter 39 (A.D. 367), which listed the twenty-seven New Testament books that became most widely accepted.[26] Bauer argues that these texts represent traditions omitted from Eusebius's orthodox list even though they were integral to the Alexandrian tradition. Particularly with the discovery of the *Nag Hammadi Library*,[27] the view that earliest Christianity, at least in Egypt, was diverse theologically has gained support through the work of a modern canon of teachers that includes Rudolph Bultmann, his student Helmut Koester, and Koester's student Elaine Pagels.[28]

Even if we don't find the critiques of Eusebius particularly convincing, accepting his testimony is still not without problems for reconstructing a canon of "orthodox" persons. Blurring the line between orthodox and heterodox are people like Origen. For Eusebius, Origen, the teacher of Eusebius's beloved Pamphilus, was ecclesial, orthodox, and a confessor to be revered and emulated. In an extended favorable account of Origen's life and work in Book Six of the *Ecclesiastical History* Eusebius says:

> But how many and how great things came upon Origen in the persecution, and what was their final result, — as the demon of evil marshaled all his forces, and fought against the man with his utmost craft and power, assaulting him beyond all others against whom he contended at that time, — and what and how many things he endured for the word of Christ, bonds and bodily tortures and torments under the iron collar and in the dungeon; and how for many days with his feet stretched four spaces in the stocks he bore patiently the threats of fire and whatever other things were inflicted by his enemies; and how his sufferings terminated, as his judge strove eagerly with all his might not to end his life; and what words he left after these things, full of comfort to those needing aid, a great many of his epistles show with truth and accuracy.[29]

---

26. *NPNF*, Second Series, vol. 4.

27. For translations of the Gnostic texts with introductions and notes see Bentley Layton, *The Gnostic Scriptures* (Garden City, NY: Doubleday & Company, 1987), and James M. Robinson, ed., *The Nag Hammadi Library in English,* 3rd ed. (San Francisco: Harper & Row, 1988).

28. From her *Gnostic Gospels* (1979) to *Beyond Belief* (2003), Elaine Pagels has done much to popularize the Bauer/Bultmann revisioning of early Christianity.

29. Eusebius, *EH* 6.39.

By the late fourth and early fifth centuries, however, Origen's status was greatly contested across the empire.[30] Origen, in fact, was also implicated as a fount of Arianism earlier in the fourth century, and he would continue to be contested up through the Three Chapters controversy of the Council of Constantinople II and beyond.

If canons of persons are merely useful for distinguishing orthodoxy from heresy then many in the mainstream institutional Christian tradition of both East and West are seriously challenged by Walter Bauer's criticisms of Eusebius's assertion of an original catholic orthodoxy with only later heretical deviations. Instead of the historically reliable path back to Jesus provided by Eusebius and other historical writers, Bauer either clouds the picture or reveals a vision of early heterodoxy. Bauer's approach has been revolutionary; the particulars have been accepted or challenged to varying degrees but they cannot be ignored or completely rejected.[31] On the other hand, if we look to canons of persons for their soteriological function, then persons whether labeled orthodox or heterodox, or whether real or even fictitious, might be appreciated to the degree that their stories have served to form people and draw them closer to God.[32]

Written histories like those of Eusebius and others are important sources for considering canons of persons as key elements in the construction of Christian memory, but they are not the only sources. Evidence that helps us reconstruct the worshiping life of Christians can be important as well.

---

30. Elizabeth Clark, *The Origenist Controversy: The Cultural Construction of an Early Christian Debate* (Princeton: Princeton University Press, 1992).

31. For a summary of almost a half century of scholarship related to Bauer see Robert Kraft, "The Reception of the Book," in Walter Bauer, *Orthodoxy and Heresy in Earliest Christianity* (Mifflintown, PA: Sigler Press, 1996), 286-316.

32. Robert Gregg and Dennis Groh have recognized the soteriology of Arius in their influential book *Early Arianism: A View of Salvation* (Philadelphia: Fortress, 1981). Additionally, "views of salvation" in distinct institutionalized or informal traditions linked with canons of persons can be found in the writings of at least four other distinct traditions that were excluded from the Nicene-Chalcedonian consensus. Donatists, Pelagians, Nestorians, and Monophysites all had institutional structures and an interest in canons of persons for the sake of Christian formation. The Donatists, for example, saw themselves as the church of the martyrs, upholding the legacy of Cyprian. The conciliar movement in fact can be seen as having been fueled by a desire to reorient and find a consensus that would include more of the excluded. This desire for consensus involved polemical aspects, but these aspects can also be seen as efforts faithfully to establish and articulate institutions and traditions that would bring people to God.

Cult of the Saints

The cult of the saints developed from the cult of the martyrs. To understand this progression we need to recognize some aspects of how Christian memory was kept in the liturgical life of Christian communities. At local levels Christians remembered their traditions in liturgical practice in at least two ways. First, since about the second century Christians remembered martyrs annually throughout the year to form a canon corresponding to the calendar.[33] Second, according to Cyril of Jerusalem, lists of martyrs and saints along with "patriarchs, prophets, and apostles" were remembered in some elaborate fourth-century liturgies of the eucharist.[34] These two aspects of the Christian tradition help point to the soteriological function of canons of persons in that these calendrical and eucharistic canons are clearly tied to formation of persons as Christians.

Early testimony of the "cult of the martyrs" which evolved into the "cult of the saints"[35] is found prototypically in the canonical Gospel accounts of the passion of Jesus and in Acts' record of the martyrdom of Stephen.[36] Other early Christian martyrdom accounts like those of the martyrs of Scillium in Africa and Lyons in Gaul, of Perpetua, Felicitas, and others also in Africa, were initially circulated regionally but gained wider fame over the centuries.[37] The martyrdom of Polycarp is particularly significant in that it gives early attestation to a celebration of the martyr's death.

> The centurion then, seeing the strife excited by the Jews, placed the body in the midst of the fire, and the fire consumed it. Accordingly, we afterwards took up his bones, as being more precious than the most exquisite jewels, and more purified than gold, and deposited them in a fitting place, whither, being gathered together, as opportunity is al-

33. Dix places this development sometime in the second century. See Dom Gregory Dix, *The Shape of the Liturgy* (London: Dacre Press, 1945), 343ff. See also W. H. C. Frend, *Martyrdom and Persecution in the Early Church: A Study of a Conflict from the Maccabees to Donatus* (New York: Anchor Books, 1967), 268ff.

34. On the innovations of Cyril see Dix, *The Shape of the Liturgy,* 350ff.

35. See particularly Peter Brown, *The Cult of the Saints* (Chicago: University of Chicago Press, 1982).

36. Interestingly, Christians also reached back and claimed the Maccabees as models of Christian martyrdom. See Frend, *Martyrdom and Persecution,* passim.

37. For texts and translations of a number of these accounts see Herbert Anthony Musurillo, ed., *Acts of the Pagan and Christian Martyrs* (Oxford: Oxford University Press, 1999).

lowed us, with joy and rejoicing, the Lord shall grant us to celebrate the anniversary of his martyrdom, both in memory of those who have already finished their course, and for the exercising and preparation of those yet to walk in their steps.[38]

The date of the death of the martyr came to be celebrated as the "birthday" of the martyr, and by the time of Cyprian in the third century we have examples of a more refined cult with liturgy and churches *(martyria)* dedicated to martyrs,[39] but it is in the fourth century that we see a quantum leap forward in the cult of the martyrs. Written accounts of the saints proliferate and circulate, the calendars become more crowded with commemorative days, liturgies are elaborated, and *martyria* multiply. Additionally, as Christianity grows correlative to waning persecutions, the number of holy men and women who are remembered expands beyond those who faced persecution and earned the title of martyr or confessor. As the term "saint" begins to emerge as a way of speaking about Christians notable for their witness, whether they suffered persecution or not, so too the "cult of the saints" extends the cultic practices that had been reserved for martyrs to a wider group. Many of these saints are seen as martyrs without blood; that is, they have put to death the worldly flesh and desires in their ascetic practice.[40] Ascetic traditions coalesce into monastic movements that serve as institutions that both develop and remember canons of saints and teachers, first in Egypt, then spreading to Palestine, Asia Minor, Italy, Africa, and Northern Europe.

Focusing on late antiquity, Peter Brown's work on saints has shown how men and women recognized for their holiness were essential agents of Christianization in that in life and death they served as mediators, intercessors, teachers, and guides to lead people to God.[41] As the empire in the West

---

38. *Martyrdom of Polycarp* 18, in *Ante-Nicene Fathers,* ed. Philip Schaff (reprint: Grand Rapids: Eerdmans, 2001), vol. 1.

39. V. Saxer, *Morts, martyrs, reliques en Afrique chrétienne aux premiers siècles. Les témoinages de Tertullien, Cyprien, et Augustin à la lumière de l'archéologie africaine, Théologie historique* (Paris, 1980), 55.

40. See for example Frend, *Martyrdom and Persecution,* 404ff.

41. Brown, *The Cult of the Saints,* and "The Rise and Function of the Holy Man in Late Antiquity," in his *Society and the Holy in Late Antiquity* (Berkeley: University of California Press, 1982), 103-52. In this case, be sure to consult Brown's own ongoing reconsideration of his work in "The Saint as Exemplar in Late Antiquity," in *Saints and Virtues,* ed. John Hawley (Berkeley: University of California Press, 1987), 3-14, and, even more fully, in "Arbiters of the Holy: The Christian Holy Man in Late Antiquity," in his *Authority and the Sacred: Aspects of the Christianisation of the Roman World* (Cambridge: Cambridge University Press, 1995), 57-78.

declined and as Christianity expanded into northwestern Europe, an excellent example of the strategic Christianizing use of saints and martyrs in a liturgical context is recorded by Bede in his *Ecclesiatical History of the English People.* There Bede records that, among instructions given by Pope Gregory to Abbot Mellitus concerning Augustine's mission, there was the direction to keep pagan temple structures and convert them to Christian use:

> . . . but let the idols that are in them be destroyed; let holy water be made and sprinkled in the said temples, let altars be erected, and relics placed. For if those temples are well built, it is requisite that they be converted from the worship of devils to the service of the true God; that the nation, seeing that their temples are not destroyed, may remove error from their hearts, and knowing and adoring the true God, may they more familiarly resort to the places to which they have been accustomed. And because they have been used to slaughter many oxen in the sacrifices to devils, some solemnity must be exchanged for them on this account, as that on the day of the dedication, or the nativities of the holy martyrs, whose relics are there deposited, they may build themselves huts of the boughs of trees, about those churches which have been turned to that use from temples, and celebrate the solemnity with religious feasting, and no more offer beasts to the Devil, but kill cattle to the praise of God in their eating, and return thanks to the Giver of all things for their sustenance; to the end that, whilst some gratifications are outwardly permitted them, they may the more easily consent to the inward consolations of the grace of God.[42]

Lives of saints like Athanasius's *Life of Anthony,* Gregory's *Life of Macrina,* Possidius's *Life of Augustine,* Sulpicius Severus's *Life of Saint Martin,* and collections of teachings like the preserved sayings of the desert fathers and mothers[43] also became sources for use in liturgy, preaching, and personal devotions. These cap what is seen in retrospect as a golden age that began with the Gospels and continued with preservation of martyrdom acts and passions like those of Polycarp up through the Constantinian inaugurated age of state-supported orthodoxy.[44]

---

42. Bede, *Ecclesiatical History of the English People,* ch. 30. Found at http://www.ccel.org/ccel/bede/history.v.i.xxix.html.

43. The Sayings were kept and transmitted in Chalcedonian and non-Chalcedonian traditions. For an English translation of one of the collections see Benedicta Ward, *The Sayings of the Desert Fathers* (Kalamazoo, MI: Cistercian Publications, 1975).

44. It should be remembered, however, that although Constantine favored Christian-

As the medieval period progressed, the two types of liturgical canons, calendrical and eucharistic, were important for Christian formation for both laity and those in religious vocations. This concern for making canons of persons an aspect of Christian formation is found in hymnody on particular days, in eucharistic worship, and in collections of saints' lives and teachings. This is evident in such far-flung examples as the *Book of Saints of the Ethiopian Church*,[45] which for the Ethiopian Monophysite tradition serves a role akin to the role collections such as Jacobus de Voragine's *The Golden Legend* served in Latin Chalcedonian Christendom.[46] This Ethiopian canon contains saints known in the Chalcedonian East and West like Antony, but there are also accounts of Ethiopian saints not known to the Chalcedonian tradition like Takla-Haymanot (c. 1215–c. 1313), known for his ascetic piety, orthodoxy, miraculous deeds, and longevity.[47]

By the eleventh century, Eastern and Western traditions diverged as distinct cultural and linguistic patterns were followed. In East and West, Chalcedonian and non-Chalcedonian Christians had calendars and liturgies rich with the memories of saints. Additionally, they saw themselves standing in theological traditions of faithful teachers that also served as a comparative point of division.

---

ity and helped enforce one form of Christianity over others in the wake of Nicaea, he did not make Christianity the only sanctioned religion in the Empire. Establishment of Christianity did not happen until the reign of Theodosius. By the close of the Council of Chalcedon at least five institutionalized forms of Christianity were outlawed: Arianism, Donatism, Nestorianism, Pelagianism, and Eutychianism or Monophysicism. I use the designations used by those who repressed these groups, but "Christian" was the name all of these groups claimed. The orthodox mainstream created a canon of heretical persons, and they were thereby able rhetorically and politically to deny the name of Christian to those who disagreed with doctrines as the institutional mainstream defined them.

45. E. A. Wallis Budge, *The Book of Saints of the Ethiopian Church*, 4 vols. (Cambridge: Cambridge University Press, 1928).

46. That is, they provide readings on saints both for liturgical and for devotional use as pious examples. Jacobus de Voragine, *The Golden Legend*, 2 vols. (Princeton: Princeton University Press, 1993).

47. According to *The Book of Saints of the Ethiopian Church*, Takla at a mere three days old confessed "One is the Holy Father. One is the Holy Son. One is the Holy Spirit"; he provided food in a famine, and he was even raised from the dead after being beaten to death by pagans. See the reading for Takla in the Ethiopian calendar on 24th of Nähasé, in Budge, *The Book of Saints of the Ethiopian Church* (Cambridge, 1928), 3:1241-46. See also E. A. Wallis Budge, *The Life and Miracles of Takla Haymânôt* (London, 1906).

From the Sixteenth Century On

The sixteenth century saw the development of new traditions in the West that established new canons of teachers that to varying degrees rejected and reinterpreted the canons of teachers that had been established over the previous thousand years. Perhaps, however, the canons of saints and martyrs received the most drastic reinterpretation from Protestants. Reflecting on the divergence between Protestants and Catholics on the understanding of the communion of saints, Donald Steele, relying on Lawrence Cunningham, presents four key aspects of the nature of sainthood:

(1) They are "sources of religious power."
(2) They are "spiritual resources."
(3) They are "models or paradigms of the Christian life."
(4) They are "intercessors."[48]

Though there can be overlap in the categories of saints and teachers. I think it is the case that aspects (2) and (3) are most relevant for understanding teachers. When, on the other hand, teachers are seen to embody "religious power" (1) or, after death, they are appealed to as "intercessors" (4), then they are clearly being recognized as saints.

Since the sixteenth century there has been divergence between Protestants, on the one hand, and Catholics and Orthodox, on the other, over the understandings of saints and teachers. Protestants, in varying degrees, leaned toward keeping the category of teacher while rejecting the category of saint, at least as framed by aspects (1) and (4) from the list above. Against the perceived excesses of the late medieval cult of the saints, two of the main points that Protestants argued were: first, that all believers were saints, and second, that those "saints" of high reputation who have died have no intercessory power and ought not to be invoked.[49] In the eyes of

---

48. Donald M. Steele, "With All God's People: Toward a Protestant Reclaiming of the Communion of the Saints," *Theology Today* 51 (January 1995): 539-47. The first three characteristics are taken from Lawrence S. Cunningham, *The Catholic Heritage* (New York: Crossroad, 1983), 207. The fourth is original to Steele. He says that (4) intercession "represents both a special obstacle and a special opportunity for a Protestant reconsideration of the subject" (Steele, "With All God's People," 540-41).

49. For the emphasis on the sainthood of all believers see, for example, Michael Whalen's "Saints and Their Feasts: An Ecumenical Exploration," *Worship* 63 (2004): 194-209. Whalen traces the liturgical affirmations of the communion of saints in Episcopal, Lu-

some Protestants the saints as viewed in medieval Christendom were not beacons guiding people to Jesus and the heart of the gospel but rather deceptive lights luring people away from safe harbor in Jesus Christ to deadly shipwreck on the crags of idolatry and superstition. Teachers, on the other hand, were safer to deal with. Standards of orthodoxy could be clearly taught, and the validity of the teaching, and thus its usefulness for guiding souls, could be easily established.

From the four main traditions that emerged from the sixteenth century and stood beside the Roman Catholic tradition — the Lutherans, the Reformed, the Anabaptists, and the Anglicans — a plethora of subtraditions emerged over the centuries that followed. Canons of saints were jettisoned as a number of Protestants argued that the cultic practices were not real Christianity but rather thinly veiled superstitions at best and demonic paganism at worst. Critics also saw these cultic practices as things that sought to displace Jesus from his unique mediatorial role.[50] This was particularly true in the case of Mary. For Protestants in the sixteenth century and beyond, Mary was the most egregious example of exaggerated attention given to a saint. Many Reformers revered Mary for her obedience but thought that it was inappropriate to invoke her or any other saint.[51]

For example, in the Lutheran tradition there was a clear rejection of the cult and intercession of the saints in Article 21 of the Augsburg Confession:

21. THE CULT OF SAINTS

It is also taught among us that saints should be kept in remembrance so that our faith may be strengthened when we see what grace they received and how they were sustained by faith. Moreover, their good works are to be an example for us, each of us in his own calling. So His Imperial Majesty may in salutary and godly fashion imitate the example of David in making war on the Turk, for both are incumbents of a

---

theran, and Presbyterian traditions. Also consider the examples from the Augsburg Confession and the Second Helvetic Confession cited below.

50. Consider the work of Jean Delumeau, *Catholicism between Luther and Voltaire* (Philadelphia: Westminster Press, 1977), and a very recent response in Scott H. Hendrix's *Recultivating the Vineyard* (Louisville: Westminster John Knox Press, 2004).

51. Protestants are starting to reconnect with Mary as a special exemplar among the saints. See, for example, the collection of essays in *Blessed One: Protestant Perspectives on Mary*, ed. Beverly R. Gaventa and Cynthia L. Rigby (Louisville: Westminster John Knox Press, 2002). See also David Van Biema, "Hail Mary," *Time*, March 21, 2005, 61-69.

royal office which demands the defense and protection of their subjects.

However, it cannot be proved from the Scriptures that we are to invoke saints or seek help from them. "For there is one mediator between God and men, Christ Jesus," I Timothy 2, who is the only savior, the only high priest, advocate, and intercessor before God, Romans 8. He alone has promised to hear our prayers. Moreover, according to the Scriptures, the highest form of divine service is sincerely to seek and call upon this same Jesus Christ in every time of need. "If anyone sins, we have an advocate with the Father, Jesus Christ the righteous."[52]

There was, however, more room in the tradition to recognize the saints as spiritual examples. In his Preface to his German translation Psalms, for example, Luther recommends the book, saying, "the Book of Psalms contains an assurance and a valid passport with which we can follow all the saints."[53]

In the Reformed tradition of Zwingli and Calvin there was a more thorough purge of the cult of the saints. Consider the title from Chapter Five of the Second Helvetic Confession and some of its paragraph headings:

CHAPTER V — Of The Adoration, Worship and Invocation of God Through The Only Mediator Jesus Christ

GOD ALONE IS TO BE ADORED AND WORSHIPPED.

GOD ALONE IS TO BE INVOKED THROUGH THE MEDIATION OF CHRIST ALONE.

THE SAINTS ARE NOT TO BE ADORED, WORSHIPPED OR INVOKED.

They then, citing Augustine, describe how the saints are to be honored.

THE DUE HONOR TO BE RENDERED TO THE SAINTS. At the same time we do not despise the saints or think basely of them. For we acknowledge them to be living members of Christ and friends of God

---

52. From the English translation of the German in Jaroslav Pelikan and Valerie Hotchkiss, eds., *Creeds and Confessions of Faith in the Christian Tradition,* 4 vols. (New Haven: Yale University Press, 2003), 3:75.

53. Luther, Preface to the Psalms, in John Dillenberger, ed., *Martin Luther: Selections from His Writings* (New York: Anchor Books, 1958), 37.

who have gloriously overcome the flesh and the world. Hence we love them as brothers, and also honor them; yet not with any kind of worship but by an honorable opinion of them and just praises of them. We also imitate them. . . . And in this respect we approve of the opinion of St. Augustine in *De Vera Religione:* "Let not our religion be the cult of men who have died. For if they have lived holy lives, they are not to be thought of as seeking such honors; on the contrary, they want us to worship him by whose illumination they rejoice that we are fellow-servants of his merits. They are therefore to be honored by way of imitation, but not to be adored in a religious manner," etc.

They reject the role of material relics asserting instead that the true relics worthy of attention are found "in their virtues, their doctrine, and their faith." They then add:

SWEARING BY GOD'S NAME ALONE. These ancient men did not swear except by the name of the only God, Yahweh, as prescribed by the divine law. Therefore, as it is forbidden to swear by the names of strange gods (Ex. 23:13; Deut. 10:20), so we do not perform oaths to the saints that are demanded of us. We therefore reject in all these matters a doctrine that ascribes much to the saints in heaven.[54]

Scott Hendrix recently has noted that the Consistory in Geneva even tried to forbid people from naming their children after saints.[55] This was an extreme example that can be contrasted with more moderate estimations.

Focusing on the understanding of true relics of the saints being found "in their virtues, their doctrine, and their faith" we can see, however, that even in the Reformed tradition there is room for some appreciation of the saints that is consistent with the canonical theism's soteriological imperative. Calvin is also helpful on this point. In his reply to Cardinal Sadoleto's letter to the Genevans he rejects the excesses of the invocation of saints, saying:

But, in regard to the intercession of the saints, we insist on a point which it is not strange that you omit. For here innumerable superstitions were to be cut off; superstitions which had risen to such a height, that the intercession of Christ was utterly erased from men's thoughts,

54. Pelikan and Hotchkiss, *Creeds*, 3:466.
55. Hendrix, *Recultivating the Vineyard*, 90-91.

saints were invoked as gods, the peculiar offices of Deity were distributed among them, and a worship paid to them which differed in nothing from that ancient idolatry which we all deservedly execrate.[56]

Yet earlier in the paragraph he conceded:

In asserting the intercession of the saints, if all you mean is, that they continually pray for the completion of Christ's kingdom, on which the salvation of all the faithful depends, there is none of us who calls it in question.[57]

Certainly it can be seen that some practices and teachings that had developed by the sixteenth century were errant distortions. Trent conceded as much while attempting to reestablish the proper role of the saints in the life of Christians: "so they may give God thanks for those things; may order their own lives and manners in imitation of the saints; and may be excited to adore and love God, and to cultivate piety."[58] It would be incorrect merely to see Trent as a response to Protestant cries for reform without acknowledging the continuance of reform within the Roman tradition. Pope Gregory VII, Bernard of Clairvaux, Savonarola, Catherine of Siena, Catherine of Genoa, Erasmus, Jacopo Sadoleto, Theresa of Avila, John of the Cross, Ignatius Loyola, and Charles Borromeo are a few of the names that a canon of reformers *within* the Roman Catholic tradition of the medieval and early modern period would include.[59] Though some traditions rejected the entire calendar and cult as well as much of the rest of the liturgical practice that had developed in Latin Christendom, there were ways in which new forms of memory developed to hold knowledge of holy exemplars.

Though less instantiated in ritual, *Foxe's Book of Martyrs,* from tumultuous sixteenth-century England, provides an early example of such

---

56. John Calvin, "Calvin's Reply to Sadoleto," in *A Reformation Debate: John Calvin and Jacopo Sadoleto,* ed. John C. Olin (reprint: Grand Rapids: Baker Book House, 1976), 72.

57. Calvin, "Calvin's Reply to Sadoleto," 72.

58. Council of Trent, Twenty-fifth Session, *On the Invocation, Veneration, and Relics, Of Saints, and On Sacred Images.*

59. Ironically, it could be said that the reform that led to the first major institutional break was in fact brought about by a saint well established in the Roman Catholic canon of the time. It was, after all, Saint Anne whom Luther asked for intercession during the storm, when he prayed, "Saint Anne, help me and I will become a monk." This, of course, set him on a path to be a biblical scholar. See Roland H. Bainton, *Here I Stand* (New York: New American Library, 1957), 15.

new forms of Protestant remembering of holy people. Foxe sought to root the stories of the martyrs of his day under so-called "Bloody Mary" Tudor in the tradition of the martyrs of the early Christian centuries.[60] By the late twentieth century the naming of buildings, organizations, institutions, and even academic chairs became well-established ways Christians, particularly Protestant Christians, remembered canons of saints and teachers.

Still, it is clear that as part of the formal teaching memory for many Protestants there has been an explicit rejection of the communion of saints conceived in terms of the above characteristics (1) and (4). Thus, although affirmed in creeds, in practice the "communion of saints" becomes something very different from what is embraced by the Orthodox and the Roman Catholics.

Where purity of doctrine has remained a concern, canons of teachers have been thrown into sharper relief. Where may these canons be found? Formally they are found in the faculties and syllabi of the educational institutions of the various traditions. Informally they are found in mentoring and personal relationships. In my African Methodist Episcopal tradition, for example, ministers often refer to the clergyperson most influential in their decision to go into the ministry as their "mother" or "father" in the ministry. As an example of mentoring there is an important parallel in the academic tradition that emerged from Germany of a *Doctorvater* or *Doctormutter* being the person who is the director of a candidate's doctoral dissertation. If Protestants rationalize sanctity by emphasizing a correct line of teachers, then the mentoring relationships in ministry and in academic institutions are perhaps a balance to draw sanctity as a model of life back into the picture.

The Future

As various traditions of Christianity — Orthodoxy, Catholicism, and Protestantism — have moved into new territories and have made Christianity a global religion, newer forms of memory have joined older forms of memory. They have variously been adopted, or imposed, on peoples depending on time and place.[61] In the twentieth century we became ever

60. To compare the editions of Foxe's work from 1563, 1570, 1576, and 1583 see the following website by the Humanities Research Institute, University of Sheffield: http://www.hrionline.ac.uk/johnfoxe/index.html.

61. On the cultural development of Christianity see Andrew Walls, *The Missionary Movement in Christian History: The Transmission of Faith* (Maryknoll, NY: Orbis, 1996).

more conscious of the interplay of differences among Christian communities. Inculturation has been an important theme in Christianity's growth since its beginning; indeed, the effort to render the gospel intelligible in different contexts partially accounts for the differences between the Gospels. Paul was also acutely aware of the need for such intelligibility:

> For though I am free with respect to all, I have made myself a slave to all, so that I might win more of them. To the Jews I became as a Jew, in order to win Jews. To those under the law I became as one under the law (though I myself am not under the law) so that I might win those under the law. To those outside the law I became as one outside the law (though I am not free from God's law but am under Christ's law) so that I might win those outside the law. To the weak I became weak, so that I might win the weak. I have become all things to all people, that I might by all means save some. I do it all for the sake of the gospel, so that I may share in its blessings.[62]

The purpose, of course, in Paul's mind was the soteriological imperative to draw people to God. In the spread of Christianity, and in Christian memories of that spread, canons of persons (as well as other canons of materials and practices) demonstrate the importance of the variety of exemplars that communities have recognized as markers or signposts showing those who come after the way to God and a Christian life. Continued recognition of this variety ought to be a central part of each Christian's formation and every Christian community's effort to know and live in God.

Additionally, an awareness of ecumenical commonalities among the various Christian traditions has developed alongside the recognition of inculturated diversity. Worship and witness are two important loci where canons of persons have found ways to move in through and across traditions. For example, in the United States the Revised Common Lectionary, the sharing of liturgies, and interdenominational worship have become avenues through which a greater appreciation for Christian memory in the form of canons of persons has developed.[63] Likewise, new liturgical occa-

---

62. 1 Cor. 9:19-23, NRSV.

63. See, for example, an important article by Clifton F. Guthrie, "Why A Sanctoral Cycle? Or, Are We Ready for Methodist Hagiography?" from the *Material History of American Religion Project* at http://www.materialreligion.org/journal/saints.html; reprinted from *Doxology: Journal of the Order of Saint Luke* 13 (1996). For Methodism broadly understood, Guthrie traces a history of the status of materials and practices as they relate to "saints." He

sions are created and saints and teachers are born and nurtured as Christians live out loving their neighbors in faithful work in the world.

In endorsing canons of persons, let me follow Paul in raising a cautionary note: teachers, saints, and martyrs have been, and always will be, imperfect signs. This fact should be always remembered as we seek to understand how members of a canon of persons function as signs. In 1 Corinthians 12, Paul, speaking of various roles that contribute to the healthy functioning of the body of Christ, cautions against conflict and offers to the Corinthians a more excellent way, the way of love. Saints have imperfections, as do we all. Perfection exists in the one to whom, by whom, and in the power of whom we are drawn. Saints and other spiritual "heroes" may have feet of clay, but this ought not to disturb us as long as some fire from these torches will direct us toward God and contribute to the increase within us of love of God and of neighbor.

---

rightly notes about my tradition that "Richard Allen's pulpit, altar, and communion jug are displayed at Mother Bethel Church in Philadelphia, the most important shrine of the African Methodist Episcopal Church"; he could have added that in the crypt underneath Mother Bethel lie the remains of Richard and Sarah Allen and Morris Brown, Allen's successor.

Imagining Theology:
The Canon of Images

Natalie B. Van Kirk

For someone reared in the ostentatious plainness of the Protestant churches of my childhood, one of the more intriguing aspects of the study of early and medieval Christianity has been the church's reliance upon material and verbal images for teaching the faith and structuring the Christian view of the world. My upbringing taught me to see statues, icons, and paintings as syncretism of the worst sort — idols perpetuating superstition and false worship. Careful reading of the reflections of those who used and supported the use of such images in the church, however, both shows an awareness of the problems and limitations of the material images and image-making in the church and simultaneously insists upon a profound theological function for those same images.

Furthermore, as I have learned to reflect more carefully on the various sorts of images employed by the church in its history, it has become apparent that even the most iconoclastic strains in Christianity have employed images, albeit sometimes unconsciously. The "unconscious" use of images does, however, often lead to a reversal of roles wherein images use us far more than we use them, and we are thus formed by unseen forces. So, the question to be argued here is not one of whether images are part of the canonical heritage of Christianity, or whether there should be images in the church. Images have always been used by the church and are already present among even the most iconoclastic of Christian traditions. The main thrust of this chapter is to uncover the various forms of images that the church has used and continues to use and argue for their intentional role in the formation of Christians.[1]

---

1. The term "images," as opposed to "art," "paintings," "statues," or "icons," is em-

This chapter will endeavor to make three related arguments: (1) When we speak of the canonical heritage of the church, we cannot avoid taking into account the images that have been used to express Christian theology and to form each new generation of Christians — all the various sorts of images used to lead Christians to true *theologia*.[2] The list includes images in liturgy and literature, painting, sculpture, architecture, and music. In other words, the canonical heritage of the church goes beyond a set of texts and the creeds and involves not only the institutional ordering of the church but also the ecclesial arts and architecture that the church used to structure and visualize its understanding of God and reality.[3] The material images that the church developed for use in worship and contemplation drew on the textual images with the intent to reinforce those images, to express the church's theology with regard to those images, and to help provide a contemplative window through which the believer could see and encounter God.[4] What the images were not intended to do, and what those who worried about their use in the church most feared they would do, is to reify the divine and confine it to a particular image or construction.

(2) While material images and specifically Christian architectural forms — i.e., in tombs, on sarcophagi, or in baptistries — develop somewhat later than the earliest Christian texts and liturgies, they too become

---

ployed throughout this chapter because the classical and medieval conceptions, for both Latin- and Greek-speaking Christians, of what an image is and the ways images function were much broader than are the modern conceptions. In the post-Enlightenment world we confine "real images" to those which have a material component — like statues, paintings, or photographs. As will be evident in the argument below, the classical and medieval thinkers saw little difference in the reality or effect between those images "painted in the mind" and those painted on a board. In both cases the image could either help lead the soul to God or be a temptation to idolatry.

2. For the fathers of the undivided church, *theologia* was not "talk about God," but rather actually "knowing the mind of God." It implied deep relationship with the Divine. For the most adept of Christians *theologia* was the result of the experience of the presence of God, or union with God. This experience was an event with epistemic implications, to be sure, but it was a knowing that came first from relationship, and the relationship was the *result* of the interplay of faith and disciplines that, through grace, led to moral and intellectual virtue and fit the believer for life with God.

3. An assertion made by Paul Gavrilyuk and William Abraham earlier in this volume.

4. This argument will be taken up in the concluding essay of this volume on the *telos* of the church and canonical theism. See also Abraham, Thesis XI, above. This essay does assume, however, that the writers of the Gospels, St. Paul, and the church's great early theologians were not talking utter nonsense when they spoke of the possibility of knowing God.

intricately woven into the dance of Scripture, creeds, liturgy, sacramental theology, ecclesiastical polity, and saints from which sprang Christian theology and the canonical heritage of the church. Images not only reflected current doctrinal teaching; they also engaged those who contemplated them in theological speculation. Images were seen not merely as visual aids, but as means of grace and transformation that helped fit the human being for relationship with God.

(3) Failure to understand the role of material and verbal image-making in the Christian tradition will lead to a misunderstanding about the ways in which images *continue* to function theologically in the church, perhaps most especially in those parts of the church most wedded to an iconoclastic ideology.

Thus, a significant portion of this essay is devoted to understanding the pedagogical work of images and the importance of the lack of distinction made in the period of the great church between material images and images created in the mind as one read a text. Indeed, it is important to note that the creation of mental images was often referred to as "painting."[5] It is only by exploring these differences in the understanding of the nature of images that we can begin to see how idolatry was understood in the first millennium or so of the church, and what role our unseen idolatry plays in the contemporary church.

The *Oikonomia* of Christian Images

There is a modern and postmodern emphasis on the creative expression or authority of the artist that tends to ignore the theological premises at work in earlier, specifically Christian art. This emphasis has led some scholars and theologians to dismiss art and architecture as mere decoration or as superstitious construction of idols when employed by the church. If we are to get past the tendency among modern theological scholarship to over-simplify the interplay of art, theology, and Christian practice, we must first explore the ways in which the canonical heritage of the church believed art and architecture could and should be used as a means of grace. What, in other words, was the economy[6] — the *oikonomia* — of images in the late antique and early medieval church?

---

5. Most famously, perhaps, in book 4 of St. Anselm's *Cur Deus Homo?*

6. A felicitous phrase and idea borrowed from Annemarie Weyl Carr, "Thoughts on

In the sixth-century chapel at the Monastery of St. Catherine on Mount Sinai[7] there is a glorious mosaic covering the apse and apse wall of the chapel. The monastery was built at the site of what was believed to be the burning bush of Exodus 3. Not surprisingly, given the chapel's location, the mosaics on the apse wall depict the great theophanies of Exodus — those times when Moses encountered God's own presence. In the center of the apse is a resplendent, much larger than life-sized Christ at the Transfiguration, surrounded by Elijah, Moses, James, Peter, and John. The relationship between the iconic images of the mosaics is a relatively simple one to make. The great theophanies of Exodus are but *typoi* of the greatest theophany of all, the glorified and incarnate God revealed in his true nature on Mount Tabor.[8]

Given its location and its themes, the *economy* of the mosaic program seems relatively simple to discern — the mosaics are intended to provide visual cues to the viewer, reminding the viewer of the stories appropriate to a setting at Mount Sinai, and to reinforce the typological reading that the theophanies to Moses were in fact but precursors to the theophany of the Transfiguration.[9] This may not be obvious to modern

---

the Economy of the Image of Mary," *Theology Today* 56:3 (October 1999): 359-78. "Economy" here refers not to what the image is in itself but rather to the way the image functions in the viewer's life, especially the way it functions soteriologically. Like the trinitarian economy it defies a linear definition. It is always polyvalent — an interplay of the intent of the creator, the situation of the work involved, and the state of the viewer.

7. I have chosen this example because the images are still *in situ*, are still in daily use, and have sufficient documentation to illuminate the ways in which the images may indeed function.

8. This reading of the mosaics is dependent upon the traditional understanding of the Transfiguration in the Eastern churches. In a tradition going back at least to Origen, the transfigured Christ is revealed in his *full* glory — as God incarnate and the fulfillment of the Law and the Prophets — to the three disciples. As his special chosen ones, they were not destroyed by the divine Light but rather had been "given eyes to see" through the disciplines of discipleship. This is not precisely how the Latin tradition in the church, following Augustine, usually understood this pericope, but the differences need not be explored here. What is important here is to see the relationship between the major iconic sections of the mosaic in their proper theological context. Moses never saw God. Those who are *true disciples of Jesus Christ* will see God.

9. It is hard to underestimate the debt owed by historians of theology to art historians at this point. Much of modern history of Christian doctrine has been concerned solely with its written expressions and, furthermore, premised upon the deeply iconoclastic impulses of Reformed theology. It has been art historians who have preserved, restored, and deciphered many of the ignored treasures of the church. Moreover, where theologians have tended to

viewers, but, to paraphrase Origen, just as providence is not abolished because we are ignorant of it, neither is the divine economy of this mosaic abolished because our weakness cannot discern the hidden splendor of its teachings.[10] The obvious didactic purposes of the mosaic will benefit the viewer, even at the most simple level; but there are, I believe, three important clues that can lead to a deeper — and Origen would say, more spiritual — understanding of the economy of the image.

The first clue is the location of the mosaics. They are in a monastery. The preeminent vocation of the monastic life has always been a life of prayer through which one will be completely reformed and come to know God — to become a friend of God as Jesus promised that those who followed him would be his friends. It is among the Christian monastics that the aphorism arose, "A theologian is one who prays, and only the one who prays is a theologian."[11] Prayer as a means of entering relationship with God and progressing on the journey to union with God was at the heart of monastic life, and all the activities and locations of monastic living were intentionally designed to support this goal. Surely something as difficult to create, as expensive, and as dominating as the mosaics in the chapel were installed not simply for decorative or narrative purposes, but intentionally to further the goals of monastic life.

The second clue is the church's teaching on *theosis* or divinization.[12]

---

take a didactic and reductionist view of Christian art, art history has asked detailed questions about what text — down to a specific verse — was used as support for a particular image. They have not neglected the relationship between scripture and art. It is, however, only of late that both art historians and theologians have begun asking about the theological economy of images in the life of the church.

10. "But just as providence is not abolished because of our ignorance, at least not for those who have once rightly believed in it, so neither is the divine character of scripture, which extends through all of it, abolished because our weakness cannot discern in every sentence the hidden splendor of its teachings, concealed under a poor and humble style." Origen, *On First Principles* 4.1.7, trans. G. W. Butterworth (Gloucester, MA: Peter Smith, 1973), 267.

11. A proverbial saying that can be found in some form in the works of Evagrius Ponticus, Maximus Confessor, and John Cassian.

12. The language of *theosis* or divinization did not drop out of the Western tradition until after the thirteenth century, and has never completely evaporated from the Catholic side of the Western church. The Reformation churches, with their doctrines of predestination, saw a doctrine of spiritual progression as pernicious, and so it has dropped almost entirely from the Protestant vocabulary. Where the concept remained among Protestants, notably among Anglicans, Wesleyans, and some Anabaptists, it was reduced to a doctrine of sanctification.

Salvation is not static but dynamic; it is not a completed state, but a constant moving toward *theosis* or deification, toward becoming like Christ. Deification need not necessarily be understood to suppress humanity, but to make each person more authentically human.[13] The fathers of the church often said that Christ became man so that humans might share in the divine nature.[14] In receiving God's fullness into his or her own life the

13. John Meyendorff, *Byzantine Theology: Historical Trends and Doctrinal Themes* (New York: Fordham University Press, 1979), 72. *Theosis* does not obliterate the distinction between Creator and creature, but focuses instead on the restoration of the divine image in human beings. Human beings do not become God or Christ Jesus, but rather are restored to share in the divine nature as it was imparted in the image given at creation. So Athanasius, *On the Incarnation of the Word:*

> What then was God to do? or what was to be done save the renewing of that which was in God's image, so that by it men might once more be able to know Him? But how could this have come to pass save by the presence of the very Image of God, our Lord Jesus Christ? For by men's means it was impossible, since they are but made after an image; nor by angels either, for not even they are (God's) images. Whence the Word of God came in His own person, that, as He was the Image of the Father, He might be able to create afresh the man after the image. But, again, it could not else have taken place had not death and corruption been done away. Whence He took, in natural fitness, a mortal body, that while death might in it be once for all done away, men made after His Image might once more be renewed. None other then was sufficient for this need, save the Image of the Father. (13.7-9)

14. See, 2 Pet. 1:4; Rom. 8 (through the Spirit we become sons of God); and John 14–17 (on the concept of the indwelling of the Trinity). Irenaeus says in *Adversus Haeresis:*

> For it is thus that thou wilt both controvert them in a legitimate manner, and wilt be prepared to receive the proofs brought forward against them, casting away their doctrines as filth by means of the celestial faith; but following the only true and stedfast Teacher, the Word of God, our Lord Jesus Christ, who did, through His transcendent love, become what we are, *that He might bring us to be even what He is Himself.* (V, praef.; emphasis added; http://www.newadvent.org/fathers/0103500.htm)

Athanasius, in *On the Incarnation of the Word*, puts it this way:

> For of His becoming Incarnate we were the object, and for our salvation He dealt so lovingly as to appear and be born even in a human body. Thus, then, God has made man, and willed that he should abide in incorruption; but men, having despised and rejected the contemplation of God, and devised and contrived evil for themselves (as was said in the former treatise), received the condemnation of death with which they had been threatened; and from thenceforth no longer remained as they were made, but were being corrupted according to their devices; and death had the mastery over them as king. For transgression of the commandment was turning them back to their natural state, so that just as they have had their being out of nothing, so also, as might be expected, they might look for corruption into nothing in the

believer is transformed into the fullness of the image of God that humans had before the Fall. The Transfiguration is, in early Christian theology, the quintessential image of the fullness of humanity realized — the promise of what human beings are called to be. To sit and worship daily under the icon of the Transfiguration in the apse of the chapel was to be reminded constantly of the journey upon which one was embarked. While *theosis* is a journey that can never be fully completed in this life, the monks at Sinai understood that they were to go as far as possible on that journey.

The third clue is found in St. John of Damascus's liturgy for the Feast of the Transfiguration.[15] While there is no evidence that St. John ever saw the mosaics at Sinai, his liturgical canticles rely on the tradition that the theophanies to Moses were types of the Transfiguration and proceed through the verbal images from Scripture in the same top-down order as the mosaics. First, the theophanies to Moses in succession and then the Transfiguration superseding them all. In both St. John's liturgy and the chapel mosaics it is as though the images — verbal and visual — function as pins on a map, anchoring the theological reflection of the one who contemplates them.

The last clue to the economy of the mosaic icons in the chapel is the iconostasis that was erected in the seventeenth century. The iconostasis was installed to bring the ancient chapel more nearly into conformity with standard Orthodox worship space and almost completely blocks the worshiper's view of the mosaics. The monks are considering removing the great cross at the top of the iconostasis. They have become concerned that since the cross and iconostasis were erected, there have been no Saints[16] at Sinai. No one among the monastic community has had his heart so changed that he lived an especially exemplary and sanctified life and was viewed as a Saint by his brothers and the greater church.[17] The monks have begun to believe that obscuring the icons in the apse has affected the formation of the community that worships in the chapel.

---

course of time. . . . Wisdom also says: "God made man for incorruption, and as an image of His own eternity; but by envy of the devil death came into the world." (4.3-6; 5.1; http://www.newadvent.org/fathers/2802.htm)

15. "Homily on the Transfiguration of Our Lord Jesus Christ by Saint John of Damascus" (Including "A Song Concerning the Transfiguration of Our Lord"), trans. Harold L. Weatherby, *Greek Orthodox Theological Review* 32:4 (1987): 26-69.

16. Capital *S* fully intended.

17. John Elsner, "The Viewer and the Vision: The Case of the Sinai Apse," *Art History* 17:1 (March 1994): 81.

The fathers of Mount Sinai understand that contemplation of these mosaic icons is part of the dance of scripture, location, material images, theology, and liturgy that transforms the viewer. The mosaics are integral to the formation of at least an occasionally monk into a Saint. This is not what we ordinarily expect of images. How can these things be?

Images as a Means of Contemplating the Divine

In modern theology and philosophy there are few ways to discuss the use of images in the church that allow for the possibility that images can be used quite deliberately to enrich a relationship with God. Nor is it commonplace to say that images can actively further the transformation of individuals into the complete and authentically human beings, in short, that images that make Saints.

My first glimmer of understanding about the source of the dissonance and incongruities between what modern scholars are willing to say about the role of Christian images and what the theologians of the Church prior to the thirteenth century[18] actually said about the uses of images lay in the interplay found at Mount Sinai between liturgy, image, and contemplation. This dissonance cropped up again in commentaries about sites like Hagia Sophia, Santa Maria Maggiore, or Notre Dame de Paris. Clearly, these were not situations in which a disinterested viewer assigned meaning to a work under inspection. Nor was exegesis of a textual image, a painting, or any other material image confined by the ancient writers to extrapolating a single meaning. A text or image of any value was understood to be polyvalent in meaning and economy — the effects varying with the spiritual condition of the viewer.

18. The argument of this essay also assumes that the undivided church did not cease to exist in the minds of the church's theologians until after the crusaders captured Constantinople in 1204. The traditional dating of the Great Schism at 1054 marks a date that seemed relatively unimportant to the parties involved. The date of 1054 is one of convenience to a certain stream of historiography but does not accurately reflect the attitudes and theology of the people who were actually there. In the high medieval renaissance of Western Europe of the mid-eleventh and twelfth centuries there was a conscious reappropriation of the patristic heritage and a deep awareness of the continuity with the minds and understandings of the previous twelve centuries of the church. It was not until the schools, with their increasing interest in Aristotelian metaphysics, flourished in the thirteenth century and the crusaders had sacked Constantinople that a rapprochement between Rome and the Eastern churches was seen as impossible and the church viewed as sundered.

Multiplying Charges

The earliest images created by Christians were frequently images from biblical stories, images of Christ, the apostles, or the Virgin and Child. The one who contemplated the images could "read" them at various levels. These levels borrowed much from Origen's understanding of the various levels of meaning in scripture.[19] There was a literal meaning connected to the actual image, recalling the story of the person depicted and a moral meaning which explored at more depth the nature of the image as exemplar and instruction for Christian living. Prolonged contemplation of the image would create the desire in the viewer to see ever more deeply into the mystery of God. The desiring viewer is then "drawn" through the "window" of the image into a deeper, anagogical (soteriological) understanding. Thus, the ultimate point of creating an image was to draw the viewer more deeply into God.

What Bernard McGinn says of Origen's way of reading scripture can also be applied to the "reading" of images. "Origen is interested not so much in determining different meanings of the text, as in using the encounter with the text as a paradigm for the spiritual education (*paideia*, training) by means of which the goal of life [the encounter with God] is attained."[20] Like scripture, images are a form of holy *paideia*.

When late antique and early medieval writers refer to the way images work, it is clear that they carry their own "charge," and it is a charge of sufficient power that it can be expected to change the viewer. Moreover, the charge in images was often expected to work with charges found in liturgical forms or the text of scripture and the cumulative effects were perceived to be far greater than the sum of the parts. Saints then were made — at Sinai and elsewhere — through the transformative effects of these charged images, liturgical rituals, and texts.

Material images became holy on this account not only because they depicted images of holy subjects, sacred stories, people, the Savior, and his mother, but also because they were perceived to have a charge or power that could help the contemplative viewer encounter the divine. The risk, of course, was always that the less theologically sophisticated would come to think a material image (painting, statue, mosaic) was intrinsically holy. More than the material image itself, it was the work of the image on the

---

19. See Origen, *De Principiis* 4.2.1-5, for an exposition of the levels of meaning in scripture.

20. Bernard McGinn, *The Foundations of Mysticism: Origins to the Fifth Century,* vol. 1, *The Presence of God: A History of Western Christian Mysticism* (New York: Crossroad, 1997), 110.

soul of the viewer, its economy, that was holy. Hence the continual distinctions made by John of Damascus and others between veneration of images, which was appropriate, and worship of images, which was not.

The mind — classical and medieval theologians believed, along with the Platonists — is formed, literally impressed, by the input of the senses, most especially sight. In this understanding, a beam of light, or the purest of non-burning fire, emanates from the eye. When this beam strikes an object, the beam is reflected back into the eye and the resulting image is burned into the mind. Because the mind is part of the soul, the soul is also marked and altered by the image.[21] Good sensory inputs — good is not necessarily synonymous with pleasurable — can turn the mind toward the Good and the Beautiful. Bad or evil sensory inputs — which may be quite pleasurable — will turn the mind and soul toward evil.

We now know that Plato's physics and physiology are in error. About his psychology we are of two minds. On the one hand, we are clear that seeing a mutant lamb with two heads will not cause a pregnant woman to give birth to a two-headed child. On the other hand, we are well aware that images can make us do things or lead us to desire certain objects or people. Modern thought tends to view the effects of images as ethical responses. In special cases, like propaganda art, advertising, violent movies, pornography, and any image that depicts an unflattering gender or racial bias, we are more than willing to believe that images can leave lasting, often negative, impressions that will configure thought patterns and morals — at least in the young and impressionable. Positive images can generate positive ethical responses, but it seems we attribute less power or appeal to the positive image. Contemplation of an image of Jesus is not usually expected to impress the soul with the image of Christ.

The canonical tradition of the church was not so double minded. At least as early as St. Paul's letter to the Philippians,[22] the church was clear that what one saw and contemplated was indeed a means for turning the soul toward the Good and Beautiful — toward God. There is no higher goal in the New Testament for this life or the next than a soul totally turned to God and lost in contemplation of the divine. When Paul says the

21. Plato, *Timaeus* 1.13 in *Timaeus and Critias,* trans. Desmond Lee (New York: Penguin Books, 1997), 62-64.
22. "Finally, brothers, whatever is true, whatever is honorable, whatever is just, whatever is pure, whatever is lovely, whatever is gracious, if there is any excellence and if there is anything worthy of praise, think about these things. . . . Then the God of peace will be with you" (Phil. 4:8-9).

God of peace will be with you, he does not mean that God will like you better if you think on such things, or reward you, but that God will be present to you and you will be able to perceive God. Thus, to "think on these things" was a way of contemplating the divine attributes and coming into God's presence.

Images could also serve as distractions which turned one away from the proper contemplation of God. Thus, it mattered tremendously how one employed the arts.[23] Art was not produced solely for its own sake. The artist had a responsibility to God and the community to depict reality, be it spiritual or material, in a way that reflected or revealed its truth. The belief in the unity of creation in God meant that artist and art were of a piece, and part of the depicted Reality. God may not be visible in the work, but God is always present, and simply cannot be dropped out of the analysis or relegated to the distant background.[24]

To say that classical and medieval people thought in images, however, is not the same thing as saying that they thought in symbols.[25] That they used images with great subtlety and imagination there is no doubt, but as realists they did not understand their mental functioning to rest upon a symbolic system. Rather, they understood that much cognition was done in relation to the images one stored in memory.[26] These images came

23. Origen, for example, in his Commentary on the Song of Songs has a long excursus on the ways in which the lewd murals found in the houses of pagans lead the mind and soul to concern for baser things and away from the contemplation of God.

24. There was also a concern for the great temptation for the artist to confuse himself with God. To volitionally create that which mimics life or reveals the divine truth, and to create that something out of almost nothing, is to do something godlike. In the other Abrahamic traditions, most particularly in Islam, the fear of confusion of the artist's self with God or the artist's creation with the Divine Reality led to absolute prohibitions on the creation of any images but verbal ones. Christianity was not unaware of these risks to artist and viewer but insisted that if God deigned to join God's self to the material then depiction of material things, or even images of the incarnate God, were entirely appropriate and served to reinforce the church's belief in the incarnate God. See John of Damascus, *On the Divine Images* 1.4 and passim, in John of Damascus, *On the Divine Images: Three Apologies Against Those Who Attack the Divine Images,* trans. David Anderson (Crestwood, NY: St. Vladimir's Seminary Press, 1980).

25. Mary Carruthers, *The Craft of Thought: Meditation, Rhetoric, and the Making of Images, 400-1200* (Cambridge: Cambridge University Press, 2000), 118-22. Carruthers opens an entire world in this extraordinary text.

26. Memory or *memoria* is not primarily a mental function that repeats or reiterates past events. That is a modern understanding that the classical and medieval thinker would have found odd at best. In their conception of *memoria,* memory functioned like a machine,

to be stored in one of four ways: (1) through sight; (2) through the hearing or reading of verbal images; (3) through the memories of events in which one had participated; and (4) through the imaginative combination of two or more images into something new.

A cognitive image is functional. This is why any art that created images was regarded functionally. It can have effects that are pedagogical or ethical, but "these effects occur within the alert mind and coloring emotion of a viewer/listener."[27] The image is a tool, but it is a tool that captures some of the essential nature of the thing imaged, and it has a reality[28] about it. Thus, the affects and intellect react to the image and are potentially changed by it. "The first question one should ask of such an image is not "What does it mean?" but "What is it good for?"[29] As classical and medieval thinkers saw it, the human mind needed images in order to think. This dependence on images was one of the basic limitations to human knowing.[30] Thus, when Christian teachers insisted that the mind concede that no image, material or verbal, could capture God *in se,* the mind and soul were forced into the ultimate act of self-transcendence, the leap into the bright darkness of God that lay beyond image or comprehension.

The images formed by engagement with the arts were to draw the mind and soul further along the path of ascent to God. Images were a means to an end, never an end in themselves. Put another way, art did not have "ontological" status. It did not exist on its own without reference to the purposes for which it was created. Such an understanding carries

---

a *machina,* classifying and sorting images, making connections between images, and creating new ones. *Memoria* is a primarily a cognitive function, not a strictly mimetic one. Carruthers, *The Craft of Thought,* 3-4.

27. Carruthers, *The Craft of Thought,* 118.

28. The reality of the image can be explained by explaining the concept of a mirror in classical or medieval thought. We know that images in mirrors are mere figments of refracted light rays that hold nothing of the essential nature of that which is reflected in the mirror. In our forebearers' understanding, the image in a mirror was a reflection of reality and contained something of the essential nature of the thing imaged. Thus, St. Paul could speak of "seeing in a mirror dimly" or later writers could speak of seeing God in the mirror of the soul, and their readers/hearers would know that it was really God that was seen in the mirror — God's essential nature was captured in the image in the mirror. A mirror image was not as good as seeing face to face, but it was not something unreal or ephemeral. See my essay "Christ Present in the Moment" later in this volume for further exploration of this theme.

29. Carruthers, *The Craft of Thought,* 118.

30. Carruthers, *The Craft of Thought,* 118.

within it a profoundly functional view of art. The arts were a means of theological speculation and doctrinal affirmation.

For example, the near simultaneous development of polyphony and the gothic in the West can be seen as a direct outgrowth of a renewed concern to incorporate the perfect ratios of mathematics into music and gothic architecture. Both were seen as means to the end of demonstrating and reflecting the perfection of God in earthly work. Thus, the church building filled with music becomes a reflection of divine perfection for multiple senses and so forms the seeker's intellect and soul.[31]

Images are constructs by which we can grasp God or a new concept and they are things that we can smell, hear, taste, touch and most especially that we *see* with the mind.[32] As St. Alcuin puts it:

> It is more remarkable, that with respect to unknown things, if they come to our ears from reading or hearing something, the mind immediately fashions a figure of the unknown thing. . . . The human mind makes up images concerning each matter; from what it knows it fashions things unknown, having all these particulars in itself. . . . By means of this swift activity of the mind, by which it thus fashions in itself all that it has heard or seen or touched or tasted or smelled, and again recalls its fashionings, by the marvelous power of God and the efficacy of its nature, from any circumstances it may acquire knowledge.[33]

This understanding of the soul-changing effects of all types of images is precisely why St. John of Damascus can use the verbal images

---

31. Medieval music was built on a Pythagorean system of intervals of fifths and fourths. The fifths were tuned on a pure ratio of 3:2. It is a mathematically elegant system and like other forms of mathematics reflected God's perfections and his impassability. The ratios trained the mind and ear. "The one potential flaw of this system is that the fourth or fifth between the extreme notes of the series, E♭-G♯, will be out of tune: in the colorful language of intonation, a 'wolf' interval. This complication arises because 12 perfect fifths do not round off to precisely an even octave, but exceed it by a small ratio known as a Pythagorean comma. Happily, since E♭ and G♯ rarely get used together in medieval harmony, this is hardly a practical problem." It was, however, a practical problem with music shifted to meantone tuning in the Renaissance, and the perfect integer notations of the Pythagorean system no longer held. The "wolf" had to be accommodated. At that point, the mathematical structure of music could not be considered "perfect." For more on the mathematical structure of Pythagorean tuning see Margo Shulter, http://www.medieval.org/emfaq/harmony/pyth.html. Much of this theory finds its origins in Plato and was transmitted to the West via the works of Boethius. See *De institutione musica*.

32. Carruthers, *The Craft of Thought*, 119.

33. Alcuin, *Liber de animae rationae*, quoted in Carruthers, *The Craft of Thought*, 120.

found in Scripture for his defense of icons. As modern thinkers we tend to see this as the weakest part of his argument. For us verbal images have no basis in reality since the only images that are "real" are those that are related to some sort of sense experience — painting or sculpture, perhaps. Words are fleeting and have only the substance of the breath it takes to utter them. Not so for St. John. The mental images one forms in the memory as one reads the Gospels, while not Truth, are stepping stones to the presence of God. It is not a reality that they lack, but a completeness of Truth.[34] In this way verbal images and the images of panel paintings or statues function analogously — they open up the intellect/soul to the reality of the divine presence.

Mary Carruthers cites St. Jerome making an argument that parallels St. John:

> For example, commenting on the verse describing the Egyptian gods painted on the exterior wall of the temple (Ezekiel 8:10), Jerome counsels that "we also may display idols painted on the walls in our [interior] temple, when we submit to all vices and we paint in our heart the conscious and various imagings of sins. . . . For indeed there in no human being who does not have some image whether of sanctity or of sin." To be sure this is a caution against mental painting for immoral purposes, but the vividness of mental picturing is, you will notice, taken for granted by Jerome's remark. More important, so is the assumption that reading will raise pictures in the mind's eye.[35]

In the above cases, it does not matter much if your images look exactly like my images. What matters is that the images can be used to anchor an entire web of associations and help us to see more deeply into the Truth. Idolatry, on this understanding of images, is a matter of allowing an image to conform one's soul to that which is not God, is less than God, or is frankly demonic. The *holy* image is the image that works to conform the soul to God's truth and to God. Thus, in the iconoclastic controversies it is not the case that the images themselves — images of Christ and his mother most especially — were evil *in se,* but that they would lead people to be-

---

34. Therefore, as St. Gregory of Nyssa and later Pseudo-Dionysius insisted, while the images will help us to approach God, in the end they all must be abandoned if we are to have union with God.

35. Jerome, *Commentarii in Hiesechielem* 3.8.7-9, quoted in Carruthers, *The Craft of Thought,* 134.

lieve that God could be conceptualized and reified as a finite image. The risk was that the "picture" of the finite image would substitute for the infinite God and become the object of worship in the soul.

Images were also volatile because they were so often ambiguous. It is not the case that the same or similar images were always interpreted the same way, or attached to same constellations of other images and ideas. Often the images had to borrow charges or power from unrelated, or not necessarily ideal images in order to have any meaning themselves.[36] The mosaics in the sixth-century baptisteries in Ravenna offer wonderful examples of the ways ambiguity could be associated with certain images.

In the mosaic depictions of Christ's baptism that fill the domes of the Arian and Orthodox baptisteries in Ravenna, Christ is depicted with clearly visible genitalia. From both sides of the theological divide art seeks to make visible and inescapable the claims each was asserting about the humanity of Jesus Christ. For the Arians, Christ's visible maleness was an affirmation that he was not God, but a man with whom the divine Logos chose to join the divine nature. For the Orthodox, Christ's maleness was affirmation that he was not simply a spiritual being, but the truly human, truly divine being affirmed in the creed. The images in the domes are very much alike in their essential elements — it would be hard to know, without knowing the history of the buildings, that they speak of different conceptions of Christ. And it is only through knowing the history of the buildings, their use, and the canonical heritage of the church in doctrine, scripture, creed, and liturgy that one can rightly interpret the images. Once again, it is the interplay of all of these elements of the canonical heritage with the image that creates meaning.[37]

It is also the case that one finds oneself unclear whether theology follows image or image follows theology. The increasing realism of depictions of the crucified Christ that begin to appear in the West in the eleventh century, for example, mark a deliberate and conscious turn from the divine

36. One cannot help but notice the visual nature of the narrative of the text. *The Life of Moses* is literally packed with vivid images nested together in sets of three like a child's set of graduated boxes, all of which are wrapped up in Gregory's metaphor of the seeker as a charioteer, disciplining and guiding the horses of the soul to run the race to God successfully. The image of the charioteer is borrowed, famously, from Plato's *Phaedrus*. Part of what is interesting in Gregory's work is the way he takes the *Phaedrus* charioteer and the constellation of associated images and completely recasts them in Christian terms.

37. The same can be said, of course, about holy scripture. How would we know what it meant without the tradition of the church, the saints and teachers, the liturgy, and its history?

Judge depicted over the doors of the cathedrals and in the manuscripts. It was a turn that spoke to an increasing concern in the West with atonement and also a desire to make Christ more human and real so that believers would seek him rather than fear him. In an eleventh-century writer like St. Anselm, we see both images held together in a necessary tension:

> Alas for me, here are sins accusing me — there is the terror of judgement. . . . Who will deliver me out of the hands of God? . . . But it is he himself, he himself is Jesus. The same is my judge, between whose hands I tremble. *Take heart, sinner, and do not despair. Hope in him whom you fear, flee to him from whom you have fled.*[38]

It is impossible, however, to tell which came first — the eleventh-century carving of a dead or dying Christ on the cross, or the change in tone and mood of the theological writing that reflects more concern with the human and crucified Christ.

One standard objection to the sort of argument raised in this section of the essay is that it confuses categories of images — concrete images and mental images are not comparable realities. Moreover, the astute historian of Christian doctrine or of art will be quick to point out that the Latin West did not share the Eastern Church's presuppositions about images. Is it not true, after all, that during the iconoclastic controversy Theodulf of Orleans wrote the definitive Carolingian (and thus Latin) statement on the use of images, saying that images had no mystical but only didactic value? Theodulf makes it clear that the value of the images was in the material and the accuracy of depiction, not in some sort of intrinsic holiness.[39] Thus, East and West did not share Neo-platonic conceptions of images, and the argument made here for a canonical heritage of images coming out of the undivided church not only confuses categories of images but also presumes a unity of interpretation that did not exist.

Perhaps the problem here is following Theodulf and, like him, misinterpreting the role and value of images and theological issues at stake in the controversy. In the greater tradition of the church, images are valuable to the extent that they make the holy accessible to the soul of the viewer, not because they are intrinsically holy. The great fear of the iconoclasts was

---

38. Anselm of Canterbury, "Meditation 1," in *The Prayers and Meditations of Saint Anselm with the Proslogion,* trans. Benedicta Ward (New York: Penguin Books, 1973), 224; emphasis added.

39. Marilyn Stockstad, *Medieval Art* (Boulder: Waterview Press, 1986), 127.

that images would lead viewers to a too small conception of the divine by making the divine seem encapsulated in a visual image. These are questions about how an image works, not questions about what it is made of. St. Augustine makes this distinction clear in *De trinitate:*

> Even the earthly face of the Lord Himself is represented differently by all the different people having thoughts about Him, even though in actuality His face was only one, whatever it was really like. *But for our faith in the Lord Jesus Christ, it is not the image which the mind forms for itself* [to use for thinking] *(which may perhaps be far different from what he actually looked like) that leads us to salvation, but, according to our mental representation, what* [sorts of thoughts we have] *about his humankind.*[40]

Making Choices about Images in the Contemporary Church

It remains only to point out the ways in which images remain a vital part of the Christian life and ways in which the unconscious use of images can affect or be affected by current trends in theology. In St. John of Damascus's defense of the holy icons he argues that icons are, like the doctrine of the *theotokos,* an important means of asserting the reality of the incarnation, preventing the church from flying off into Arianism or worse. The divine Logos really was incarnate as a human being, and as such, the divine can be depicted in the human form of Christ. It is a very deliberate use of imagery for theological expression.

Likewise, when the iconoclasts seized the Church of the Nativity in Bethlehem, they stripped the mosaics from the walls and replaced them with a suitable "icon." In place of the Theotokos and Child they installed a depiction of an altar, a cross, and the Bible — an icon of the Trinity without human form. This too was a deliberate use of iconography for theological purposes. For both John and the iconoclasts, however, there remains an insistence that the Trinity be depicted as present in the church. The abstraction or figurative nature of the image is what is at issue, not the value and place of images of any kind. Both iconoclasts and iconodules understood that images were powerful shapers of theological perception and each was determined to use them to shape theology in particular ways.

---

40. Augustine, *De Trinitate* 8.4.7, quoted in Carruthers, *The Craft of Thought,* 121; emphasis added.

Think now of the early Methodist, Anglican, and Presbyterian parishes in the eastern United States — the ostentatiously plain churches
among which I was raised. These are churches without color on the walls
or in the glass. The interiors are painted white; the windows are large and
clear. There were no Bibles, no crosses, no altars, no candles, and certainly
no graven images in these churches. The focal point of these churches is
an elevated pulpit placed high in the center of the wall facing the congregation. Still the churches themselves, as much as any gothic cathedral, are
an image. There is a particular God worshiped in such spaces, and the
spaces tell of the God one expects to encounter. This God is a being of
light and transcendence, and, given much of the rest of Protestant theology, a God of power. But such a space raises some questions about the reality of a God who is a personal being, much less triune or incarnate. In
some ways the God to be found in these churches seems Arian — so far
removed from the messiness of real human existence that it seems impossible that God could have been so involved. God is Light and Spirit, but is
this a God to whom one can have hope of ascending? Is the pristine God
of such spaces a God who would deign to be involved in the messiness of
incarnation? In this case, I think our church architecture both reflected
and accelerated the breakdown and abandonment of the doctrine of the
Trinity and a sense of the human being as seeking and being sought by a
loving God.

I want to be careful to avoid insisting that anyone who desires to be a
canonical theist must adopt and make use of a particular set of images, or
that canonical theists must reappropriate the Neo-platonic understandings of images from the pre-Scholastic world. I do, however, want to make
it clear that even those of us who do not think we are using images are indeed surrounded by them, and when the images with which we surround
ourselves contradict the words that we speak or read, we are in great danger of creating such cognitive dissonance that the entire message becomes
incomprehensible. The spaces in which we worship, for example, do form
our conceptions of God, for we learn from childhood that our church is
God's house. Incongruence between the spatial or material image and the
proclaimed images heard from the pulpit will not long survive, and generally it is the visual image that will triumph.

The verbal images of hymns provide another example of the way in
which images can operate below the level of consciousness as formers of
theology. Protestants tend to have regular, internecine fights about hym-
nals. Where the use of images is covert or idling, the images created by

hymn texts and tunes become powerful teaching tools. It is more than just "theology" — it is the image of divinity that they promulgate which becomes precious. This is why mainline Protestants have argued so vehemently over hymns like "Washed in the Blood of the Lamb." The arguments against the continued presence of the hymn in a hymnal are made not because the hymn is scripturally unsound, but because it creates an image that its opponents do not want to reinforce or promulgate within the church. The argument is not that Christ's blood isn't saving, but that the hymn is too gory.

Further, willful ignorance of the nature of our own idolatry where images of God are concerned and the refusal to take the power of images seriously enough in the church leaves the field open for all sorts of false images and false gods to take residence in the hearts and minds of human beings. Instead of images of those who have surrendered themselves to the transforming power of the Holy Spirit, who have sought to live as closely with God as possible, and so in their lives have helped make God incarnate for others — instead of Saints — we leave room for idols from the secular world like professional athletes, product logos, and entertainers to fill our hearts and minds and shape the deepest desires of our souls. Out of our fear of the risks of idolatry associated with the contemplation of the image of Christ Jesus — the risk of confusing the image with the reality of Christ — we set our children up to run the risks associated with the idolatry of modern popular musicians or the athletes in the posters on their walls. Indeed, these people are openly referred to as "cultural icons," and we keep relics like photographs, used baseballs, clothing, and many stranger things than these to help us remember those we have idolized. With the image of the holy in such peril, would it not behoove us to think again about the sorts of images we wish Christians to use as they think?

In an age of movies, television, and photographs, what does "idolatry of graven images" really mean? Can Christianity hope to evangelize in the postmodern cultural milieu without making use of images? It may be that the decision has already been made. Those churches which have been most successful at evangelizing in modern North Atlantic culture have made it standard practice to use movie clips as part of the sermon to illustrate virtues and characters in parallel with scriptural texts. They intend them to be tools to help people think about holy things and holiness.

In another example, the movie *The Passion of the Christ* became a visual and emotional window into the reality of the last hours of Christ's life for many people who had little experience contemplating crucifixes, paintings, or the scriptural texts, creating for them indelible images and under-standings of the horror and pain of Good Friday.[41]

The question we face as modern canonical theists is not really whether the model of mental function in use for most of the church's history was correct, nor whether their understandings of physics and physiology were accurate. What we must carefully consider is whether or not their psychological insights into the way images work and shape the divine-human interaction illuminate the way the images that surround us work on us. Further, we must make a choice. We live in a culture that uses images in extremely powerful ways to get people to act in particular ways, to form ideas of beauty, or to show us who and what heroes are. It is only the church that fails to make such deliberate use of images. Are we going to cede to the interests of the commercial and secular forces of society such a powerful tool for the formation of human beings?

The majority of the Christian church for two thousand years has been "stuffed" with images and employed them quite deliberately. What is truly remarkable is the brevity and limited nature of the spasms of icono-clasm in Christianity. For canonical theists the challenge will be to find ways of incorporating the images of the canonical heritage and asking the right questions about the use or lack of use of such images among the present-day body of Christ.

41. Critics, of course, have had much to say about the scriptural inaccuracies, the possible anti-Semitism, and the violence of the film. All of these are, in fact, tacit (and sometimes explicit) admissions that the images presented will shape religious understanding and experience for the viewer. In this case, it was the images of the movie — the blending of gospel narratives and the possible misinterpretations — that underlay the critics' objections. In other words, critics often criticized the movie precisely because it presented compelling, convincing images of theological positions with which they took issue.

PART II

The Emergence of Canonical Theism

WILLIAM J. ABRAHAM

Canonical theism as a living option for both church and academy emerged over time as a fruit of intense personal struggle within the contours of contemporary Protestantism. Having expressed its claims elsewhere in this volume in terms of cold-blooded, impersonal theses, my aim in this chapter is to provide a brief account of the spiritual and intellectual journey that lies behind it. Clearly others who find it helpful to embrace the central convictions of canonical theism or who are happy to explore this or that element within it, will have very different stories to tell. In a way nothing critical hangs on the particularity of the narrative that follows, for many can come to embrace a vision of the Christian faith from very different backgrounds and angles; the journey is not in itself constitutive of the position adopted. The value of such testimony lies in this: canonical theism is not one more speculative effort in systematic theology; it is an attempt to find an expression of the faith that nourishes the soul and that provides shape and motivation for lively involvement in the life and ministry of the church. There is merit, then, in providing a more personal take on the issues at stake. While every element within canonical theism is subject to appropriate intellectual analysis, reflection, and rigorous criticism, these intellectual practices are intimately joined to a robust commitment to the kingdom of God in the church and the world. So speaking openly and personally about such matters may help illuminate what is at stake. I shall begin at the beginning with my initial conversion but will then work less chronologically and more thematically.[1]

---

1. For a somewhat different take on my intellectual pilgrimage see "Faraway Fields Are Green," in *God and the Philosophers,* ed. Tom Morris (New York: Oxford University Press, 1994), 162-72.

My conversion to the Christian faith took place in my mid- to late teens within the warmth and honesty of a very strong version of pietism in the south of the North of Ireland mediated through Irish Methodism.[2] As a teenager from the countryside of Fermanagh, I was introduced to the Christian faith through religious education in the public schools, through caring Sunday School teachers, and through sensitive ministers who visited our home. My family was opposed to any kind of living faith; they were very clearly Protestants but not Christians. The early death of my father in a bad truck accident at a railway bridge outside Enniskillen had made us a focus of concern to the members and leaders of the local church to which we nominally belonged. I have a legion of memories of kind Methodist ministers and laity who brought the orphan money every quarter, prayed for us in the home, lured us to Christmas parties and to annual Sunday School excursions in Bundoran, and helped out in times of need and crises. The result was a deep impression of the Christian faith as something healthy, positive, cheerful, and open to truth. To be sure, these experiences also brought home how difficult it was to be a Christian; yet the overall impression was unfailingly attractive.

All this contrasted sharply with the sectarianism that was a constitutive part of social and political life. Like everyone else in my setting, I knew such sectarianism intimately; it was pervasive and inescapable. Yet exceptionally close relations tempered the sense of national and external religious identity. In my family's case we lived face to face with Roman Catholic neighbors, playmates in the fields, fellow travelers by bus to school, and everyday helpmates. In my childhood I can remember only once being subject to sectarian abuse.[3] On the way home from Sunday School we were stopped by a car load of vulgar Irish nationalists from an area called Coa where my maternal grandparents lived. They tried to intimidate us by calling us Orange bastards, but after a short time sped off.

Within this world, under the influence of evangelical lay preachers I did make a personal commitment of faith to the gospel when I was nine or ten. However, there was no serious initiation or follow-up; the difficulties

2. For a very good general treatment of the history of Christianity in Ireland I recommend Michael Staunton, *The Voice of the Irish* (Mahwah, NJ: Hiddenspring, 2001). The classic history of Irish Methodism is that of C. H. Crookshank, reprinted in six volumes as *Days of Revival: History of Methodism in Ireland* (Clonmel, Ireland: Tentmaker Publications, 1994).

3. Later, when I lived and worked in Belfast, my phone was tapped by Protestant paramilitaries.

of Christian discipleship and the pressure to reject the faith at home were simply too great; the seed sprouted and quickly died. By my teen years the faith was dead. I had won a scholarship as a dayboy to Portora Royal School, a place committed to exacting study and learning. I loved intellectual work and did relatively well in my studies; I was drawn to the humanities side of the curriculum, most especially to the study of literature and languages. However, in a quiet way cosmic and metaphysical issues that eroded any theistic or religious commitments that had been picked up in my childhood haunted me. The fundamental problem was simply that if God was not visible, then he was unreal. As a result I found it liberating to cast off any lingering fear of the divine. Knowing that sliding into even a befuddled form of atheism was a very serious move, I gave myself a period of three months at church to make sure I was doing the right thing. It was precisely this sense of freedom and discipline that set me free to have a fresh look at the Christian faith.

Within those three months I had become a convinced Christian. I read the New Testament for myself, followed with increasing dread and then joy the content of the sermons and the poetry of the Methodist hymnbook, and finally took the plunge publicly for myself in a mission in my local church. I was immediately taken under the spiritual care of the church and its ministers, most especially that of Shaun Cleland, whose integrity, wit, intellectual rigor, and passionate faith were then and remain to this day a tonic. I immersed myself in Wesley and the story of Methodism and found there some of the additional spiritual and intellectual nourishment I sorely needed. Sensing a very clear call to the ordained ministry of the church, I went off to Queen's University in Belfast to study philosophy and psychology. From there I went to seminary at Asbury Theological Seminary in Wilmore, Kentucky, an independent Wesleyan seminary committed to the renewal of the Wesleyan heritage. Given that I had as many questions as I had intuitions and answers, I then went to Oxford to work with Basil Mitchell and take up again my primary interest in issues in philosophy of religion.[4] As we have already crossed the border into philosophy and theology, it is time to shift gears and refocus more thematically.

To date philosophy has been the bedrock discipline that I cherish and enjoy the most. While I find myself working across the whole spectrum of sub-disciplines that feature within Christian theology, philosophy is where I

---

4. When I arrived at Oxford, Mitchell had just published *The Justification of Religious Belief* (London: Macmillan, 1973), a text that has had a profound impact on my thinking.

am most comfortable intellectually. My formation within it has been clearly within the Anglo-American analytical tradition. While I appreciate the drive to conceptual clarity and intellectual rigor that are the hallmarks of this tradition, I have never received its treasures in an exclusivist or doctrinaire fashion. Thus one of my earliest tutors in philosophy was a French phenomenologist and existentialist; moreover, I have always kept an eye and ear open to the rival Continental tradition. Happily, it is now clear that while the concepts, forms of argument, and general styles may be radically different, these traditions represent cousins operating in the wake of Kant that often have very similar concerns.[5] Thus both traditions in their own way have been wrestling with the loss of faith in the modern world, with the nature of natural science as an intellectual and cultural enterprise, with the nature of language and meaning, and with appropriate contact with the world of everyday experiences and agents, especially human agents. The greatest failings of analytical philosophy have been its intellectual narrowness, insularity, and arrogance, its failure to come to terms with the creation and transposition of concepts in history, and its prejudice against religion.[6] Recent developments, especially in the United States, have made such prejudice look increasingly intellectually insensitive and partisan.

The developments I have in mind lie within the region of epistemology and philosophy of religion; while they remain ignored or sidelined in contemporary theology, they have had a profound bearing on the emergence of canonical theism. In my own journey I was immersed initially in an epistemology that was thoroughly evidentialist in orientation.[7] Thus the standard approach to the rationality of religious belief consisted of a threefold strategy. First, one argued for the meaningfulness and coherence of general theism. Second, one mounted some kind of natural theology either from various proofs or from religious experiences. Finally, one turned to divine revelation to finish off the job and get to a more robust version of

---

5. This theme is explored with exemplary clarity in Simon Critchley, *Continental Philosophy: A Very Short Introduction* (Oxford: Oxford University Press, 2001).

6. This is not to say that there is no work of exceptional sensitivity on issues that matter deeply to religious believers. See, for example, Jonathan Glover, *Humanity: A Moral History of the Twentieth Century* (New Haven, CT: Yale University Press, 1999); Bernard Williams, *Truth and Truthfulness* (Princeton: Princeton University Press, 2002); and Susan Neiman, *Evil in Modern Thought: An Alternative History of Philosophy* (Princeton: Princeton University Press, 2002).

7. Anthony Flew, *God and Philosophy* (London: Hutchinson, 1966), summed up this tradition neatly.

theism. As I was committed to a robust version of theism, I was clearly interested in proposals about divine revelation, and much of my early work was taken up with the nature of inspiration and the status and content of divine revelation. Given that these notions were intimately related to conceptions of the Bible, I was also fascinated by the impact of historical investigation on scripture and explored this arena both as a topic of interest in its own right and as a way into the wider debate about the justification of Christian belief. At the same time I was exposed in person as a student at Oxford to the early work of Richard Swinburne and Alvin Plantinga. In between these two towering giants, I pursued with enthusiasm the work of my supervisor, Basil Mitchell, who in turn opened up a line to the brilliant insights of John Henry Newman. Another figure that made a lasting impression on my thinking while at Oxford was Isaiah Berlin, whose seminar with Patrick Gardiner in the philosophy of history reinforced my convictions about the irreducibility of human action in metaphysics and of the indispensability of human judgment in the life of the mind.

These thinkers are but the tip of an iceberg in recent philosophy, more specifically in epistemology.[8] The crucial streams that swirl around them can only be mentioned in passing here. One stream is the reemergence of externalism as a rival to internalism. Externalism puts human agency, human capacities, trust, and intellectual virtue back on the table in the quest for rationality, justification, and knowledge. While it does not displace the proper use of logic, rational principles, and the like, externalism undermines the standard version of evidentialism that I had implicitly and none too happily embraced. A second stream is that of particularism as a rival to methodism. For me the importance of particularism, that is, of focusing ruthlessly on the particulars of our actual intellectual endeavors, emerged most sharply in the impossibility of reducing history to science as an intellectual enterprise. The search for one method of inquiry, whether of deductive logic or of the patterns of reasoning exemplified in natural science, is a chimera and a snare. The third stream fastens on the claims of foundationalism over against coherentism. Initially I was deeply drawn to coherentism, in that it fitted with the attraction of cumulative case arguments and with the clear character of historical reasoning. However, it be-

---

8. Robert Audi's work is but one example of a splendid list of texts that might be cited. See his *The Architecture of Reason: The Structure of Rationality* (Cambridge: Cambridge University Press, 2002), and *Epistemology: A Contemporary Introduction* (London: Routledge, 2003).

came all too clear over time that I was generalizing too quickly from the critical place of judgment in certain areas of inquiry and failing to distinguish between classical and moderate forms of foundationalism. I had confused the discovery of cumulative case arguments with coherentism and have since abandoned it as a global theory.

The crucial point to register at this stage is this. While I have my own vision of the epistemology of theology, one that puts a premium on the place of divine revelation in our knowledge of God, we now have at our disposal an extraordinary range of epistemological options in thinking through the topics of rationality, justification, and knowledge not just as these apply generally to critical inquiry but as these apply to theology. Thus the breakup of the standard evidentialism that was prevalent in my training in philosophy has been matched by the development of better options in the philosophy of religion. This is a revolutionary development. Something akin to this observation shows up in talk about a shift from modernity to postmodernity, but this way of speaking fails to do justice both to the range of options that have emerged and to the philosophical rigor that accompanies them. I find reference to postmodernity as a cultural artifact or development helpful in making sense of the recent past. It is much less helpful as a guide in sorting through the epistemological options available because it makes too much of the failures of classical foundationalism, makes too little of the real diversity available, too quickly dissolves the debate into one about the dynamics of contemporary politics and culture, and tends to undermine the need for careful, detailed epistemological work from all the contestants in the current debate. Worst of all it fails to note that robust Christian theists have worked up a network of competing epistemologies all of which are clearly compatible with the Christian gospel. Christian intellectuals need no longer be on the defensive, as they have been throughout the modern period; they no longer have to feed off scraps dropped from the philosophers' table; they have at their disposal a full range of competing menus, each with its own feast on offer.

The importance of this development for Christian theology is simple. Epistemology has at one and the same time been radically diversified and radically relativized. Consequently, the church can be thoroughly substantial in its theology and practices without making the integrity or legitimacy of its claims depend on the formal or canonical adoption of this or that epistemology. More generally the worry, if not obsession, of having the right theological method is now sidelined. Equally, the quest for some kind of absolute certainty can also be seen for what it is, that is, an imposition from without on the faith of the church. Expressed differently, Christian intellectuals have been freed up to explore a host of epistemological options. Most important, they are liberated to articulate and develop the various epistemological suggestions that show up in scripture and in the wider canonical heritage. We might capture the salient point in this manner. The internal life of the church has been turned upside down, or more aptly, the right way up. Where before the first order of business was to settle the issue of canon, conceived as getting the right criterion of truth in theology, now the first order of business is Christian formation in the full life of the church. Questions of apt criteria, rationality, justification, and the like are secondary; inescapable as such questions may be, they are not constitutive of the life of faith.

I have sketched this conceptual revolution by way of recent developments in recent epistemology. In my own journey they coincided with my own spiritual and ecclesial experiences. The point to register at this juncture is my encounter with the Methodist tradition in North America. Given that it was Irish Methodists who first brought Methodism to North America, there is more than a passing interest for me in this journey. Having come to know the ecclesial scene in United Methodism from top to bottom and from one end of the Continent to another, the critical observation is this. While the Methodist tradition is very much alive and its renewal is much further along that its critics acknowledge, it has enormous difficulty securing a sufficiency of content and practice to nourish one's spiritual life over time.

When I came to Perkins School of Theology in 1985 the prevailing orthodoxy was unmistakably liberal. I had been invited to apply for a position, and I agreed to be interviewed only after I was convinced that I would have real freedom in my teaching and thinking. The first couple of years at Perkins were exhilarating, not least because of a splendid faculty. Clearly the leading voice in theology was that of Schubert M. Ogden, a scholar of such intense clarity and ferocity that he had become legendary in his impact. While we were poles apart, we routinely roomed together at faculty retreats, and I came in time to judge Ogden one of the greatest liberal Protestants of the twentieth century. As is well known, Ogden demythologized the demythologizers.[9] By the time he was finished there was nothing left of the Christian faith that held any interest for me, much less that would have

9. See most notably his *Christ without Myth* (San Francisco: Harper and Row, 1961).

been minimally adequate for Christian discipleship.[10] The problem this posed for me was historical. How did it come about that a whole stream of Methodism had failed to preserve critical components of the Christian faith over time? The standard reply on the part of conservatives was that this stemmed from either lack of piety or lack of theological and intellectual integrity. Neither explanation applied to Ogden. He was pious to the core in his own liberal way, and he was a paradigm case of intellectual integrity, that is, of exploring and of articulating the relevant options and following the evidence where it led. Over time the conclusion that emerged was this: there was something fundamentally flawed at the origin and core of the tradition itself.

Critics of Methodism will reach naturally for the usual causal suspects: the anti-intellectualism of its pietism, its obsession with experience, its suffocating moralism, its unhealthy pragmatism, its liturgical antinomianism, its lust for respectability, its artificial anthropomorphism, its corrupting institutionalism, and the like. All these worries strike me as superficial. The really deep problems stem from a much wider development in Western Christianity, namely, the obsession with right epistemology as critical and constitutive of the life of the church. The immediate expression of this in modern United Methodism is the unconstitutional and canonical adoption of a quadrilateral of scripture, tradition, reason, and experience as the solution to the problem of the criterion in theology. As a serious piece of epistemology, this proposal is intellectually naïve, a manifestation of both bad judgment and of intellectual incompetence. As a rendering of the theology of John Wesley it is false, for Wesley was thoroughly medieval in his conception of scripture and in the role he gave to reason and experience in its interpretation. What is critically important, however, is that both Wesley and those moderns who project their own views back on him by means of the Quadrilateral share the same fundamental vision in that they have privileged epistemology as constitutive and canonical for faith. While any appeal to a single causal origin of our current woes is clearly mistaken, this mistake is critical in any accurate account of the thinning out of the life of the church and its inability to provide adequate resources for robust forms of Christian discipleship.[11]

10. Ogden's positive contribution to Christology can be found in *The Point of Christology* (Dallas: Southern Methodist University Press, 1982).

11. For my interpretation of some of the issues in the neighborhood see *Waking from Doctrinal Amnesia: The Healing of Doctrine in The United Methodist Church* (Nashville: Abingdon Press, 1995).

This growing conviction coincided with two other developments that I can only mention in passing. First, this discovery was given flesh and bones in my work on the intersection of theology and epistemology at the beginning of the Enlightenment. As I have argued at length elsewhere, the turn to epistemology and the forms of its proposals in the modern period are only fully intelligible when the connections between theology and philosophy are visited with care. It is surely no surprise that Christianity has been decimated at the hands of modern critics in the name of intelligibility and rationality. Modernity was invented initially by Christian intellectuals to resolve the problems thrown up by an obsession with epistemology that took hold of the Western Church after the Great Schism. Once the epistemology changed, the faith had to be changed to make it fit, until so much change has been produced that there is sometimes nothing left to believe or disbelieve. The same set of problems has already emerged with the arrival of postmodernity. Postmoderns are modern to the core in their obsession with epistemology; we should expect a rerun of the standard diseases as we move into the future.

Second, the place of spiritual formation and discipleship in the development and formation of Christian doctrine was driven home in a powerful way in my conversations and work with Ellen Charry, who was then a colleague at Perkins.[12] It became very clear to me that the adoption of a body of official doctrine was not simply a clever intellectual exercise designed to secure tenure but a brilliant exercise in spiritual and intellectual formation that was intimately related to human healing and recovery from evil. Moreover, the church that evangelized the Roman Empire needed more than a canon of scripture to get the job done; minimally, it also needed a canon of doctrine. The whole canonical enterprise, including the adoption of a canon of doctrine, was driven by soteriological and theological concerns; the place of epistemology was relative and secondary.

Reference to the practice of evangelism naturally takes me to another dimension of my journey. Thus far I have touched on my conversion, my formation in philosophy and theology, and my encounter with the weal and woe of modern Methodism. I had come to Perkins only on the condition that I would teach philosophy, and over time I began to work intentionally in systematic theology. My primary brief, however, was to do serious work and research in evangelism. While this appeared to be a

---

12. See Ellen T. Charry, *By the Renewing of Your Minds: The Pastoral Function of Christian Doctrine* (New York: Oxford University Press, 1999).

distraction at first, it very quickly took on a life of its own, bearing fruit in arenas I neither imagined nor anticipated. In some ways I now credit my work in this territory as every bit as important as my work in philosophy or my experiences cross-culturally.

I took as two critical areas of historical investigation the history of revivalism and the evangelization developed over the first four to five centuries of the church. The former provided a window unto the vicissitudes of spiritual formation in the modern period, most especially as that related to conversion. Both the success and failure of various forms of revival brought home to me the critical place of Christian formation in any contemporary vision of evangelism. This dovetailed with the crucial place of catechesis in the formation of Christians in the patristic period. The obvious analogies between our current marginalization in a pluralist world with the place of the church in the ancient world only serve to drive home how wise the ancient church was in its evangelistic patience and practice. Yet this was not the most startling or exciting element in my fresh encounter with the early and developing tradition.

I had studied the history of the church with great interest in seminary, and I had been keenly engaged intellectually with the work of Maurice Wiles, a first-rate teacher I had encountered in my time at Oxford, but the historical material from the early centuries always struck me as foreign and even artificial.[13] I now read the early history and patristic theology as part of my interest in evangelism. As a result the debates and intellectual developments of the early tradition were totally transformed. I came to see the life of the church in all its complexity and fragility as incredibly relevant, intellectually fecund, and spiritually nourishing. Where before I was reading ancient texts professionally and following the institutional developments sociologically or merely historically, the whole life of the church came alive as a place where folk were brought to faith, nourished in holiness, helped in the battle against evil, motivated to persevere, and energized to plumb the full depths of gospel conviction. The great fathers, teachers, and saints were no longer distant figures drowned out by my critical preoccupations and concerns; they became mentors and living inspirations of the Holy Spirit.[14] The creeds of the church ceased to be

13. For a sampling of Wiles's work in patristics, his *The Making of Christian Doctrine* (London: Cambridge University Press, 1967) is especially attractive.

14. For a splendid recent text that captures this possibility in reading the fathers see Robert Louis Wilken, *The Spirit of Early Christian Thought* (New Haven: Yale University Press, 2003).

mere summaries of scripture; they took on a life of their own in the formation and preservation of authentic discipleship. In turn this kind of encounter expanded into a fully orbed vision of the internal life of the church as constituted and formed not just by scripture, but also by the content of Nicene Creed, by a canon of teachers, by lists of saints, by rich liturgical practice, by normative forms of iconography, and the like. Moreover, it was both fitting and essential that there be forms of episcopacy that ensured the preservation and proper use of this complex canonical heritage.

Within this encounter, I naturally took a keen interest in the relation between theology and philosophy, a well-worn topic in the history of theology. What became patently obvious over time was that the church could beg, borrow, and steal from philosophy without canonizing any particular vision of philosophy or theory of knowledge. Of course, the standard line I had been taught and had accepted was that the great doctrines of the church were an amalgam, say, of divine revelation and Neo-platonism. However, aside from its naïve simplicity, this vision did not begin to do justice to the way the church's teachers skillfully deployed a variety of intellectual resources to express the truth of the gospel. What struck me most forcibly was the way the church kept its own counsel and insisted on its own convictions in the teeth of intellectual challenge and ridicule. What also struck me dramatically were the official omissions. Thus while the church was adamant about such matters as the Trinity and the nature and person of Christ, such issues as the nature of divine revelation, atonement, and the doctrine of the Christian life were left to be carried in diverse vessels in the sea of faith. In short, I came to see that the life of the church was the reverse of what it had become in the West. The canonical faith of the early church focused on a diverse body of materials, practices, and persons that were critical and instrumental in spiritual formation and left epistemological matters to be taken up as needed; the medieval and modern church reversed this over time by reducing canon to scripture, by treating canon as a criterion of truth, and by subjecting everything to a highly artificial process of intellectual validation. Thus while I began my work in evangelism by exploring the evangelization of the ancient world as a way of exploring Christian initiation, I ended up with a fresh reading of the tradition that dovetailed both with my philosophical intuitions and discoveries with my spiritual struggles in the contemporary church.

One obscure person had a truly dramatic role in this journey and reference to him will round off this section of my comments. As I was ruminating one afternoon on the extraordinary thinning out of the doctrines and practices of Methodism and on the etiological narrative of Protestantism I sketched above, I turned by accident to Aleksei Khomiakov's polemical account of developments of Western Christianity after the division between East and West. I found the early part of his paper, "On the Western Confessions of Faith," uninteresting and even boring.[15] Then in the course of reading a few pages I was suddenly gripped and thunderstruck. After insisting that the division of the church was essentially a matter of bad manners, in that the West had changed the creed without consultation and then went on to invent suitable theories to defend its lack of affection, he proceeded to develop a picture of theological developments in the West. I was immediately taken with his sketches of what had happened, in that one painted a pre–Vatican II Roman Catholic, and the other looked like a vivid portrait of Schubert Ogden. Having reread the relevant section of Khomiakov several times, I am not all that sure how far my chain of thought was prompted more by my background beliefs at the time than by the content of the text itself. What hit me with incredible force was that it was possible to conceive of the life of the church in terms not of theory, or of epistemology, or even of truth, but of affection, of mutual love, of a community of sanctity, of a people called out and equipped by the Holy Spirit to bring us to Christ, the Son of God, and through him to lead us to the Father, the Creator of the universe.

Even though I have no illusions about Khomiakov's shortcomings and polemical intensity, and even though, equally, I have no illusions about the Eastern Orthodoxy he so dearly loved, I consider him a theologian of acute perception.[16] When I stumbled upon his grave in a Moscow cemetery in the summer of 1997, I counted that discovery as an act of extraordinary providence and an occasion for deep gratitude. After reading his paper on that memorable afternoon, I picked up the phone and found the telephone number for St. Seraphim's Cathedral in Dallas, a temple of God that has become something of a second spiritual home for my thirsty soul and my aching intellect. It has also provided a point of entry for ongoing encounter with the treasures of the Eastern Orthodox tradition. Taken

15. Khomiakov's paper can be located in Alexander Schmemann, *Ultimate Questions: An Anthology of Modern Religious Thought* (New York: Holt, Reinhart and Winston, 1965), 31-69. For further access to Khomiakov see Boris Jakim and Robert Bird, eds., *On Spiritual Unity: A Slovophile Reader* (Hudson, NY: Lindisfarne, 1998).

16. For those desiring an affectionate but sobering description of contemporary Orthodoxy I recommend Victoria Clark, *Why Angels Fall: A Journey Through Orthodox Europe from Byzantium to Kosovo* (New York: St. Martin's Press, 2000).

in the round my encounters with Eastern Orthodoxy have served to confirm the conviction that the church in the New Testament and patristic period was first and foremost a school and haven of salvation rather than a seminar in religious epistemology. The full ecclesiological implications of this judgment remain for me murky and undeveloped.

We might summarize the outcome of this thematic journey as it relates to canonical theism in terms of three comments. First, there is a high price to pay for the privileging of epistemology in the life of the church. Canon becomes an item in epistemology; hence its nature and its scope must be reworked to fit the demands of the favored epistemology. This is bad for both canon and for epistemology. This move reduces canon to scripture, and then reconfigures scripture so that it is first and foremost an infallible foundation for theology. Equally, it is bad for epistemology, for it casts epistemology in terms of a search for the right criterion or criteria, a strategy that impoverishes the field by limiting our options. Second, the way out of this intellectual cramp and captivity is to revisit the topic of canon and over time to find a way to recover the full canonical heritage of the church. This means that we must come to terms with the complexity of canon, relating it afresh to the practice of spiritual formation and to growth in grace. This move in turn frees up the church to be both more relaxed and more disciplined in its epistemological endeavors: more relaxed, in that the church eschews the need to canonize any epistemology; more disciplined in that it expects the highest standards of performance that can be mustered in any generation. Third, we must revisit our vision of the church as a community brought into existence and equipped to do its work in the power of the Holy Spirit. The whole canonical heritage is the fruit of the Spirit's inspiration in and through the life of the faithful. Its fresh appropriation and ongoing usage depends critically on the human side on prayer, humility, repentance, and trust; on the divine side these depend on the constant anointing of the grace and Spirit of God. What has been lost needs to be rediscovered; what has been neglected needs to be revisited; what has been despised needs to be celebrated; and what has been kept and used to good effect needs to be cherished and sustained. In pursuing this vision we start from where we are and not where we would like to be; we gladly acknowledge the gifts we do possess and add to that stock as providence and the work of the Spirit give wisdom and guidance. As different ecclesial communities have sinned differently in the use and abuse of the canonical heritage of the church, renewal will be intergenerational and tradition-relative. The goal in the end is the full visible unity of the people of God fully equipped to minister in and to the world in the power of the Holy Spirit.

Canonical theism is then both a discovery and a project in the making. It seeks to come to terms with the theism canonized and adopted by the church and that as such shines through its complex canonical heritage. Thus it cannot but engage in sensitive reception of the treasures of the church. Yet that reception is a project that calls for extended labor on all sides and from every quarter of the Christian fold. Thus the canonical theist welcomes every effort to retrieve and renew the faith of the church. We might legitimately relate such hospitality to the extraordinary efforts extended currently across the length and breadth of the church to recover vibrant and generous forms of orthodoxy. Orthodoxy has of late become like a fleet of new cars; there are many models that share the same general form and function. Consider what we might call Narnia orthodoxy unleashed by the writings of C. S. Lewis, or the paleo-orthodoxy of Thomas Oden, or the radical orthodoxy of John Milbank and his allies, or the post-Barthian orthodoxy of Colin Gunton and John Webster, or the classical orthodoxy of Alvin Plantinga and Richard Swinburne, or the feminist orthodoxy of Sarah Coakley and Ellen Charry, or the soft liberationist orthodoxy of Jürgen Moltmann and Miroslav Volf, or the distinctive Anglican contributions of David Brown and John Polkinghorne. Clearly many theologians and intellectuals in the Christian tradition are hard at work refurbishing and replenishing the intellectual treasures of the church.

Canonical theism differs from these versions of Christianity in two ways. First, while all of them are interested in retrieval and reappropriation of the past, canonical theism has its own way of thinking about this retrieval. Thus canonical theism is very intentional about retrieving the canonical heritage of the church in the context of extended spiritual and ecclesial renewal. We are not just interested in some sort of patristic consensus, or a vague orthodoxy, or generic Trinitarianism, or classical Christianity. We are interested in the very particular components of the heritage, that is, in the scriptures, the rule of faith, the iconography, the canon of saints, and so on. Moreover, we receive these as precious gifts of the Holy Spirit given by God to incorporate us into the life of Christ. Second, canonical theists are resolute in exploring the best epistemological prospects for Christian theology, all the while refusing to canonize such epistemological projects. We believe that theology, as much as science or common sense, give us access to truth, that it has a rightful place in the academy, that it is a demanding and rigorous disciple, and that it should aggressively make good on its claim to knowledge in the marketplace of ideas. Yet every effort to secure its status in epistemology or in the wider culture should remain in the bosom of the church, deployed appropriately in its catechesis, preaching, and apologetics, but treated as midrash rather than as constitutive of ecclesial identity.

Furthermore, canonical theists welcome the interaction with contemporary culture missiologically and intellectually. Missiologically the task of spreading the gospel, of forming robust disciples, and of being salt and light in the world calls for extensive engagement with contemporary political, social, and cultural realities. New and old forms of ministry are needed to take the gospel to the world in an effective and faithful manner. In this engagement, and in the renewal of the church that it entails, fresh insights will be formed and developed. In some cases this will lead to new and innovative understandings of the canonical heritage. In other cases such engagement will lead to new midrash and to new interpretive commentary that will become part of the contingent, ongoing life of the church. Either way we can expect resistance, criticism, and even fierce opposition. Yet what is at issue is no mere secular effort to win this or that intellectual debate or to score this or that polemical point. What is ultimately at issue is the comprehensive renewal of the church, and this work lies in the hands of God. It is enough on our part to see things as clearly as we can, to articulate the faith of the church with as much flair as we can muster, to offer a reason for the hope that is within us, and to live humbly before Almighty God, the triune God of Father, Son, and Holy Spirit.

Canonical Theism and the Primacy of Ontology: An Essay concerning Human Understanding in Trinitarian Perspective

Jason E. Vickers

Canonical theism, as distinguished from other forms of theism, is "the robust form of theism manifested, lived, and expressed in the canonical heritage of the Church."[1] To be sure, other forms of Christian theism are often deeply conversant with the canonical heritage of the church. How then does canonical theism differ from these other forms? In what sense is canonical theism a "living form of theism and a substantial theological experiment for today" (Thesis I)?

Distinguishing Features of Canonical Theism

Canonical theism distinguishes itself from other forms of theism only when four features of canonical theism are taken together. First, canonical theists refuse to cast a sideways glance at the soteriological function of ecclesial canons. Instead, canonical theists insist that the primary function of ecclesial canons is *to occasion and facilitate entry into the life of the triune God*. From the standpoint of canonical theism, the Holy Spirit works through ecclesial canons to facilitate the healing of individuals, of the church, and ultimately of the whole creation.[2] Further, canonical theists contend that modern theology's obsession with epistemology has largely sidelined this conception of the canonical heritage and that contemporary

---

1. The canonical heritage is comprised of a whole network of canonical materials, persons, and practices. These include canons of scripture, images, saints and relics, creeds and sacraments, liturgy, and the practice of episcopacy.

2. See my essay in this volume on the Holy Spirit.

exceptions are now difficult to find.[3] By contrast, canonical theists give "intellectual primacy to ontology over epistemology" (Thesis XXII). On this view, the Holy Spirit works in and through ecclesial canons, initiating persons into the fullness of the triune life of God. Through scripture, creeds, sacraments, images, saints, the practice of episcopacy, and the liturgy, the Holy Spirit occasions our entry into and participation in the humanity that is ours in Christ, which is, of course, also the divinity that is ours in Christ.[4]

Second, canonical theists resist all efforts to transform ecclesial canons into epistemic criteria. Otherwise put, they insist on making and maintaining a critical conceptual distinction between ecclesial canons and epistemic criteria. From the standpoint of canonical theism, it is wrong-headed to ask icons, scripture, and sacraments, for example, to do the epistemic work customarily done by inference, memory, perception, and the like. Thus canonical theists are vigilant in their efforts to expose even the subtlest of appeals to an ecclesial canon (e.g., the canon of scripture) as an epistemic criterion in theology.[5] When epistemic worries arise, Christian theologians can and should turn not to ecclesial canons but to relevant work in epistemology, i.e., to canons of rationality, justification, truth, and knowledge.[6] Repeated failure to do so has led to deep divisions in the church itself. From the standpoint of canonical theism, discarding an epistemic conception of ecclesial canons is vital for reconciliation within the body of Christ.

---

3. One such exception can be found in the work of the Catholic *ressourcement* theologian Yves Congar. See especially his *Tradition and Traditions: An Historical and a Theological Essay* (London: Burns & Oates, 1966). Also see his *I Believe in the Holy Spirit*, trans. David Smith (New York: Crossroad Herder, 1999). For a helpful essay that calls attention to precisely those features of Congar's work that canonical theists find most attractive, see John Webster, "Purity and Plentitude: Evangelical Reflections on Congar's *Tradition and Traditions*," *International Journal of Systematic Theology* 7:4 (October 2005): 399-413.

4. On the Holy Spirit's sacramental use of "creaturely realties" such as the church fathers, see Congar, *Tradition and Traditions*, 436ff.

5. For an account of the shift from scripture as ecclesial canon to scripture as epistemic criterion in the history of Christian theology, see William J. Abraham's *Canon and Criterion in Christian Theology: From the Fathers to Feminism* (New York: Oxford University Press, 1999).

6. Fortunately, there is an abundance of work available in this area. In fact, the last twenty-five years of scholarship in religious epistemology constitute something of a golden era in the field. Among others, William Alston, Basil Mitchell, Alvin Plantinga, Richard Swinburne, and Nicholas Wolterstorff have made outstanding contributions.

One concern that tends to arise here has to do with the status of divine revelation. For canonical theists, revelation is an appropriate epistemic concept to which theologians can and should appeal when epistemic worries arise. In doing so, however, it is of crucial importance that theologians not confuse revelation with ecclesial canons, including the canon of scripture. At best, ecclesial canons mediate divine revelation; they do not themselves constitute divine revelation *tout court.*

Third, having rejected the epistemization of ecclesial canons, canonical theists go further and reject the canonization of epistemological proposals, regardless of the level of technical sophistication or the extent to which we find such proposals intellectually compelling. This includes formal and informal theories of justification, rationality, truth, and knowledge. Canonical theists recognize and, when appropriate, appeal to epistemic canons, but we think it deadly to baptize them into the life of the church. Thus we are quick to point out that, while one can find many rich epistemological insights and suggestions in the early fathers, we think that the early fathers were wise not to canonize any particular epistemic theories alongside, say, the doctrine of the Trinity.[7]

Canonical theism distinguishes itself from other forms of theism in a fourth and decisive way. While canonical theists refuse to canonize epistemological proposals, we also take epistemological questions very seriously.[8] For us, *Christian beliefs constitute genuine knowledge;* we are not prepared to stake our lives on mere opinions or preferences. Further, we recognize that some things count against Christian beliefs, e.g., the problem of evil. Consequently, we are committed to dealing with queries and challenges regarding the rationality, justification, and truth of Christian beliefs. This commitment, in turn, motivates us to explore theories of justification, rationality, truth, and knowledge. We are intrigued by and take seriously epistemic theories like externalism and internalism in justification, foundationalism and coherentism in rationality, and correspondence, coherentist, and pragmatist conceptions of truth. We are, in a word, committed to rigorous work on the epistemology of Christian theology, and we want to create a new sub-discipline in theology under that name.

---

7. For an example of the rich epistemic insights and suggestions embedded in the work of the early fathers, see the essay on the *Philokalia* by Frederick Aquino in this volume.

8. Canonical theists are particularly interested in the epistemic hints and suggestions that emerge in the Christian tradition itself.

Such a sub-discipline differs considerably from religious epistemology insofar as the latter tends to concern itself with the justification or rationality of mere or generic theism, while the former takes up, both internally and externally, far more specific theological claims. Internally, the epistemology of Christian theology assumes the robust vision of God embedded in the canonical heritage of the church. Otherwise put, canonical theists are committed to addressing epistemic issues that emerge not only with regard to the existence of an all-powerful, all-knowing, and benevolent God, but also with regard to the belief that God became incarnate in Jesus of Nazareth, that God sent the Holy Spirit to be with us and instruct us and to make us one, holy, catholic and apostolic church, that Christ will come again, and similar specific claims integral to canonical theism. Externally, the epistemology of Christian theology will also evaluate critically the precise theological claims associated with other, non-trinitarian forms of theism.

Unmasking *Methodist* Commitments

At this stage, we can imagine Christian theologians objecting that there is a deep incongruence between the third and fourth distinguishing marks of canonical theism, i.e., between our refusal to wed the canonical heritage of the church to any epistemological proposal and our commitment to rigorous work on the epistemology of theology. Surely canonical theists are trying either to disguise formal and material epistemic commitments, or they are trying to avoid submitting their beliefs to public criticism. Either canonical theists should submit Christian beliefs to publicly agreeable epistemic criteria for evaluating propositions, or they should admit that they do not take epistemic challenges to their beliefs very seriously after all.

The apparent incongruence between these two features of canonical theism actually reflects the extent to which Christian theologians remain committed to methodism in epistemology.[9] A methodist in epistemology holds that a person cannot know anything until she provides an acceptable general method or criterion for distinguishing true and false beliefs. But why have Christian theologians been so deeply committed to methodism? The answer is simple. Christian theologians are partly responsible

---

9. For the classic definition of "Methodism" in epistemology, see Roderick Chisholm's *The Problem of the Criterion* (Milwaukee: Marquette University Press, 1979).

for the birth and subsequent flourishing of methodism in epistemology and, good parents that they are, they find it very difficult to abandon their own children.

Before we identify the theological origins of methodism in epistemology, it will help if we identify four options vis-à-vis the epistemic status of Christian beliefs that are available to us under methodist conditions. As we will see, these options can be found within theology itself.

First, one can embrace methodism in its simplest and most straightforward form. On this option, a single, all-encompassing theory of knowledge is developed and used to judge the truth of all beliefs regardless of domain.

Second, one can name and defend the criteria that one will use to distinguish truth from falsity in various domains of learning. On this option, one seeks an appropriate epistemic fit between criteria and subject matter. One recognizes that different types of propositions, e.g., propositions in mathematics versus propositions in ethics, often require different criteria by which to judge truth from falsity. Yet, while one recognizes this, one remains adamant that an acceptable method or criterion is necessary in order to ascertain whether a belief counts for knowledge in a given domain.[10] On the second option, then, methodism in epistemology is wed to a principle of appropriate epistemic fit.

The third and fourth alternatives are similar and can be treated together. On the one hand is skepticism. Skeptics acknowledge methodism but deny that any acceptable method or criterion exists. Until such a criterion turns up, skeptics urge us not to assent wholeheartedly to any proposition. On the other hand is fideism. The fideist rejects the idea that certain fundamental beliefs are subject to rational assessment, and therefore sidesteps the problem of the criterion altogether. We are entitled to hold these beliefs regardless of whether we have to hand evidence or reasons in support of them.

To be sure, the overriding purpose of canonical theism *is to clear the way for theological renewal.* Before we can do that, however, we must engage in what, in another context, Nicholas Wolterstorff has called "the archaeology of cultural memory," the aim of which is "[to tell] the story of

---

10. It is possible that a belief might be construed as knowledge and be false. It is also possible that a belief might be true and yet not count as knowledge. For the time being, it will suffice to register these technical problems in epistemology. For a first-rate treatment of these and other problems, see Robert Audi's *Epistemology* (New York: Routledge Press, 1998).

how we got to where we are in our thinking."[11] Thus we need to chronicle briefly the way in which the commitment to methodism in epistemology emerged within theology.

Theological Origins of *Methodism* in Epistemology

The rise of methodism in epistemology is intimately related to three inter-connected factors. These factors include the loss of confidence in ancient learning about creation, the need for resolution concerning the location of the one true church and therefore of salvation, and the rediscovery of ancient, Pyrrhonian skepticism. If we are to come to grips with the emergence of methodism in epistemology, then we must account for each of these developments.

Among other things, the sixteenth century was marked by a growing loss of confidence in the learning about and approach to creation that was available in the Christian tradition. Whatever value this learning and approach might have held for the Christian's journey toward God, it was proving increasingly unreliable for navigating the day-to-day world. For example, in an increasingly mobile world, there was a growing awareness that the locations of places like Jerusalem, Rome, and the Garden of Eden on Christian maps were of little, if any, use for persons wanting to move about the world. Similarly, there was a growing awareness that, whatever Christian teaching about the great seas and oceans might contribute to the human understanding of evil and providence, such teaching was of no use for seafaring persons who valued their lives.

In response to the need for more scientifically accurate ways of understanding the world, there emerged an entire network of low-grade technological and scientific developments in areas such as mapmaking, time-keeping, botany, and the like. These developments further undermined confidence in the utility of the learning available in the Christian tradition concerning the world itself.[12] The loss of confidence in the utility of an-

11. Nicholas Wolterstorff, *John Locke and the Ethics of Belief* (New York: Cambridge University Press, 1996), xiv.

12. For an account of how low-grade developments undermined confidence in the utility of Christian teaching about creation, see especially Peter Harrison's *The Bible and the Rise of Modern Science* (New York: Cambridge University Press, 1998). Also see Alfred W. Crosby, *The Measure of Reality: Quantification and Western Society, 1250-1600* (New York: Cambridge University Press, 1997).

cient learning about creation was so great that, by the turn of the seventeenth century, Sir Francis Bacon called for a total reworking of the very foundations of knowledge and learning. Bacon's life and work, perhaps more than that of any other single individual, reflects the extent to which persons were losing confidence in an entire way of apprehending and approaching the created order.[13] In the years that lay ahead, spiritual or sacramental ways of understanding the created order would be viewed primarily as interfering with more profitable and therefore more useful scientific understandings.

At the same time that confidence in the usefulness of the knowledge of creation embedded in the Christian tradition was ebbing away, the Protestant Reformation was calling into question ancient claims concerning the location of the one true church and with it the location of salvation. Unfortunately, the soteriological implications of the Reformation are often lost on modern readers. We simply forget that, for many persons, the choice between the Catholic and Protestant churches had eternal implications. In order to see this we must recall that, for many persons in the sixteenth and seventeenth centuries, the thought of joining a Protestant church could precipitate a crisis of assurance. It was no small thing, after all, to leave behind the church into which one had been baptized and confirmed for an upstart, renegade church that had either eliminated or severely revised the various rituals and daily practices to which one's family and friends had for years turned for assurance.[14]

Among the practices that the Reformers eliminated were the cult of the saints, the use of images, the sacrament of penance, and devotion to Mary. Practices associated with the Virgin that were designed to bring consolation to believers' hearts must have been especially difficult to abandon, as many persons took comfort and consolation in the daily cycle of prayers to the Virgin made available in the widely popular Books of Hours. Similarly, absolution in penance and the real presence of Christ in the eucharist

13. See "The Great Instauration," in Francis Bacon, *Novum Organum and Related Writings* (Upper Saddle River, NJ: Prentice Hall, 1960). For an outstanding account of these developments, see William S. Babcock's "The Commerce Between the Mind and Things: A Re-shaping of the World in the Seventeenth Century," in *The Unbounded Community: Papers in Honor of Jaroslav Pelikan,* ed. William Caferro and Duncan G. Fisher (New York: Garland Press, 1996), 163-86.

14. For the elimination of various rituals and practices, see John Calvin, "On the Necessity of Reforming the Church," in *Calvin: Theological Treatises,* LCC, vol. XXII, trans. J. K. S. Reid (Philadelphia: Westminster Press, 1954), 184-216.

provided for many a deep sense of assurance that the benefits of the aton-ing sacrifice of Christ, indeed even Christ himself, were readily available to all who were truly contrite for their sins. Upon feeling the hand of the priest on one's head or the body and blood of Christ in one's mouth, one could be hopeful, even confident, about one's standing before God. In-deed, the entire late medieval penitential and sacramental system reflected a deep conviction among Catholic priests and laity alike that, as Madeleine Gray puts it, "God had promised to bestow grace on all those who did their best."[15]

By contrast, questions abounded concerning the efficacy of baptism, of the sacrament, of ministers' orders, indeed of the whole vision of salva-tion on offer in Protestant churches. As a result, the Magisterial Reformers had little choice but to identify the marks of a true church. For example, Luther argued that what constituted a true church was the word of God, the sacraments of baptism and eucharist rightly administered, the office of the keys and of the ministry, public worship, and the bearing of the cross.[16] Despite the protestations of the Reformers, Catholic theologians and priests publicly denied the legitimacy of the salvation on offer in Protestant communions. Thus the very existence of a rival church with ri-val sacraments and a rival vision of salvation triggered a crisis of assurance that would have been felt by many persons in deep and profoundly per-sonal ways.

Finally, it is important to remember that the romantic notion that what matters most is not the truthfulness of one's beliefs but the sincerity with which one holds them was not available to persons in the sixteenth and seventeenth centuries. Isaiah Berlin captures the point brilliantly, saying:

> Suppose you had a conversation in the sixteenth century with some-body fighting in the great religious wars which tore Europe apart at that period, and suppose you said to a Catholic of that period, engaged in hostilities, "Of course these Protestants believe what is false; of course to believe what they believe is to court perdition; of course they are dangerous to the salvation of human souls, than which there is nothing more important; but they are so sincere, they die so readily for their cause, their integrity is so splendid, one must yield a certain need

15. Madeleine Gray, *The Protestant Reformation: Beliefs and Practices* (Brighton: Sus-sex Academic Press, 2003), 18-19.

16. For this list and for Calvin and Zwingli on the marks of the true church, see Gray, *The Protestant Reformation,* 72-94.

of admiration for the moral dignity and sublimity of people who are prepared to do that." Such a sentiment would have been unintelligible. Anyone who really knew, supposed themselves to know, the truth, say, a Catholic who believed in the truths preached to him by the Church, would have known that persons able to put the whole of themselves into the theory and practice of falsehood were simply dangerous persons, and that the more sincere they were, the more dangerous, the more mad.[17]

Given that the one, holy, catholic, and apostolic church had fractured over the vision of salvation, the question was invariably raised, how can one know which church and which vision of salvation is the right one? Thus the Reformation triggered a crisis of assurance in and around the issue of ecclesial authority in an unprecedented way. To be sure, the Great Schism between East and West had raised the question of ecclesial authority with considerable force in the eleventh century. However, the problem of authority brought about by the Reformation was most likely felt with even greater force and intensity than had been the case during the Great Schism, due to the sheer fact that Catholic and Reformation churches were in much closer proximity to one another than many Eastern and Western churches had been. For eleventh-century clergy and ordinary believers alike, there were no daily reminders of the Great Schism across the street or on the other side of town.

We have seen that the sixteenth century was marked by deep disagreements over both the location of things, i.e., over how best to map the creation, and over the location of the one true church and therefore of salvation. In the midst of these disagreements, a third factor emerged that contributed directly to the rise of methodism in epistemology, namely, the rediscovery of ancient, Pyrrhonian skepticism in the late Renaissance period.[18] The timing could not have been worse. A sheer historical coincidence, skepticism reemerged on the intellectual scene via the discovery, translation, and distribution of the writings of Sextus Empiricus, Cicero, and Diogenes Laertius. Amid the deep disagreements over the nature of world and the location of salvation, interlocutors on all sides were coming

---

17. Isaiah Berlin, *The Roots of Romanticism* (Princeton: Princeton University Press, 1999), 9.

18. For a history of the impact of skepticism on theology during and after the Reformation, see Richard Popkin's *A History of Skepticism: From Erasmus to Spinoza* (Los Angeles: University of California Press, 1995).

into contact with the principle of ancient skepticism that, when faced with such disagreements, the path to intellectual stability lay in the providing of a reliable method for obtaining knowledge. The skeptical tradition appeared a perfect fit for the times.

In response to questions having to do with the authority of the Protestant church and especially with the Protestant vision of salvation, theologians on both sides proposed a "rule" or criterion by which to identify the one true faith. Luther took his stand on scripture over against the received tradition of the church.[19] Thus Luther developed the famous Protestant principle of *sola scriptura* primarily with the Protestant vision of salvation or justification *sola fide* in mind. On the Catholic side, theologians generally defended a combination of scripture and tradition. The same problem, of course, applied equally to Catholic and Protestant criteria. Neither criterion was self-justified nor universally held. In fact, the issue was precisely that each rule of faith was vociferously contested. Consequently, any appeal to either the Catholic or Protestant epistemic criteria faced two problems. First, if one refused to appeal to anything beyond the criteria themselves, one's argument would take the form of circular reasoning or begging the question. Second, if one appealed to another criterion in order to show the validity of one's criteria, one's argument would take the form of a regress ad infinitum. Despite these difficulties, the temptation to meet the challenge of skepticism and to secure once and for all an infallible criterion in theology proved too great for most to resist.[20]

In time, many Catholic theologians tried to defeat the Protestant rule of faith by pointing out disagreement among the Protestants themselves over the meaning of scripture.[21] Amid rival interpretations, they asked, how could one be sure that one had understood scripture correctly? Isolated from tradition, they argued, scripture proved to be an inconsistent and unreliable criterion. To meet this challenge, John Calvin attempted to secure the Protestant rule of faith by appealing to a doctrine of divine illumina-

19. See especially Martin Luther, *On the Councils and the Churches,* in *Selected Writings of Martin Luther, 1539-1546,* ed. Theodore G. Tappert (Philadelphia: Fortress Press, 1967), vol. 4, 325-42.

20. See Popkin, *A History of Skepticism,* ch. 1.

21. A case can be made that the concept of a rule of faith was itself epistemized during this journey. Originally, the rule of faith was regarded as a summary of the material content of the faith. Sometime after the Reformation, however, it became natural to think of a rule of faith as an epistemic criterion or a guarantor of truth. For the former conception and usage of "rule of faith," see Douglas M. Koskela's essay in this volume.

tion. According to this doctrine, the inner witness of the Holy Spirit provided self-validating evidence that scripture is the Word of God. Further, the same illumination by the Holy Spirit that secures scripture as the Word of God also enables the reader to grasp its meaning. This, of course, only moved the problem to another level. Instead of registering doubts about whether one had both the right divine revelation and a proper understanding of it, the Counter-Reformation propagandists could now call into question whether what one identified as the inner witness of the Spirit was in fact the inner witness of the Spirit. Consequently, right down to the present day, the heirs of Luther and Calvin have expended considerable energy fine-tuning and propping up the appeal to scripture; they have developed rather elaborate doctrines of illumination, inspiration, and inerrancy.

In many respects, the same story can be told concerning post-Protestant Catholic theology. Whereas Protestants transformed scripture into an epistemic criterion designed to secure the Protestant vision of salvation, Catholics appealed to the episcopacy and the canon of teachers as epistemic criteria in theology. This appeal is enshrined in the doctrine of papal infallibility on the one hand and the canonical status accorded to Thomas Aquinas on the other.[22] Sadly, the obsession with making scripture, the Bishop of Rome, and the canon of teachers into serviceable epistemic criteria in theology caused many to lose sight of *the therapeutic and restorative function of these ecclesial canons*. Rather than healing and restoring human beings to God, scripture, the Bishop of Rome, and a great teacher in the church are appealed to primarily to underwrite or to secure the truthfulness of Christian doctrine. In a penetrating analysis of this development, the nineteenth-century Russian Orthodox theologian Alexei Khomiakov noted that, in Catholic and Protestant arguments about authority, "the premises are identical." Most telling in Khomiakov's analysis is his perceptive remark concerning both Catholic and Protestant theology in the modern period, namely, that in both of these traditions, "authority became external power" and "knowledge of religious truths [was] cut off from religious life."[23]

22. For a helpful summary of the epistemization of the episcopacy via the doctrine of papal infallibility, see Mark Powell's essay in this volume. On the canonical status afforded Thomas Aquinas, see David Burrell, *Friendship and Ways to Truth* (Notre Dame: University of Notre Dame Press, 2000), esp. ch. 3. Also see Abraham, *Canon and Criterion*, ch. 4.

23. As quoted by John Meyendorff in "Doing Theology in an Eastern Orthodox Perspective," in *Eastern Orthodox Theology: A Contemporary Reader*, ed. Daniel B. Clendenin (Grand Rapids: Baker Academic, 2003), 87. The original quotation can be found in English in A. E. Morehouse's translation of Khomiakov's *Quelques mots d'un chretien orthodoxe sur*

At this stage, we cannot lose sight of the first crisis that we identified above, namely, the crisis over the right method or criterion for a right apprehension of the natural world. Here, it is important to note that neither Luther nor Calvin proposed scripture as a general criterion for resolving disputes in all domains. Rather, they urged that epistemic criteria follow a basic distinction in the order of being; this distinction can be variously described as a distinction between the heavenly and the earthly, the eternal and the temporal, the infinite and the finite, the supernatural and the natural, the Creator and the creation. On the one hand, the Reformers adopted scripture as their criterion for knowledge of the heavenly realm. Reason, on the other hand, did the relevant epistemic work with efficiency in the earthly realm. Indeed, Luther and Calvin insisted on having the right criterion for knowledge of each respective order. Formally, they were methodists in epistemology; materially, they proposed different criteria for different kinds of knowledge. Thus Luther and Calvin developed the second option available within methodism, wedding methodism to a principle of appropriate epistemic fit.

We do not have time to trace the many developments that follow from here that are pertinent to the rise of methodism in theology. We need rather to focus on one crucial development, namely, the difficulty that theologians have had maintaining the commitment to a principle of appropriate epistemic fit, especially when religious beliefs appear to contradict knowledge derived from reason. One episode in the story of modern theology that is especially revealing of this difficulty is the trinitarian controversy in late seventeenth-century England, to a brief summary of which we now turn.[24]

It is often noted that, in Book IV of *An Essay concerning Human Understanding,* John Locke argues that religious beliefs can be above but not contrary to reason.[25] Given that our epistemic capacities have limits, it fol-

les confessions occidentals. For Morehouse's translation, see Alexander Schmemann, ed., *Ultimate Questions* (Crestwood, NY: St. Vladimir's Theological Seminary Press, 1975).

24. For a more extensive summary of this controversy, see Philip Dixon, *'Nice and Hot Disputes': The Doctrine of the Trinity in the Seventeenth Century* (London: T&T Clark, 2003). Also see Jason E. Vickers, *Invocation and Assent: The Making and Remaking of Trinitarian Theology* (Grand Rapids: Eerdmans, forthcoming 2008); William S. Babcock, "A Changing of the Christian God," *Interpretation* 45 (1991): 133-46; and William Placher, *The Domestication of Transcendence: How Modern Thinking about God Went Wrong* (Louisville: Westminster Press, 1996), ch. 10.

25. John Locke, *An Essay concerning Human Understanding,* ed. Peter H. Nidditch (Oxford: Oxford University Press, 1975).

lowed for Locke that reason could be "assisted and improved, by new Discoveries of Truth, coming from the Eternal Fountain of all Knowledge."[26] Yet, because the capacity to reason is God's good gift to human beings at creation, it also followed that we cannot "reject a greater Evidence to embrace what is less evident," and we cannot "entertain Probability in opposition to Knowledge and Certainty." Locke could not have been clearer: "Nothing that is contrary to, and inconsistent with the clear and self-evident Dictates of Reason, has a Right to be urged, or assented to, as a Matter of Faith, wherein Reason hath nothing to do."[27]

Locke was, of course, not the first to maintain that the content of divine revelation could not be contrary to reason. Edward Stillingfleet had argued the same thing in the debate over transubstantiation almost forty years earlier.[28] Ultimately, few took comfort from the idea that the content of divine revelation was not contrary to reason. Stillingfleet himself, among others, simply could not resist the urge to demonstrate that central Christian doctrines given in divine revelation were actually in accordance with reason. The results were devastating. As William S. Babcock puts it, the outcome of the debate was nothing short of "a changing of the Christian God."[29]

Initially, Stillingfleet, William Sherlock, and a host of others set out to prove that the Trinity did not contradict reason. Before they were finished, however, they were arguing that the Trinity could be shown to be in accordance with reason. Thus, on the one hand, Sherlock tried to show that the Trinity was in accordance with a Cartesian conception of reason.[30] On the other hand, Stillingfleet sought to vindicate the Trinity on Lockean grounds.[31] When the Trinity proved itself ill-suited for both Cartesian and Lockean conceptions of reason, theologians were confronted with a terrible choice. They could either discard the Trinity, or they could keep it and

---

26. Locke, *Essay,* 4.28.10.

27. Locke, *Essay,* 4.28.10.

28. Edward Stillingfleet, *Origenes Sacrae, or a Rational Account of the Grounds of Christian Faith, as the Truth and Divine Authority of the Scripture, and the Matters therein Contained* (London, 1662).

29. Babcock, "Changing of the Christian God," 135.

30. For a helpful essay on Sherlock's approach, see Udo Thiel, "The Trinity and Human Personal Identity," in *English Philosophy in the Age of Locke,* ed. M. A. Stewart (Oxford: Clarendon Press, 2000), 217-44.

31. For Stillingfleet's approach, see M. A. Stewart, "Stillingfleet and the Way of Ideas," in Stewart, ed., *English Philosophy in the Age of Locke,* 245-80.

forfeit the epistemic citizenship of Christian beliefs. By century's end, a significant number of Anglican clergymen had joined the ranks of the deists and Unitarians, discarding the Trinity in favor of a conception of God more palatable to reason. Thus to the extent that the chief mark of modern Christian theology is the accommodation of theology to epistemology, this episode, and not the episode involving the work of Schleiermacher, marks its beginning.

Beginning with the trinitarian controversy in late seventeenth-century England, one could survey the history of modern Christian theology by identifying the various conceptions of reason on which theologians have tried to secure full epistemic citizenship for Christian doctrines. If particular doctrines like the Trinity did not fit neatly, they were trimmed, altered, or discarded altogether. In time, thanks largely to Hume, Descartes's and Locke's theories gave way to Kantian idealism. Promptly, Christian theologians scurried about to evaluate how Christian doctrines might fare on this new and presumably more secure conception of reason. Once again, doctrines that proved uncooperative were altered, relegated to an appendix, or abandoned outright. When idealism proved problematic, it did not occur to theologians that Christian doctrines might be at least as secure as the epistemological proposals or speculative metaphysics to which they repeatedly turned for approval.

In many ways, a large number of Christian theologians today are still hard at work trying to gain epistemic citizenship for Christian doctrines. In fact, we can identify entire movements within Christian theology that continue to accommodate Christian beliefs to all-encompassing theories of knowledge or speculative metaphysics. Chief among these groups is process theology, but one can also count open theism and perhaps even radical orthodoxy among their ranks.[32] Most recently, some theologians are turning from epistemology and metaphysics to aesthetics in an effort to secure the truthfulness of Christian doctrine.[33]

The failure of one all-encompassing theory after another has been, for many, a source of deep disillusionment and confusion. In the wake of the repeated failures of all-encompassing theories of knowledge or specu-

---

32. One way to understand radical orthodox theology is to see it as canonizing "the Augustinian vision of all knowledge as divine illumination." John Milbank, Catherine Pickstock, and Graham Ward, eds., *Radical Orthodoxy: An Introduction* (London: Routledge, 1999), 2.

33. See David Bentley Hart, *The Beauty of the Infinite: The Aesthetics of Christian Truth* (Grand Rapids: Eerdmans, 2003).

lative metaphysics, many persons argue that no method or criterion is available and that it is therefore impossible to say whether Christian doctrines rise to the level of knowledge. For this group, hermeneutics performs the tasks once reserved for epistemology. Doctrines are reducible to locally produced and locally meaningful discourse because, without a criterion, there simply is no context-free way to evaluate them. It is rarely noticed that these theologians remain committed to methodism in epistemology. In fact, their work depends entirely on the continued failure of methodism. They simply do not bother to ask whether there might be an alternative to methodism.

An Alternative to *Methodism* in Epistemology

From the standpoint of canonical theism, it is astonishing that theologians have rarely challenged methodism itself. Doing so would open up new pathways for thinking about the epistemology of theology. Before we get to those, however, we need quickly to identify three reasons for rejecting methodism in epistemology.

First, epistemology is itself a highly contested field; there is a multitude of ways to develop all-encompassing theories of knowledge and there has been little agreement down through the centuries as to which is best.[34] Consequently, all-encompassing theories in epistemology that rule out particular religious beliefs may turn out to be more highly contested and controversial than religious beliefs themselves. Canonical theists maintain that the robust, trinitarian theism that is embedded in and facilitated by the canonical heritage of the church is at least as secure as any single, all-encompassing theory of knowledge.

Second, methodism in epistemology has historically excluded what a large majority of persons count as knowledge. For example, methodism may or may not allow us to believe in the past, in material objects, or in the external world. Further, methodism has never been able to establish the existence of other minds.[35] When confronted by these difficulties, meth-

34. For example, one is free to mix and match theories of rationality with theories of justification and theories of truth and knowledge. Thus, if we had only two theories in each of these domains, there would be sixty-four all-encompassing theories of knowledge. Needless to say, there are more than two theories in each of these domains.

35. For this issue, see Alvin Plantinga, *God and Other Minds* (Ithaca, NY: Cornell University Press, 1967).

odists tend to refine and qualify their positions in a variety of ways. In the end, however, the original proposal is so over-qualified that it appears less secure than the propositions for which the qualifications were made in the first place.

Third, as we have seen, methodism came about largely in response to radical skepticism in the midst of a massive cultural crisis. In our view, radical skepticism is deeply flawed, and it should never have been allowed to set the standard for success in epistemology. It is, like classical foundationalism, self-referentially incoherent. Radical skeptics are certain that we cannot know anything with certainty. However, they rarely bother to inform us of how they came to know with certainty that we cannot know anything with certainty. Moreover, in order to sustain their position, radical skeptics regularly rely on the very things that they claim are not reliable, namely, memory, induction and deduction, inference, and the like.

If we reject methodism, then what options are available for the epistemology of theology? First and foremost, canonical theists are intrigued by particularism. Unlike methodism, which assumes that we cannot know something unless we can first show how we know it, particularism assumes that we know all sorts of things and that we may or may not be able to show how we know them. The particularist is sure that she knows, and when problems arise, she is willing to explore the options regarding how she knows. Thus, if a general theory in epistemology calls into question what the particularist takes to be a secure proposition, then she will be more likely to call the theory or method into question before she abandons the proposition itself. We can imagine specific beliefs that she would refuse to abandon regardless of what might be going on in epistemology in the philosophy department of her local university. For example, if on the basis of a new and widely heralded theory in moral epistemology, a philosopher challenges her belief that it is everywhere and always wrong to kill babies after midnight for fun, she will maintain her belief and rightly assert that something has gone wrong in that particular moral epistemology. The particularist will look patiently for other epistemic options, but she will be slow to abandon what she takes to be good and sound knowledge.[36]

36. In some ways, Bruce Marshall provides just such an account with regard to the doctrine of the Trinity. On Marshall's analysis, if the Trinity is judged to be false, irrational, unjustified, or otherwise unacceptable on a new theory or justification or knowledge, then the Christian will nonetheless be extremely slow to give up her belief that the Trinity is true/truth. See Bruce Marshall, *Trinity and Truth* (New York: Cambridge University Press, 1999). On the other hand, see the following curious remark by Marshall: "When it comes to truth,

Second, it follows that canonical theists are drawn to the principle of appropriate epistemic fit. Thus, when it comes to the rationality of Christian beliefs or the justification of canonical theism itself, any epistemic deliberations should be appropriate to the subject matter on hand. In the end, however, canonical theists insist that an even more significant alternative awaits us. It is time to put epistemology in its proper place with respect to the canonical heritage of the church.

Canonical Theism and the Primacy of Ontology

Having identified *particularism* and the principle of *appropriate epistemic fit* as options for the epistemology of theology after methodism, it is crucial to note that canonical theists have no interest in canonizing these proposals. Formally, canonical theism is restricted to the theism embodied in the canonical heritage of the church. Within that heritage, *there are no epistemic canons as such.* Rather, when one consults the canonical heritage of the church, one finds a thick description of the order of being. To be sure, epistemic suggestions are embedded throughout the canonical heritage, and canonical theists take these very seriously. Nevertheless, the church fathers did not see fit to canonize those suggestions and neither do we.

We are delighted that the early church fathers did not add a fourth major clause to the Nicene Creed requiring Christians to confess their belief in an epistemic theory. To see how badly astray things have gone in modern theology, one only need imagine what this might look like. After confessing our belief in God the Father, God the Son, and God the Holy Spirit (and in the church, the resurrection, the life to come, and so on), we would go on to say, "And we believe in the principles of Cartesian rationalism, in the cogito," or in whatever theory of knowledge we might be keen on.

Canonical theists recognize that both inquirers into Christianity and mature Christians sometimes raise epistemic questions, and we are prepared to explore a variety of options when this happens. Indeed, it is precisely because such questions come up in evangelism and even in the day-to-day lives of Christians that we remain interested in and committed to the epistemology of theology. What we reject is twofold. On the one hand,

---

as to any other matter, theology should seek to bring under its own discipline the most plausible account currently available to it, not the account that makes its own job go more smoothly" (233).

we reject the use of ecclesial canons as epistemic criteria to address these situations. Among the reasons for rejecting this is the simple fact that appeals to say, the canon of scripture, often turn out to be question-begging arguments that rarely resolve deep epistemic queries. On the other hand, we reject any attempts to canonize epistemologies properly so called. The reason for this, as we have just seen, is that such proposals have rarely, if ever, enjoyed a long shelf-life in the history of philosophy.

From the standpoint of canonical theism, ecclesial canons are first and foremost the media through which we encounter the triune God. In and through our encounter with the scriptures, creeds, doctrines, images, and saints in catechesis and baptism, the Holy Spirit brings us to a saving knowledge of Christ, convicts us of our sins, breathes the breath of new life into us, assures us of our forgiveness, purifies our hearts, renews our spirits, fills us with the love of God the Father, and the like. Similarly, in and through our encounter with the eucharist, the Spirit enables us to perceive, to enjoy, and to be cleansed and restored to our full humanity by the presence of Christ.

When canonical theists speak of the primacy of ontology over epistemology, we intend to call attention to the transforming presence and work of the triune God in the life of the church. As we see it, the church fathers canonized precisely those materials, persons, and practices by means of which they had themselves encountered the living God and been restored to the image of God. To use Augustine's metaphor for scripture and doctrine, ecclesial canons function first and foremost as vehicles that the Holy Spirit uses to carry persons to God.[37] Thus, even when we think of ecclesial canons as having a soteriological rather than an epistemological function, it is crucial, as Augustine himself observes, that we not become so enamored with the vessels that we forget their instrumental status, turning canonical images, for example, into idols.

It also needs to be said that canonical theists welcome the full range of metaphors and images that have emerged across the years for describing the Holy Spirit's work in bringing us to God. Thus we welcome the language of justification, regeneration, new birth, adoption, healing, forgiveness, conversion, restoration, reconciliation, sanctification, holiness, Christian perfection, the baptism of the Spirit, liberation, theosis or deification, and the like. Indeed, we fully expect and embrace the Johannine-like imagery that emerges naturally when we think about the ways in

---

37. Augustine, *De Doctrina Christiana* 1.4.

which we encounter God through the canonical heritage of the church. For example, we celebrate and embrace the images of hearing the Holy Spirit speak through the scriptures, doctrine, and preaching, of seeing God in images, of holding Christ with our hands and tasting Christ in the eucharist, and the like.

Finally, we regard a recovery of the primacy of ontology and of the soteriological function of ecclesial canons as crucial not only for the healing of individual persons but also for the healing of the ecumenical church throughout the world. On this front, it is crucial to recall that the canonical heritage of the church is a gift of the Spirit and that the presence and work of the Spirit through that heritage is also a gift. Throughout the world the church must ever remind itself that the church does not possess the canonical heritage so much as it receives it — and with this heritage the life-giving presence of the Holy Spirit — anew and afresh each day.

Epistemic Virtues of a Theologian in the *Philokalia*

FREDERICK D. AQUINO

THESIS XI

The canonical heritage of the church functions first and foremost soteriologically. It operates as a complex means of grace that restores the image of God in human beings and brings them into communion with God and with each other in the church. Each component is primarily an instrument to be used in spiritual direction and formation.

THESIS XIII

The ongoing success of the canonical heritage of the church depends on the continuing active presence of the Holy Spirit working through the relevant persons, practices, and materials.

THESIS XIV

The canonical heritage of the church is to be received in genuine repentance and lively faith. The effective operation of the various components depends on an open and contrite heart and a readiness to practice in the light of God that one encounters.

THESIS XXII

The canonical heritage generates rigorous epistemological reflection and theorizing. Such work needs to be pursued at the highest intellectual level. There is no drawing back from the epistemology of theology

---

I want to express appreciation to the canonical theism group, Paddy Roche, Mark Hamilton, and Chris Dowdy for their valuable comments on this chapter.

into some kind of naïve credulity or a shutting down of the question of meaning and justification rightly raised by philosophers in the twentieth century. Canonical theists are interested in pursuing the implications of epistemologies compatible with canonical theism for the understanding of the history of the church and the study of scripture. Canonical theism may lead to the development of epistemological insights that have overtones for all of human thought and existence that are as yet unidentified and unexplored.

This essay connects the four stated theses of canonical theism with a proposal on the formation of theological judgment, highlighting and linking its soteriological and epistemological dimensions. Since the canonical heritage functions "first and foremost soteriologically," the essay examines what this means for the nature of theological reflection and the formation of a theologian (Thesis XI). Since the ongoing success of the canonical heritage presupposes "the active presence of the Holy Spirit working through relevant practices, people, and material," it also pursues the role of theological practices and agents of theological reflection in the proposal of canonical theism (Theses XIII and XIV).

Reconnecting the intellectual dimension of theological judgment to the process of spiritual formation is key for constructing a more robust understanding of theology. In this regard, the *Philokalia* furnishes some epistemic hints about habits that are requisite for vibrant, healthy theological reflection. It links habits of the mind and spirituality.[1] In general, the texts of the *Philokalia* share the assumption that virtuous and contemplative practices are indispensable for forming theological judgment and securing knowledge of God. With this in mind, the essay offers a brief introduction to the *Philokalia,* clarifies some of its basic assumptions about cultivating theological judgment, identifies some key epistemic virtues, and probes some implications for theological education. It also offers a preliminary suggestion on how relevant practices, persons, and materials

---

1. Pierre Hadot, *Philosophy as a Way of Life: Spiritual Exercises from Socrates to Foucault* (Oxford: Blackwell, 1995), offers a persuasive argument for the integration of philosophy and spirituality in ancient philosophy and the subsequent traditions of Greco-Roman thought and Christian thought. For additional reading on the connection between spirituality and philosophy, see Pierre Hadot, *What Is Ancient Philosophy* (Cambridge, MA: Harvard University Press, 2002), and Sarah Coakley, *Powers and Submissions: Spirituality, Philosophy, and Gender* (Oxford: Blackwell, 2002).

nurture praiseworthy dispositions and produce a reliable belief-forming process that inducts people into the life of God. In this sense, theology is a healing enterprise, connecting knowledge of God and the formation of character.

What Is the *Philokalia?*

The *Philokalia* is a vast collection of writings from spiritual exemplars of the Orthodox Christian tradition, ranging from the fourth to the fifteenth centuries. In the eighteenth century two Greek monks, St. Nikodimos of the Holy Mountain (1749-1809) and St. Makarios of Corinth (1731-1805), gathered and compiled these texts into an anthology on spirituality. The texts were originally published in Greek and subsequently translated into Slavonic, Russian, and most recently into English. They guide people in the practice of the contemplative life and the internalization of the logic of the Jesus Prayer ("Lord Jesus Christ, Son of God, have mercy on me, a sinner"). As the editors of the English translation note, "although the *Philokalia* is concerned with many other matters, it would not be too much to say that it is the recurrent references to the Jesus Prayer which more than anything else confer on it its inner unity."[2]

The writers of the *Philokalia* share the basic assumption about the process through which people come to know God. The primary goal of these texts is to show how "love of the beautiful, the exalted, the excellent" (the meaning of the word *Philokalia*) undergirds the purification, illumination, and perfection of the intellect.[3] Through virtuous and contemplative practices people become more attentive to God as the ground and source of their being. Thus, learning is not merely the recollection of facts but the transformation of the whole person, melding intellect and heart so that our highest possibility — assimilation to God — becomes an actuality.

The *Philokalia,* then, is a guide for practicing the contemplative life, enabling Christians to cultivate post-baptismal habits and grow into the "full stature of Christ" (Eph. 4:13). It also presupposes that the spiritual journey is rooted in the sacramental life of the church. The spiritual journey is pursued with others and not primarily in isolation from others. As

---

2. G. E. H. Palmer, Philip Sherrard, and Kallistos Ware, eds., "Introduction," in *The Philokalia,* vol. 1 (London: Faber & Faber, 1983), 15; henceforth cited as *The Philokalia.*

3. "Introduction," *The Philokalia,* 1:13.

we will see, spiritual progress depends upon following the logic and insights of those who have cultivated a life of spirituality. Yet, the writers of the *Philokalia* live out their spiritual journey within a monastic setting. This environment provides more focused conditions under which people can pursue the path of purification. Nevertheless, communities and individuals outside this context may practice the teachings of the *Philokalia*. Obviously some settings are more conducive to a deliberate and ongoing experience of interior silence, but the basic precondition for any context is "inner stability," not external conditions.[4]

Cultivating Theological Judgment

The *Philokalia* roots theological judgment in the triune God. Though divine knowledge is initiated and sustained by God, a properly disposed mind is indispensable for acquiring this knowledge.[5] Theology entails contemplation of God coupled with a right state of the heart. It may include academic discourse about doctrinal matters, but its deeper dimension entails participation in and perception of the divine world.[6] For some,

4. Kallistos Ware, *The Inner Kingdom* (Crestwood, NY: St Vladimir's Theological Seminary Press, 2000), 95. Ware cites St. Gregory of Sinai who "sent his disciple Isidore back into the world; many of his closest companions on Mount Athos and in the desert of Paroria became patriarchs and bishops, leaders and administrators of the Church" (106-7). In "'Seek First the Kingdom': Orthodox Monasticism and Its Service to the World," *Theology Today* 61 (2004): 16-17, Ware adds that "St. Nikodimos insists in his preface that the book is addressed 'to all of you who share the Orthodox calling, laity and monks alike.'"

5. The editors of the English translation point out that different understandings of the nature of human personhood exist in the *Philokalia* (e.g., the relationship between the soul and the body), but in this essay I follow the one that sees the integration of affective, moral, and cognitive dimensions of human personhood. For example, Maximus says, "the body is deified along with the soul through its own corresponding participation in the process of deification" (*The Philokalia*, 2:160). See Kallistos Ware, "The Soul in Greek Christianity," in *From Soul to Self*, ed. M. Lames C. Crabbe (London: Routledge, 1999), 49-69, and Panayiotis Nellas, *Deification in Christ: Orthodox Perspectives on the Nature of the Human Person* (Crestwood, NY: St. Vladimir's Theological Seminary Press, 1987).

6. "By 'perceiving Him directly,' I mean experiencing divine or supernatural realities through participation" (*The Philokalia*, 2:242). For good philosophical treatments of religious experience, see William Alston, *Perceiving God: The Epistemology of Religious Experience* (Ithaca, NY: Cornell University Press, 1991); Caroline Franks Davis, *The Evidential Force of Religious Experience* (Oxford: Clarendon Press, 1989); Jerome Gellman, *Mystical Experience of God: A Philosophical Inquiry* (London: Ashgate, 2001); Gellman, *Experience of God*

theological judgment stems from scripture, liturgy, tradition, and one's own immediate experience of the divine (e.g., Symeon the New Theologian). Essentially, theology is an ongoing participation in the life of God, thus creating growth of awareness within the deiform person.

The cultivation of theological judgment also presupposes the phenomenon of epistemic dependence. The deiform person follows socially established practices that foster "a constellation of dispositions or habits."[7] Such an endeavor reflects a social process by which people acquire insights from mature agents of theological wisdom. A theologically mature person engages in "higher spheres of contemplative activity" and becomes a source of theological wisdom for others.[8] Thesis XIII of canonical theism resonates with the *Philokalia*'s insistence on the indispensable role of practice for forming and sustaining theological judgment. Practicing the moral virtues is a pre-condition for acquiring knowledge of God,[9] thereby cleansing the intellect of epistemic vices and cultivating a properly focused intellect.

The key is experience; true knowledge is rooted in experiential understanding and is perfected by habitual practices. Proficiency in theological judgment is a skill that must be cultivated and refined.

---

and the Rationality of Theistic Belief (Ithaca, NY: Cornell University Press, 1997); and Alexei V. Nesteruk, *Light from the East: Theology, Science, and the Eastern Orthodox Tradition* (Minneapolis: Fortress, 2003).

7. Alston, *Perceiving God*, 153, 163, refers to the constellation of habits and dispositions as doxastic practices. See also Frederick Schmitt, ed., *Socializing Epistemology: The Social Dimensions of Knowledge* (Lanham, MD: Rowman & Littlefield, 1994).

8. Nikitas Stithatos, "On Spiritual Knowledge, Love and the Perfection of Living: One Hundred Texts," *The Philokalia*, 4:143, 152. Linda Zagzebski, "Phronesis and Religious Belief," in *Knowledge, Belief, and Character,* ed. Guy Axtell (Lanham, MD: Rowman & Littlefield, 2000), 216, connects judgment with *phronesis.* "To be a phronimos is, in part, to be recognized as a person of good judgment. The phronimos is a person who is imitated and his judgment consulted" (216). In *Virtues of the Mind: An Inquiry into the Nature of Virtue and the Ethical Foundations of Knowledge* (Cambridge: Cambridge University Press, 1996), Zagzebski argues: "we acquire intellectual virtues, just as we acquire moral virtues, by imitating those who are practically wise" (228). Connecting ethics and epistemology in this way shifts "the focus of analysis away from the belief to the agent's traits," thus "the concept of intellectual virtue does most of the normative work in the evaluation of cognitive processes and states" (267). Her move parallels the focus on cultivated judgment in the *Philokalia*. Environment, dispositions, and practices enhance the process of deification.

9. Knowledge in the *Philokalia* fits under the category of "knowledge by acquaintance." Knowledge comes through immediate awareness (non-inferential perceptual knowledge) of objects and people. See Bill Brewer, *Perception and Reason* (Oxford: Oxford University Press, 2002); and Alston, *Perceiving God.*

For reading and listening are one thing and experience is another. One cannot become a craftsman simply by hearsay: one has to practice, and watch, and make numerous mistakes, and be corrected by those with experience, so that through long perseverance and by eliminating one's own desires one eventually masters the art. Similarly, spiritual knowledge is not acquired simply through study but is given by God through grace to the humble.[10]

Watchfulness, discrimination, stillness, and dispassion distinguish a mature reservoir of theological wisdom from a novice. Well-formed theological judgment demands longstanding practices that solidify proper dispositions of the mind into skillful evaluation of and application of spiritual matters to particular situations. In other words, attaining spiritual knowledge is connected to "a rich store of virtue gained through" practicing the virtues.[11]

The *Philokalia* depicts the spiritual journey as a three-stage process: practice of the virtues *(praktiki),* contemplation of nature *(physiki),* and contemplation of God *(theologia).*[12] The aim is to grow in knowledge and wisdom so that one may attain "the measure of the full stature of Christ" (Eph. 4:13). The path of deification is "the spiritual and truly sacred rite in which the Logos of unutterable wisdom makes Himself a sacred offering and gives Himself, as far as is possible, to those who have prepared themselves."[13]

The first stage involves moral preparation. The baptized Christian practices the virtues and sheds old habits in order to move to contemplation and continue on the path of assimilation to God. By pursuing and embodying the Christian virtues, the deiform person grows in moral dis-

---

10. St. Peter of Damaskos, "A Treasury of Divine Knowledge," *The Philokalia,* 3:92.

11. St. Maximus the Confessor, "Two Hundred Texts on Theology and the Incarnate Dispensation of the Son of God" and "Various Texts on Theology, the Divine Economy, and Virtue and Vice," *The Philokalia,* 2:129.

12. E.g., Evagrius the Solitary, "On Prayer," *The Philokalia,* 1:61-62; St. Maximus the Confessor, "Four Hundred Texts on Love," *The Philokalia,* 2:63-64, 90; and Nikitas Stithatos, "On the Practice of the Virtues: One Hundred Texts," "On the Inner Nature of Things and on the Purification of the Intellect: One Hundred Texts," and "On Spiritual Knowledge, Love and the Perfection of Living: One Hundred Texts," *The Philokalia,* 4:79-174. For a fascinating connection between Orthodox spirituality and virtue ethics, see Joseph Woodill, *The Fellowship of Life: Virtue Ethics and Orthodox Christianity* (Washington, DC: Georgetown University Press, 1998).

13. Nikitas Stithatos, "On Spiritual Knowledge, Love and the Perfection of Living: One Hundred Texts," *The Philokalia,* 4:148.

cernment and fosters praiseworthy dispositions (e.g., purity of heart, humility, watchfulness, passionlessness, and uninterrupted prayer). This stage does not entail passive reception of the gifts and graces of God, but an active purging of distractions. Hence, the first stage is called the active life. Unlike the notion of salvation as an exclusively divine matter, the *Philokalia* presupposes a collaborative and relational process. The baptized Christian is surely a recipient of divine grace, but realizing deification (salvation) does not happen without human cooperation.

The second stage is contemplation of God in and through nature, connecting the intellect and the senses.[14] The intellect reconnects the natural and divine; it perceives the sacramental presence of God and recognizes "things and persons and every material body as they are according to nature."[15] Events, people, places, and objects are no longer divorced from but connect the deiform person with the divine. Here, the person becomes keenly aware of how the divine works in nature and within one's own life. However, virtuous practices are indispensable for engaging in the second stage of the process; they enable the person to engage in focused contemplation of God, nature, and the world.

The third stage is contemplation of God in which the deiform person receives knowledge (immediate awareness, perceptual knowledge) of the triune God — awareness of the object of the intellect's union. To be a theologian in the fullest sense is to attain stillness and undistracted prayer. At this stage, the deiform person no longer experiences God exclusively through nature but encounters "the Creator face to face in an unmediated union of love. The full vision of the divine glory is reserved for the Age to come, yet even in this present life the saints enjoy the sure pledge and firstfruits of the coming harvest."[16] Theology here is not primarily rational deduction from revealed data, but the experience and perception of God. The final goal of the third stage "is our initiation into the hidden mysteries of God and our being filled with ineffable wisdom through union with the Holy Spirit, so that each becomes a wise theologian in the great Church of God, illuminating others with the inner meaning of theology."[17]

14. St. Maximus the Confessor, "Various Texts on Theology, the Divine Economy, and Virtue and Vice," *The Philokalia*, 2:204.

15. Nikitas Stithatos, "On the Practice of the Virtues," *The Philokalia*, 4:92.

16. Kallistos Ware, *The Orthodox Way,* rev. ed. (Crestwood, NY: St. Vladimir's Theological Seminary Press, 1995), 106.

17. Nikitas Stithatos, "On Spiritual Knowledge," *The Philokalia*, 4:152. For the writers of *The Philokalia*, a theologian in the strictest sense of the word is one who has traveled

The result of the three-stage process is the formation of theological judgment. Appropriate motivation and reliable practices link people to their proper end — assimilation to God. Knowledge implies participation in the life of God, "not only intellectual knowledge, but a state of the entire human being, transformed by grace, and freely cooperating with it by the efforts of both will and mind."[18] Participation also presupposes gradual levels of awareness of one's spiritual life and of one's knowledge of God. Moreover, virtuous and contemplative practices are not the end but the means for achieving assimilation to God. Virtue furnishes epistemic stability, enabling the deiform person to pursue the contemplative life and "spiritual knowledge solely for the sake of truth."[19] Consequently, virtuous and contemplative practices are truth-conducive to the extent that they are appropriately motivated and they function as reliable belief-forming processes in leading the deiform person to union with God.

Underlying this understanding of theology is a particular conception of the nature, function, and focus of the intellect. The intellect is the highest faculty of humanity, though it is not to be confused with discursive, conceptual, and explicitly logical modes of reasoning. It is the faculty that secures understanding of theological truths through affective knowledge, immediate experience, or intuition. The result is the reaffirmation of the natural state of the intellect in which it functions properly and realizes the "state in which it was created."[20] The proper state of the intellect establishes its activity in the life of God, hence viewing thought, not as some autonomous reality or merely a set of formal propositions, but as an ever-increasing representation of the disclosure of the God in whom the deiform person is now a participant (2 Pet. 1:4).

The natural state of the intellect is now rooted in the prime example of the Logos incarnate. As the paragon of the new humanity, Jesus Christ points to the true sense of what it means to be created in the image and likeness of God (Eph. 2:12-18). The union of the divine and the human in Jesus is now what defines and sets before it the full maturity of the new

---

through the threefold stages of moral purification, contemplation, and direct experience of God. Consequently, to be a theologian in the broader sense of the word means that one has to trust the insights of these exemplars.

18. John Meyendorff, *Byzantine Theology: Historical Trends and Doctrinal Themes* (New York: Fordham University Press, 1974), 8-9.

19. St. Maximus the Confessor, "Various Texts on Theology, the Divine Economy, and Virtue and Vice," *The Philokalia*, 2:215.

20. St. Hesychios the Priest, "On Watchfulness and Holiness," *The Philokalia*, 1:194.

humanity to which the deiform person is growing (Eph. 4:15; 2 Cor. 3:17f.). The deifying grace of the Holy Spirit moves us and we with an ever-increasing process make this grace our own. In other words, the natural state of the intellect reflects collaboration between the divine and the human. The deiform intellect exercises its freedom so that it either "reaffirms its true nobility or through its actions deliberately embraces what is ignoble."[21]

The *Philokalia* grounds its implicit epistemological claims in soteriology (Thesis XI). Though the appeal to the natural state of the intellect needs further investigation, the assumption here is that a proper understanding of soteriology includes the reconnection of human beings to their intended noetic state — the intellect's true nature, dignity, and nobility. There is where deification factors into the discussion. Deification involves the reconstitution of the intellect perhaps in a fuller sense than its original created state. This process of receiving Christ's intellect "does not come to us through the loss of our intellectual power; nor does it come to us as a supplementary part added to our intellect; nor does it pass essentially and hypostatically into our own intellect. Rather, it illumines the power of our intellect with its own quality and conforms the activity of our intellect to its own."[22] The basic opposition between nature and grace does not apply here. Our humanity is not absorbed or overcome; participation in God is our "very nature, not its abolition."[23] The economy of God's salvation infuses within the intellect an ever-growing desire for union with God, "from whom it had its origin, by whom it is activated, and toward whom it ascends by means of its natural capabilities."[24] Thus, God's gift of shared life is an invitation to be fully human.

The *Philokalia* connects epistemology and soteriology by way of virtuous dispositions and practices. It is by means of virtuous practices that the intellect prepares for and comes to knowledge of God and "the new Adam is formed, made again according to the image of [its] Creator."[25] An

21. St. Maximus the Confessor, "Two Hundred Texts on Theology and the Incarnate Dispensation of the Son of God," *The Philokalia*, 2:116.

22. St. Maximus the Confessor, "Two Hundred Texts on Theology and the Incarnate Dispensation of the Son of God," *The Philokalia*, 2:158.

23. Meyendorff, *Byzantine Theology*, 153.

24. Nikitas Stithatos, "On Spiritual Knowledge, Love and the Perfection of Living: One Hundred Texts," *The Philokalia*, 4:143.

25. Evagrius the Solitary, "On Discrimination," *The Philokalia*, 1:40.

epistemically virtuous lifestyle solidifies dispositions and forms an intellect that intensely longs for and ceaselessly pursues God. A key component of virtue is constancy, the "mother of habit; once acquired, it rules us like nature."[26] Moreover, the formation of virtue and spiritual knowledge enables the theologian to view things correctly and according to their true nature: "A pure intellect sees things correctly. A trained intelligence puts them in order."[27] Underlying the process is the triune activity of God. It is only when the intellect is deeply immersed in the life of God that "it is granted direct vision of what pertains to God and, through the indwelling of the Holy Spirit, becomes in a true sense a theologian."[28] A properly disposed mind "apprehends, through the grace and wisdom of the Holy Spirit, the knowledge of things both human and divine."[29]

A basic assumption of the *Philokalia*, then, is that long-term practices form and sustain knowledge of God. The deiform person "should cultivate and practice what is good, so that it becomes an established habit operating automatically and effortlessly when required."[30] Practice helps us keep mindful of our new identity that is rooted in the knowledge of God. Moreover, the cultivation of the intellect requires exemplars of theological reflection; the underlying assumption is that epistemic trust, sustained by cultivated experience, creates a reliable process of belief formation. The basic rationale is that exemplars of theological wisdom are apt to offer skillful application of the knowledge of God. The experienced have "the best method and teacher of all: the activity, discernment, and peace of God Himself."[31]

---

26. St. Hesychios the Priest, "On Watchfulness and Holiness," *The Philokalia*, 1:178.

27. St. Maximus the Confessor, "Four Hundred Texts on Love," *The Philokalia*, 2:82.

28. St. Peter of Damaskos, "A Treasury of Divine Knowledge," *The Philokalia*, 3:143.

29. St. Peter of Damaskos, "A Treasury of Divine Knowledge," *The Philokalia*, 3:100.

30. St. Peter of Damaskos, "A Treasury of Divine Knowledge," *The Philokalia*, 3:87.

31. St. Peter of Damaskos, "A Treasury of Divine Knowledge," *The Philokalia*, 3:169. For example, St. Peter of Damaskos says, "we learn from the divine Scriptures and from the discrimination of the fathers how to conquer the passions and acquire the virtues" (*The Philokalia*, 3:91). St. Gregory of Sinai adds, "no one can learn the art of virtue by himself, though some have taken experience as their teacher. For to act on one's own and not on the advice of those who have gone before us is overwhelming presumption — or, rather, it engenders such presumption. . . . One should therefore listen to those who have experienced the hardships involved in cultivating the virtues and should cultivate them as they have" (*The Philokalia*, 4:274).

The *Philokalia* and Virtue Epistemology

Virtue epistemology is a multifaceted enterprise but the predominant conversation surfaces in reliabilist and responsibilist versions. While this overview acknowledges the nuances and variations of virtue epistemology, it highlights the fundamental distinction between these two versions.[32] Both relocate epistemic evaluation from properties of beliefs to properties of epistemic agents. One basic difference, for example, lies in the extent to which they ground their epistemic proposals in virtue theory.

The reliabilist strand connects virtue and epistemology through the logic of outcome. Faculties, people, practices, and processes are reliable to the extent that they produce true rather than false beliefs. Success is the epistemic glue that solidifies means and end. An independent standard of reliability serves as the criterion for determining whether faculties, people, practices, and processes are deemed epistemically virtuous. In the purest sense, most reliabilist treatments of virtue epistemology fail to derive their accounts from a virtue theory of ethics. The focus on truth-conduciveness is independent of this conception of virtue. The appeal to virtue has greater continuity with consequentialism than with the Aristotelian conception of virtue ethics.[33] Internal factors are not indispensable for secur-

---

32. For a good overview of various options in epistemology, see John Greco, "Virtue Epistemology," in *The Stanford Encyclopedia of Philosophy*, http://plato.stanford.edu/archives/fall1999/entries/epistemology-virtue.html. See also Linda T. Zagzebski, *Virtues of the Mind: An Inquiry into the Nature of Virtue and the Ethical Foundations of Knowledge* (Cambridge: Cambridge University Press, 1996); Michael DePaul and Linda T. Zagzebski, eds., *Intellectual Virtue: Perspectives from Ethics and Epistemology* (Oxford: Clarendon Press, 2003); Abrol Fairweather and Linda Zagzebski, eds., *Virtue Epistemology: Essays on Epistemic Virtue and Responsibility* (Oxford: Oxford University Press, 2001); John Greco, *Putting Skeptics in Their Place* (New York: Cambridge University Press, 2000); Matthias Steup, ed., *Knowledge, Truth, and Duty: Essays on Epistemic Justification, Responsibility, and Virtue* (Oxford: Oxford University Press, 2001); Michael Brady and Duncan Pritchard, eds., *Moral and Epistemic Virtues* (Oxford: Blackwell, 2003); Guy Axtell, ed., *Knowledge, Belief, and Character: Readings in Virtue Epistemology* (Lanham, MD: Rowman & Littlefield, 2000); Jonathan Kvanvig, *The Intellectual Virtues and the Life of the Mind* (Lanham, MD: Rowman & Littlefield, 1992); Kvanvig, *The Value of Knowledge and the Pursuit of Understanding* (New York: Cambridge University Press, 2003); James A. Montmarquet, *Epistemic Virtue and Doxastic Responsibility* (Lanham, MD: Rowman & Littlefield, 1993); Lorraine Code, *Epistemic Responsibility* (Hanover, NH: University Press of New England for Brown University Press, 1987); and Ernest Sosa, *Knowledge in Perspective: Selected Essays in Epistemology* (Cambridge: Cambridge University Press, 1991).

33. David Solomon, "Virtue Ethics: Radical or Routine," in *Intellectual Virtue,* makes

ing reliable results. Thus, most equate the reliabilist approach with virtue consequentialism.

For example, Alvin Goldman's reliabilist approach, though couched in the language of virtue, follows more of a consequentialist approach to belief formation than one rooted in virtue theory. Epistemic practices are evaluated by "their veritistic outputs," not by appropriate motivational states. In fact, Goldman disputes the connection between epistemology and virtue ethics, contending first of all that they are different fields. One should not assume that what holds in ethics must likewise follow in epistemology. Rather, "a process, trait, or action is an epistemic virtue to the extent that it tends to produce, generate, or promote (roughly) true belief."[34] Though Goldman may see a parallel between epistemology and ethics, this connection is not limited to virtue ethics but may have consequentialist and deontological connotations. Consequently, the internalist component of properly disposed motivation is not a precondition to Goldman's conception of virtue epistemology.

The responsibilist strand situates virtue at the center of the epistemological enterprise. It sees a greater connection between virtue theory and epistemology, stressing the importance of internal motivation (e.g., dispositions) and epistemic habits for acquiring knowledge. The stress on epistemic primacy here departs from the reliabilist accounts insofar that it sees motivation as indispensable to the process of knowing. The epistemically best kinds of beliefs cannot be specified independently of the proper exercise of intellectual virtues. Though the alternatives for this approach vary, the common ground lies in the connection between epistemology and virtue theory.

---

an astute point about the need for understanding the diversity and complexity of discussion in virtue ethics as epistemologists try to connect it with epistemology. For example, Solomon claims that Ernest Sosa's proposal of virtue epistemology falls into the "pattern of distributed assimilation. His virtues are faculties or dispositions by which a subject can reliably distinguish the true from the false within a field of proposition" (79). Reliability serves as an independent standard by which one determines whether faculties and dispositions are virtues. Thus, Sosa's virtue epistemology resembles consequentialism. Sosa, *Knowledge in Perspective*, 225, seems to confirm Solomon's observation here: "An intellectual virtue is a quality bound to help maximize one's surplus of truth over error . . . or so let us assume for now, though a more just conception may include as desiderata also generality, coherence, and explanatory power, unless the value of these is itself explained as derivative from the character of their contribution precisely to one's surplus of truth over error."

34. Alvin I. Goldman, *Pathways to Knowledge: Private and Public* (Oxford: Oxford University Press, 2002), 52.

For example, Linda Zagzebski's unified responsibilist version combines the internalist component of responsibility and the reliabilist component of epistemic success.[35] Good epistemic habits link the internal motivation of the epistemic agent and a reliable process of belief formation. The cultivation of epistemic virtues "requires that an agent's motivational states bear an appropriate relation" to the desired end.[36] Thus, Zagzebski's approach focuses on "the cognitive life of the agent rather than on episodes of cognitive activity in isolation. It would view inquiry as a practice, or a set of practices, always with a determinate form influenced by the historical and social circumstance within which the inquiry was carried out."[37]

The point of this brief overview is not to resolve current disputes in virtue epistemology or conflate the contemporary scene and the context of the *Philokalia*. Such moves would be premature and anachronistic. The *Philokalia* does not provide a fully developed virtue epistemology. Rather, it reflects the work of mystical theologians. Hence, my constructive suggestion merely highlights a possible connection between the *Philokalia* and virtue epistemology.

Retrospectively speaking, the responsibilist version is present, though not formally, in the *Philokalia*. Though the texts of the *Philokalia* are not philosophical in the technical sense of the word they do offer philosophical insights. Moreover, they would agree in principle with the claim that a robust version of virtue epistemology combines appropriate motivation and a reliable belief-forming process. Both aspects are indispensable to making progress on the path of deification. Pursuing deification without moral preparation (stage 1) is as incoherent as attaining knowledge of God without reliable contemplative practices (stages 2 and 3). Deification presupposes reliable processes/faculties/agents and an appropriate state of mind. In other words, appropriate motivation connects with practices that lead to the transformation of character and mystical union with the divine.

---

35. Not all responsibilist versions combine these components. For example, Code and Montmarquet focus on the primacy of epistemic responsibility and do not extend this focus to the externalist route. For further discussion of both components, see Gary Axtell, "Virtue Theory and the Fact/Value Problem," in *Knowledge, Belief, and Character*, 177-93; Frederick D. Aquino, *Communities of Informed Judgment: Newman's Illative Sense and Accounts of Rationality* (Washington, DC: The Catholic University of America Press, 2004), esp. ch. 4.

36. Abrol Fairweather, "Epistemic Motivation," in *Virtue Epistemology*, 68.

37. Solomon, "Virtue Ethics," 80.

The *Philokalia* offers, perhaps implicitly, an epistemology of theological judgment. A properly disposed mind sustained by healthy practices and habits enables a person to attain knowledge of God and render skillful judgment about particular situations. The result is the formation of a theologically mature mind.

Some Virtues of the Mind

The *Philokalia* sees prayer, repentance, and humility as significant cognitive practices that enable the deiform person to incorporate other epistemic virtues into its formative process (Thesis XIV). Theological knowledge without prayer is insufficient for forming theological judgment. "If you are a theologian, you will pray truly. And if you pray truly, you are a theologian."[38] Prayer's primary task is to immerse the intellect in divine matters so that that union with God becomes a reality and not merely a possibility.[39] Communion with God in prayer involves setting aside distracting thoughts and waiting for divine illumination. The remembrance of Jesus saturates the deiform person's diet; "for when the intellect with fervor of heart maintains persistently its remembrance of the precious name, then that name implants in us a constant love for its goodness, since there is nothing now that stands in the way."[40] Through stillness and silence the deiform person acquires skills of listening, thus enabling the heart to receive God's transformative love and grace.[41] Without purity of heart, the deiform intellect cannot reach its goal — transformation into the image and likeness of God.

Repentance re-centers the focus around the triune life of God. It is not to be confused with a list of negative rules but creates a properly disposed intellect, rooted in the work of the Second Adam. In Christ we experience a change of mind and receive a new way for understanding God, self, others, and the rest of creation. We discover, by divine grace, the new humanity we are called to become. In this sense, repentance is an ongoing

---

38. Evagrius the Solitary, "On Prayer," *The Philokalia*, 1:62.

39. Nikitas Stithatos, "On the Inner Nature of Things," *The Philokalia*, 4:129.

40. St. Diadochos of Photiki, "On Spiritual Knowledge," *The Philokalia*, 1:270-71.

41. Andrew Louth, *The Origins of the Christian Mystical Tradition* (Oxford: Clarendon Press, 1981), 98, points out that "Prayer is something done, rather than something thought about, and while all theology should relate to prayer, mystical theology does so directly in being reflection on the way of prayer, the way to union of the soul with God."

process that translates praiseworthy dispositions into union with God. "To repent is to look, not downward at my own shortcomings, but upward at God's love; not backward with self-reproach, but forward with trustfulness. It is to see, not what I have failed to be, but what by the grace of Christ I can yet become."[42]

Humility is an outgrowth of repentance, implanting a contrite heart in the deiform person and ensuring that the beginning of its illumination is healthy. The key is to recognize one's limits while pursuing the richness of divine knowledge. The deiform person "who fears the Lord has humility as his constant companion and, through the thoughts which humility inspires, reaches a state of divine love and thankfulness."[43] Without humility, a person will fail to make progress in the life of God. Claiming more than one is entitled to is an epistemic vice and hinders spiritual progress. Appropriate motivation is essential, not merely reliable practices, to continuing along the path of deification and the pursuit of divine knowledge and wisdom.

Self-awareness comes with stages 2 and 3 of the journey, though practice of the virtues clearly prepares the way for receiving divine knowledge and wisdom. In cultivating self-awareness, the deiform person enters "into the very sanctuary of God, into the noetic liturgy of the Spirit, the divine haven of dispassion and humility."[44] Inner awareness of the knowledge of God clarifies the "mysteries of the kingdom of heaven and the inner essences of created things."[45] The more one is deeply immersed in the life of God through the illuminating power of the Holy Spirit the more one sees one's own limitations and greater empathy for others.

The practices of prayer, repentance, and humility foster watchfulness. The practice of watchfulness regulates the path to knowledge of God and guards the intellect from distraction, homing in on the moment at hand. It connects holiness and truth, fostering a continuity of attention that "produces inner stability; inner stability produces a natural intensification of watchfulness; and this intensification gradually and in due measure contemplative insight into spiritual warfare."[46] In essence, watchfulness signals a disposition of attentiveness that recognizes epistemic distractions and guards the heart and intellect from improper images of the divine. It creates greater possibilities for discerning truth-conducive practices. Thus, the deiform per-

---

42. Ware, *The Inner Kingdom,* 45.
43. St. Maximus the Confessor, "Four Hundred Texts on Love," *The Philokalia,* 2:57.
44. Nikitas Stithatos, "On the Inner Nature of Things," *The Philokalia,* 4:117.
45. Nikitas Stithatos, "On the Inner Nature of Things," *The Philokalia,* 4:117.
46. St. Hesychios the Priest, "On Watchfulness and Holiness," *The Philokalia,* 1:163.

son pursues "the virtue of attentiveness — the guard and watch of the intellect, that perfect stillness of heart and blessed state of the soul."[47] Through stillness, the heart will discern "the heights and depths of knowledge; and the ear of the still intellect will be made to hear marvelous things from God."[48]

One result of watchfulness is discrimination. This entails the capacity to perceive spiritual truths, weighing and weaving insights into a new locus of knowledge. A deiform intellect pursues truth over falsity and good over evil. The "power of discrimination" scrutinizes every thought and activity, distinguishing and setting aside "everything that is base and not pleasing to God," keeping the deiform intellect "free from delusion."[49] Part of discrimination involves the capacity to glean from the wisdom of other exemplars of faith (e.g., the fathers). It is the result of a trained intellect that unites "wisdom, intellection and perceptiveness." Without it, "no virtue can stand or remain firm to the end, for it is the mother of all the virtues and their guardian."[50] Consequently, a mature theological agent of discrimination also knows how to assess the spiritual maturity of the questioner and apply rightly knowledge of God to different situations.

Implications for Theological Education

The work of the *Philokalia* embodies to a degree the integration of philosophy (though not formally) and spirituality. The mind and heart are interwoven into the life of God, thus reorienting the human self about the purpose for which God created humanity.[51] As a way of life, theology

47. St. Hesychios the Priest, "On Watchfulness and Holiness," *The Philokalia*, 1:182.

48. "Spiritual discourse fully satisfies our intellectual perception, because it comes from God through the energy of love. It is on account of this that the intellect continues undisturbed in its concentration on theology. It does not suffer then from the emptiness which produces a state of anxiety, since in its contemplation it is filled to the degree that the energy of love desires. So it is right always to wait, with a faith energized by love, for the illumination which will enable us to speak. For nothing is so destitute as a mind philosophizing about God when it is without Him" (*The Philokalia*, 1:254).

49. St. John Cassian, "On the Holy Fathers of Sketis and on Discrimination," *The Philokalia*, 1:99.

50. St. John Cassian, "On the Holy Fathers of Sketis and on Discrimination," *The Philokalia*, 1:100.

51. Andrew Louth, *Discerning the Mystery: An Essay on the Nature of Theology* (Oxford: Clarendon Press, 1983), 4, points out that there is "no division between theology and spirituality, no dissociation between the mind which knows God and the heart which loves

apprehends God through virtuous and contemplative practices, transforming the person into the image and likeness of God. Consequently, separating the cognitive, moral, and affective dimensions of human personhood is an inadequate depiction of the theological enterprise. Theology is the process of assimilating the whole person into the life of the triune God. The knower and the known collaborate and form a new humanity.

Theological education, however, has become so compartmentalized that integrating cognitive, moral, and affective dimensions of learning is a complex and difficult task to accomplish in theological institutions (e.g., seminary). Though the formational dimension of theological education does exist in some settings, it has become devalued in status. Specialized training in different fields of knowledge has largely eclipsed the cultivation of Christian character as a part of theological education. Researchers have replaced exemplars of theological wisdom.[52] Theological curricula are "so highly compartmentalized and teaching so committed to 'speed learning' (covering large chunks of content quickly)" that little time is committed to the cultivation of requisite intellectual virtues for acquiring wisdom.[53] Students shaped by this pedagogical move, then, assume that understanding (wisdom) comes by digesting and regurgitating large amounts of material. As we have seen, however, forming theological judgment requires induction into long-standing practices that solidify praiseworthy dispositions. The cultivation of the deiform intellect does not occur by digesting isolated facts but connects the relevance of these facts to their ultimate referent through habit and imitation.

A change in perspective is both necessary and relevant. Severing knowledge and wisdom has disastrous consequences for the enterprise of theological education.[54] When the former becomes the dominant concern,

---

him. It is not just that theology and spirituality, though different, are held together; rather theologia is the apprehension of God" by a person "restored to the image and likeness of God, and within this apprehension there can be discerned two sides (though there is something artificial about such discrimination); what we call the intellectual and the affective."

52. Peter Hodgson, *God's Wisdom: Toward a Theology of Education* (Louisville: Westminster John Knox Press, 1999), 129. Hodgson's chapter on transformative pedagogy is close to what I have in mind in this section.

53. Richard Paul, "Critical Thinking, Moral Integrity, and Citizenship: Teaching for the Intellectual Virtues," in Axtell, ed., *Knowledge, Belief, and Character,* 164.

54. See Ellen Charry, *By the Renewing of Your Minds: The Pastoral Function of Christian Doctrine* (Oxford: Oxford University Press, 1997), and William Abraham, *Canon as Criterion in Christian Theology: From the Fathers to Feminism* (Oxford: Oxford University Press, 1998).

theology essentially entails reflection on the coherence and justification of theological ideas, thus eclipsing focus on how these ideas, grounded in concrete practices, initiate and sustain the deiform person (the transformative dimension of theology). When the latter becomes the dominant focus, theology essentially becomes a superficially transformative enterprise without a cognitive basis. The *Philokalia* provides a wonderful example of how the cognitive and transformative dimensions of theological education are merged. Theological education is not simply the process of informing students, though this is an important aspect, but fosters the capacity to understand and connect items, especially the knower and the known. Connecting virtue and knowledge enables people to grow into the kind of people God calls them to be.

Thus, the goal of Christian education is deification, not simply dissemination of information. This, however, is not an escape from rigorous or critical thinking but a redirection of priorities. Theological education includes conversation with different disciplines (e.g., history, philosophy, and science). Nevertheless, we are called to inform but also be formed by the knowledge acquired. Consequently, students should see the process of deification actualized through a set of pedagogical practices, displayed by exemplars of theological wisdom (e.g., teachers) both in and outside of the classroom.[55]

The process of theological education also should reflect the various stages of formation. Professors should employ what Newman described as the principles of reserve and economy in which exemplars of theological judgment apply teaching according to the intellectual demeanor of the learner.[56] This takes time and interaction, reminding us that theological education is a communal enterprise. Professors should provide concrete practices through which students can learn together. For example, pedagogical discernment correlates multiple methods of teaching with the actual learning styles of students (e.g., lecture, discussion, and group projects). Deification is not personality-specific, and so the plurality of methods is warranted. It also calls for other epistemic practices such as finely honed inquiry for knowledge, open-mindedness in appraising data

---

55. See Frederick W. Schmidt's essay in this volume, "What Is Being Asked of You? Canonical Theism and Theological Education," for a proposal for implementing such a program of theological education.

56. John Henry Newman, *Apologia Pro Vita Sua*, ed. David DeLaura (New York: Norton, 1968), and Newman, *The Arians of the Fourth Century* (London: Longmans, 1919). For further treatment of this notion, see Robin C. Selby, *The Principle of Reserve in the Writings of John Henry Cardinal Newman* (Oxford: Oxford University Press, 1975).

and other arguments, epistemic humility, intellectual honesty, and the capacity to solidify various pieces of data into a synthetic judgment.[57]

Such a pursuit fosters an epistemically virtuous habit of mind, enabling people to understand and experience the unveiling of God's wisdom. Moreover, it connects the cognitive, moral, and affective dimensions of theological education. Separating the head and heart fails to see the integrative reality of the deiform life. In essence, "our own minds and experiences must become the subject of our study and learning. Indeed, only to the extent that the content of our own experiences becomes an essential part of study will the usual subject matter truly be learned."[58]

Connecting virtue and epistemology in this way "humanizes" the enterprise of theological education, showing the nuances, challenges, and blessings of an open-ended process of learning.[59] Tying education into deification sees learning as ongoing search for and participation in the pursuit of knowledge, truth, and the formation of character. Teaching is not simply apt communication of ideas but includes a display of epistemic virtues requisite for acquiring knowledge, truth, and wisdom. It is an experiment in transformation.

The Next Step

In my estimation, the *Philokalia* provides rich material on the formation of theological judgment. The next step is to unearth and develop further these hints in conversation with current work in social and virtue epistemology. My suggestion here is not the attempt to canonize an epistemology, but to pursue the implications of these resources both for understanding Christian thought/practice and for developing "unidentified and unexplored" epistemological insights that are relevant to the broader scope of human thought (Thesis XXII).

Clearly, the *Philokalia* sees a connection between virtue and knowledge. However, it does not offer a formal theory of knowledge, but rather lived and experienced wisdom cultivated through virtuous and contemplative practices. These practices enable the deiform intellect to focus on

57. I unpack these epistemic virtues in "The Craft of Teaching: The Relevance of Newman for Theological Education," *Christian Higher Education* 2 (2003): 269-84.

58. Paul, "Critical Thinking, Moral Integrity, and Citizenship," 173.

59. Aquino, "The Craft of Teaching," 278.

the right things and to guard the heart from distractions, remembering the new humanity to which God has called it to embody. Consequently, the aim of the Christian life is deification, a process in which humans consciously participate in the life of God. Our participation is an open and dynamic process; the gift of the *imago dei* calls for assimilation to God. The deiform person's search for immediacy with God, not simply knowledge about God, results in conformity to God — the subject and object of its virtuous and contemplative practices.

The *Philokalia* affirms that the economy of salvation reconstitutes the intellect, but we have yet to unpack the implications for a post-Reformation and post-Cartesian setting. Such investigation may help clarify how canonical theism will prescribe these practices for the church and theological schools today and avoid the epistemic pitfalls of the past. Though the epistemic hints are rich, retaining the practices of canonical theism without uncritical adoption of their varied epistemological and cosmological assumptions is an important task. Fusion of virtuous and contemplative practices should furnish vibrant safeguards.

Canonical Theism and the Challenge of Epistemic Certainty: Papal Infallibility as a Case Study

MARK E. POWELL

While the debates over biblical inerrancy and papal infallibility are complex, at least one familiar pattern has emerged. On the one hand are opponents of these doctrines who expose errors and contradictions in the biblical text or papal teaching, only to reject orthodox Christian beliefs in favor of a revisionist version of the faith. On the other hand are defenders of these doctrines who offer ingenious explanations for the supposed errors and contradictions and warn that rejecting these foundational epistemic doctrines is the first step to denying the Christian faith as a whole. As one who shares the concern to defend a broadly orthodox understanding of the Christian faith, these debates have led me to two conclusions. First, biblical inerrancy and papal infallibility are highly problematic as epistemic doctrines, and intellectual virtue demands that this fact be faced. And second, the assumptions underlying this debate, which is currently at a standstill, need to be questioned. Is it true that the Christian faith stands or falls with an inerrant scripture or infallible teacher? Or with epistemic doctrines that, in their mature form, occur for the first time in the second half of the nineteenth century?[1] A new paradigm for conceiving these issues is desperately needed.

Canonical theism offers a new way of envisioning religious epistemology that overcomes this impasse in the traditional debates over biblical inerrancy and papal infallibility. For one, canonical theism gives primacy to a

---

1. While there are precursors to these doctrines, the doctrine of biblical inerrancy appears in mature form with the Old Princeton theologians Charles Hodge (1798-1878) and B. B. Warfield (1851-1921), and papal infallibility receives extensive attention just before, and definitely after, Vatican I (1869-70).

basic Christian ontology instead of a particular epistemic method that is intended to secure this ontology. In other words, canonical theists are more interested in the faith that one confesses than in the method one uses epistemically to secure the faith. This shift corresponds well with recent developments in philosophy, where the pursuit of a "one-size-fits-all" epistemic method has been largely abandoned as an unattainable goal of classic modernity.[2] This, though, does not mean that we are left with a choice between relativism and fideism. Many contemporary philosophers suggest another option that is much more viable. Instead of beginning with an epistemic method and then proceeding to particular knowledge claims (methodism), we can begin with particular knowledge claims and defend the rationality of these claims using various *ad hoc* arguments (particularism).[3] Canonical theism advocates beginning with particular Christian beliefs, specifically the theism found in the canonical heritage of the church, and defending these beliefs using *ad hoc* arguments from scripture, the other canons of the church, and contemporary claims to knowledge.

Biblical inerrancy and papal infallibility are reflective of classic modernity's desire for epistemic certainty. For conservative Protestants, epistemic certainty is found in an inerrant scripture as interpreted by the individual Christian under the guidance of the Holy Spirit. More recently conservative Protestants have emphasized the importance of the church community for good biblical interpretation in an attempt to avoid excessive individualism.[4] However, since the beginning of the Reformation, Catholics have rightly argued that an inerrant scripture alone is inadequate for epistemic certainty. Devout believers, and communities, interpret scripture differently, and this in turn leads to divisions in the body of Christ. Catholics contend that, in addition to an inerrant scripture, an infallible judge is needed who properly interprets scripture with the assistance of the Holy Spirit.[5] The modern desire for an epistemic method that would secure religious certainty culminated in the definition of papal in-

2. See Jason E. Vickers, "Canonical Theism and the Primacy of Ontology," in this volume for a crucial distinction between *methodism* and *particularism* in epistemology.

3. For a concise discussion of *methodism* and *particularism,* see Roderick Chisholm, *The Problem of the Criterion* (Milwaukee: Marquette University Press, 1973).

4. See Douglas M. Koskela, "The Authority of Scripture in Ecclesial Context," in this volume.

5. A good account of this debate, especially during the Reformation, is found in the first chapter of Richard H. Popkin's *The History of Skepticism from Erasmus to Spinoza* (Berkeley: University of California Press, 1979).

fallibility at Vatican I in 1870. Canonical theism contends that the repeated quests for epistemic certainty on the part of both Protestants and Catholics have been a costly mistake.

Rather than viewing scripture, the creeds, and the episcopacy[6] as epistemic criteria, canonical theists view them more appropriately as means of grace which function soteriologically to lead one into communion with God and a new life founded on the gospel. This is not to say that scripture and the other canons of the church cannot be appealed to in arguments for the rationality of particular beliefs. Scripture, which provides access to divine revelation, and the other canons of the church can and should be appealed to in such cases. However, it is one thing to appeal to scripture, for instance, because it provides access to divine revelation; it is another thing to appeal to scripture as an epistemic criterion. Scripture and the other canons of the church are first and foremost means of grace that, through the working of the Holy Spirit, lead one to salvation.

This chapter will seek to demonstrate the conceptual advance canonical theism offers contemporary theology in comparison to theories of inerrancy and infallibility. The Catholic doctrine of papal infallibility will be taken as an example for two reasons. As already mentioned, it represents the culmination of the desire for religious epistemic certainty that characterizes the modern period. In addition, papal infallibility has been canonized in the Roman Catholic tradition, a move that canonical theism strongly warns against. Since the definition of papal infallibility offers a significant ecumenical challenge, this chapter will end with a consideration of how Catholicism might incorporate the proposals of canonical theism found in this book.

The Doctrine of Papal Infallibility

Papal infallibility is a remarkable epistemic proposal whose complexity and subtlety is often underestimated. The definition of papal infallibility in *Pastor Aeternus* reads,

---

6. I use the term "episcopacy" in the broad sense for any legitimate ecclesial authority who oversees and cares for the church (cf. the New Testament use of the word ἐπίσκοπος), not in the specific sense of a particular form of church government. In my usage, "episcopacy" could refer to elders in a congregational or presbyterian church, as well as bishops in an episcopal church.

Therefore, faithfully adhering to the tradition received from the beginning of the Christian faith, to the glory of God our Savior, for the exaltation of the Catholic religion and for the salvation of the Christian people, with the approval of the sacred council, we teach and define as a divinely revealed dogma that when the Roman pontiff speaks *ex cathedra,* that is, when, in the exercise of his office as shepherd and teacher of all Christians, in virtue of his supreme apostolic authority, he defines a doctrine concerning faith or morals to be held by the whole church, he possesses, by the divine assistance promised to him in blessed Peter, that infallibility which the divine Redeemer willed his church to enjoy in defining doctrine concerning faith or morals. Therefore, such definitions of the Roman pontiff are of themselves, and not by the consent of the church, irreformable.[7]

According to *Pastor Aeternus,* the pope enjoys the infallible assistance of the Holy Spirit when he speaks *ex cathedra,* or "from the chair [of Peter]." An exegetical clause explains that the pope speaks *ex cathedra* when, "in the exercise of his office as shepherd and teacher of all Christians, in virtue of his supreme apostolic authority, he defines a doctrine concerning faith or morals to be held by the whole church." Therefore the pope is not infallible in all of his statements. He may make a doctrinal error in his teaching as a private theologian or in his exercise of ordinary papal magisterium.[8] He may err in his judgment on issues outside the scope of "faith or morals," such as political and scientific matters. He is still susceptible to sin. But when the pope issues a solemn judgment on an issue of faith or morals for the whole church, he enjoys "the divine assistance promised to him in blessed Peter, that infallibility which the divine Redeemer willed his church to enjoy in defining doctrine concerning faith or morals." Since the pope has the *charism* of infallibility, his *ex cathedra* definitions are "of themselves, and not by the consent of the church, irreformable."

---

7. *Pastor Aeternus,* in *Creeds and Confessions of Faith in the Christian Tradition,* ed. Jaroslav Pelikan and Valerie Hotchkiss, vol. 3 (New Haven: Yale University Press, 2003), 358.

8. Catholic theologians distinguish "extraordinary papal magisterium," when the pope exercises his infallible teaching authority to solemnly define a doctrine, and "ordinary papal magisterium," when the pope teaches a doctrine authoritatively but not infallibly. A helpful glossary of terms is found in J. Robert Dionne, *The Papacy and the Church: A Study of Praxis and Reception in Ecumenical Perspective* (New York: Philosophical Library, 1987), 17-25.

A number of beliefs undergird the doctrine of papal infallibility, as the context of *Pastor Aeternus* demonstrates. First of all, Catholics agree with Protestants that God has been decisively revealed in the history of Jesus of Nazareth and that apostolic writers reliably recorded this divine revelation in scripture under the inspiration of the Holy Spirit. The infallible decisions of the pope are not viewed as new revelations, and the *charism* the pope enjoys is not conceived as inspiration, even if papal definitions are clearly found in scripture and early church tradition. Rather, the *charism* is conceived as a negative one that keeps the pope, and the church, from error in interpreting and applying scripture and tradition in each new generation. Second, Catholics agree with many Protestant and Orthodox Christians that the church is indefectible, since Jesus promised that the gates of hell would not prevail against his church (Matt. 16:18). Catholics, though, believe that an infallible interpreter is needed for the church to remain faithful to the gospel and to maintain unity. So the doctrine of papal infallibility is placed within the context of the indefectibility of the church. Third, Catholics argue that the *charism* of infallibility was given to the apostle Peter for the benefit of the church (Matt. 16:18-19; Luke 22:31-32; John 21:15-17), and this *charism* continues today in the pope. The pope serves as an infallible belief-producing mechanism who properly interprets scripture and tradition. Therefore, while the modern doctrine of papal infallibility does not view the pope as an epistemic criterion *per se,* the doctrine logically follows from conceiving scripture and tradition as epistemic criteria. An infallible pope is the capstone of an epistemic tower built on scripture and tradition.[9]

It is clear that the Ultramontanes, the proponents of papal infallibility at Vatican I, were concerned with epistemic certainty. For example, Henry Edward Cardinal Manning (1808-1892), archbishop of Westminster and an outspoken leader of the Ultramontanes, said, "Surely divine truth is susceptible, within the limits of revelation, of an expression and a proof as exact as the inductive sciences."[10] He further maintained,

Of two things one at least: either Christianity is divinely preserved, or it is not. If it be divinely preserved, we have a divine certainty of faith.

---

9. For a more detailed account of the magisterium and papal infallibility in Catholic theology, see Francis A. Sullivan, *Magisterium: Teaching Authority and the Catholic Church* (New York: Paulist Press, 1983), and Richard R. Gaillardetz, *Teaching with Authority: A Theology of the Magisterium in the Church* (Collegeville: Liturgical Press, 1997).

10. As quoted by Robert Gray in *Cardinal Manning: A Biography* (London: Weidenfeld and Nicolson, 1985), 103.

If it be not divinely preserved, its custody and its certainty now are alike human, and we have no divine certainty that what we believe was divinely revealed.[11]

Manning paints a stark contrast. Either God has preserved Christianity and we can have a "divine certainty of faith," or we do not have religious certainty and Christianity has not been preserved. He argues that epistemic certainty is attained not by an inerrant scripture, nor by scripture and tradition, for such proposals rest on private judgment. Rather, epistemic certainty is attained by an infallible pope who is able to discern and apply the meaning of scripture and tradition for the church today.[12]

Manning's maximal interpretation of papal infallibility has lost support among many contemporary Catholic theologians, but his concern for epistemic certainty remains. For example, Avery Cardinal Dulles, a contemporary Catholic theologian, defends a moderate interpretation of papal infallibility. Dulles is aware that Manning's desire for precise theological expression, modeled after scientific and mathematical statements, is no longer tenable. Science and mathematics are no longer viewed as providing objective, certain knowledge, not to mention theology. Thus Dulles turns to the discipline of hermeneutics to provide insight into the nature of papal pronouncements. Dulles writes,

Even infallible statements do not escape the limitations inherent in all human speech. Dogmatic statements, insofar as they bear upon the divine, contain an element of special obscurity. The formulations of faith necessarily fall short of capturing the full richness of the transcendent realities to which they refer. Furthermore, as already stated, dogmatic pronouncements are inevitably influenced by the presuppositions, concerns and thought-categories of those who utter them, as well as by the limitations in the available vocabulary. Without contradicting Vatican I's teaching on infallibility, therefore, one may admit that all papal and conciliar dogmas, including the dogma of papal infallibility, are subject to ongoing reinterpretation in the Church.[13]

---

11. Henry Edward Manning, *The True Story of the Vatican Council* (London: Henry S. King, 1877), 181.

12. See James Pereiro, *Cardinal Manning: An Intellectual Biography* (Oxford: Clarendon Press, 1998), 68, 69.

13. Avery Dulles, "Papal Authority in Roman Catholicism," in *A Pope for All Christians*, ed. Peter J. McCord (New York: Paulist Press, 1976), 62.

The discipline of hermeneutics not only allows Dulles better to explain the nature of papal pronouncements, it also allows him to reformulate doctrines that are no longer plausible, including papal infallibility.

Since papal pronouncements and papal infallibility can be continually reformulated, one might wonder how they bring epistemic certainty. Dulles insists that the fluidity of Catholic doctrinal statements does not detract from the infallibility of the Catholic Church. He later states,

> Minimalistically, or even strictly, interpreted, [the definition of papal infallibility] is hardly more than an emphatic assertion that the pope's primacy, as defined in the first three chapters of *Pastor aeternus*, extends also to his teaching power. He is not only the first pastor but also the first teacher in the Church. In view of his special responsibility for the unity of the whole Church in the faith of the apostles, it is antecedently credible that in him the infallibility of the whole Church may come to expression.[14]

For Dulles, papal infallibility is an "emphatic assertion" of papal primacy in teaching. Still, he views an infallible pope as a necessary part of an infallible church, thus maintaining an epistemic understanding of the canons of the church. His carefully nuanced position, though, betrays the difficulties that arise in seeking epistemic certainty in the teachings of the papacy.

Papal Infallibility and Epistemic Certainty

As a proposal to secure epistemic certainty, papal infallibility has obvious shortcomings. One that was recognized early on by Protestant critics is the problem of interpreting papal pronouncements. While scripture and tradition are preserved in texts and must be interpreted using private judgment, papal pronouncements are also preserved in texts that must be interpreted. W. E. Gladstone, the British statesman and devout Anglican, observed,

> These are written definitions. What are they but another Scripture? What right of interpreting this other Scripture is granted to the Church at large, more than of the real and greater Scripture? Here is

14. Dulles, "Papal Authority in Roman Catholicism," 64.

surely, in its perfection, the petition for bread, answered by the gift of stone.[15]

An example of the problem is seen in the fate of *Pastor Aeternus* itself. After Vatican I, the terms of the definition, especially *ex cathedra* and "faith or morals," were given several interpretations by Catholic theologians. Some, like Manning, held a maximal interpretation of the doctrine that allowed for a large number of papal pronouncements to be held as infallible. Historical difficulties with the maximal view led others, like the German bishop Joseph Fessler, to propose a moderate interpretation of the doctrine that views infallible pronouncements as rare.[16] Many contemporary Catholics, like Dulles, hold the moderate view that the pope has spoken infallibly on only two occasions, the definition of the Immaculate Conception of the Blessed Virgin Mary (1854) and the definition of the Assumption of the Blessed Virgin Mary (1950). Again, the problem of interpreting *Pastor Aeternus* itself was recognized by Gladstone.

> There is no established or accepted definition of the phrase *ex cathedra* and [the Catholic individual] has no power to obtain one, and no guide to direct him in his choice among some twelve theories on the subject, which, it is said, are bandied to and fro among Roman theologians, except the despised and discarded agency of his private judgment.[17]

Gladstone makes an important point that should not be lost in his rhetorical banter. Instead of solving the problem of interpretation and private judgment, the doctrine of papal infallibility only pushes the problem one step back. The only way out of this infinite regression is for each individual to possess infallibility so that each person can know that one has properly interpreted infallible papal pronouncements. But if each individual must possess infallibility to attain epistemic certainty, there is hardly a need for the pope to have a special *charism* of infallibility.

A second problem with papal infallibility, which is interrelated to the problem of interpretation and extends beyond *Pastor Aeturnus,* is the

---

15. W. E. Gladstone, *Vaticanism: An Answer to Replies and Reproofs* (London: John Murray, 1875), 99.

16. See Joseph Fessler, *The True and False Infallibility of the Pope* (New York: Catholic Publication Society, 1875).

17. W. E. Gladstone, *The Vatican Decrees and Their Bearing on Civil Allegiance* (London: John Murray, 1874), 34-35.

problem of identifying infallible doctrines. The Catholic Church professes epistemic certainty for a whole host of doctrines besides the two Marian dogmas, which are secured under a moderate interpretation of *Pastor Aeternus*. An important question, then, is how epistemic certainty is attained in these numerous other instances as well. The Second Vatican Council addressed this issue by affirming that doctrinal infallibility extends to the bishops in communion with the pope in two circumstances. First, when the bishops in communion with the pope, though ministering throughout the world, agree on a doctrine of faith or morals, that doctrine is infallibly taught. This exercise of infallible teaching authority is called "ordinary universal magisterium." Second, when bishops gather in ecumenical councils in communion with the pope and define a doctrine of faith or morals, the bishops can teach infallibly. This exercise of infallible teaching authority is called "extraordinary universal magisterium."[18] As can be imagined, questions often arise over whether a doctrine has been infallibly taught by means of the ordinary universal magisterium or extraordinary universal magisterium. One well-known example will suffice to demonstrate the confusion that can ensue.

In 1970 the controversial Catholic theologian Hans Küng published his work, *Unfehlbar? eine Anfrage*, which was translated into English the following year as *Infallible? An Inquiry*.[19] In this work Küng made a bold move for which he would ultimately lose his canonical mission to teach — he challenged the Catholic doctrine of infallibility in all of its forms. While Küng offers numerous examples that make the infallibility of the Catholic Church difficult to maintain, such as the condemnation of Pope Honorius I by an ecumenical council and several subsequent popes, he focuses his attention on the more recent example of *Humanae Vitae*, which bans artificial birth control.[20] He maintains that, even though *Humanae Vitae* is not an infallible papal pronouncement, it still functions infallibly. The restriction against artificial birth control has been taught by the bishops of the church scattered throughout the world, a condition which, according the Vatican II, makes a doctrine infallible though not infallibly defined. Küng's argument is that the immorality of artificial birth control is based on faulty natural law reasoning rather than scrip-

18. See *Lumen Gentium* 25, in Pelikan and Hotchkiss, eds., *Creeds and Confessions of Faith in the Christian Tradition*, 3:596-98; Sullivan, *Magisterium*, chs. 5-7.

19. Hans Küng, *Unfehlbar? eine Anfrage* (Zurich: Benziger, 1970); ET: *Infallible? An Inquiry*, trans. Edward Quinn (Garden City, NY: Doubleday & Co., 1981).

20. Küng, *Infallible?* 33.

ture, and it is not accepted by the majority of the scientific community, non-Catholic Christians, and even Catholics. So he feels he has a good contemporary case where the teaching office of the Catholic Church has made a wrong decision. Küng suggests that the reason the Catholic Church continues to maintain the immorality of artificial birth control is not the material aspect of the doctrine — the immorality of artificial birth control — but the formal aspect of the doctrine, the infallibility of the Catholic Church.[21]

The fascinating thing about Küng's work is not the merits or demerits of his argument. What is fascinating is the response Küng's work elicited from Catholic theologians, especially regarding the example he chose to highlight. For instance, Richard McBrien states,

> I agree with Avery Dulles and others that Küng is mistaken when he argues that the teaching of *Humanae Vitae* and the doctrine of papal infallibility stand or fall together. . . . Küng certainly knows that this encyclical does not fulfill all the conditions for an infallible pronouncement as set down by Vatican I.[22]

Here we find ourselves in the midst of a debate over the meaning of *ex cathedra* and whether or not *Humanae Vitae* should be identified as an *ex cathedra* definition. To defend Küng against McBrien's charge, there is nothing in *Pastor Aeternus* that prevents *Humanae Vitae* from being an infallible pronouncement if one maintains a maximal interpretation of *Pastor Aeternus*. Manning would have viewed *Humanae Vitae* as an infallible papal pronouncement. Of course, *Humanae Vitae* is excluded under a moderate interpretation of *Pastor Aeternus*.

Küng's argument is not, however, that *Humanae Vitae* is an infallible papal definition, but that it is an infallible teaching of the bishops scattered throughout the world. Once again there is disagreement. Francis Sullivan notes, "Karl Rahner and most other Catholic theologians . . . do not agree that, according to the official Catholic doctrine on the infallibility of the ordinary universal magisterium, the sinfulness of artificial contraception has been infallibly taught."[23] Sullivan is overstating the case, for a number of conservative Catholic theologians believe the sinfulness of artificial contraception has been infallibly taught. Küng and his supporters agree.

---

21. Küng, *Infallible?* 43-52.
22. John J. Kirvan, ed., *The Infallibility Debate* (New York: Paulist Press, 1971), 39.
23. Sullivan, *Magisterium*, 120.

Again, we find ourselves in the midst of a disagreement among Catholic theologians over identifying the infallible teachings of the ordinary universal magisterium.

Unfortunately, Küng falls into the same trap that was presented at the beginning of this chapter. After rejecting papal infallibility and biblical inerrancy he adopts another theological method based on an epistemic understanding of the canons of the church, the historical critical exegesis of scripture. Based on this methodology he questions whether the pre-existence of the Son and the ontological divinity of Jesus are actually found in the original apostolic preaching, although both are found in the New Testament, the Nicene Creed, and the Chalcedonian definition, and both are foundational for the traditional Christian belief in the incarnation. Küng adopts a functional Christology where God acts in a dynamic way in the man Jesus, but he never affirms the ontological divinity of Jesus.[24] Thus Küng adopts a revisionist version of the faith that, ironically, gives ammunition to the defenders of papal infallibility. From the standpoint of the defenders of papal infallibility, Küng becomes a textbook example of what happens when one denies the epistemic doctrine of papal infallibility — one eventually denies material doctrines of the faith such as the ontological divinity of Jesus. While Küng is helpful in exposing problems with papal infallibility, his own solution is mired in the same search for a methodology that views the canons of the church as epistemic criteria.

In summary, the Catholic Church claims to have an infallible teaching whenever the pope speaks *ex cathedra,* the bishops throughout the world teach a doctrine, or the bishops gather in council and pronounce a doctrine. However, there is disagreement on the identification and interpretation of *ex cathedra* pronouncements, as well as the infallible teachings of the ordinary universal magisterium and extraordinary universal magisterium. Further, if we take Dulles's suggestion, identified infallible teachings can be reformulated and developed if such teachings no longer appear plausible. Such problems over identifying and interpreting infallible doctrines make claims to epistemic certainty appear unconvincing, if not plain dubious. At least it is difficult to see how Catholic doctrines of infallibility bring more epistemic certainty than what is enjoyed by other Christians. Canonical theists believe there is a better way to conceive the canons of the church and the epistemology of theology.

---

24. See, for example, Hans Küng, *On Being a Christian,* trans. Edward Quinn (London: Collins, 1978), 131-33.

Analysis

The doctrine of papal infallibility involves at least four conceptual errors. The first two, which have already been discussed in the beginning of the chapter, also characterize doctrines of biblical inerrancy.[25] First, the doctrine of papal infallibility is deeply wedded to the quest for epistemic certainty in theology. The quest for epistemic certainty is clearly seen in Manning, who argued that the only two options are "the divine certainty of faith" as secured by papal infallibility or total uncertainty. Dulles's desire for epistemic certainty is more subtle but nonetheless present — without an infallible pope the church cannot remain in the truth of the gospel. Küng does not clarify matters when he rejects papal infallibility only to adopt another epistemic method that leads him to revision fundamental Christian beliefs.

Canonical theists argue that Christians should begin with the theism found in the canonical heritage of the church, rather than first devising a method or criterion that will secure this theism. The doctrine of the Trinity can be accepted as true without having a method or criterion to secure this and all other Christian doctrines. Further, arguments for the rationality of the Trinity and other beliefs can be presented and evaluated in numerous ways. But an infallible method for securing religious doctrine is neither available nor necessary.

Second, the doctrine of papal infallibility makes a conceptual error by turning an ecclesial canon, the episcopacy, into an epistemic criterion. As noted above, it is more accurate to say that papal infallibility conceives scripture and tradition as epistemic criteria and the pope as an infallible belief-producing mechanism who properly interprets these criteria. Canonical theists argue that canons like scripture, tradition, and the episcopacy are better conceived as means of grace whose primary function is soteriological. The canons of the church reveal God to the believer, transform the believer, and lead the believer into a relationship with God and the people of God. The role of the episcopacy, then, is not to secure epistemic certainty, but to teach the faith, shepherd believers, and lead the church, all the while looking to the Holy Spirit for guidance. Further, the Holy Spirit is looked to as the only one who can secure the truth of the gospel and bring unity in the church.

25. A recent example of biblical inerrancy that is committed to methodism and that views the canon of scripture as an epistemic criterion is the "Chicago Statement of Biblical Inerrancy," *Journal of the Evangelical Theological Society* 21:4 (December 1978): 289-96.

Third, papal infallibility canonizes an epistemology. The collapse of classic modernity in the century following Vatican I demonstrates why canonizing an epistemology is a mistake. While the content of the gospel does not change, intellectual currents do. The church needs the flexibility to present and defend the gospel in light of contemporary philosophical developments and challenges, although the gospel will also be critical of these developments. Further, papal infallibility is widely considered to be the chief obstacle in ecumenical dialogue. But, as has been argued here, agreement on religious epistemology is not necessary for ecumenical unity on particular beliefs. The church does not seek to present an epistemology to the world, but the gospel of salvation.

Fourth, papal infallibility confuses epistemic certainty with the effective exercise of teaching and organizational authority.[26] Many Catholic theologians insist that infallibility is needed effectively to exercise authority in the church, which in turns secures church unity. Infallibility, it is maintained, gives the pope the right to decide doctrinal disputes regarding the authentic teaching of the church, to admonish and correct, and to protect the church through discipline. But epistemic certainty is not logically required for the effective exercise of teaching and organizational authority. For example, legal courts make effective and binding interpretations of the law, which in turn police officers effectively enforce, without claims of infallibility and irreformability. The Catholic Church itself maintained teaching and organizational authority without definitive claims of papal infallibility until 1870. The maxim that papal pronouncements should be obeyed even if they are not infallible supports the notion that infallibility is not logically required for effective teaching and organizational authority.[27]

The Promise of Canonical Theism

As an epistemic proposal, papal infallibility leads to insoluble problems. More important, papal infallibility has undoubtedly become a leading obstacle in recent ecumenical discussions. How, then, might Catholic theolo-

---

26. A thorough philosophical analysis of authority is found in Richard T. De George, *The Nature and Limits of Authority* (Lawrence: University of Kansas Press, 1985).

27. See, for example, *Lumen Gentium* 25, in Pelikan and Hotchkiss, eds., *Creeds and Confessions of Faith in the Christian Tradition*, 3:597.

gians proceed given the insight of canonical theism? Let me suggest two possibilities.

First, papal infallibility could be viewed as a local epistemic proposal of the Catholic Church that is not binding on other Christians within a larger ecumenical union. While canonical theism takes epistemological issues seriously, it does insist that "no single epistemological vision should be offered or sanctioned as canonical in the Church." Further, "various and internally competing epistemological visions and theories are compatible with the content of the canonical heritage."[28] Therefore the Catholic theologian may affirm that papal infallibility offers the best available method for securing religious knowledge. Canonical theism simply argues that epistemological theories must be "decanonized in the ecumenical arena."[29] A Catholic theologian could affirm papal infallibility and canonical theism by (1) confessing the theism found in the canonical heritage of the church, and (2) refusing to canonize an epistemology in the ecumenical arena.

Second, and by far more preferable, the doctrine of papal infallibility could be further interpreted or developed within Catholic theology in light of the suggestions of canonical theism. Dulles's work in hermeneutics and Catholic proposals for doctrinal development give Catholic theologians significant leeway in affirming past doctrinal statements while recognizing the philosophical limitations of those statements. While earlier I suggested that such moves make claims to infallibility and epistemic certainty look unconvincing, they could be used to relocate *Pastor Aeternus* outside the field of epistemology. Therefore, *Pastor Aeternus* could be interpreted or developed in light of philosophical developments that question the possibility of epistemic certainty. Taking Dulles's suggestion, *Pastor Aeternus* could be interpreted to give the pope primacy in his teaching ministry in the Catholic Church. The pope would serve as the final judge in doctrinal disputes in the Catholic Church, but this exercise of teaching and organizational authority would not be conceived in epistemic terms. It would be recognized that the desire for an infallible method and epistemic certainty found in *Pastor Aeternus* is culturally conditioned and unnecessary.

These suggestions alone do not solve all of the ecumenical issues the papacy poses. For one, it does not deal with the issue of primacy.[30] Never-

---

28. Thesis XXV in "Theses on Canonical Theism," above.

29. Thesis XXX in "Theses on Canonical Theism," above.

30. See J. Michael Miller, *What Are They Saying about Papal Primacy?* (New York: Paulist Press, 1983).

theless, if the episcopacy is reconceived along the lines suggested here, the issue of primacy will be easier to address. The pope could still exercise primacy in the Catholic Church while exercising a different role of leadership in any potential ecumenical union, as the Bishop of Rome did in the first millennium of the church's existence. Even if ecumenical union is not a possibility, the insights of canonical theism offer viable resources for Catholic theologians in their conception of the episcopacy.

The Authority of Scripture in Its Ecclesial Context

Douglas M. Koskela

There is perhaps no better introduction to our topic than the words of Joseph T. Lienhard: "To say that the Bible is authoritative is to begin a discussion, not to end it."[1] Indeed, virtually all Christian traditions attribute some degree of authority to the Christian scriptures. But roughly two centuries of concentrated debate (and increasing confusion) about what this means have raised some troubling questions, particularly for Protestant communions: What *sort* of authority do the biblical texts hold? Are there features in the texts themselves which demand such authority, or is their status conferred by some external entity?[2] Are there certain conditions which must be met for scripture's authority to obtain (or conditions under which its authority might be lost)? It is the last question in particular that will occupy our attention in what follows. For, at a very basic level, the biblical texts are considered authoritative because they are thought to yield special revelation to the community of faith.[3] But the process of interpreting the scriptures such that revelation is faithfully received is a very complex matter indeed. To compound the problem, one significant consequence of the Protestant Reformation was the detachment of the Bible from the ecclesiastical practices that were intended to facilitate healthy interpretation. Embracing mottos such as *sola scriptura*, heirs of the Refor-

---

1. Joseph T. Lienhard, *The Bible, the Church, and Authority* (Collegeville: Liturgical Press, 1995), 78.

2. See Richard Bauckham's helpful discussion of "intrinsic" and "extrinsic" authority in "Scripture and Authority," *Transformation* 15 (April 1998): 5-11.

3. For a lucid discussion of the relation between authority, inspiration, and revelation, see William J. Abraham, *The Divine Inspiration of Holy Scripture* (Oxford: Oxford University Press, 1981), 74-90.

mation espoused a notion of an authoritative Bible that stood alone, free from the entanglements and distortions of church tradition. The problem, of course, was that their Bible proved to be anything but self-interpreting, and competing interpretations of scripture abounded.[4]

In light of the ensuing confusion, the question of scripture's authority came to the fore. How could a collection of texts hold significant purchase on a community if the meaning of those texts could not be unambiguously determined? Furthermore, two developments of modernity pushed proponents of biblical authority into deeper water. The first was a growing skepticism of the notion of authority itself, as it was seen to compromise the fundamental value of genuine autonomy. The second was the rise of biblical criticism, illustrating with increasing clarity the human involvement in the production of the biblical texts.[5] While theologians often bent over backwards to offer convincing accounts of scripture's authority in light of these difficulties, their proposals consistently fell victim to a fatal presumption: they understood the canon of scripture primarily as an epistemic norm.[6] The driving concern was to describe precisely how the Bible served as a criterion of truth, thus yielding the sort of reliability needed for an "authority." What such proposals failed to recognize was the place of scripture within the broader canonical heritage and the importance of the Bible's ecclesial context.

For the canonical theist, the history of this discussion raises the temptation to jettison the term "authority" altogether. It has become habitual upon hearing the term to think immediately of some sort of epistemic guarantee. Whatever version of biblical authority is on offer, the tendency is to understand it as a surefire mechanism of deciphering truth. It is precisely this type of move that canonical theism resists. However, I

---

4. James Barr, *Holy Scripture: Canon, Authority, Criticism* (Oxford: Clarendon Press, 1983), 32-33. Of course, this should not have been news. To take but one of many examples from the church fathers, Irenaeus's dispute with the Gnostics in the second century was essentially a debate about the interpretation of the scriptures. His appeal to the rule of faith as an interpretive key already indicates the problem with the notion that scripture is authoritative on its own. See Lienhard, *The Bible, the Church, and Authority,* 49ff.

5. Abraham, *Divine Inspiration,* 77. See also Clark Pinnock, "Three Views of the Bible in Contemporary Theology," in *Biblical Authority,* ed. Jack Rogers (Waco, TX: Word Books, 1977), 49.

6. William J. Abraham, *Canon and Criterion in Christian Theology: From the Fathers to Feminism* (Oxford: Oxford University Press, 1998). While the entire work traces this development in Western Christianity, see particularly the opening chapter, "Orientation: Authority, Canon, and Criterion," for the place of biblical authority in this discussion.

propose in this essay that a notion of biblical authority can indeed be embraced within the logic of canonical theism. When scripture is considered as a means of grace with a specific place in the life of the church, new possibilities open for this entire discussion. "Authority" in this sense is not understood as an epistemological proposal intended to secure truth in a failsafe manner. Rather, authority reflects the unique role the biblical texts play as the community of faith seeks the guidance of God in spiritual formation, addressing ethical questions, and settling doctrinal disputes. In this process, the scriptures cannot be detached from the various practices and patterns that foster the apprehension of divine revelation. Thus I would suggest that scripture's authority is best conceived as "conditional authority."[7] My thesis is as follows: the Bible is authoritative for the community of faith if and only if it functions in its proper ecclesial context. Clearly, serious reflection is needed to delineate precisely what this context entails. I would suggest that there are at least three essential dimensions: the church's rule of faith as the interpretive key to the scriptures, a particular teaching practice within the church, and the immersion of the interpretive community in worship and the means of grace. Before we address these, however, more reflection is needed on what a conditional conception of authority involves.

The Contours of "Conditional Authority"

A conception of biblical authority does not *confer* the authority it describes. Rather, it attempts to elucidate how scripture functions authoritatively in the life of a given community of faith. Surely Darrell Jodock is correct when he writes, "Whatever else the Bible may accomplish, it serves the community and its purposes. Therefore the Scriptures function as an authority in the community before any theory describes their authority. The theory serves a practical end: the proper exercise of an already existing authority."[8] It is crucial to recognize the significance of Jodock's appeal to the "proper" exercise of authority. As history so clearly attests, scripture might function as a practical authority for a community in unhealthy or

---

7. A more precise term might be "contextual authority," but such a phrase would leave itself open to easy misinterpretation, given the prevalence of the term "contextual theology" (which refers to something altogether different).

8. Darrell Jodock, *The Church's Bible: Its Contemporary Authority* (Minneapolis: Fortress Press, 1989), 11.

even morally reprehensible ways.[9] Quite obviously, just as there are misguided theories of authority, there are faith communities with harmful appropriations of biblical authority in practice. If a conception of scripture's authority is to be fruitful, then, it will include both descriptive and normative components. Specifically, it will describe the role that the Bible *does* and *should* play in guiding a community in truthful belief and practice.

The appeal to *truthful* belief and practice might suggest that we have arrived back on the tracks we sought to avoid — namely, a primarily epistemic conception of the canon of scripture. However, a few key distinctions will show that this is not the case. First, we must make the distinction between divine revelation and the collection of biblical texts. As noted above, the Bible is recognized as authoritative generally because it provides access to divine revelation. It plays a role in providing the community of faith with truthful knowledge about God and the world as well as a faithful way of living in relation to God and the world. However, to say that the Bible has a part in yielding divine revelation is far from saying that this collection of texts and divine revelation are identical (which would be an odd confusion of categories). As William J. Abraham notes, the operative epistemic concept at stake is divine revelation, and not the canon of scripture.[10]

A second distinction is also in order: to recognize that scripture is not an epistemic criterion is not to suggest that scripture is irrelevant to the church's appropriation of truth. On the contrary, precisely because it has a key role in the mediation of special revelation, the Bible is central to the church's deliberations on right belief and practice. In other words, the conviction that the biblical texts function primarily as means of grace does not preclude the special significance of scripture in the church's attempt to discern truth. It is only because of this special role that we can even speak of the conditional authority of scripture. The question that remains is clear: under what conditions — or, in what context — does the Bible fulfill its proper role in the church's apprehension of divine revelation?

At this point it is evident that what I am calling a conditional conception of biblical authority is a formal proposal that might involve any number of material suggestions. That is, two people might agree that the

9. One of the clearest examples in the North American context is the biblical justification of the institution of slavery. Thought experiments on this point are relatively easy to come by as well: one only has to imagine taking the end of Psalm 137 as "authoritative" without recognizing its place within the broader context of the Psalter.

10. Abraham, *Canon and Criterion in Christian Theology*, 6.

authority of scripture depends upon specific conditions but disagree as to what those conditions are. Given that biblical authority became particularly problematic *after* the Protestant detachment of the biblical texts from their ecclesiastical context, it is instructive to explore the initial place of scripture within that context. Indeed, as Abraham demonstrates, the biblical texts emerged within a rich collection of canonical materials in the first millennium of the Christian church.[11] The ways in which this canonical heritage served to enrich and instruct the community of faith were complex, rather fluid, and ultimately dependent upon the work of the Holy Spirit. However, certain specific patterns did emerge in the church's utilization of scripture. If any of these were missing, then the potential for misinterpretation could emerge quickly and sharply. Thus, I would suggest that these patterns are the key to delineating the conditions under which the Bible's authority obtains within the community of faith. They include the rule of faith, the teaching vocation of the church, and particular spiritual and doxological practices. Let us explore each in turn.

The Rule of Faith as Interpretive Key

From very early in the church's history, it was recognized that interpretations of scripture could vary in alarming degrees. It simply was not the case that *any* reading of scripture yielded divine revelation — in fact, teachings that were considered quite dangerous by the mainstream Christian community were underwritten by appeals to biblical texts. Some sort of guide was needed, then, to aid the church in its reading of scripture. Robert W. Wall describes the role that emerged for this rule of faith:

> Tertullian . . . — and others beginning in the mid-second century, including Irenaeus, Clement of Alexandria, Hippolytus, Origen, and Novatian — appealed to a "Rule of Faith" or "Rule of Truth" in order to determine the significance of what the Jesus of history said and did (Acts 1.1) and also to make sense of the church's ongoing experience with the living Jesus. The results were statements of core theological affirmations, which might continue to serve the church as criteria for assessing the coherence of one's interpretation of Scripture. These for-

---

11. See Abraham's chapter, "The Emergence of the Canonical Heritage," in *Canon and Criterion in Christian Theology.*

mulations are many, but all set out to administer the lines of scriptural faith.[12]

The notion that the biblical texts could be conceived as authoritative apart from such a hermeneutical key would have quickly proven untenable. In reference to Irenaeus's conflict with the Gnostics, Lienhard writes: "what enables Irenaeus to arrange all the jewels in the Bible into a mosaic of the comely king is the rule of faith; without the rule of faith, the biblical gems can be remade into the picture of anything one wishes, no matter how ugly, foul, or lowly."[13]

What gave the church's rule legitimacy as an appropriate guide for biblical interpretation? Historically, it is crucial to note that the church recognized this core set of affirmations *before* it recognized a canon of New Testament books as scripture. In fact, one major criterion of inclusion in the canon of any given book was its accordance with the rule of faith.[14] Thus it is quite natural to regard the rule — which emerged from the community's experience and remembrance of the incarnate Son — as that which shapes the church's reading of the biblical texts.[15] Wall argues that biblical authority rests on the apprehension of special revelation in light of the rule:

> The church's christological "grammar of theological agreements" came first with and was fashioned by the life and teaching of Jesus, not first with and because of the Christian Bible. Scripture's authority for Christians is predicated on the congruence of its subject matter with the revelation of God's Son.[16]

12. Robert W. Wall, "Reading the Bible from within Our Traditions: The 'Rule of Faith' in Theological Hermeneutics," in *Between Two Horizons: Spanning New Testament Studies and Systematic Theology*, ed. Joel B. Green and Max Turner (Grand Rapids: Eerdmans, 2000), 89.

13. Lienhard, *The Bible, the Church, and Authority*, 52.

14. Lienhard, *The Bible, the Church, and Authority*, 40-41.

15. It is crucial to avoid a potential misunderstanding at this point. The term "rule of faith" has often been taken to mean an epistemic criterion or something that guarantees truth if used properly. To understand the rule in this sense would lead one into the very problems we noted with viewing scripture itself as such a criterion. Thus I share Wall's contention that "rule of faith" refers to a set of core theological affirmations. In other words, the rule of faith summarizes the *content* of the faith in such a way that our reading of scripture is appropriately focused. I am not proposing that the church's rule of faith is a surefire truth-detection mechanism.

16. Wall, "Reading the Bible from within Our Traditions," 97.

Thus a conditional conception of biblical authority that does not recognize the utilization of the rule of faith as an essential condition will be severely diminished. Reading scripture to discern adequately the nature and purposes of God as revealed in Jesus demands careful attention to the church's theological "grammar."

What do we make, then, of Protestant communities that continue to champion an appeal to the authority of "scripture alone"? Two comments are in order at this point. First, it is important to note that the Reformers recognized to some degree the necessity of interpretive guides, and they often cited patristic sources. While deeply skeptical of a particular institutionalization of interpretive authority, the classical branches of the Reformation accepted the major creeds of the church and compiled their own confessions of faith.[17] Second, the ecclesiastical descendents of these classical Reformers are very likely to qualify significantly the notion of *sola scriptura*.[18] One is far more likely to encounter unapologetic appeals to the authority of scripture alone in independent congregations in which the pastor wields the primary interpretive authority.[19] Thus, under the guise of appealing directly to the text of the Bible, such communities (and often just the pastors) are actually engaging internalized or subconscious "rules" that may or may not accord with the classical rule of faith. As the evangelical theologian Clark Pinnock writes, "for all our talk about '*sola scriptura*,' the Bible is seldom left 'alone.'"[20] It behooves the community of faith, then, to be conscious and intentional in employing the hermeneutical key that helped shape the biblical canon itself.

What is the content of this rule of faith? Undeniably, a variety of

17. D. H. Williams, *Retrieving the Tradition and Renewing Evangelicalism: A Primer for Suspicious Protestants* (Grand Rapids: Eerdmans, 1999), 173-204. See also the illuminating discussion of Luther and Calvin on church and tradition in David C. Steinmetz, *Luther in Context* (Bloomington: Indiana University Press, 1986).

18. For one example of a "reconstruction" of *sola scriptura*, see John R. Franke, "Scripture, Tradition and Authority: Reconstructing the Evangelical Conception of Sola Scriptura," in *Evangelicals and Scripture: Tradition, Authority and Hermeneutics*, ed. Vincent Bacote, Laura C. Miguélez, and Dennis L. Okholm (Downers Grove, IL: InterVarsity Press, 2004), 192-210.

19. See Nancy Tatom Ammerman's account of this phenomenon in *Bible Believers: Fundamentalists in the Modern World* (New Brunswick, NJ: Rutgers University Press, 1987). In particular, chapter 7 ("The Shepherd and His Flock: Authority, Structure, and Ritual") offers a helpful sociological perspective on the nature of pastoral authority in particular independent congregations.

20. Pinnock, "Three Views of the Bible," 80.

instantiations of this rule emerged in the discourse of the early church. The set of affirmations offered by Irenaeus, for example, differs slightly but not dramatically from that offered by Origen. While the various versions of the rule served as precursors to the more fixed form of the creed, the rule of faith was not restricted to written form.[21] Wall describes the general pattern as "narrative in shape, Trinitarian in substance, and relat[ing] the essential beliefs of Christianity together by the grammar of christological monotheism."[22] The rule delineates a particular view of and orientation to God and creation. When scripture is interpreted apart from this vision, claims to authority are rendered dubious for the community of faith. When engaged in accordance with this orientation, the biblical texts play a pivotal role in the church's process of apprehending divine revelation. In such a capacity is its authority grounded.

The Teaching Vocation of the Church

It is one thing to have an interpretive key to the scriptures; it is quite another to delineate which members of the community of faith are ultimately responsible for the proper use of this key. Indeed, the presence of a material rule of faith does not automatically guarantee interpretive agreement or preclude disputes. It is therefore crucial for Christian communities of faith to designate particular persons within the church to regulate and order their interpretive judgments.[23] What is needed, that is, is a specified "teaching vocation" of the church.[24]

A cautionary note should be sounded at this point, for we are touching on a very delicate matter. On the one hand, it is becoming clear that it

21. Lienhard, *The Bible, the Church, and Authority,* 51. He notes that Irenaeus insisted on the adequacy of the rule of faith even for the illiterate, for whom it is "written on their hearts."

22. Wall, "Reading the Bible from within Our Traditions," 101.

23. The use of the plural (communities of faith) here is intentional. In the tragic context of ecclesial disunity, it is impossible to speak of one teaching office for the church universal. We can think only in terms of concrete communities or denominations.

24. I use the term "teaching vocation" here to refer to persons or structures within a community whose responsibility it is to delineate legitimate teaching or belief within the community, be they bishops, councils, or whoever. Within Roman Catholicism, for example, this is primarily the role of the magisterium. However, I consciously avoid the more familiar term "teaching office," which may signal some sort of epistemic machinery intended to secure truth for the community.

is perhaps more precise (on a conditional conception of biblical authority) to speak of authoritative *readings* of scripture than of authoritative texts that stand alone. And yet, on the other hand, it would be unwarranted simply to transpose biblical authority unambiguously to the authority of particular persons within the church. As we will see, what is ultimately authoritative is a dynamic process of the church's reception of revelation as demonstrated in particular beliefs and practices. That specific leaders in the church are entrusted with the responsibility of overseeing this reception (and the preservation of what has been received) does not mean that they have the latitude to wield authoritarian or careless judgments. Rather, the role of the teaching vocation is to remain attentive to the movement of the Holy Spirit through the canonical materials in guiding the faithful into the divine life. Avery Dulles, whose own Roman Catholic tradition entrusts remarkable authority to its teaching vocation, makes clear the accountability of the magisterium:

> Catholics continue to hold, in accordance with Vatican I and Vatican II, that the ecclesiastical magisterium is a divinely given guide that enables the truth of revelation to be authoritatively heralded by the church. But as the Councils also point out, the teaching of the magisterium is not itself the word of God; rather, it is under the word of God, which it serves.[25]

For Dulles, then, the ecclesial authority of the magisterium is grounded in its relation to the revelation of the nature and purposes of God.

Despite the accountability of the teaching vocation, one landmark development in the Roman Catholic tradition suggests a reluctance to leave any uncertainty about its effectiveness. I refer of course to the doctrine of papal infallibility, implicit in Catholic teaching for centuries but promulgated as dogma at the First Vatican Council in 1870. This dogma moves beyond imploring the faithful to trust its leaders as reliable guides to something far more bold: epistemic certainty. Indeed, with infallibility in place, the teaching vocation is no longer merely one part of an authoritative and dynamic process; it is the center of the Roman Catholic Church's effort to secure truth. Abraham writes:

---

25. Avery Dulles, "Scripture: Recent Protestant and Catholic Views," in *The Authoritative Word: Essays on the Nature of Scripture*, ed. Donald K. McKim (Grand Rapids: Eerdmans, 1983), 260.

The development of a doctrine of infallibility brings with it a certain reading of the canonical heritage of the church. . . . It amounts to a quiet revolution in the conception of canon. Now one of the canons — namely, that related to Episcopal oversight — has become a foundation for everything else. It has become a norm of truth which can be assumed in the pursuit of knowledge, and in this instance historical knowledge.[26]

The emergence of this doctrine demonstrates just how strong of a desire there is to secure certainty for the teaching of the church. But building such safeguards into the episcopacy (or any dimension of the church's canonical heritage) is a dubious move on both epistemological and spiritual grounds.[27] Perhaps just as important, foolproof epistemological machinery is simply not needed for trustworthy teaching practices. Taking our cue from the ancient church, we might recognize that it is entirely reasonable to trust leaders with particular gifts and character to guide the faithful into the soteriological riches offered by God through the community of faith.

What shape should the teaching vocation take? It is clear that the episcopacy developed very early in the church's history to provide both ministerial and doctrinal oversight.[28] It was the role of the bishops to provide the necessary order in the life of the church so that it would remain faithfully engaged in the worship and service of God. Since the Protestant Reformation, of course, many varieties of church government structures have emerged. Some of these do not have bishops, and many communities relegate to bishops purely administrative roles, without any responsibility for the interpretation of the canonical materials or the preservation of doctrine. This diversity raises a whole host of ecclesiological questions. Should such a variety of ecclesiastical forms be affirmed, or is a traditional episcopacy necessary for reliable leadership in faith and practice? Should the teaching office be concentrated in one or a few central figures, or is a conciliar or even a communal model more appropriate? Suffice it to say at this point that, while there are better and worse structures of ecclesial oversight, it is crucial that a community has some explicit pattern of interpretive authority in place. What is central is the recognition that specific persons within the church need to be entrusted with the responsibility for

---

26. Abraham, *Canon and Criterion*, 79-80.
27. See the essay by Mark E. Powell in this volume.
28. See Abraham, *Canon and Criterion*, 39.

ultimate decisions of doctrine and practice. Moreover, significant attention must be paid to the gifts and graces of those who take such leadership. In other words, the condition of authority is not simply that there is *someone* in place to provide oversight. Rather, effective and authoritative leadership requires mature, patient, and wise leaders who are deeply immersed in the life of faith.

The Practice of Worship and the Means of Grace

The recognition of the need for leaders who are engaged in Christian practice leads to a third condition for biblical authority. The role of oversight is not best understood as interpreting the canonical tradition *for* the community, as if their work were done in isolation from the rest of the faithful. Rather, ecclesial leadership aims rightly to order the deliberations of an *interpretive community.* And the scriptures are properly authoritative only when such a community is regularly engaged in worship and is immersed in the means of grace.[29] Particularly in the Eastern Christian tradition, there has been a deep-seated conviction that specific Christian practices orient and enable a person to apprehend "divine things" that could not be apprehended otherwise.[30] One's appropriation of any experience or material — including canonical materials — is affected by the spiritual and doxological practices in which that person is engaged. Thus one who reads scripture from outside the practicing community of faith will inevitably experience something very different than one immersed in the full range and riches of the canonical heritage. Once again, the detachment of the biblical texts from their proper ecclesial context erodes the appropriate conditions for authoritative readings.[31]

29. I am not using "means of grace" in any technical sense at this point. Rather, I have in mind any number of practices of the church by which God's grace is mediated to the faithful in formative and nurturing ways. Such practices would include — but are not limited to — the sacraments, prayer, liturgy, and works of mercy.

30. For one fascinating example, see St. Symeon the New Theologian, *First Ethical Discourse* XII, and *Discourse on Spiritual Knowledge* 3.

31. I avoid the language of "necessary conditions" because it might be somewhat misleading, if technically accurate. For while I would suggest that the foregoing are indeed necessary conditions for biblical authority, the Holy Spirit could certainly render *truthful* and/or *fruitful* readings if any or all of these conditions are missing. In such a case, the reading would not be properly authoritative for a community even though it might be beneficial for a given individual in a particular situation.

The practices of the Christian life do not yield authoritative interpretations simply because they are effective exercises. Rather, the aim of engaging in worship and the means of grace is ultimately to encounter the presence of God. In an insightful essay, Trevor Hart suggests that it is the presence and activity of God in such a context that endows the biblical texts with authority.

> In a Christian reading of scripture, there is another dimension of presence to be reckoned with — namely, the supposition that this text does not only speak about God, but that in and through the medium of this text God has spoken and speaks. It is here that we must finally discern the root of the claim that scripture is authoritative for the structuring of Christian identity.[32]

In a sense, we have come back to the general proposal that the Bible is authoritative because it provides access to divine revelation. What Hart makes clear, however, is that scripture is not merely a transmitter of past instances of revelation (though it certainly is that). It is also a means of grace through which God continues to speak to the faithful who delve wholeheartedly into the life of faith.

It is not sufficient to make haphazard or hardhearted use of the canonical materials if one wishes to experience the soteriological and spiritual riches of the community of faith. Rather, a particular posture of humility and openness to the leading of the Holy Spirit is a clear necessity. Abraham argues that "the various elements of the church's canonical heritage will be of little or no value if those who receive them do not approach them in a spirit of repentance and humility."[33] A similar appeal is made by Richard Bauckham, who suggests that God's authoritative word is available in scripture for the one who approaches it with a reverent willingness to listen.[34] Pride and hard-heartedness are clear enemies of fruitful and faithful apprehension of the guidance of the Holy Spirit. Thus the *manner* in which scripture is approached is a crucial factor in an adequate discussion of biblical authority. If the Bible is interpreted in isolation from the practices of the Christian community or in an inappropriate spirit, then a crucial condition for its authority has been missed.

---

32. Trevor Hart, "Tradition, Authority, and a Christian Approach to the Bible as Scripture," in Green and Turner, eds., *Between Two Horizons,* 201.

33. Abraham, *Canon and Criterion,* 54.

34. Bauckham, "Scripture and Authority," 11.

Conclusion

In the preceding pages I have argued that scripture's authority is not primarily a function of a text but of a text in a particular context. Specifically, authority requires that the Bible function in its intended ecclesial context, as marked by conditions that can be clearly identified. These conditions are material (the rule of faith), formal (the teaching vocation), and dispositional (participation in worship and the means of grace). Some might respond that such an argument merely favors a Roman Catholic notion of canonical authority over against a Protestant conception. This is not the case, for at least two reasons. First, it is indeed true that the Catholic Church has maintained a clearer understanding of the importance of scripture's ecclesial context. However, I have aimed to describe the contours of this context in rather fluid and organic terms. Indeed, any number of Protestant communities could embrace these proposed conditions of authority without a great deal of restructuring (though reorienting assumptions about scripture would likely prove much more difficult). Second, as has been made clear, one element of the Roman Catholic system of authority — specifically, the dogma of infallibility — has transposed the ecclesial canon of episcopacy into an epistemic criterion. From the perspective of canonical theism, such a move is quite problematic. Not only does it represent a confusion of categories, but it carries the potential of throwing a delicate arrangement of canonical materials, persons, and practices out of balance.

While there are notable differences between my proposal and the full-scale Roman Catholic vision of authority, I certainly do not wish to feed the fire of Protestant misconceptions of scripture's authority. I have sought to provide a practicable and fitting way to preserve the language of the authority of the Bible, so central to the identity of many Protestant communions. I would suggest, however, that we might generate a more precise formulation than the mere affirmation that the Bible has authority under these conditions. Specifically, these conditions suggest that what is ultimately authoritative is the symphony of canonical materials of which scripture has a central role. These materials are not authoritative because they yield epistemic certainty; as a matter of fact, they do no such thing. They are authoritative because the one who humbly desires participation in the life of the triune God will immerse herself in them and allow her life to be shaped by their riches. The primary function of the church's canonical heritage is soteriological. One who submits to the authority of God generally and embraces the full range of the Christian canons specifically can trust that he will not be denied the salvation he seeks.

The Jesus of History and Canon:
Some Thoughts on Interdisciplinary Scholarship

DAVID F. WATSON

The aim of canonical theism is to reclaim the church's rich canonical heritage that was established prior to the Great Schism of 1054. This canonical heritage, while not precisely delineated,[1] contains not only scripture, the Nicene-Constantinopolitan Creed, and the Chalcedonian definition, but a number of other elements as well.[2] William J. Abraham broadly describes the canonical heritage as "constituted by a network of materials, persons, and practices which mediated divine revelation, encounter with the living God, the bread of heaven and wine of fellowship, forgiveness of sins, instructions in holy living, directions for the corporate life of the church, a host of insights for the life of obedience to God, and various epistemic suggestions."[3]

Given this aim, canonical theism and critical biblical scholarship may seem strange bedfellows initially. By "critical biblical scholarship," I mean biblical scholarship that does not assume (1) that when biblical texts portray past events they always represent history accurately, or (2) that the faith claims expressed within the Bible must cohere with faith claims of a particular later tradition (such as the doctrinal tradition of Christian orthodoxy). With the rise of critical biblical inquiry informed by the insights of the Enlightenment, the dogmatic systems of Christian tradition came to be regarded as outdated, pre-critical, mythological, and irrelevant. Over the last two centuries, critical biblical scholarship, and especially historical

---

1. See William J. Abraham, *Canon and Criterion in Christian Theology: From the Fathers to Feminism* (Oxford: Oxford University Press, 1998), 29-30.

2. See Abraham, *Canon and Criterion*, 37-38.

3. Abraham, *Canon and Criterion*, 470.

criticism, has constructed a divide between itself and the theological claims of the church, partly in the interest of preventing "confessional" readings that would impose upon the text foreign and anachronistic theological concepts. This divide has been notably visible in the branch of New Testament scholarship that deals with the life and teachings of Jesus.[4] An account of the life and teachings of Jesus of Nazareth constructed according to modern canons of rationality could have nothing to do with such theological concepts as the Trinity and the incarnation. Although the term "historical Jesus" has meant different things in different contexts,[5] in almost all cases the classical doctrines of the Christian faith are regarded as inappropriate for consideration in historical Jesus research. Doctrine and theology are usually thought to contaminate, rather that illuminate, accounts of what "actually happened."[6]

Yet for many Christians, including many Christian academics, historical Jesus reconstructions are inadequate precisely because they tend to exclude the possibility of God's acting uniquely and directly through the person of Jesus.[7] Those who hold the ideas of the Trinity and incarnation to be soteriologically valuable and to express true claims about God draw upon the insights of a formative time in the history of the church, a time when questions of proper Christology were debated and the resolutions of these debates were codified in the statements of the ecumenical councils. In this essay, I will explore the possibility of bringing historical research into dialogue with these canonical christological affirmations. Such a dialogue would involve interdisciplinary work between biblical scholars and scholars in other fields, such as systematic theology, historical theology, church history, and philosophy of religion. I will proceed in two major parts: First, I will discuss the importance of critical biblical scholarship for Christian faith, as well as the appropriateness of bringing

---

4. Cf. Marcus J. Borg, *Jesus in Contemporary Scholarship* (Valley Forge, PA: Trinity Press International, 1994), 188.

5. For a concise account of the development of historical Jesus scholarship over the last two-and-a-half centuries, see Mark Allan Powell, "Historians Discover Jesus," ch. 1 in *Jesus as a Figure in History: How Modern Historians View the Man from Galilee* (Louisville: Westminster John Knox Press, 1998).

6. Cf. *The Oxford Dictionary of the Christian Church*, 3rd ed., s.v. "Historical Jesus, Quest of the."

7. Undoubtedly, there are many options for thinking about Jesus other than the historical Jesus; see *Dictionary of Biblical Interpretation,* ed. John H. Hayes (Nashville: Abingdon, 1999), s.v. "Jesus, Quest of the Historical," especially 581-84.

critical biblical scholarship into dialogue with the canonical theological tradition. Second, I will discuss the canonical claims about Jesus and the possibility of bringing these into dialogue with historical scholarship on the life of Jesus.

Critical Biblical Scholarship and Christian Faith

Critical biblical scholarship has tended to proceed apart from reference to the classical doctrines of Christian faith and specific concepts of scriptural authority. The intentional divide between critical biblical studies on the one hand and doctrine and theology on the other has caused some Christians to question the value of critical biblical studies for the life of the church. At times, when the results of critical scholarship have conflicted with important Christian claims or called into question the historical accuracy of scripture, Christians have responded by appealing to theological proposals that render critical scholarship irrelevant or inappropriate. The philosopher Peter van Inwagen offers one example of such an appeal. He writes, "[T]here is no reason for me to think that [Critical Studies of the New Testament] have established *any* important thesis about the New Testament."[8] By "Critical Studies," he means "those historical studies that either deny the authority of the New Testament, or else maintain a methodological neutrality on the question of its authority, and which attempt, by methods that presuppose either a denial of or neutrality about its authority, to investigate such matters as the authorship dates, histories of composition, historical reliability, and mutual dependency of the various books of the New Testament."[9] Van Inwagen excludes from the category of Critical Studies "purely textual studies and studies of aspects of the New Testament that . . . take the texts at face value."[10]

He is concerned in this essay with "users of the New Testament," by which he means "first, ordinary church-goers who read the New Testament and hear it read in church and hear it preached on, and, secondly, the pastors who minister to the ordinary churchgoers, and, thirdly, theologians who regard the New Testament as an authoritative divine revela-

8. Peter van Inwagen, "Critical Studies of the New Testament and the User of the New Testament," in *Hermes and Athena: Biblical Exegesis and Philosophical Theology,* ed. Eleonore Stump and Thomas P. Flint (Notre Dame: University of Notre Dame Press, 1993), 186.

9. Van Inwagen, "Critical Studies," 159.

10. Van Inwagen, "Critical Studies," 164; see also 160.

tion."[11] He argues that if users of the New Testament have good independent grounds for accepting the New Testament as historically and theologically reliable, they need not attend to Critical Studies, since Critical Studies reject or remain neutral regarding the authority of scripture. "The conclusion of the argument is not that users of the New Testament must not or should not have an extensive acquaintance with Critical Studies, but that they need not."[12]

There are a few problems with van Inwagen's argument that deserve discussion.[13] One problem relates to his understanding of the "authority of the New Testament," by which he means "what the church has presupposed about the New Testament,"[14] viz., its "historical and theological reliability."[15] Van Inwagen does not attempt to clarify what he means by "theological reliability" because, he says, the space limitations of his essay do not permit his doing so. However, since the rejection of theological reliability is part of what he finds so objectionable with regard to Critical Studies, he needs to explain what he means by this term in order to substantiate this part of his objection. Theological reliability could be thought of in many different ways, and some who would question the historical reliability of the New Testament would hold some notion of its theological reliability (for example, Bultmann).

He does, however, clarify what he means by "historical reliability." Restricting his attention to "descriptions of the words and actions of Jesus," he explains historical reliability in three ways: formally, functionally, and ontologically. His formal explanation is "that (i) Jesus said and did at least most of the things ascribed to him in [the New Testament] narratives and (ii) any false statements about what Jesus said and did that the narratives may contain will do no harm to those users of the New Testament who accept them as true because they occur in the New Testament."[16]

Functionally, "the narratives are historically reliable if they are historically accurate to a degree consonant with the use the church has made

---

11. Van Inwagen, "Critical Studies," 159.

12. Van Inwagen, "Critical Studies," 165.

13. In the same volume as the one in which van Inwagen's paper appears, Ronald J. Feenstra offers a response to van Inwagen's essay; see Ronald J. Feenstra, "Critical Studies of the New Testament: Comments on the Paper of Peter van Inwagen," in Stump and Flint, eds., *Hermes and Athena*, 191-97.

14. Van Inwagen, "Critical Studies," 162.

15. Van Inwagen, "Critical Studies," 164.

16. Van Inwagen, "Critical Studies," 169.

of them. . . . If these narratives were indeed largely a product of the imaginations of various people in the early church, then the church has, albeit unwittingly, been guilty of perpetrating a fraud."[17]

His ontological explanation "proceeds by describing the basis in reality of the fact (supposing it to be a fact) that the New Testament narratives possess the degree of historical accuracy that I have characterized formally and functionally."[18] Although human beings may offer fallible accounts of historical occurrences, God "has guided the formation of the New Testament historical narratives by acting on the memories and consciences and critical faculties of those involved in their formation."[19] He also offers the following examples:

> I suppose that if, say, St. Luke was told one of the bizarre stories about Jesus' boyhood that survive in the apocryphal infancy gospels, the Holy Spirit took care that his critical faculties, and, indeed, his sense of humor, were not asleep at the time. I suppose that if an elder of the Christian community at Ephesus in A.D. 64 was tempted by want of funds to twist the story of the widow's mite into an injunction to the poor to buy their way into the Kingdom of God, the Holy Spirit saw to it that his conscience was pricked, or that no one believed his version of the story, or that the changed story never got out of Ephesus and soon died out.[20]

Van Inwagen's formal and ontological explanations present some real problems. One issue that renders these explanations problematic is the anti-Jewish polemic that we find in the New Testament. For example, in Matthew's passion narrative we read that Pilate brings Jesus before the people, and that they shout that the governor must release Barabbas and crucify Jesus. Pilate proclaims his own innocence of Jesus' death, but "the people as a whole" answer, "His blood be on us and on our children!" (27:25).[21] Donald Senior makes a very significant observation about this passage: "Matthew no longer uses the term *ochlos*, 'crowd,' but *laos*, a collective term used in the

---

17. Van Inwagen, "Critical Studies," 171.
18. Van Inwagen, "Critical Studies," 173.
19. Van Inwagen, "Critical Studies," 175.
20. Van Inwagen, "Critical Studies," 174.
21. As noted above, van Inwagen restricts his attention to descriptions of the words and actions of Jesus. Since his larger argument is intended to show that Critical Studies of the New Testament are unnecessary, however, it seems fair to bring a broader group of passages into consideration.

Gospel to refer to people as a whole (see, e.g., 1:21, 'for he will save his *people* from their sins' or the repeated phrase, 'elders of the people').["22] We might also consider the rhetoric against "the Jews" that we find in John's Gospel. For example, in John 8:44 Jesus says to "the Jews," "You are from your father the devil, and you choose to do your father's desires."[23] Passages such as these have contributed to devastating attitudes and occurrences in the history of the relationship between Christians and Jews.[24] I take it for granted that passages that have contributed directly to anti-Jewish attitudes are harmful not only to Jews, but to the Christians who hold them.

Yet in thinking through these examples we might consider certain claims that critical New Testament scholars commonly make regarding both Matthew and John: that they were written after the destruction of the Jerusalem temple, and that they reflect intra-Jewish disputes between Jewish Christians and Jews who rejected Jesus' messiahship and status as the Son of God. Considering the circumstances that may have affected the content of these Gospels — attempting to account for their historical contingency — may help us in the life of faith much more than simply taking these passages at face value as historically or theologically reliable. For example, we may see in these passages a reflection of the painful break between the church and the synagogue and consider the tragic history of the relationship between Christians and Jews. We may ponder the fractures that occur within our own families of faith and be led to seek reconciliation with those from whom we are estranged. We may give serious thought to the best ways to handle theological disagreement, not only within our own faith communities, but between different faith traditions as well. These are just a few examples of the kinds of considerations that might emerge from thinking through these texts in ways that do not simply pre-

---

22. Donald Senior, *Matthew* (Nashville: Abingdon Press, 1998), 324. There is debate, however, with regard to the meaning of "the people as a whole," and "on us and on our children." Some scholars would not take this as an indictment of the Jewish people as a whole; see Senior, *Matthew*, 325.

23. In fairness to van Inwagen, he would likely not be persuaded by the line of argument that I am pursuing. See his critique of redaction criticism in "Critical Studies," 185. In support of this criticism, he draws on Morna Hooker's article, "On Using the Wrong Tool," *Theology* 75:629 (1972): 570-81. Hooker's article, however, deals mainly with form criticism rather than redaction criticism.

24. As Daniel J. Harrington has written, "This text has often been used to base the idea of a divine curse upon the Jewish people, condemning them to wandering and persecution, for having put to death the Son of God" (*The Gospel of Matthew* [Collegeville: Liturgical Press, 1991], 392).

suppose their historical reliability or assume the theological appropriateness of a "face-value" reading of the texts. The point here is not that we should explain away passages with which we are uncomfortable, but that we should account for the historical contingency of the writings of scripture in order better to understand their significance in our own historically contingent circumstances.

To summarize, the point in criticizing van Inwagen's argument is to indicate a larger problem with appeals to theological understandings of scripture that render critical scholarship insignificant. At this point in the history of our faith, critical readings of scripture are of real importance for the ongoing life of the church. Simply presupposing that all of scripture is historically reliable and theologically appropriate for our communities of faith may hinder our understanding of their literary history, the historical contexts in which they developed, the political concerns that they reflect, and other circumstances and dynamics that affected their formation. Therefore, we deprive ourselves of certain resources that we may use in order to understand these texts more fully, an unproductive move given scripture's central place in shaping the Christian life.

As van Inwagen specifically deals with the words and actions of Jesus, his comments are especially relevant for this discussion of interdisciplinary work on Jesus. Can we not understand Jesus more fully by making use of the results of historical research? Might we cut ourselves off from important resources by simply presupposing the historical reliability of the New Testament stories about Jesus? This is not to say that each Christian must become familiar with historical research on the life of Jesus, but that such research has the potential to enrich the life of the church and deepen the faithfulness of its witness.

Critical Inquiry and Christian Theology in Dialogue

Rejecting theological understandings of scripture that render critical scholarship insignificant does not mean that we must entirely detach our reading of scripture from Christian theology. Joseph Fitzmyer offers a reasonable alternative to van Inwagen's position.[25] Fitzmyer points out that

25. See Joseph A. Fitzmyer, S.J., "Historical Criticism: Its Role in Biblical Interpretation and Church Life," *Theological Studies* 50 (1989): 244-59. Feenstra endorses Fitzmyer's position; see "Comments," 197.

while the Roman Catholic Church under the leadership of Pope Leo XIII was suspicious of historical-critical scholarship through the first third of the twentieth century, "the cloud of negative reaction was finally lifted when Pope Pius XII published his encyclical *Divinio afflante Spiritu* in 1943."[26]

Fitzmyer's description of the historical-critical method is worth quoting:

> The method is called "historical-critical" because it borrows its techniques of interpreting the Bible from historical and literary criticism. It recognizes that the Bible, though containing the Word of God, is an ancient record, composed indeed by a multiplicity of authors over a long period of time in antiquity. Being such an ancient composition, it has to be studied and analyzed like other ancient records. Since much of it presents a narrative account of events that affected the lives of ancient Jews and early Christians, the various accounts have to be analyzed against their proper human and historical backgrounds, in their contemporary contexts, and in their original languages. In effect, this method applies to the Bible all the critical techniques of classical philology, and in doing so it refuses a priori to exclude any critical analysis in its quest for the meaning of the text.[27]

Given Fitzmyer's understanding of the Bible as containing "the Word of God," why is the historical-critical method sometimes regarded with suspicion by Christians? Fitzmyer holds that "it was tainted at an important stage in its development with [rationalist] presuppositions that are not necessarily part of it,"[28] especially by those scholars who engaged in the *Leben-Jesu Forschung,* so powerfully present in the religious academy of the nineteenth century. Therefore, he argues, an "otherwise neutral" method came to be tainted by presuppositions of rationalists who sought to divest Christianity of any and all dogmatic influence. By "rationalist" Fitzmyer refers to the methodological exclusion of traditionally Christian "dogmatic" claims about Jesus, including any claim regarding the "supernatural aspects" of Christianity.[29] This approach would be modified in the

---

26. Fitzmyer, "Historical Criticism," 248. He notes that this suspicion was manifested in the oversight of the Pontifical Biblical Commission which was established in 1902.

27. Fitzmyer, "Historical Criticism," 249.

28. Fitzmyer, "Historical Criticism," 252.

29. Fitzmyer, "Historical Criticism," 252.

twentieth century within the demythologizing, existential, theological framework of Rudolf Bultmann.

Although Fitzmyer does not specifically mention Van Harvey, his work, built upon that of Ernst Troeltsch, offers a sophisticated argument for the position that historical research must be carried out apart from the "falsifying influence of belief."[30] Harvey developed an idea of the "radical autonomy of the historian," whereby the historian is not constrained in his or her judgments by any authority that might limit the results of historical study. Harvey states, "If the historian permits his authorities to stand uncriticized, he abdicates his role as critical historian. He is no longer a seeker of knowledge but a mediator of past belief; not a thinker but a transmitter of tradition."[31] Harvey's arguments are too complex and too well-argued for any extended treatment in this essay, though his position has been thoroughly critiqued in other works.[32] I will point out, however, that the type of historian who follows Harvey's guidelines for historical research is also a transmitter of tradition, even if not a theological tradition.[33]

Fitzmyer, conversely, encourages a partnership of Christian belief and rigorous historical investigation. He states, "Modern Christian practitioners of the [historical-critical] method . . . also use the method with presuppositions — but presuppositions of a rather different sort."[34] He argues that, along with the philological tools of the historical-critical method, the Roman Catholic biblical interpreter will presuppose

---

30. See Van A. Harvey, *The Historian and the Believer: The Morality of Historical Knowledge and Christian Belief* (1966; Urbana: University of Illinois Press, 1996); for a brief account of Troeltsch's position, see *Encyclopaedia of Religion and Ethics,* ed. James Hastings (Edinburgh: T & T Clark; New York: C. Scribner's Sons, 1908–26), s.v. "Historiography" (6:716–23).

31. Harvey, *The Historian and the Believer,* 42.

32. For critiques of the positions of Harvey and Troeltsch, see C. Stephen Evans, "Critical History and the Supernatural," ch. 8 in *The Historical Christ and the Jesus of Faith* (Oxford: Clarendon Press, 1996); as well as William J. Abraham, "Divine Intervention and Historical Warrants," ch. 6 in *Divine Revelation and the Limits of Historical Criticism* (New York: Oxford University Press, 1982). For further critiques of the rationalist position, see Alan G. Padgett, "Advice for Religious Historians: On the Myth of a Purely Historical Jesus," in *The Resurrection: An Interdisciplinary Symposium on the Resurrection of Jesus,* ed. Stephen T. Davis, Daniel Kendall, and Gerald O'Collins (New York: Oxford University Press, 1997), 287-307.

33. Basil Mitchell understands positions such as Harvey's as representative of particular "schools of thought"; for his very interesting discussion of this issue, see "Faith and Reason: A False Antithesis?" in *How to Play Theological Ping-Pong,* ed. William J. Abraham and Robert W. Prevost (London: Hodder & Stoughton, 1990), 137.

34. Fitzmyer, "Historical Criticism," 254.

the elements of faith: that the book being critically interpreted contains God's Word set forth in human words of long ago; that it has been composed under the guidance of the Spirit and has authority of the people of the Jewish-Christian heritage; that it is part of a restricted collection of sacred, authoritative writings (part of a canon); that it has been given by God to His people for their edification and salvation; and that it is properly expounded only in relation to the Tradition that has grown out of it within the communal faith-life of the people.[35]

As a result, "historical criticism assists the Church in its ongoing life, by helping it to uncover the essence of the revelation once given to it — the meaning of the Word of God in ancient human words."[36]

It is noteworthy that, for Fitzmyer, to bring the "elements of faith" into the critical study of scripture is not to assign a particular substantive content to the scriptures. He discusses the significance of the Bible for people of faith, but not its message(s). Yet crucial for his argument is that the Bible is "properly expounded only in relation to the Tradition that has grown out of it within the communal faith-life of the people." Protestants have at times attempted to maintain their commitment to *sola scriptura* alongside a commitment to doctrines such as the Trinity by loading the whole doctrinal freight of the faith into the scriptures. According to the position that Fitzmyer lays out, however, later theological developments that we find in Christian tradition provide a set of faith claims with which it is proper to bring the Bible into dialogue, but these later developments are also recognized as logically distinct from scripture. One has a set of revelations (such as the creed) that function in concert with scripture and that are in particular ways organically related to scripture, but which provide a set of truths which scripture alone does not provide. The position of canonical theism is similar to Fitzmyer's in three important ways: (1) it rejects both a rationalist perspective and *sola scriptura,* (2) it views the creed and other canonical sources of doctrine as deeply valuable for the life of faith, and (3) it can easily accommodate critical engagement with the scriptures.

---

35. Fitzmyer, "Historical Criticism," 254-55.

36. Fitzmyer, "Historical Criticism," 258; Evans endorses a position very much like Fitzmyer's (see *Historical Christ,* 20).

Jesus Christ and Canon

Our images of Jesus, like our readings of scripture, help to shape the ways in which we think about and conduct our lives as Christians. Marcus Borg writes that "images of Jesus *in fact* very much affect images of the Christian life. . . . Because of his central place in the Christian tradition, how we as Christians think of Jesus shapes our understanding of the Christian life itself."[37] Scholars who work in the field of historical Jesus scholarship have amassed a tremendous amount of information regarding the world in which Jesus lived, including his social and political environment and the cultural characteristics of first-century Palestine and the wider Mediterranean world. They have carefully scrutinized ancient sources of information about Jesus, including both Christian (canonical and extra-canonical) and non-Christian sources. They have delved deeply into the development of Jewish and Christian eschatology; the functions and literary forms of parables; the phenomena of miracle-working and exorcism in the ancient world; the practices and activities of popular ancient teachers; and other sources of information that might cast light on the life, activities, and teachings of Jesus.[38] Scholarship on the Jesus of history is abundant, detailed, and diverse. Surely this scholarly field offers much that may enrich our images of Jesus.

At times historical Jesus scholars have attempted to discuss the theological significance of their work or to bring their work into dialogue with particular theological claims. For example, John Dominic Crossan claims that "Christian belief is (1) an act of faith (2) in the historical Jesus (3) as the manifestation of God."[39] John P. Meier offers a very helpful analysis of the ways in which scholarship on the life of Jesus can be useful for contemporary Christian theology.[40] Yet in reconstructing the historical Jesus, scholars tend to adopt the kind of rationalist position that Fitzmyer criticizes in connection with the historical-critical method. Some scholars, like Meier, adopt an approach "which prescinds from what the believer knows

---

37. Borg, *Jesus in Contemporary Scholarship*, 193.

38. For a very thorough treatment of the approaches, sources, and topics of historical Jesus scholarship, see Gerd Theissen and Annette Merz, *The Historical Jesus: A Comprehensive Guide*, trans. John Bowden (Minneapolis: Fortress Press, 1998).

39. John Dominic Crossan, *Jesus: A Revolutionary Biography* (San Francisco: HarperSanFrancisco, 1994), 200; for a contrasting opinion, see John P. Meier, *A Marginal Jew: Rethinking the Historical Jesus*, vol. 1 (New York: Doubleday, 1991), 197-98.

40. See Meier, *Marginal Jew*, 196-200.

or holds by faith" because this is considered to be proper to the historical-critical endeavor.[41] For others, a rationalist approach appears to be more of a matter of conviction about the way in which the universe operates. For example, in discussing the widespread ancient belief in spiritual powers and miracles, E. P. Sanders refers to the "rationalist" protest of Cicero (unusual among the ancients), who states that "nothing can happen without cause; nothing happens that cannot happen, and when what was capable of happening has happened, it may not be interpreted as a miracle. Consequently, there are no miracles."[42] After quoting Cicero, Sanders states, "The view espoused by Cicero has become dominant in the modern world, and I fully share it. Some reports of 'miracles' are fanciful or exaggerated; the 'miracles' that actually happen are things that we cannot yet explain, because of ignorance of the range of natural causes."[43] In his popular work *Jesus: A Revolutionary Biography,* Crossan takes a metaphorical approach to the issue of healing: "I presume that Jesus, who did not and could not cure that disease [leprosy] or any other one, healed the poor man's illness by refusing to accept the disease's ritual uncleanness and social ostracization." Crossan sees his interpretation as offering a redefinition of miracle. "Such an interpretation may seem to destroy the miracle. But miracles are not changes in the physical world so much as changes in the social world."[44] In *Jesus the Magician,* Morton Smith remarks rather pejoratively, "[Jesus] could not glow in the dark. But he could and probably did persuade himself and his disciples that he would appear in glory, and eventually they all 'saw' (by hallucination) what they hoped to see."[45]

Extending the logic of Fitzmyer's argument about scripture to the study of Jesus, however, two important insights emerge. First, if we reject rationalism it allows us to rethink the kinds of background beliefs that are appropriate for historical investigation, including investigation of the Jesus of history. For the Christian interpreter, background beliefs (or presuppositions) that take into consideration the possibility of God's acting in the world are entirely appropriate. Second, if we bring historical investigations of Jesus into dialogue with church tradition, we open our thinking

41. Meier, *Marginal Jew,* 197.

42. Cicero, *De Divinatione,* quoted in E. P. Sanders, *The Historical Figure of Jesus* (London: Penguin, 1993), 143.

43. Sanders, *Historical Figure,* 143.

44. Crossan, *Revolutionary,* 82.

45. Morton Smith, *Jesus the Magician: Charlatan or Son of God?* (1978; Berkeley, CA: Seastone, 1998), 196-97.

about Jesus to a broad network of theological and philosophical resources that do not fall within the purview of historical scholarship as it is traditionally conceived.

Basic Contours of a Canonical Christology

The Bible is an early source for canonical traditions about Jesus. Certain claims about Jesus in the New Testament became central for later Christian reflection. In his discussion of the "incarnational narrative," C. Stephen Evans identifies some of the claims in the Gospels that have proved most significant in shaping Christian doctrine. By "incarnational narrative" Evans means to indicate "the Church's story," which is presented in a "*basically* coherent" way in the four Gospels, and which "is an account of how the divine Word took on human flesh, was born as a baby, lived a life characterized by miraculous healing and authoritative teaching, died a cruel and voluntary death for the sake of redeeming sinful humans, was raised by God to life, and now abides with God, awaiting the time of his glorious return and ultimate triumph." He sees this as "common ground among orthodox Christians, be they Catholic, Orthodox, or Protestant."[46] Evans locates this story in the four Gospels, and one could certainly locate each of the elements of this narrative in at least one of the four (though no single Gospel contains all of the elements of this narrative). The canonical heritage involves the elements of Evans's narrative, but the substantive content of these elements is shaped in the canonical tradition by a network of christological affirmations and denials that build upon the scriptural witnesses to Jesus.

As stated earlier, the contours of the canonical heritage are not set in stone, but the christological claims established in the ecumenical councils of the church offer a baseline inventory of the elements of a canonical Christology, since these elements are the product of a clear process of canonization.[47] Of those councils that established particular christological

---

46. Evans, *Historical Christ*, 5.

47. These seven ecumenical councils all took place before the end of the eighth century, during the period when the Eastern and Western churches still made up a single communion. Two of these councils, the Council of Ephesus (431) and the Second Council of Nicaea (787), did not result in specific christological formulations, although the Council of Ephesus, the third of the seven councils, denounced a christological formulation, that of Nestorianism. The statements of the fourth, fifth, and sixth councils are understood to be refinements of the basic ideas laid out in the Nicene-Constantinopolitan Creed.

formulations, the first was the Council of Nicaea (325), and the creed in which it resulted was refined at the First Council of Constantinople (381). This creed was developed in response to the Arian controversy, and therefore affirms that the Son is "begotten from the Father before all time" *(ton ek tou patros gennēthenta pro pantōn tōn aiōnōn)* rather than created, and is of one substance *(homoousion)* with the Father. For our salvation, the Son descended from heaven, "was incarnate by the Holy Spirit and the Virgin Mary, and became human [*enanthrōpēsanta*]. He was crucified for us under Pontius Pilate, and suffered and was buried, and rose on the third day, according to the Scriptures, and ascended into heaven, and sits on the right hand of the Father." Jesus will come again as a judge, and "his Kingdom shall have no end."[48] Underscored in this creed are both Jesus' real consubstantiality with the Father and his real humanness.

Building upon the Nicene Creed of 381, the definition of Chalcedon was developed over against the claims of the Eutychianism and emphasized Christ's full humanity alongside of his divinity.[49] The definition claims that Jesus Christ is perfect in "Godhead" as well as in "humanness." The consubstantial nature of the Father and the Son are emphasized again, as is the idea that the Son was "begotten before all ages of the Father according to the Godhead." Yet this time around Jesus is also said to be consubstantial with humankind, and Jesus' birth to the Virgin Mary (who is now called the Mother of God) is said to have taken place "in respect of his human-ness [*anthrōpotēta*]."[50] Jesus possessed both a rational soul and a body, though he was without sin. The definition wrestles with the tension between Jesus' humanity and divinity, claiming that he should be acknowledged as possessing two entirely indivisible natures that exist in perfect union with one another: Jesus bears simultaneously the nature of the Godhead and the nature of humankind. It is this Lord Jesus of whom the prophets spoke, about whom Jesus himself taught, and about whom the fathers wrote.

During the fifth and sixth councils, both of which were held in Constantinople and took place in 553 and 680-681 respectively, there were further christological refinements. The fifth council dealt with the monophysite controversy,[51] and the sixth dealt with the monothelyte controversy.

48. This translation from John H. Leith, ed., *Creeds of the Churches: A Reader in Christian Doctrine from the Bible to the Present*, 3rd ed. (Atlanta: John Knox Press, 1982), 33.

49. See Leith, ed., *Creeds of the Churches*, 34.

50. Leith, ed., *Creeds of the Churches*, 36.

51. This fifth council was intended to resolve the issues of the "Three Chapters" controversy. The Three Chapters were "the three subjects condemned by the Emperor Justinian

Both reaffirmed the hypostatic union, the fifth council by establishing that in Christ two natures, one human and one divine, were united; and the sixth council by stating that these two natures were accompanied by two natural wills.

One might say that the debates that resulted in these statements mainly concerned the interpretation of scripture. Trevor Hart writes that at Nicaea the issue was "a dispute about the interpretation of the text of Scripture, a dispute that extended beyond the particulars of the case to general considerations." He also notes, however, that "Arius' appeal to the New Testament was every bit as thorough and detailed as that offered by his opponents. It was so thorough, in fact, that it proved impossible to re-fute Arius on the basis of the biblical texts alone. Any biblical text supplied in order to do so proved capable of an Arian reading."[52] Interpretation is a crucial concept as we think about these canonical christological claims. Scripture does not offer us a definitive picture of the Christ of the creedal faith, though this is not to say that scripture precludes such a reading. Those who crafted the doctrines set forth in the statements of the councils drew on a variety of resources, including the traditions of the church and the philosophical resources available to them. The issue was not simply, "What do the texts say about Jesus?" but rather, "Given that we hold as sa-cred these scriptural texts, what interpretation of them is most faithful to what God has done in Jesus?"[53]

To put the matter in somewhat different terms, the debates that led to and took place within these councils were not only about the proper in-terpretation of scripture but also about the ontology of Jesus. Or, more simply, the focus of these debates was not just a set of texts, but a person. Just as our modern Jesus scholars have set out to tell us about various as-pects of Jesus' life and teachings, the statements of the councils attempt to

---

in an edict of 543-4, namely (1) the person and works of Theodore of Mopsuestia, (2) the writings of Theodoret against Cyril of Alexandria, and (3) the letter of Ibas of Edessa to Maris. As all three were considered sympathetic to Nestorius, Justinian issued the edict in the hope of conciliating the Monophysites by a display of anti-Nestorian zeal" (*Oxford Dic-tionary of the Christian Church*, 3rd ed., s.v. "Three Chapters").

52. Trevor Hart, "Tradition, Authority, and a Christian Approach to the Bible as Scripture," in *Between Two Horizons: Spanning New Testament Studies and Systematic Theol-ogy*, ed. Joel B. Green and Max Turner (Grand Rapids: Eerdmans, 2000), 188.

53. On this issue, see Robert Morgan, "The Bible and Christian Theology," in *Cam-bridge Companion to Biblical Interpretation*, ed. John Barton (Cambridge: Cambridge Uni-versity Press, 1998), 120.

articulate, based largely on scripture, who Jesus is in relationship to the Godhead.

It is important to note here that the Nicene-Constantinopolitan Creed and other statements of the ecumenical councils are not immune from rigorous historical investigation. Like the writings of scripture, the decisions of the councils are historically contingent. Critical scholars are fully within their rights to inquire regarding the philosophical and theological presuppositions of the statements of the councils, political factors by which these statements may have been affected, their implicit polemics, and other such factors that played into their development. As with scripture, we may construe the decisions of the ecumenical councils theologically without assuming that they must have an authority that renders them immune to critical inquiry.

Canonical Christology in Dialogue with the Study of Jesus

With regard to the teachings of the Nicene Creed, Borg writes that "historical scholarship about the pre-Easter Jesus affirms essentially none of this. We are quite certain that Jesus did not think of himself as divine or as 'Son of God' in any unique sense, if at all. If one of the disciples had responded to the question reportedly asked by Jesus in Mark's Gospel, 'Who do people say that I am?' with words like those used in the Nicene Creed, we can well imagine that Jesus would have said, 'What???'"[54] Borg's claim that historical scholarship affirms none of the claims of the Nicene Creed seems reasonable; traditionally, historical scholarship has methodologically excluded the kinds of claims that are present in the Nicene Creed. His claim about Jesus' self-understanding is another matter altogether. The extent to which historical scholarship is capable of ascertaining the specifics of Jesus' self-understanding is questionable, but more is at stake here than sound methodology. Borg's comments could be taken as an implicit denial of the truth of the claims in the creed, since if those claims were true one would expect Jesus to be aware of them, or at least not to be shocked by them. David Friedrich Strauss, perhaps the most significant nineteenth-century scholar of the historical Jesus, went much further than Borg does. Near the end of his landmark work *The Life of Jesus Critically Examined* he wrote, "The results of the inquiry which we have now brought to a close,

54. Borg, *Jesus in Contemporary Scholarship*, 182-83.

have apparently annihilated the greatest and most valuable part of that which the Christian has been wont to believe concerning his Saviour Jesus, have uprooted all the animating motives which he has gathered from his faith, and withered all his consolations."[55]

Yet these judgments seem rather one-sided. In cases in which the historical study of Jesus is said to give the lie to the church's theological claims about him, it behooves us to give serious consideration not simply to the results of historical Jesus research but to various aspects of the theological traditions in question, including the history of their development, the reasoning that lies behind them, their epistemological underpinnings, and alternative proposals. In other words, historical research should not have a line-item veto with regard to the affirmations of the creed and other important Christian statements of faith. Rather, historical research should provide one set of data to consider within the much larger discussion of what (if anything) God has done in Jesus Christ. Biblical studies is a rich and diverse field, and biblical scholars are no strangers to interdisciplinary work. Scholars of the Bible bring into dialogue such areas of analysis as anthropology, literary criticism, reader-response criticism, deconstruction, African American hermeneutics, and feminist hermeneutics, to name a few. Given the many and varied methods of analysis that inform the study of the Bible and early Christian history, it seems strange to enforce a strict separation of traditional Christian faith claims from the historical study of Jesus, especially in cases in which the latter is said to upend the former.

N. T. Wright argues that "rigorous history (i.e. open-ended investigation of actual events in first-century Palestine) and rigorous theology (i.e. open-ended investigation of what the word 'god', and hence the adjective 'divine', might actually refer to) belong together, and never more so than in discussion of Jesus."[56] The particular contribution that canonical theism might make to the kind of investigation that Wright describes would be in its engagement with the canonical faith of the church. Our answers regarding what words such as "God" and "divine" might mean, while not wholly determined in advance, will be informed by dialogue with Christians who have gone before us, and especially by the decisions of the ecumenical councils. Canonical theism is not tied to a particular

---

55. David Friedrich Strauss, *The Life of Jesus Critically Examined,* ed. Peter C. Hodgson, trans. George Eliot (Philadelphia: Fortress, 1972), 757.

56. N. T. Wright, *Jesus and the Victory of God* (Minneapolis: Fortress Press, 1996), 8.

epistemological perspective or theological method, but it does involve certain theological commitments, such as belief in the Holy Trinity and the incarnation. Thus in work that brings historical inquiry and theological inquiry into dialogue with one another, this concept of the Trinity who has acted decisively in the world through Jesus Christ would provide important resources for understanding who God is and what God does.

There are also important ethical implications for this kind of interdisciplinary research. In instances in which our historical investigations lead us to believe that Jesus taught a certain ethical way of living, regarding other people and regarding God, we will better understand the claim that Jesus makes upon our lives today by understanding his theological significance. Again it is helpful to turn to Borg, who writes:

> [I]f a Christian becomes persuaded that Jesus taught a subversive wisdom, it affects how that person sees the conventional wisdom of his or her own day; if a Christian becomes persuaded that Jesus countered the purity system of his day, it affects how she or he sees purity systems in our day; if a Christian becomes persuaded that Jesus indicted the ruling elites of his day, if affects how domination systems are seen in the present. Note that I am not saying that these perceptions *ought* to have an effect, but that they do. I have seen this happen again and again: a significant change in a Christian's perception of Jesus in fact affects that person's perception of the Christian life.[57]

The "ought to," however, is of some significance. Why should anyone living today follow a first-century teacher from Galilee? Why should this teacher occupy any special place of significance? Research on Jesus that takes into account theological and philosophical insights, as well as historical ones, has the potential to speak in deeply meaningful ways about the actions and attitudes that Christians should adopt. To bring the study of Jesus into dialogue with the canonical faith of the church is not the only way to understand Jesus' significance, but it does provide an important set of resources for Christians who believe the Trinity and the incarnation to be meaningful theological categories.

I want to emphasize that I am not advocating a move to an uncritical understanding of the Bible or history.[58] As twenty-first-century West-

---

57. Borg, *Jesus in Contemporary Scholarship*, 194.

58. Cf. Green, "Scripture and Theology: Uniting the Two So Long Divided," in Green and Turner, eds., *Between Two Horizons*, 42.

erners, we have our own social locations and our own sets of concerns and intellectual commitments that we bring to our inquiries regarding Jesus. We have to be realistic about the fact that critical inquiry may lead us in unexpected, and even uncomfortable, directions. For instance, in bringing the voices of historians and scholars of other fields together, we must face realistically the possibility of conflicting sets of claims. The results of our historical investigations may come into conflict with our theological commitments. The ways in which these conflicts are worked out will depend on a number of issues, including the epistemological positions of the scholars involved in the disagreement; but this does not mean that we should stop talking to one another.

Conclusion

Although there has long existed a significant divide between critical scholarship and the canonical tradition, this need not be the case. Critical scholarship can contribute much to Christians who wish to hold up the creedal faith as a powerful expression of the Christian witness. Fitzmyer has shown us that historical-critical inquiry may be fruitfully carried out in dialogue with a network of theological claims. With regard to the person of Jesus, critical biblical scholarship has much to say. Yet, extending Fitzmyer's logic somewhat, if it is proper to read scripture in conversation with these theological commitments, it is equally proper to bring theological voices into our inquiries regarding the person and work of Jesus. Such inquiries will be interdisciplinary in nature, and scholars may undertake them in various ways. Inquiry into the life, teachings, death, resurrection, ontology, and significance of Jesus should be seen as an ongoing task, rather than a "quest" with some ostensibly attainable goal. Bringing critical scholarship into dialogue with the canonical faith of the church will be a very involved task, and it will most certainly complicate the task of understanding of the person and work of Jesus of Nazareth. Nevertheless, I am convinced that this type of dialogue is a worthwhile undertaking with great potential to enrich the life of the church and to contribute to scholarly discussion.

In the last sentences of *The Historical Jesus*, Crossan writes, "For a believing Christian both the life of the Word of God and the text of the Word of God are alike a graded process of historical reconstruction. . . . If you cannot believe in something produced by reconstruction, you may have nothing left to believe in."[59] To a certain extent, we all depend upon reconstructions. The question is not whether we employ them, but what sources we use in devising them.

59. John Dominic Crossan, *The Historical Jesus: The Life of a Mediterranean Jewish Peasant* (San Francisco: HarperSanFrancisco, 1992), 426.

The Canonical Heritage of the Church
as a Means of Grace

Charles Gutenson

Introduction

Canonical theism is not committed to any particular epistemology, but rather recognizes that different epistemologies have, historically, led to right belief and right practice. Consequently, canonical theists are interested in and affirm the importance of epistemic matters even if they are not monolithically committed to this or that epistemology. In what follows, I explore the manner in which one operating in the Wesleyan tradition might understand important epistemic matters and how one might, then, outline the contours of a "Wesleyan" epistemology. Even at that, as one committed to canonical theism, I do not deny the possibility, nay, likelihood, of alternative Wesleyan epistemologies.

William J. Abraham's book *Canon and Criterion in Christian Theology* serves as the programmatic work that lies behind this collection of essays, a collection aimed at working out some of the consequences of affirming the central thesis of that earlier work.[1] That thesis has both a positive and a negative aspect, and it can be summarized as follows: The canonical heritage of the church, taken broadly as that group of materials, persons, and practices canonized by the early church, functions primarily soteriologically. Hence, the canonical heritage of the church is firstly to be taken as "means of grace" and not as "epistemic criterion."[2]

---

1. William J. Abraham, *Canon and Criterion in Christian Theology: From the Fathers to Feminism* (New York: Oxford University Press, 1998).

2. This particular wording has been created by the author to capture, in summary fashion, the claim of *Canon and Criterion*.

Interestingly, whenever I use Abraham's book as a text for one of the classes I teach, the most common questions relate to this thesis, and they are: (1) What does it mean to say that the canonical heritage of the church is intended primarily as "means of grace"? And (2) What is being denied when it is claimed that the canonical heritage is not intended to function as "epistemic criterion"?

It is my intention is this chapter to deal with these questions, though I shall deal with them in reverse order, and I shall spend the bulk of my time addressing the first question. Hence, we shall begin by exploring what follows from the claim that the canonical heritage of the church is not intended primarily as "epistemic criterion." This section will be brief, and then we shall turn to a more detailed consideration of the claim that the proper way to see this heritage is as "means of grace."

Canonical Heritage Is Not an Epistemic Criterion

In actual fact, it seems that Abraham is quite clear on what he means by this claim, though from time to time questions arise that require comment. For example, is Abraham denying that the category "truth" any longer has meaning or usefulness? Or, is the denial that, say, Scripture functions as an epistemic norm really a way of denying that Scripture makes truth claims? Or, methodologically speaking, is Abraham suggesting that all those are mistaken who consider Scripture, in some sense, to be normative for the theological enterprise? I think the answer to each of these questions is an unreserved "no!" However, this only heightens the question: If he does not mean any of these things, what exactly does he mean? Rather than merely repeat Abraham's own words, let us try to come at this from a couple of different directions in an attempt to clarify the claim.

The premier epistemic category is "knowledge." One engages in epistemic ruminations with the ultimate goal of being able to identify and to possess knowledge. Given the importance of the concept of knowledge, a clear set of criteria are necessary to determine whether a particular proposition, say P, constitutes knowledge for us. The generally accepted definition of knowledge is "warranted (or, justified), true belief." This definition identifies three requirements that must be satisfied if P is to be knowledge for us. First, I must believe P, and to see this, one only need consider how bizarre it would be to say, "I know P, but I do not believe it." Second, it must be warranted or justified for me. Now, there are a variety of theories about what confers warrant for our beliefs, and I am not inclined to be side-tracked onto that well traveled road. So, let us simply observe that warrant/justification is an indicator of my right to believe P. To be warranted in believing P is to have satisfied the antecedents of that right; to be unwarranted is not to have satisfied them. Finally, for P to be knowledge for me, P must be true. (This has an interesting consequence, given that in many, many cases, *knowing* whether P is true or not is quite difficult, but alas, another side road of importance for which we do not have time.) So, if our believing P satisfies these three criteria, we "know" P.

Now, try to imagine what it would mean to say that, in addition to these requirements, the canonical heritage of the church constituted another requirement for some proposition to count as knowledge. Would it not be inappropriate and wrong-headed to add a fourth criterion to this set that went something like, "and must be contained in the canonical heritage of the church"? There are a good many P's that constitute knowledge for me about which the canonical heritage of the church says nothing. For example, I know that, in Euclidian geometry, the three angles of a triangle add up to 180 degrees. I can demonstrate this deductively without any appeal to the canons of the church whatsoever. Likewise, I know that I am currently sitting here with my laptop in my lap, and again, I did not need to consult the canons of the church to come by this knowledge.

"Okay," you may say, "the canons of the church are not a requirement for knowledge in that sense, but they are an epistemic requirement, say of 'truth' rather than 'knowledge,' such that if P is contained in the canonical heritage of the church, then P is true." Well, this is all well-intentioned I suspect, but it is, nevertheless, clearly false is it not? For example, if one peruses the writings of the early fathers, one finds that most are orthodox on many points and yet either heretical or mistaken on other points. Hence, if P were one of *those* propositions, then it would not be the case that P's being in the canonical heritage of the church guarantees its truthfulness.

"Well," you might add, "my real concern is with scripture. It is the norming norm of the theological enterprise, and so, if some proposition P is contained in scripture, then P is true." In order to make this a meaningful claim, one would need a good deal more specificity. For example, apocalyptic literature is highly figurative, and if one does not understand the nature of the symbols, figures, etc. *and* their likely referents, one will not even be clear about what the truth claim being made (if one is being made) *is*, much less whether or not it is true. Examples could be multiplied. However, let us say that what you really want to affirm is that if some proposition P is affirmed in scripture and if we have properly understood scripture so that we have accurately captured the textual intent, genre, meaning, etc., then P is true. The claim might then be: scripture is a requirement for truth such that if, say, scripture affirms the resurrection of Jesus, then the proposition "Jesus was raised from the dead" is true. But, one must ask, does this really make scripture a *criterion of truth?* Is it the case that this proposition's being contained in scripture is what *makes* it true? Rather, is it not the case that what makes the proposition "Jesus was raised from the dead" true is the fact that Jesus, after dying, came back to life? Texts merely report; they do not serve as epistemic criteria, either of truth or of knowledge.

If we must think of scripture vis-à-vis the question of truth, is it not better to think of scripture along the lines of witness or evidence or some such? As Abraham notes, lying behind attempts to deploy scripture as an epistemic criterion is an appeal to Scripture as access to the mind of God. The real criterion of truth one has in mind, then, is something like, "being believed by God." Hence, we might say, "If God thinks P is true, then P is true." And, to this, most would readily enough concur. However, this is a far cry from straightforward appeal to scripture; rather, it is an appeal to revelation or to divine speaking, an appeal that carries its own difficulties — for example, where is the authoritative revelation? Even if one can satisfactorily answer this query, difficulties remain, for one must now engage the hermeneutical set of questions raised above, develop a theory of inspiration such that we can easily get from "affirmed by Scripture" to "affirmed by God," *and* show why God's primary intent in granting scriptural texts to his children was to convey propositional truths. In fact, it is precisely reflection on this last question that opens the door to seeing matters in a rather different light — i.e., what did God intend to accomplish with the canonical resources of the church? Abraham argues that God's primary intent is *soteriological.* Scripture was not given us to serve as a storehouse of propositional truth; rather, it was given, as were the other canonical materials, for the express purpose of initiating one into the life of God and, ultimately, bringing one to conformity to the image of Christ. Finally, the categorization of the canonical heritage as "means of grace" rather than "epistemic criterion" is not to suggest that the canonical heritage does not contain truth; instead, it is merely to say that the canonical heritage does not constitute a "test" for truth. The same "criteria" of truth that apply anywhere else (correspondence and coherence, for example) apply with regard to truth claims coming from within the church canons. To affirm the canons of the church as "means of grace" is to raise an entirely different set of questions.

Canonical Heritage as Means of Grace

A common definition of the term "grace" as used by Christians is something like "unmerited favor." However, this oft-deployed definition does not do justice to the nature of the claim being made when we say that the canons of the church are first and foremost intended as "means of grace." In this locution, the intent of "grace" is more like empowerment for initiation into and living out participation in the life of God. Of course, the phrase "means of grace" is not uncommon in the life of the church; in fact, it is generally deployed with the sacraments in mind — at least baptism and the eucharist. By calling these sacraments "means of grace," the church has affirmed that in some mysterious way, by participating in these means of grace, individual believers and the church as a whole are changed through an inner working of God's Spirit. We shall not take time to develop a theory regarding the manner in which this mysterious change is effected; rather, we will be happy to note that it is grace in this sense that canonical theists have in mind. In similar fashion, canonical theists argue that God intends the church to use the canonical heritage bequeathed to it by the Holy Spirit expressly for the formation of persons into the image of Christ. The communication of valid truth claims will, in some cases, be a part of that formative process, but canonical theists argue that this is coincidental to formation rather than being an end in itself.

The theology of John Wesley will be instructive at this point. Wesley spoke of five different kinds of grace that God makes available to humans. (I prefer to think of them as five different *functions* of divine grace rather than as actually different *types* of grace.) These are: prevenient grace, convicting grace, justifying grace, sanctifying grace, and glorifying grace. Let us see if we can make sense of the claim that the canonical heritage of the church is intended to function as a complex means of grace by utilizing these categories from Wesley. With regard to each function of grace, we shall consider if this grace is mediated through the canons of the church, and, if it is, how it is mediated.

Let us turn our attention first to what Wesley calls "prevenient grace" and "glorifying grace." In an interesting claim during his debate with the Calvinists, Wesley said that there was a point at which he came within a "hairsbreadth" of Calvinism. He went on to say that this was because he agreed with the Calvinists that natural humanity could only sin and that all good works were attributable to God. It would seem to follow that Wesley would, likewise, affirm theological determinism, and yet there was that "hairsbreadth," which turned out to be prevenient grace. Wesley believed that every individual ever born (and, hence, every *actual* human being) was the recipient of irresistible, prevenient grace that restored human faculties to the point that humans were enabled to respond to God's offer of salvation, and thus, theological determinism was denied. As we can see, this function of grace is irresistibly given to every human that has ever lived (before and after Christ), and thus we can readily affirm that God mediates prevenient grace to us outside the canons of the church. So, we dismiss the important concept of prevenient grace from further consideration.

Glorifying grace is that function of grace that allows, to use Paul's words, this mortal to take on immortality. It is the final act whereby God graciously transforms us from merely human, corruptible creatures to the incorruptible creatures that will live with him throughout eternity. This transformative act is one that God directly imparts, and thus it is given to humans outside the canons of the church. As with prevenient grace, while this function of grace is of remarkable importance, it need receive no further attention in our present considerations. Let us turn to the other three, each of which, I believe, we shall find is mediated through the canonical heritage of the church.

The Christian doctrine of original sin, however it is taken, intends to communicate the fact that humanity as it is does not correspond to humanity as God ultimately aims for it to be. To say that humans are "sinful" or "fallen" is to affirm this and to point out the fact that humans stand in need of transformation. Of course, before one can *be* transformed, one must *see the need* for transformation, and it is at precisely this point that what Wesley called "convicting grace" comes into play. The function of convicting grace (sometimes also called "convincing grace") is to bring to conscious awareness the disparity between the actual human condition and the condition intended by God. Christians, then, deploy the concept of "sin" as a way to identify the cause for this disparity. Properly understood, sin is a profoundly relational notion, for it is precisely the relationship between humans and God that is ruptured as a consequence of human sin. Consequently, the condition that exemplifies this disparity between humans as they are and humans as God intended can best be characterized as one of estrangement or alienation — i.e., humanity stands estranged or alienated from God. Convicting grace functions to help humans see their sinfulness and the alienation from God that is the inevitable consequence. I have suggested that this function of grace is mediated to humans through the canonical heritage of the church. Let us see how.

Since convicting grace functions to create both cognitive and affective awareness, one of the most obvious ways this function can be accomplished is by bearing witness to the fact of human sinfulness. Of course, spread throughout the canonical resources are materials, persons, and practices aimed to raise this awareness to consciousness as well as to create the appropriate affect. Within the liturgical tradition, there are rituals for confession and repentance, which mark the beginning of response to convicting grace. Within the writings of the early fathers, there are sermons as well as other theological treatises that highlight human sinfulness and explain how this state of sinfulness is related to estrangement and alienation from God. Within the scriptural traditions, one finds many, many affirmations both of human sinfulness and of God's requirement for transformation. In fact, the central narrative of the canonical heritage, the narrative of the incarnation, death, resurrection, and ascension of Jesus, is cast, within both scripture and the other canonical traditions (including eucharist, baptism, or the church's iconography), as primarily about restoration of sinful humanity to right relationship with God. In Jesus' own words, "The Son of Man came to seek and to save those who are lost" (Luke 19:10). To say that the canons of the church are intended to function as a means of grace is, partly, to say that the Holy Spirit, either directly or indirectly,[3] uses the materials that comprise those canons to bring to awareness the need for transformation, and one way to understand this function is to speak of convicting grace.

Since God intends to transform persons so as to make possible the restoration of a right relationship between God and humans and among humans, the divine intention would not yet be satisfied merely through convicting grace. In other words, while awareness of the need for transformation precedes the transformative acts themselves, a fundamental transformation of humanity is necessary for restoration to occur. Wesley called the function of grace that begins the process of transformation "justifying grace." Historically, to set one upon the path of participation in the life of God has been characterized by confession of and repentance for one's sins

---

3. For our purposes, we really need not say much more than that the Spirit uses these resources either "indirectly" or "directly." Whether the intended outcome of convicting grace is accomplished through humans reading and reflecting upon the canonical materials (and, hence, these materials are used indirectly) or whether the Spirit is actively involved in guiding the understanding of the reader to the intended outcome (and, hence, these materials are used directly) is of no substantive consequence for this presentation. Consequently, we shall treat that question with agnosticism.

and by forgiveness of those sins by God. Hence, the sinful person is initially made right with God, or "justified," and the function of grace that accomplishes this is categorized as "justifying" grace. Now, we must be clear: justifying grace is not an end in itself, but rather points beyond itself to the telos that God has in mind — namely, conformity to the image of Christ. In a sense, justifying grace and the concomitant conversion is merely the beginning of one's journey in the participation in the life of God. Of course, it builds upon the functions of grace that have preceded — prevenient grace and convicting grace — but it marks a significant point of transformation, for just as prevenient grace overcomes the worst effects of the Fall, thereby enabling human response to God's call, justifying grace changes the believer's whole orientation from one closed to God to one open and responsive to further gracious acts on God's part. In a very real sense, the receipt of justifying grace marks a clear and distinct point in the person's restoration to God.

Just as with convicting grace, what we have, following Wesley, called justifying grace is also mediated to humanity through the canonical traditions of the church in a wide variety of ways. Let us consider just a few. First, even a casual perusal of the writings of the early fathers demonstrates the extent to which they were concerned to understand and articulate the great change in humanity that was made possible through the incarnation of the eternal Son. For example, Athanasius, in *The Incarnation of the Word of God*, comments upon sin's damage to human nature, the need to have that damage healed, and the fact that only through the ministry of the Son was such healing possible. Athanasius uses a number of rich metaphors and images to communicate these claims. One utilizes the image of the artist and a painting. Since the Son was the initial agent of creation, the Son is the one most fitting to undertake the re-creation and restoration of sinful humanity. Irenaeus has similar notions in mind when he deploys his concept of recapitulation, i.e., the Son takes on sinful humanity and makes possible its re-establishment upon proper footings. While the images and concepts used by both Irenaeus and Athanasius easily extend beyond mere justifying grace, since the path to restoration must *begin,* these concepts include justifying grace.

Within the liturgical traditions, plentiful are the rituals involving initial conversion. Of course, the most significant is probably Christian baptism; it is through this ritual that one stands before the community, makes confession of one's faith in Christ, and is "reborn" through being "buried and raised" with Christ. In similar fashion, there are catechetical processes that are oriented toward instructing one in the basics of the faith, thus preparing one for entry into the Christian community, practices such as baptism, confirmation, and so forth. Believers are repeatedly called, during the Christian life, to revisit the moment of conversion when they are instructed to "remember your baptism."

The scriptural traditions themselves are replete with instruction, narrative, and commentary upon what it means to become a "new person in Christ." Instruction is given or implied in such passages as "all who call upon the Lord shall be saved" (Acts 2:21), and "believe with your heart and confess with your mouth" (Rom. 10:19), and "work out your own salvation with fear and trembling" (Phil. 2:12). Stories such as the conversion of the Ethiopian eunuch (Acts 8:27) and the conversion of Saul (Acts 9:4) recount for us, in narrative form, the conversion experiences of some. Finally, the epistles of the New Testament frequently comment upon the need for, as well as the meaning and implications of, conversion. In short, given the centrality of initial conversion into the family of God, the canons of the church are chockfull of materials that aim to instruct and guide one to salvation. To say, then, that the canons of the church are intended as means of grace includes saying that, by our reading and reflecting upon them, we open ourselves to that work of the Holy Spirit, which we have characterized as justifying grace, whereby we enter into the community of faith and become characterized as believers.

As noted above, justifying grace marks that point in our return to God where, in essence, we turn about from a walk away from God to a walk toward God. Just as empowerment for that change of direction had to come by God's gracious actions, we cannot walk toward God without further bestowals of grace. Wesley used the term "sanctifying grace" to capture that function of grace whereby we are empowered for ongoing growth toward God's ultimate goal for us: conformity to the image of Christ. While justifying grace marks the point of our turn toward God, sanctifying grace engages, guides, and directs us throughout eternity, as we begin a participation in the life of God that never ends. Interestingly, many of the early church fathers described this process using terms such as *apotheosis* and *deification*, whereby they intended to claim that it was the destiny of saved humanity to become as much like God as is possible for humans. Of course, for this to have concrete meaning for us we have to move beyond merely repeating the phrase "be conformed to the image of Christ," and at some point we have to inquire into what that means. What would it look like for a human to become completely conformed to the image of Christ?

How is a sanctified life lived? What priorities does it observe? How is it empowered? Is the life that "conforms to the image of Christ" one that imitates the life of Christ in every detail, thus suggesting that only single itinerants can be Christ-like? If not, what does imitating Christ look like?

While we will not take the time to answer each of these questions, the reader knows by now where one looks for the answers: the canonical heritage of the church. Yet, one looks not to the canonical heritage merely to receive satisfaction of one's inquisitiveness; rather, one consults the canonical heritage of the church in order to have sanctifying grace mediated to one in such a way that one is actually sanctified, i.e., one is empowered to live the life that pleases God. One does not read, pray, reflect, and act upon the canons of the church so as to *know* what it means to be conformed to the image of Christ; one does these things *so as to be conformed* to the image of Christ. The canons of the church mediate sanctifying grace to us in a variety of ways. First, by reading, say, certain parts of Scripture, one is instructed as to what acts are pleasing to God, and which are not. This opens the door to our asking for the Spirit's empowerment to live out what we have come to know. Second, Alasdair MacIntyre, in *Three Rival Versions of Moral Enquiry,* reflects upon the importance of apprentice/mentor relationships in our coming to be virtuous people.[4] The emphasis here is not so much upon having an exhaustive knowledge of the sorts of acts that are acceptable in different situations as upon being able *to reflect Christianly* upon specific moral questions. The first step in learning to live Christianly is being able to think Christianly, and this is often most effectively conveyed to us, not propositionally, but rather through mentoring relationships. In essence, to be guided by the canons of the church is to be mentored by the tradition. As we read the narratives of the faith, whether those contained in scripture or those found elsewhere in the canonical heritage, we observe the process of "thinking Christianly," and we find ourselves being formed to so think ourselves by virtue of our "living in" those narratives. In essence, the goal of engaging the canons of the church is not knowledge, per se, or certainty; rather, it is to be formed so as to live out a particular kind of life — namely, one that God intends humans to live. Again, we return to the idea of telos, specifically, the telos that God intends to result from our engagement with the canons of the church. Actions are not chosen abstractly, but rather for a reason, in order to get

---

4. Alasdair MacIntyre, *Three Rival Versions of Moral Enquiry* (Notre Dame: University of Notre Dame Press, 1990).

somewhere; hence, to reflect upon what it means to act Christianly, without reflection upon the goal God intends for us, is to reflect abstractly, and perhaps legalistically. To say that the canons of the church are intended as means of grace is, partly, to say that the Spirit mediates sanctifying grace to believers through their engaging those materials, whether they be Scripture, liturgy, creeds, and the like.

It is hard to imagine that one can exaggerate the significance of the role of sanctifying grace in one's growing participation in the life of God. The path to ever-increasing degrees of sanctification is one that must be every Christian's goal, and the full resources of the canonical heritage of the church ought to be available to each and every believer. We are formed by our interaction with the saints of the church, by their writings, as well as by the distinctively Christian practices of baptism and eucharist. In the final analysis, the goal of the Christian life is not primarily to become a people who know a particular set of propositions (though they may secondarily become such people); rather, the Christian life is primarily about being formed to be a particular kind of people — a people who think and act like God! That complex set of materials we reference as the canonical heritage of the church are those materials provided through the leadership of the Holy Spirit and intended by the Spirit to transform us into the people of God, in the fullest sense of the term.

Conclusions/Implications

In our argument so far, we have examined what it means to deny that the canons of the church are to be conceived as epistemic criterion and what it means to affirm that they are to be conceived as a rich, variegated, and complex means of grace. We have deployed the Wesleyan conception of the various functions of grace as a tool for getting at these questions. At this point, however, I must point out that, while I am a Wesleyan and while I consider Wesley's access to these questions instructive, I do not mean to suggest that there are no other appropriate ways of explicating and defending the claims laid out herein. Rather, I leave it as an exercise to the reader to reflect upon other ways to analyze these matters. By now, the reader will recognize that the intent of our two-pronged thesis is not to deny that knowledge is important, but rather to suggest that, to the extent that the tradition has focused upon knowledge to the exclusion of formation, the tradition has, at best, given a shortsighted picture of the Christian life. The devolution of Scripture to serve first and foremost as epistemic criterion was too fateful for the life of faith, and canonical theists aim to offer correctives to that mistake.

Before closing, however, it is appropriate to consider one further matter. At this point, one might respond by saying, "Well, that constitutes a very interesting proposal, but why should I accept it? What would be the decisive warrant for claiming that the canonical heritage is first and foremost intended to be a means of grace?" I suggest that the answer is very straightforward: the thesis is to be accepted to the extent that so conceiving and utilizing the canonical heritage, in fact, results in transformed lives, which increasingly conform to the image of Christ. One might be inclined to reject this test on the grounds that it is too pragmatic, though I think this would be mistaken. Generally, to say that a justification for something is pragmatic is to say that it "works," with "works" meaning something like "if it enables one to get along in the world." However, being conformed to the image of Christ, if the actual life of Christ is any indicator, will not likely result in one's getting along better in the world. Rather, it will likely result in one's being judged "out of touch" with reality. Saving your life by giving it away, turning the other cheek, reversing the normal power paradigms of the world, these are what result from being conformed to the image of Christ, and we would be foolish to expect anyone to applaud — except, of course, the God who so calls us!

Canonical Theism and Evangelicalism

WILLIAM J. ABRAHAM

The aim of this chapter is to explore the potential relation between evangelicalism and canonical theism. Positively, I shall argue that many if not most of the best insights of evangelicalism as a movement in modern Protestantism can readily be preserved within the contours of canonical theism. Canonical theism enriches the content and practices of evangelicalism. Negatively, I shall argue that canonical theism can help evangelicalism avoid one of its besetting sins, namely, its tendency to spawn forms of liberal and radical Protestantism that constantly erode precious components of the Christian faith and that foster various intellectual vices. I shall begin by offering an initial description of evangelicalism that does justice to its historical and theological complexity.[1]

Evangelicalism is a rich, essentially contested tradition.[2] We can see

1. Donald Dayton, *Discovering an Evangelical Heritage* (New York: Harper and Row, 1976), remains a landmark study of evangelicalism. So too does George Marsden, *Fundamentalism and American Culture: The Shaping of Twentieth Century Evangelicalism, 1870-1925* (New York: Oxford University Press, 1980). Two general recent studies worth consulting are Mark A. Noll, David W. Bebbington, and George A. Rawlyk, eds., *Evangelicalism: Comparative Studies of Popular Protestantism, the British Isles, and Beyond, 1700-1900* (New York: Oxford University Press, 1994), and Kenneth Collins, *The Evangelical Moment: The Promise of an American Religion* (Grand Rapids: Baker Academic, 2005). Gary J. Dorrien, *The Remaking of Evangelical Theology* (Louisville: Westminster John Knox Press, 1998), is a very insightful review of the evangelical tradition in theology.

2. For the meaning of this notion see W. B. Gallie, "Essentially Contested Concepts," in *Philosophy and Historical Understanding* (London: Chitto and Windus, 1964), 157-91. I have deployed the idea of essentially contested concepts in exploring the unity and diversity within evangelicalism in *The Coming Great Revival: Redeeming the Full Evangelical Experiment* (San Francisco: Harper and Row, 1984).

this initially by noting that the term "evangelical" came to life at three very different moments in the history of Protestantism. It emerged at the Reformation to capture the insights of the Reformers, in the eighteenth century as a way of identifying the core interests of the First Great Awakening, and in the twentieth century in efforts to move out of fundamentalism into a richer and more intellectually serious version of the Christian faith. It is a mistake to flatten these different movements into expressions of a common essence or to treat them simply as developing expressions of a common core of ideas and practices. Each moment has its own way of summing up the heart of the Christian faith, often distilled into short slogans and formulae that are not commensurable with each other.

We can best see this crucial insight by noting that the great heroes of the evangelical tradition differ quite significantly in their convictions and practices. Thus Martin Luther, John Calvin, Jonathan Edwards, John Wesley, Charles Finney, Phoebe Palmer, P. T. Forsyth, Billy Graham, and Carl F. H. Henry provide strongly contrasting visions of the Christian faith. To be sure, it would be easy to draw up a list of what they hold in common, like, the authority of scripture, the importance of personal faith, the privileging of preaching, the centrality of evangelism in mission, the doctrine of the Trinity, and the like. Yet any such list would miss what is distinctive and vital to the theologies developed by these contrasting evangelical heroes. Hence evangelicalism is marked by an inner contest and rivalry to bring to birth the heart of the Christian faith theologically and spiritually. Within the one family, the members have their own way of articulating its treasures and resources. This accounts for the internal tensions, the polemical edge, and the genuine differences of tone, practice, and content that are visible to the serious student.

One of the paradoxes of evangelicalism over the years is its tendency to give birth to new generations of liberal and radical Protestants.[3] Many contemporary liberals and radicals began life within evangelicalism. There are many reasons for this development, but two are worth citing at this juncture. First, insofar as evangelicalism self-identifies as being "biblical," it makes epistemology primary in its rendering of the Christian faith, and thus directs its converts to the search for adequate foundations, proper in-

---

3. I am using the categories "liberal" and "radical" here broadly to denote those who find the traditional or classical faith of the church wrong, misplaced, inadequate, and the like, and who then proceed to significant revision of the faith in order to render it intelligible, credible, appropriate, and the like. There is no neutral way to describe what is at stake, but the general tendency is well known and sufficiently clear for present purposes.

tellectual grounding, intentionally formed beliefs, and the like. In many instances, being "biblical" means treating the text as inerrant and infallible, so that once difficulties arise in this arena, there is invariably a deep crisis of faith. The encounter with historical-critical investigation of scripture readily forces the issue for many, and given that liberal and radical Christians have owned this work as their special property, evangelicals are ready targets for conversion away from what first brought them to faith. Some version of liberal Protestantism or radical Protestantism appears initially as the obvious alternative to embrace.

Second, insofar as some evangelicals attempt to develop a full theology or full-scale ecclesiology out of a volatile movement, they very quickly bump up against the inadequacies of the tradition as a whole and thus become vulnerable to deconversion from the evangelical tradition. Given that the main alternative in the Western tradition involves an untenable appeal, say, to papal infallibility, the temptation to turn to liberalism or radicalism as the only way forward is especially intense.[4] It is surely no accident that some of the most vociferous critics of evangelicalism are lapsed fundamentalists, like Bishop John Shelby Spong, whose own version of the faith becomes a kind of mirror-image of the faith they abandoned. Liberal and radical Protestants often turn out to be very disillusioned and lapsed evangelicals.[5]

This disquieting feature of evangelicalism deserves much more attention than it has received. Happily many contemporary evangelicals have intuited that there must be a better way than turning to liberal or radical Protestantism to preserve the best insights and riches of the evangelical tradition across the years. Recent evangelicalism has been marked by a search for wider horizons of thought and practice that has born much fruit. Thus the tradition as a whole is marked by an intellectual patience, humility, and rigor that was missing a generation or so ago. Evangelicals have done exceptionally good work in biblical studies, history, and philosophy, and are poised to make lasting contributions to systematic theology. To be sure, there are deep stresses and strains below the surface. Thus the doctrine of God has become an acute matter of contention in some circles. There are intense debates about the nature of liturgy and worship, about

4. I am not here downplaying the great attraction of Roman Catholicism to some evangelicals. In fact, turning to Roman Catholicism is one way to shore up the problems that became visible over time in the Protestant versions of *sola scriptura*. Nor do I want to downplay the continuing attraction of Barth for many evangelicals.

5. Any list might begin with Maurice Wiles, John Hick, and Elaine Pagels.

how best to deal with secular church growth strategies, about the gifts of the Holy Spirit brought to light within Pentecostalism, and about how best to be involved in political and cultural life. Clearly the question about what to do with postmodernism will take years to resolve.[6] These internal struggles are signs of life and health rather than of death and demise. At times they spill over into a nasty exclusivism and alienation, but we should keep a sense of intellectual proportion about such developments; however unwelcome, they make manifest a seriousness about the content of the faith that is laudable.

One way to bring out the fertility of canonical theism is to indicate how it can enrich some of the lasting virtues, practices, and theological insights that have surfaced within evangelicalism. Within this I shall argue that those evangelicals who set great store by epistemic conceptions of scripture can still find a place at the table, despite the fact that canonical theism raises fundamental questions about such an approach to scripture. My strategy up ahead will be simple. I shall suggest that six crucial features of the evangelical tradition taken in the round can be preserved and even strengthened within canonical theism. The six crucial areas I shall explore are as follows: scripture, fellowship in the local church, evangelism and mission, conversion and piety, the gifts of the Spirit, and commitment to divine revelation.[7] I shall begin in each case with reflections on these topics as they show up within evangelicalism and then suggest how they can be enriched by the concerns of canonical theism.

Evangelicals have always set enormous store by scripture. They believe that it is divinely inspired, that its exposition is central in good preaching, and that it is designed by God to make us wise unto salvation.[8] In recent years it has become common to focus on the soteriological significance of scripture, so much so that Gary J. Dorrien has rightly called attention to post-conservative forms of evangelicalism that make this the core of an adequate conception and use of scripture.[9] In this version of evangelicalism, the focus is not on inerrancy but on scripture as a means of grace.[10] This vi-

---

6. Much of the discussion currently centers in and around the legacy of Stanley Grenz.

7. I leave aside for now the concern with social justice.

8. I have dealt with the topic of divine inspiration in *The Divine Inspiration of Holy Scripture* (Oxford: Oxford University Press, 1981).

9. Dorrien, *The Remaking of Evangelical Theology*, ch. 5.

10. The soteriological purpose of scripture in pietism and beyond is exceptionally well brought out in Donald Dayton, "The Pietist Theological Critique of Biblical Inerrancy,"

sion clearly captures the critical place of scripture in preaching and in the extensive use of scripture both in Bible study groups and in the personal devotional life of the believer. Equally, this vision dovetails with the slogans of *sola scriptura, sola gratia, solus Christus,* if we see these rallying cries not as a full-blown theory of scripture but as a corrective to the neglect of scripture in the everyday life of the church. On this analysis scripture has its own magnificent way of depicting the beauty of grace and of the full expression of that grace in Jesus Christ.

All this is fully transportable into the vision of canonical theism. Scripture retains its full place in the life of the church. The great virtue of canonical theism at this point is that it insists on taking scripture as it stands. There is no need to place scripture within an artificial theory of origin or function that forces it into a particular mold or pattern; the text can be read naturally in its historical context. Yet the aim is not to read scripture merely historically but to receive it within a rich theistic vision that is unapologetic about its ontological and metaphysical commitments.[11] Whatever the historical origins of the texts, scripture is now read as recontextualized within the life of faith, functioning in a host of ways to bring one to a vibrant faith in God and to sustain one in that faith. Thus scripture is not pitted against, say, the trinitarian faith of, say, the Nicene Creed but as complementary to it. Nor need one worry about deriving the creed from the scriptures; indeed the very decision about the content of the New Testament was in part determined by the compatibility of the proposed canonical text with the rule of faith. Thus the drive to see scripture as a foundation of the creed is sidelined, so that both scripture and creed can do the job that they do best in their singularity and particularity.[12] The same applies to the other components of the canonical heritage. More generally we might say that scripture is read within the full life of the church and allowed to play its unique role in fostering faith and in equip-

---

in *Evangelicals and Scripture: Tradition, Authority, and Hermeneutics,* ed. Vincent E. Bacote, Laura C. Miguelez, and Dennis L. Okholm (Downers Grove, IL: InterVarsity Press, 2004), 76-89.

11. See, for example, the fine study by John Webster, *Holy Scripture: A Dogmatic Sketch* (Cambridge: Cambridge University Press, 2003). Rather than derive the doctrine of the Trinity from scripture, Webster assumes the doctrine and then relocates scripture in the activity and ministry of the triune God.

12. Ellen Charry's landmark study of theology as a soteriological enterprise has had a wide impact on recent evangelicals. See Ellen T. Charry, *By the Renewing of Your Minds: The Pastoral Function of Christian Doctrine* (New York: Oxford University Press, 1997).

ping the saints to engage in the work of ministry. There is a liberty here that is bracing in its own way. Scripture is set free as an instrument of the Spirit to bring about holiness, faithfulness, and competence in ministry.

The tendency of evangelicals to rest content with merely local and even occasional attention to the life of the church needs repairing at this point. Clearly, it was the church that decided the content and limits of the canon of scripture. Hence to pit the canon of scripture against the life of the church is in principle wrong-headed. To be sure, we can understand why evangelicals are wary of those church leaders who have used their power to hamper or even forbid the free use of scripture among the laity. It is perfectly natural that evangelicals have been skeptical of a robust vision of the church because they have been hounded at times from pillar to post by corrupt church authorities who have persecuted the faithful.[13] The prejudice against evangelicals in the mainline denominations and in major segments of the academy shows that they should be cautious and wary of cheap talk about inclusivism in the mainline denominations and in the culture as a whole. Yet it is shortsighted to deduce from this that the church is secondary to the life of faith or that historical continuity across the ages should be maligned. Critical as local Christian communities are, they should not be set in opposition to the translocal unity that is given to the people of God as a whole. Clearly, as things stand, the divisions among Christians means that the expression of the translocal unity of the church remains a hope rather than an empirical reality. Yet just as believers are ineluctably drawn to fellowship in local communities, that same sense of communion cannot be restricted to merely local expression.

Canonical theists are inescapably ecumenical in their orientation. While they lament the lack of organic unity in the faith, they see in the gradual reappropriation of the canonical heritage of the church one significant way to transcend the narrowness of both party spirit and ecclesial arrogance. It is patently clear that the Holy Spirit has breathed through the manifold heritage of the church wherever that heritage has been used in faith and repentance. It is a sin against the work of the Holy Spirit to deny or disparage that healing and saving encounter with Christ that has been pivotal to vibrant forms of evangelicalism. Some of that work has been carried out in the teeth of opposition from those who claim an exclusive connection to the church of the apostles and deserves deep gratitude. For

---

13. Sadly, this continues today in some countries with long histories of Eastern Orthodoxy and Roman Catholicism.

their part evangelicals have had their own brand of exclusivism that limits the Holy Spirit to their own favored doctrines and practices; they have developed their own version of the slogan, *extra ecclesiam nulla salus*. We now need to acknowledge the work of the Holy Spirit across our current ecclesial divisions. It is empirically clear to those with eyes to see and ears to hear that the Holy Spirit has drawn to Christ countless hosts of believers who exist outside the boundaries of the great historic Christian communities. The challenge surely is to find a way to recognize this fact and to find fresh ways to express the full unity of the faith willed by God.[14]

Given that the official ecumenism of the twentieth century is now brain dead and that its recent instrumentalities have become partisan and divisive, there is a need to rethink the work of ecumenism and to find fresh instrumentalities of unity in the Spirit. For a time the great hope was that the scriptures would be pivotal if not sufficient as the instrument for securing unity. Since the 1960s appeal to scripture has in fact become the basis as much for a false form of ecclesial pluralism as for unity. Given that appeal to scripture became a source of endless division in Protestantism after the Reformation, it is clear that we need a wider network of materials and practices to make headway in the future. Attempts to find the unity of church in religious experience or in agreed moral and political agendas have fared no better. It is at this point that the canonical heritage can perhaps exercise a valuable role in drawing Christians together into one body. Rather than work from a minimalist vision of the lowest common denominator, we should work instead from a maximalist vision that seeks consensus around the agreed canonical traditions of the undivided church.

Not surprisingly, evangelicals have been as ambivalent in their commitment to church unity as they have been in their commitment to the church. The time is ripe for them to find a new way to own both. Beginning with their zeal for healthy forms of fellowship and local church life, they need to expand their range of vision and work patiently for translocal and even worldwide identity in one body that stretches back in time to the apostles and across space to the ends of the earth. Embracing the canonical faith and practice of the church as a whole is clearly a significant step in this direction.

Happily, spreading the gospel across the face of the earth has been

---

14. John Wesley's sermon "Catholic Spirit" remains a splendid testimony to this aspiration. See Albert C. Outler and Richard P. Heitzenrater, *John Wesley's Sermons: An Anthology* (Nashville: Abingdon, 1991), 299-310.

one of the great virtues of evangelicalism, ancient and modern. Indeed the commitment of evangelicals to evangelism has been one their great strengths over the centuries. While they wobbled for a time about world mission, once they crossed the Rubicon on this issue there has been little let-up since the beginning of the nineteenth century. One reason why evangelicalism is a major force to be reckoned with in terms of sheer numbers stems from their intensity and tenacity.[15] Whatever the faults and mistakes in mission may have been, the inspiration for the work of evangelism has been enduringly theological. One can think of evangelicals at one level as being gospel people who believe that Christ's coming is of decisive significance for the whole world. Failure to share the faith is not just a dereliction of duty in mission; it is a deep betrayal of the faith itself. More positively, evangelicals have been driven by an enduring sense of joy and passion that cannot be contained in parochial and national vessels. To be sure, evangelicals have been exporters of Western culture in their sharing the gospel, but they long ago repented of their imperial past. They have readily come to terms with the need for contextualization of the faith — so much so that there are intense internal disputes on how to handle indigenization. Anyone acquainted with the spirited discussion they hold, say, at the Overseas Ministries Study Center will know how diverse and civilized the discussion can be. The desire to allow national Christians to work through issues of gospel and culture is matched by a desire to engage in reflection on the relation between gospel and culture in the West. In this arena the work of Lesslie Newbigin has made a lasting mark.[16]

As to practice of evangelism, evangelicals are at heart radically pragmatic. The legacy of revivalism lingers on, but it is now a spent force. Evangelicals can no longer rely on culture to transmit the faith, and revivalism depended crucially on the preparatory work carried out by the public schools and by the culture more generally. In the period of degenerative Christendom, a gospel sermon topped off by the call to decision and repentance was often sufficient to connect folk personally to the gospel for a lifetime. Given the loss and thinness of faith in the contemporary world and the rapid embrace of pluralism in the political arena, this strategy has faltered. Some still hold out for a great revival, but we now know that re-

---

15. We are only beginning to take note of developments in China. See, for example, David Aikman, *Jesus in Beijing* (Washington, DC: Regnery, 2003).

16. See especially Lesslie Newbigin, *Foolishness to the Greeks: The Gospel and Western Culture* (Grand Rapids: Eerdmans, 1986).

vivals were something of a historical construct that masked some of the critical factors at work in the birth of faith. In the most recent past evangelicals have been keenly interested in church-growth strategies, in postmodernism, and in various forms of Pentecostalism as the way ahead. There has been a fresh rush of interest in evangelism in declining mainline circles, especially among British Anglicans and American United Methodists, which has led to very significant cross-fertilization of theology and practice.

If one thing has become patently clear over the last generation, it is that faithful evangelistic practice requires a recovery of small group ministries, many of which have become the location for extremely important new ventures in catechesis. Few evangelicals would use the language of catechesis, for it sounds too much like the old and tired use of a catechism, but the reality is that modern evangelicals have stumbled into the practices of catechesis without realizing what they are doing. Given that the contemporary scene in the West is strikingly similar to the ancient pluralist world of the Roman Empire, there are no surprises here for the careful observer.[17] The Christian gospel has been driven from the public square, is despised in many academic circles as superstitious and intellectually backward, and must now compete in an intellectual market that is sometimes extremely volatile and vulgar. New believers simply cannot survive in this world without intentional spiritual formation and instruction. Handing out Bibles without other aids to reflection and spiritual development is of very limited value. Scripture alone failed to work in the second century in the midst of the aggressive work of Gnostics who were only too ready to provide their idiosyncratic and tendentious reading of the sacred text. Scripture alone will not work today in the midst of the whole range of voices that compete for attention and allegiance; the new Gnostics, whether sophisticated like Joseph Campbell, or more popular, like Shirley McClaine, will readily gobble up the text of scripture and make it fit their prearranged schema. As Wesley remarked, to leave new converts without help at this point is to create children for the murderer.

> I was more convinced than ever, that the preaching like an Apostle, without joining together those that are awakened, and training them up in the ways of God, is only begetting children for the murderer.

17. There are, of course, important differences between Europe and the United States, but this is not the place to explore these.

> How much preaching has there been for these twenty years all over Pembrokeshire! But no regular societies, no discipline, no order or connexion; and the consequence is, that nine in ten of the once-awakened are now faster asleep than ever.[18]

Hence healthy and creative forms of catechesis are imperative.

Clearly this provides a lively point of contact with canonical theism. We now know that the creation of the canonical heritage was intimately tied to the kind of formation that prepared folk to survive in a hostile and even persecuting world. The creed was developed by hard-pressed teachers, priests, and bishops who were seeking for a way to build new believers up in the faith. Strange as it may seem, the rule of faith was the equivalent of the Four Spiritual Laws of Campus Crusade; that is, it provided a way to summarize the core convictions of the faith in a way that would be accessible and memorable to new converts. The teachings of the fathers were in part intended to take the convert from there and unpack the intellectual content of the faith so that the whole of human existence was brought under the light of the gospel. Liturgical practice taught the faith dramatically. The lives of the saints set up powerful models of behavior and inspiration. Icons displayed the great events of salvation history in a way that captured and transformed the imagination. Current efforts to make use of images on screens are pale reflections of this practice; they are a fumbling way to recover a lost art in the life of the church. Thus evangelicals can benefit enormously from exploring how the canonical heritage of the church may be invaluable in providing fresh and effective ways of communicating the gospel and sustaining its content in a hostile environment.

We can say the same for working through issues related to conversion and piety. Evangelicals have been fascinated by conversion and deeply concerned about piety. Contrary to the popular stereotype, they have not collapsed conversion into a dramatic once-for-all event in the life of the believer. Some have done this, but the weight of the tradition has always recognized that the spiritual journey has twists and turns that defy analysis and simplistic summary. Even the Wesleyan tradition, a tradition that was obsessed in its own way with personal commitment, developed a very rich set of theological concepts in its effort to make sense of the reception of the gospel. Thus it wrestled with various shades of grace and with such no-

---

18. Reginald Ward and Richard P. Heitzenrater, eds., *The Works of John Wesley* (Nashville: Abingdon, 1992), 21:424.

tions as justification, regeneration, sanctification, baptism in the Holy Spirit, assurance, repentance, and faith. It even developed a robust doctrine of double predestination that is now buried in the archives.[19]

The latter effort represented one way of countering the endemic tendency within evangelicalism to collapse into an anthropomorphic vision of the Christian faith. All too often evangelicals started out staring into the glory of God in the face of Jesus Christ but ended up staring at themselves staring at God. One sees this even in such a brilliant theologian as Jonathan Edwards whose trinitarian theology has recently been rediscovered, but whose account of religion relocated it decisively in the affections of the heart. However understandable originally, the effects of this radical turn to the subject have been devastating spiritually. We might capture this accurately by saying that evangelicals were tempted in three directions at once. On the one hand, say, in the holiness traditions, they collapsed the faith into patterns of spiritual development that fail to work over time.[20] At that stage folk turned to the externals of piety, to the shibboleths of religious orthodoxy, and to moral legalism as strategies of survival. Reacting against this, liberal evangelicals turned to moral and political activism as the heart of the faith, dropped wide swaths of Christian doctrine, and became equally suffocating in their legalism and moralism. Much of this still lives on in vulgar forms of liberal and radical Protestantism today. In turn both these developments fostered a drift to polemical forms of orthodoxy and biblicism that bet the store on an arid textualism that has been inadequate to sustain either the orthodoxy or spirituality that inspired it.

Clearly one way beyond all this is to recover the full canonical heritage of the church and come to terms with the spiritual practices and complexity it enshrines. The content of the creed is a perfect antidote to the narcissism and anthropormorphism of much contemporary evangelicalism. The lives of the saints supply an extraordinary diverse set of mentors in coming to terms with the ingenuity of human evil and the matching intelligence of the grace of God. The quest for holiness and the transformation of the whole cosmos shines through the heritage as a whole, as does a gritty realism that refuses to be diminished or discouraged by the battle against the world, the flesh, and the devil. There is no need here to aban-

---

19. I draw particular attention to this in *Wesley for Armchair Theologians* (Louisville: Westminster John Knox Press, 2005), ch. 9.

20. My colleague Elaine Heath has convinced me that such a development may well have represented a serious reduction and misreading of the theology of Phoebe Palmer.

don the quest for personal faith; on the contrary, that quest is now lodged in a historic and communal horizon that has its own way of evoking and sustaining a profound trust in God for salvation. Many flowers thrive best when they are removed from direct sunlight and allowed to sprout and flourish in the shade provided by trees and fences. Likewise, mature faith is more likely to grow strong if it is taken out of the glare of the spotlight and allowed to come to fruition within the intentional traditions and practices of the church across the years.

The same applies to the recovery of the gifts of the Holy Spirit that has been pioneered by Pentecostalism but that has now quietly found a home within so much of contemporary evangelicalism. In its own way this has been revolutionary for evangelicalism in the twentieth century. We cannot here chart the fascinating migration of this challenging "supernatural" vision from Pentecostalism to the charismatic movement and then on to the leavening of the tradition as a whole. What is clear is that, while the more "supernatural" gifts of the Spirit remain an agenda issue for further exploration, the place of such gifts is in the bosom of the church and on the frontlines of evangelistic practice. How long it will take the church to get to this point is unpredictable; but in making this journey we shall be recapitulating the journey of the apostolic communities and acknowledging the wisdom of the church as a whole. The gifts of the Spirit serve the church as a whole, they are strictly subordinate to the life of the Son, and they are not ends in themselves. Their exercise needs the context and tempering of the wider heritage of the church.

In pursuing this line of inquiry, it is pivotal that the fullness of the Holy Spirit's work be acknowledged. The tendency to freeze the work of the Holy Spirit, say, in the days of the apostles, in the sacraments, in regeneration, in ecstatic experience, and now in a favored list of ministries, is an understandable but common mistake. The antidote to this reductionism is to come to terms with the ingenuity of the Spirit in matching the maddening complexity of human need and sin with a full range of experiences and ministries that act as medicine. It is crucial to recognize this salient fact: the Holy Spirit is not intimidated by common ecclesial practices or by institutional developments; on the contrary, the Holy Spirit seeks to be at work throughout the whole life of the church personally, liturgically, institutionally, sociologically, and culturally. Coming to terms with the network of gifts given in the manifold canonical heritage of the church is one way of coming to terms with this gracious reality.

Openness to the work of the Holy Spirit as found in Pentecostalism stands somewhat in tension with another feature of the evangelical tradition, namely, its passion for divine revelation as a bedrock foundation for Christian theology. The tension stems in part from a tendency to play off the once-for-all revelation given in Christ and in scripture with contemporary appeals to divine speaking or the gift of prophecy. So long as the latter works within the boundaries and constraints of the former, I see no serious problems in insisting on both sorts of claim being entirely compatible, so I set the issues that arise in this arena aside. What needs attention is how far the standard evangelical vision of revelation is compatible with canonical theism.[21] Perceptive readers will have noted that I have deliberately skirted this whole topic in my earlier comments on evangelical visions of scripture. There I emphasized those soteriological dimensions of the doctrine of scripture that have clearly played a pivotal role in the tradition. It is surely critical to take up the other side of almost all evangelical visions of scripture, namely the strong tendency to reduce canon to scripture and the equally strong tendency to treat canon as a criterion of truth in theology. Surely, it will be said, canonical theism involves a radical break with the evangelical tradition rather than its enrichment.

Tempting as it is to draw this conclusion, we need to pause before we accept it. Everything at this point depends on whether we collapse a robust doctrine of divine revelation into a doctrine of scripture and whether evangelicals are prepared to distinguish logically between their vision of scripture and their doctrine of divine revelation. For the canonical theist this is where the deeper issues have to joined with care. The debate about scripture is more often than not a debate about divine revelation. Once we recognize that scripture and revelation are logically distinct categories then we can make immediate progress on the issues that need attention.

There is no question but that standard accounts of scripture in the evangelical tradition confined canon to scripture and construed scripture as a criterion. However, what really drives this move is a very particular vision of divine revelation that gives a critical place to divine speaking as securing access to the mind of God. Thus in treating scripture as the oracles of God or as the Word of God, evangelicals have wanted to insist that God really has spoken to us and that there is a faithful rendering of the Word in scripture. I have argued on a number of occasions that this thesis is on tar-

---

21. Carl F. H. Henry supplied the benchmark work in this terrain, but many others appropriated his position. See his multivolume *God, Revelation, and Authority* (Waco, TX: Word Books, 1976-79).

get; indeed I consider a robust doctrine of divine revelation to be an essential feature of any acceptable epistemology of theology; moreover, there are deep dimensions of this vision that remain underdeveloped in the history of theology to date. Hence I fully identify with and endorse the tenacity and resolution of evangelicals in articulating a vision of divine revelation. It is a mistake, however, to go further and collapse any such vision of divine revelation into a doctrine of scripture.

We can develop the crucial issues clearly and sharply by noting that it is possible to hold the following four propositions at once:

(1) Scripture is first and foremost a list of books developed as a means of grace and designed for use within the church within a wider canonical network of materials, practices and persons.

(2) Christian doctrine should be exclusively derived from a vision of special revelation that is enshrined in a unique way in scripture.

(3) The theory of revelation articulated in the second hypothesis constitutes a creative contribution to the epistemology of theology.

(4) All epistemologies of theology (including the one identified in 2 above) are matters of midrash in the life of the church and should not be canonized.

In this scenario I have posited for the sake of argument a maximalist account of the relation between scripture and divine revelation. It proposes that every other element in the canonical heritage, beginning, say, with the Nicene Creed, can in fact be intellectually derived from scripture. It involves then a thesis about how scripture is to be related to the other components of the canonical heritage. So long as this proposal is carefully restricted to the domain of the epistemology of theology, and so long as the epistemology of theology is given a status below that of the canonical heritage of the church, there is no problem whatsoever in preserving a maximalist evangelical vision of scripture and being a versatile canonical theist.

For the record, it is important to note that I do not think proposition two can be sustained. It strikes me as epistemologically bizarre for a theologian to limit herself to staking everything on an exclusive appeal to a divine revelation enshrined in scripture. I also think that this move acts as a virus to destroy the faith of the church again and again. Furthermore, I do not think that the theological content of the canonical heritage of the church can be derived exclusively from any doctrine of divine revelation.

So I am not diffident about the status of this epistemological option. However, the critical factor to note is that both the acceptance and the negation of proposition two are epistemological proposals that we can discuss with care at our leisure. If some evangelicals want to continue to pursue the aforementioned option, then let it be done with flair and rigor. Other evangelicals will want to pursue a very different epistemology of theology. Still others will want to locate the core of the evangelical tradition not in epistemology but in soteriology and spirituality. However we go in these matters, these pursuits are secondary to the renewal of the full canonical heritage of the church in our day and generation. Canonical theists gladly welcome any help they can receive from those committed to a robust and healthy version of evangelicalism. They are also convinced that the best insights of evangelicalism can best be retained within the contours of canonical theism. Indeed, given the contested character of evangelicalism, canonical theism might well be described as a new and surprising version of evangelicalism.

PART III

What Is Being Asked of You?
Canonical Theism and Theological Education

FREDERICK W. SCHMIDT

One great benefit of a religious vocation is that it helps you concentrate.
It gives you a good basic sense of what is being asked of you and also
what you might as well ignore.[1]

A religious vocation is not of greater value than any other vocational
choice one might make. It is, however, a life's work that takes those who
bear its mantle straight into questions of what does and doesn't matter. By
engaging those questions, clergy acquire "a good basic sense" of the answers, and, if they have learned what they should, the experience equips
them to assist those in other vocations to identify the same choices in their
own walk of life.

But do seminaries engage their students in a conversation about the
gravity of the choices that they will face or prepare them to make those
choices? Does the larger shape of theological education draw their attention to the formative character of the questions asked and answered by its
professors? Does the shape of their preparation help them to grasp the difference between a vocation that demands a certain kind of *performance*
from them and the vocation into which they have been called, which requires them to *be* the kind of people who are possessed by that "basic
sense" of what is being asked of them? Are their professors prepared to
shape souls as well as intellects? When they graduate, do students have the
sense that they have already embarked on that vocation?

---

1. Marilynne Robinson, *Gilead* (New York: Farrar, Strauss and Giroux, 2004), 7.

Forgetting What Is Being Asked of Us

As a product of, and participant in, theological education for over three decades, I am inclined to think that the answer to these and other questions is, more often than not, "no." Successive and disparate influences have diverted theological education from deeply nurturing vocations to ordained life. As a result the clergy who emerge from our seminaries often lack a clear sense of their vocational identity or the work that is essential to it.

They are as likely to resort to sociological, psychological, political, or emotional arguments in the pulpit and elsewhere, as they are to offer a theological justification for the assertions that they make. Theological and spiritual considerations are often belatedly introduced, looking more like a rationalization than a rationale.[2]

A glance around the libraries of most priests and pastors reveals a telling difference. The yellowed bindings of theological textbooks from a seminary education give way to the bright, new bindings of countless how-to books. And a pragmatism not unlike that of their colleagues in the business world governs decisions about program and ministry.

Having been exposed to a highly eclectic curriculum, around the content of which there is little consensus, clergy often leave seminary with a superficial introduction to basic theological disciplines. So, in spite of the fact that most seminaries have, for example, assembled credible faculties in the area of biblical studies, the average seminarian often graduates without studying a biblical language or taking a course in exegesis.

The design of most Protestant curricula requires no regular exposure to patristic literature. So, more often than not, the exposure students receive to the development of systematic theology leaps from Scripture to the patron saint of a given tradition or teacher, to some part of the modern conversation. The net result is a grab bag of insights, often marked by omissions that would not be tolerated in any other field of study and preparation.

Missing too is any preparation for the spiritual practice that clergy are meant to inculcate in the lives of others. An increasing number of spiritual formation programs are, thankfully, cropping up in Protestant seminaries. A decade or a little more ago, they were all but nonexistent. But in

---

2. The politicized roots of much that passes for theology are traceable in large part in the United States to the colonial roots of mainline Protestantism, which was born hip to hip not just with colonial convictions about the nature of democratic governance, but with a "politics of leverage" that now governs both the body politic and the church. See Frederick W. Schmidt, "Politicking in Purple," unpublished article.

most seminaries the leadership for such work is still relegated to clergy leading nearby parishes without deep consideration of the goals of such formation. As a result, the content is often eccentric, and students are sent the clear message that such demands are not as important as the rest of their instruction.

Most disturbing of all is the failure of an ever larger number of clergy to grasp the basic narrative and tenets of the Christian faith. Ask a group of ordinands the meaning of the word "gospel" and, in my experience, many are often hard-pressed to answer the question beyond repeating the widely known fact that the word in Greek can be translated "good news." Press for an explication of the Nicene Creed and the results are even more disheartening.

Not all of these trends are traceable, of course, to the character of seminary curricula. Standards of admission are not nearly selective enough, and in most quarters grade inflation is rampant. But the disorganized nature of the curriculum is unarguably a factor and widespread concern about the shape of theological education has been acknowledged now for years.[3]

What We Don't Know We Don't Know

More than one factor has contributed to this state of affairs, but for a variety of reasons they often go unnamed and/or their cumulative significance goes unnoted. Canonical theists tend to see the following three issues as constitutive of the disorganization of theological education:

3. Robert K. Martin, "Theological Education in Epistemological Perspective: The Significance of Michael Polanyi's 'Personal Knowledge' for a Theological Orientation of Theological Education," *Teaching Theology and Religion* 1 (1998): 139. Martin observes: "Theological education is currently, and has been for some time in a peculiar state of dis-ease. It is common knowledge that in the university, theological education is considered intellectually suspect, and its presence and voice is trivialized within the prevailing 'culture of disbelief.' . . . There is a palpable feeling in theological schools that something is seriously wrong with the preparation of students for lay and clerical ministries, the predominance of the schooling paradigm in the academy, and the relations between the theological academy and ecclesial bodies and other religious and nonreligious institutions. Certainly we should be wary of overgeneralizations, for the situation of theological education in North America is extremely complex with more going on than we can account for. But the fact is that quite a bit of time, effort, and money have been devoted to sorting out the troubling issues and addressing the problematics of theological study in the academy."

- The *quest for credibility* in the larger academy prompted theologians to adopt the models used by sociologists, psychologists, and students of comparative religious studies for use in a wide array of traditionally theological disciplines. The application has been fruitful, but the methods often overshadowed explicitly theological and spiritual discourse. So, for example, in the field of biblical studies it has only been recently that scholars have begun to ask questions about the spiritual experiences of Christians whose lives are discussed everywhere in the New Testament, but have rarely attracted the attention of those who study biblical texts. Doctrinal approaches to the text gave way to historical discussions, historical discussions yielded to sub-disciplinary approaches, and the faith of the people in the story itself was obscured.[4]
- The *adoption of the university model* for graduate education and the preparation of faculty atomized the curriculum, driving professors into narrowly specialized disciplinary approaches without either the means or the motivation to articulate the larger vocational dimension of their efforts.[5] The result is an education which is less a coherent window into what was once considered a truly formative experience and more akin to what H. Richard Niebuhr once described as "'a series of studious jumps in various directions.'"[6] As a result the process of acquiring a theological education is a bit like assembling a child's toy on Christmas Eve: pieces everywhere, arcane if not fragmentary instructions for inserting "part a" in "slot b" spread out before the beleaguered parent, and little or no idea about what the result should resemble. (Sadly, seminaries often lack any sense that assembly instructions should be included.)[7]

4. See Luke Timothy Johnson, *Religious Experience in Earliest Christianity: A Missing Dimension in New Testament Study* (Minneapolis: Augsburg Fortress, 1998).

5. The rise of the university model is well documented by David H. Kelsey, *To Understand God Truly: What's Theological about a Theological School* (Louisville: Westminster/John Knox, 1992) and *Between Athens and Berlin: The Theological Education Debate* (Grand Rapids: Eerdmans, 1993).

6. H. Richard Niebuhr et al., *The Purpose of the Church and Its Ministry* (New York: Harper & Brothers, 1956), viii.

7. See Frederick W. Schmidt, *Conversations with Scripture: Revelation* (Harrisburg: Morehouse Publishing, 2005), xv-xvi. So also, Edward Farley observes, "Education in the theological school is not so much a matter of 'the study of theology' as a plurality of a number of types of study each with its own method." See Edward Farley, "The Reform of Theological Education as a Theological Task," *Theological Education* 17 (Spring 1981): 93.

- Successive trends in theological education that were designed to address legitimate issues in the *praxis* of the Christian life also tended to redefine ordained ministry in ways that diverted theological education from its formative task. During the closing decades of the twentieth century, seminaries focused resources and research first on the corporate or social character of sin, then on the significance of the psychological for spiritual self-understanding, and finally on the importance of leadership and administrative prowess. Each effort addressed genuine needs, but changes to the curriculum loomed large in the education offered to students and the message was not lost on several generation of seminarians. As a result clergy educated during the second half of the twentieth century embraced a succession of alternative identities, assuming the mantles of social prophet, therapist, and administrative leader instead.

These are not necessarily the only developments that diverted seminaries from their task, but for canonical theists it seems natural to ask the question, "What is theological formation of clergy supposed to do and how did it come to stop doing it?" Equally important are the ecclesial developments reflected in seminary education. Churches emphasize functional definitions of ordination to the exclusion of ontological understandings — forcing seminaries to *service* the needs of their congregations, rather than *form* future clergy.[8] Further, policies emphasizing originality as the key to tenure and promotion lead all too often to little more than novelty; and novelty, in turn, shapes the curriculum of seminary courses, leaving students with an often eccentric exposure to the Christian tradition.

What is clear is that the current state of theological education is, as sociologists would put it, over-determined. That is, so many factors have

8. Cf. Howard Worsley, "Problem-based Learning (PBL) and the Future of Theological Education: A Reflection Based on Recent PBL Practice in Medical Training Compared to Emerging Trends in Residential Ministerial Training for Ordination," *The Journal of Adult Theological Education* 2:1 (2005): 71-81. Worsley celebrates "problem-based learning" as "the future of theological education," arguing that it encourages retention and integration, while motivating students to learn (73). While all three goals are certainly laudable, it is also striking how thoroughly functional are both the method and its goals; and it is no surprise to discover that when PBL is transferred to a theological setting, education is seen as "empowerment" (80). It is no surprise that the method is appropriated from medical training in the United Kingdom. While it is possible to construe the primary purpose of medical education as creating "healers," that is neither the necessary, nor primary goal of a medical school education. Technical competence is, instead, the hallmark of that world.

contributed to the current state of affairs that it is all but impossible to identify a single factor that has brought us to this point. If a sharp, clear diagnosis was all that was missing we would not face the impasse that is ours to navigate. Even the challenge of unraveling the attendant causes would not present an insurmountable obstacle to fixing theological education.

The complexity of the diagnosis is hardly the greatest problem. Unexamined and unmeasured, the impact of these influences has gone largely unnoticed as an aggregate, and together they pulled the curriculum with competing force in a variety of directions that are difficult to accommodate or reconcile. To make matters worse, in most seminaries there is no one clearly charged with the responsibility to think about it, let alone do something about it. President-deans are saddled with fundraising, academic deans are overwhelmed with maintaining the apparatus of the status quo, and members of the faculty attend to the challenges of their individual disciplines.[9] As a colleague once observed, "It is not what you don't know that gets you, it's what you don't know that you don't know that gets you." Theological education is the victim of unexamined influences.

The Four Loci of Theological Education

Mustering both the energy and institutional focus needed to make any kind of change in the shape of seminary curricula is an administrative consideration that need not occupy us here. Even the task of dislodging the alternative views of theological education now so firmly ensconced in most seminaries raises a different set of issues than those raised by the larger question of how seminaries might go about reclaiming and nurturing the deep connections between the curriculum and vocation.

While anyone committed to changing the architecture of theological education will need to address all three issues, it is to this last challenge of imagining the new architecture that the balance of this essay is devoted. To paraphrase the words of Marilynne Robinson, how do we ask anew, "What is being asked of clergy and what might they just as well ignore?"

In drawing upon the contribution made by canonical theism to answer that question, no half measures will suffice. Restoring an older ap-

9. Edward Farley, "Why Seminaries Don't Change: A Reflection on Faculty Specialization," *Christian Century*, 5-12 February 1997, 138-39.

proach to theological education will not be enough. The fourfold "'theological encyclopedia' of Bible, church history, dogmatics, and practical theology" dominated a great deal of the history of seminary education. Melanchthon refers to the fourfold encyclopedia in *Brevis ratio discendae theologiae*. K. R. Hagenbach popularized it among European Protestants. In the United States Phillip Schaff gave it wider attention.[10]

But, as Edward Farley observes, it is precisely the fourfold encyclopedia that has been co-opted by the changing trends in theological education. During the sixteenth and seventeenth centuries Melanchthon's fourfold divisions were treated "as 'dimensions' of the one enterprise, the study of Divinity." But from 1780 to 1914 they were treated as "quasi-independent branches of study in the 'age of encyclopedias'" and after that they were treated "as independent scholarly 'sciences.'"[11] Simply to duplicate or attempt to recapture Melanchthon's encyclopedia is to enter the same vortex with little hope of a different outcome.

An approach that leaves a largely disciplinary-specific core intact by simply commending an interest in vocation to faculty will substantially fail to change the shape of theological education.[12] Likewise, an approach that simply adds a course devoted to the subject of the church's canons will fail to inform the logic of the curriculum in a manner that genuinely changes the place that canons assume in the lives of the students who enroll in theological education. Even an approach that simply "breaks out" the individual components of canonical authority into a separate constellation of disciplinary foci (e.g., creeds, liturgy, scripture) runs the risk of creating an equally fragmented curriculum.[13] As Rebecca Chopp observes: "If knowing God is as much a matter of right relationships as it is the mastery of correct ideas, then the present crisis of theological education cannot be fixed merely by reordering the curriculum. . . . Indeed, the task for the subjects of theological education may be as much the doing of new forms of

10. See Farley, "The Reform of Theological Education," 95-96. Cf. Melissa Harrison, "Searching for Context: A Critique of Legal Education by Comparison to Theological Education," *Texas Journal of Women and the Law* 11 (2002): 262.

11. Farley, "The Reform of Theological Education," 96.

12. As Robert Banks observes, theological education has been largely shaped by the uncritical adoption of professional models that remain uninformed by a distinctively theological perspective. See Robert Banks, *Reenvisioning Theological Education: Exploring a Missional Alternative to Current Models* (Grand Rapids: Eerdmans, 1999), 6-7.

13. See Part I of this volume for an overview of the several canons upon which Christianity relied during the first five centuries.

relationships to God, self, others, traditions, and society as it is the articulation of right ideas."[14]

The key to the transformation of theological education lies instead in attending to four considerations, the twin purposes of theological education:[15]

- formation or the cultivation of a *habitus*;[16]
- discernment;[17]

14. See her *Saving Work: Feminist Practices of Theological Education* (Louisville: Westminster/John Knox, 1995), 110.

15. As Robert Banks observes, it is not enough to focus on discernment alone as an antidote to the failure of both the so-called "classical" and "vocational" approaches to theological education, because "discernment is only one aspect of moral formation" and can remain a largely cognitive enterprise. However, Banks's restriction of the term "formation" to the moral sphere reflects a less than adequate and, finally, more *functional* understanding of what I would argue is the *ontological* complexity of a vocation to ordained ministry. See Banks, *Reenvisioning*, 56, 60. This goes a long way toward explaining why, in offering his own alternative, Banks is content to describe his own proposal as "missional" in character (69ff.). Cf. the way in which language about leadership, competence, and professionalism continues to dominate the proposal offered by Kelsey, *To Understand God Truly*, 237ff.

16. In the case of most professional educations, the demonstration of competence is paramount and formation of character or identity is secondary, if not entirely dispensable. In the case of theological education for ministry, formation of character is indispensable. It could be argued, in fact, that the disappearance of that concern from the heart of seminary curricula is precisely one of the reasons that the curriculum is no longer well-integrated. See Edward Farley, *Theologia: The Fragmentation and Unity of Theological Education* (Philadephia: Fortress, 1983), 44. Farley observes that perhaps the most significant development in theological education has been "the disappearance of theology as wisdom and theology as discipline (science) from the theological school — the disappearance, that is, as the overall unity and rationale. . . . It is not too strong to say that the theological school will make little progress in understanding its present nature and situation if it overlooks the disappearance of the very thing which is supposed to be its essence, agenda, and telos." See also Richard Neuhaus, ed., *Theological Education and Moral Formation* (Grand Rapids: Eerdmans, 1992), vii and ff. Neuhaus observes: "from the New Testament era to the present the church has always expected its leadership to be morally exemplary, or, as some ordinals put it, 'to adorn the gospel with a holy life.' . . . Today's disputes about the moral expectations of church leadership are not about what is *permissible* but about what is *exemplary*."

17. Discernment embraces but is not limited to the definition of one's vocation. In addition to asking "I-questions," the discerning Christian also asks and seeks answers to "God-questions" and "we-questions." In fact, the task of discernment is first and foremost about asking where and how God is at work in the world. For a fuller definition of discernment, see Frederick W. Schmidt, *What God Wants for Your Life: Finding Answers to the Deepest Questions* (San Francisco: HarperSanFrancisco, 2005). Cf. Charles Wood, *Vision and Dis-*

and the paired, inner logic of the church's canonical authority:

- its *skopos,* or outline of the faith;[18]
- salvation history or the story of redemption.

The first two considerations define the purpose of a theological education. The second pair defines the means of realizing that purpose by suggesting the lineaments of a new curriculum.

Together all four loci reflect the purpose of the church, which is to make disciples or, as Paul puts it, to foster a faith that leads to the renewing of minds (Rom. 12:1-2) — a process that the Wesleyan tradition refers to as "sanctification" and the Orthodox tradition describes as "Christification."[19] Now, to some minds, the assumption that this is what a seminary education should do will draw into question the shape of this proposal. Some will argue that the students who attend seminary should already be disciples. Others will argue that a seminary curriculum cannot afford to be so narrowly focused, insisting that allowances should be made for students who are not disciples and have no interest in being disciples.

The second of these objections is irrelevant to this proposal. For those who believe that, even in offering a master's of divinity, seminaries should accommodate a variety of academic goals and wide-ranging confessional commitments, including the absence of any Christian commitment at all, the religious studies model will work well. To such objections

---

cernment: An Orientation in Theological Study, Studies in Theological Education (Atlanta: Scholars Press, 1985), who uses the terms "vision" and "discernment" to comprehend the challenges described here.

18. See Natalie Van Kirk, "For the Sake of the Joy That Lay Before Him," unpublished paper, 2005. Van Kirk observes: "Increasingly I have come to see that Saint Bernard, like Origen and Saint Augustine upon whom he relied so heavily, has a *skopos* or outline of the faith — a sense of the whole of Christianity and its meaning — formed by the creeds, by Scripture, by the teaching of the church, and his own experiences of the Risen Christ in prayer (not necessarily in that order), and that his use of scripture is determined by that *skopos* rather than the other way round."

19. Drawing on Acts 1:6ff., William H. Willimon observes, "The Matthias episode at the beginning of Acts reminds us that ministry begins in the heart of God, in God's relentless determination to have a people, a family. . . . Ministry is therefore something that God does through the church before it is anything we do." See Willimon, *Character and Calling: Virtues of the Ordained Life* (Nashville: Abingdon, 2000), 16. Cf. L. William Countryman, *Living on the Border of the Holy: Renewing the Priesthood of All* (Harrisburg: Morehouse Publishing, 1999), 137ff., and Donald B. Cozzens, *The Changing Face of the Priesthood: A Reflection on the Priest's Crisis of Soul* (Collegeville: Liturgical Press, 2000), 10ff.

one can only observe that this is precisely the function of a religious studies program, and we would do well not to confuse its goals with those of a divinity school.

By contrast, the first objection is rather more developmental. One might imagine students who are already disciples, but they are rarely if ever so fully prepared. Even those who are nominally prepared are usually far from ready to embrace the sacramental responsibility that they will assume for God's people.[20] Indeed, it has been my experience that an increasing number of seminarians enroll in courses of theological study, seeking to backload the catechetical instruction in the Christian faith that the church failed to provide them.

Add to this the fresh learning that needs to be placed in the context of a growth in grace and it becomes obvious that whatever value there may be in the acquisition of new knowledge, the central challenge remains to make sense of that learning as a person of faith. That is why, as Charles Wood observes, what the church expects from the graduates of seminaries are students with a "thorough self-knowledge and self-possession as Christians."[21]

The twinned loci of formation and discernment, an outline of faith and an account of salvation history make that uniquely Christian self-knowledge and self-possession possible. These four loci place at least five elements that are essential to such knowledge at the heart of Christian education:

- an introduction to and practice with the spiritual disciplines that make a life of prayer and surrender to the purposes of God possible;
- the knowledge of God that the church has learned will accompany such practices;
- a theology of discernment that can guide both priest and congregation in defining the precise shape of their baptismal vocation;
- an understanding of Christian doctrine that will assist the body of Christ in the explication of its faith;
- lastly, a grasp of the Christian story that helps the seminarian locate both herself and the church in the history and progress of the larger Christian pilgrimage into the kingdom of God.

20. Such are the findings of students and faculty at both Candler School of Theology and Duke Divinity School. See Harrison, "Searching for Context," 269ff.

21. Charles Wood, "Theological Inquiry and Theological Education," *Theological Education* (Spring 1985): 79.

A Canonical Approach to Theological Education

In an ideal world, the resources of the church's canonical authorities would play fluidly and freely in helping to shape this experience. Toward that end, many of the courses would be team taught by faculty from a variety of disciplines. One possible outline of a four-year curriculum might unfold as follows:

YEAR ONE
Spiritual formation, including an introduction to spiritual disciplines with the expectation that students will participate
Basic orientation to scripture and the Christian narrative
Basic church history

YEAR TWO
Basic catechesis and introduction to the loci of systematic theology, not as a school of thought, but as a means of organizing the study of theology
Intensive study of the history of doctrine, including familiarization with the basic content of the church's theology; the shape of ongoing debate; as well as practice with synthesizing and applying doctrine:
The Trinity
Christology
Pneumatology
Ecclesiology
Sin and salvation

YEAR THREE
Continued catechesis and introduction to the loci of systematic theology
Intensive study of:
Eschatology
The sacraments
Moral theology
Study of denominationally specific history
Synthesis

YEAR FOUR[22]
Canon law and polity
Cure of souls (pastoral care)
Liturgical theology and practice
Evangelism (making disciples)
Homiletics and catechesis (teaching)
Internship/fieldwork
Formation in a specific tradition

The specific suggestion outlined here is not the only way in which the contributions of canonical theism could be developed in the seminary.[23] Nor is it unrecognizable when compared with other curricula, particularly those found in some Roman Catholic seminaries. This proposal does, however, have the advantage of breaking with the long-established patterns that are so easily co-opted by existing trends in theological education; and while it allows for the contributions made by modern academic specialization, it is also more rigorously confessional in character. In this way the approach taken here reconnects the curriculum with its deeper purposes. What is being asked of those with a religious vocation is clear in such a curricular design:

First, those called to vocational ministry are being asked to think in new ways about spiritual and theological authority. The nature of authority in canonical theism and the formational dynamic described here is not coercive in nature or autocratic. Far from relying upon a brand of authority that is infallible, irresistible, and imposed from "on high," the canons of authority constitute a creative space in which theological learning and inquiry can thrive.[24] As such the courses taught are not meant to indoctrinate the students enrolled in them, but are meant to introduce students into that space, equip them with the necessary vocabulary, and familiarize them with the Christian story.[25]

22. A year of applied ministry, drawing on previous years of theological work.

23. As with other suggestions about the possible shape of theological education, it probably amounts more to "utopian fantasy" than "sober expectation." So, Charles M. Wood, "Theological Education: Confessional and Public," available at: http://www.resourcing-christianity.org/WhatsBeenLearned.aspx?ID=60&t=1&i=77.

24. Cf. Schmidt, *What God Wants,* 40ff.

25. This construal of theological authority is at variance with the view advanced by Edward Farley, who rightly criticizes the fairly wooden version of ecclesial authority to which he objects. To be sure, as Farley notes, authority — as exercised in some parts of the

For that reason, however, the *second* and necessary corollary is that students are asked to acquire a knowledge of the entire Christian story. As valuable as critical tools and a variety of hermeneutical perspectives can be, they do not serve the student well when offered in a vacuum devoid of a basic understanding of the Christian faith. That story is to theological understanding what music theory is to advanced courses in composition or improvisation. One cannot do Christian theology without a thorough-going knowledge of the Christian narrative.

This does not mean that a representation of the Christian story need take a single approach to the telling or that the inherent complexity and diversity of the story need be suppressed. A curriculum of this kind could and should still make room for a study of biblical criticism and a diverse range of hermeneutical approaches. It does mean, however, that the larger sense of the church's history as communicated by the church's canons provides a necessary orientation to any study that might rightly lay claim to being Christian in nature.

Third and finally, they are being asked to remember that it is not enough to learn what it is that clergy do. They need to be in touch with what it is that clergy are meant to become. Their own relationship with God, their growth in faith, and the practice of spiritual disciplines are keys to that becoming and to the knowing that accompanies it. In turn, those same experiences are indispensable to the seminarians' own ability to make disciples of others.

A witness to the experience of God and the theological enterprise are not separate efforts. They are part of the same task, both of which require an encounter with God as framed by the canons of the church. Neither the positivism, nor the radical relativism of some approaches to knowing (many of which were bequeathed to schools of theology by the modern university) will ever lead to a knowledge of the divine that can sustain those called to a vocation in the church. As Robert Martin observes:

---

church — can be coercive. But such an approach is neither representative nor inevitable as Farley seems to believe. See his *Ecclesial Reflection: An Anatomy of Theological Method* (Philadelphia: Fortress, 1982). See also Ted Grimsrud, "A Pacifist Way of Knowing: Postmodern Sensibilities and Peace Theology," *Mennonite Life* 56 (March 2001), available at http://www.bethelks.edu/mennonitelife/2001mar/grimsrud.html. Borrowing from Farley's work, Grimsrud hints at the violence done by the kind of ecclesial authority that Farley critiques, but like Farley, he fails to consider other ways that authority might exercise its influence.

No longer should theological education take its bearings from other disciplines or other sciences, though it converses with them and utilizes their insights. *The legitimation and validation of theological education cannot come from a parasitic dependence upon social science, secular philosophy, the interests of the guild or the academic institution, or any other nontheological point of reference. To be true to itself, theological education must derive its content, ecology, and pedagogy from its faithful orientation to the ultimate Object of its inquiry.* Theological education must, therefore, take its bearings from One who in fact chooses to communicate to us and welcomes us into communion. In so far as theological education takes as its ultimate point of reference the actual, historical event of the incarnation, and is organized in the communion of ecclesia, the Body of Christ, it is objectively oriented to the one True Subject.[26]

In sum, then, the task of a theological faculty is to form Christians who possess the spiritual disciplines to sustain them. They should be capable of critical and synthetic work, but they must also be members of the body of Christ, devoted to the life of that body. A pedagogy that is focused only upon a critical examination of the faith will always perform an autopsy on the one True Subject, without first taking note of its life. Only those who are devoted to that life are capable of teaching others what is being asked of them and what they might as well ignore.

---

26. Cf. Martin, "Theological Education in Epistemological Perspective," 145ff.; emphasis mine. Martin, depending upon the epistemological paradigm developed by Michael Polanyi, offers a perspective on theological education that complements the approach to theological education outlined here.

Canonical Theism and the Future of Systematic Theology

WILLIAM J. ABRAHAM

A Dilemma in Search of a Resolution

Contemporary systematic theologians are faced with a dilemma at the core of their work. On the one hand, they are committed to certain essential themes, like creation, redemption, the church, the last things, and so on. To be sure, various topics get dropped or fall out of favor. Thus in recent years pneumatology tends to be sidelined despite the extraordinary attention given to it in various quarters.[1] However, it is clear that if one is to be a systematic theologian the course as a whole is set. Furthermore, the origin of the network of topics in systematic theology is obvious. They are derived from the articles of the great creeds of the church.[2] Thus the themes of systematic theology run naturally through a narrative from creation to the eschaton.

On the other hand, the contemporary systematic theologian cannot really start from the creeds with a good conscience. To do so is to be doomed to being archaic and to being hopelessly repetitive. Worst of all, it is to be doomed to begging the whole question of truth from the outset. A minority, perhaps more than a minority, would go so far as to be hostile to

---

1. This is the case in two recent anthologies. See William B. Placher, ed., *Essentials of Christian Theology* (Louisville: Westminster John Knox, 2003); Francis Schüssler Fiorenza and John P. Galvin, eds., *Systematic Theology: Roman Catholic Perspectives*, 2 vols. (Minneapolis: Fortress, 1991).

2. Clearly the only creed ever canonically accepted by the whole church was the creed of Nicea-Constantinople. For the purposes of this essay I shall speak more generally of the three main creeds that operated in the patristic tradition. At times I shall speak of the creed in the singular, but nothing hangs on this in the argument that follows.

the creeds. At best any kind of creedal materials, even its schema, can start the conversation. At worst creedal materials get in the way of truth, and maybe they are morally poisonous.

The standard way to resolve this is to develop a prolegomenon. Here the theologian provides a method at getting at the truth or, better still, a criterion for settling issues of truth and falsehood in theology. So he or she begins work on an epistemology of theology. With this in place, the theologian works through the articles of the creed and defends them if he or she is a conservative. If the theologian is a revisionist, then he or she sets about fixing the tradition, doing his or her best to keep the themes intact, even if some fancy footwork is needed, or even if a doctrine is lost here or there. Some theologians toggle back and forth between conservation, rejection, and revision, never really thinking about what they are doing with the loci. They flit back and forth with nowhere to lay their heads.

What has to be faced here is this: there is no guarantee that the epistemology of theology adopted will secure any of these themes in any robust sense. Either the epistemology will be finessed to give the results desired, so that the epistemology is artificial and constrained; or, if we keep the epistemology independent of the results it yields, we will have to shoehorn the tradition and its themes into the epistemology adopted.

So we have a very serious dilemma right at the start of systematic theology. It is an understatement to say that something has gone badly wrong here. In this chapter I shall indicate how a canonical theist might fruitfully work his or her way out of this dilemma. I begin with some historical comments that will get to the core of the proposed resolution. What follows is not a blueprint for systematic theology within canonical theism but one way of thinking about how to do systematic theology from this angle of vision.

Catechesis and Systematic Theology

The church began in an outburst of evangelistic activity after Pentecost. Empowered by the Spirit, the church took on the might of the Roman Empire and eventually broke its persecuting power and zeal, winning hosts of its citizens to become disciples of Jesus Christ. Evangelism had two components or hands. With one hand the church reached out to gossip and herald the good news of the kingdom of God. This heralding was accompanied by healing, by miracles, and by exorcism. From the beginning the church was a dynamic, charismatic community proclaiming the gospel. Robust proclamation of the gospel was the work of one hand. With the other hand the church reached out and brought new converts into the church; this was the task of catechesis. In the circumstances there had to be substantial, lengthy, serious formation; folk had all sorts of intellectual, moral, and spiritual baggage that had to be sorted out. The kind of wishy-washy initiation we find, say, in much of contemporary Christianity in the West would strike our ancestors in the faith as ludicrous. The faith had to be learned, tried on like a new dress, and worked into the fabric of one's existence. So catechesis and formation were crucial. This was the second component or hand of evangelism. Evangelism was both proclamation and catechesis.

Systematic theology began as a further exploration, unpacking, and defense of this faith of the church. This was the case, for example, in the great school of Alexandria led by Clement (A.D. 150-215) and Origen (A.D. 185-254). This sort of development was entirely natural. Contrary to contemporary prejudices, a robust creed does not close off inquiry. Taken seriously, it will give an acute pain in the brain. Receiving the creed of the church and then exploring its content is like taking a subject to a deeper and higher level. The lower levels both prepare for this work and provoke this work. Hence the work of catechesis naturally led into the serious task of systematic theology. What we need in our current situation is a retrieval of this vision of systematic theology.

We do not need to have an explicit epistemology to do this work. At this point we can even leave open the desiderata of a good epistemology. However we think of epistemology, we can become Christians in good standing without buying into any epistemology.[3] We receive the faith and

---

3. This is one of the deep problems that emerges in Paul J. Griffiths and Reinhard Hütter, eds., *Reason and the Reasons of Faith* (Edinburgh: T&T Clark, 2005). This is a splendid set of essays that seek with befitting diversity to develop a theological vision of reason. Whatever the particular difficulties in the various material suggestions on offer, the deep problem lies in the status predicated of their proposals. Thus the editors seek to develop nothing less than a Christian syntax and semantics of reason. After insisting that "we are rational (only to the extent that we are) only because we have been created in the image of the Holy Trinity and thus participate in God's *ratio*," they continue: "Talk of human reason and reasonableness cannot, therefore, be finally divorced from talk of God as principle of all reason — this is a basic syntactic rule the violation of which rejects orthodoxy" (4). Later the editors appear to make the following epistemic proposal essential to the syntax of Christian talk: scripture under the tradition of its interpretation by the church is cognitively authoritative (10). It is one thing to provide a rich theological vision of reason; it is another matter

then, willy-nilly, get to work with the materials to hand. We go deeper into what we have already been doing, that is, we start paying attention to the church's faith owned in baptism and celebrated liturgically every Sunday. We naturally ruminate on this faith. In time we begin making distinctions, following through on various insights, looking for internal connections, dealing with objections, discovering arguments which support our initial conversion and attraction to Christ, wondering what counts as a good argument, pondering whether we need any arguments, identifying problems that we and others have noted, making a speculative move here and there, tracing connections and contradictions between the Christian faith and other beliefs we have, and the like. Thus we find ourselves with all sorts of suggestions and queries.

Let's pursue this idea further. We receive our faith in baptism from the tradition of the church that emanated in one way or another from the apostles. The church gave us that faith without giving us an epistemology. The church gave us food for thought straight from the kitchen, not a recipe on how it got that faith. The church in its faith gave us a bridge to God, not a course in engineering on how to build bridges. The church gave substance rather than process, content rather than form, meat rather than meat-producers. The church laid out what it was convinced it knew and for which its members and leaders were often prepared to die in martyrdom; the church did not in the same way lay out how it knew what it knew. In fact the church never worked out an agreed criterion of truth, or a reflective theory of rationality, or a theory of justification or knowledge.

We can approach this suggestion from a different and more traditional angle. Many theologians think that the church had from the beginning a criterion for its theology, and that criterion was its canon of scripture. Most proponents of traditional Protestantism and Roman Catholicism agree on this; the differences center essentially on what hermeneutical authorities are in play in the reading of scripture and how they are related.[4] Scripture, the biblical canon, it will be said, is the foundation, the criterion for Christian theology; this is the proper epistemology of all good theology. Hence the obvious way to resolve our dilemma is to develop a prolegomenon to systematic theology that defends the thematic

---

entirely to make such epistemological proposals, however hedged around with qualifications, the very condition of Christian speech and the test of orthodoxy.

4. This is the picture that emerges in Colin E. Gunton, Stephen R. Holmes, and Murray A. Rae, eds., *The Practice of Theology: A Reader* (London: SCM, 2001).

composition of systematic theology by arguing that it is derived indirectly from an epistemic vision of scripture. The church effectively identified a criterion of proper theology and from that criterion offered the creeds as a summary of scripture.

This claim is historically false. The church was doing theology long before it had any fixed canon of scripture. This would be impossible if the theory under review were true. Furthermore, the church was far more concerned to secure the content of its creed, its list of teachings or doctrines, than it was in fixing the limits of its canon of scripture. In fact the issue pretty much lay dormant until the Council of Trent. Moreover, the church's rule of faith was critical in deciding the content of the canon of scripture, so the relation is the reverse of what we usually claim. Thus one of the reasons why the church rejected various Gnostic gospels was precisely because they went clean contrary to the church's developing doctrines. In addition, when it came to the epistemology of theology, the great theologians of the church were simply not on the same page; the church tolerated significant diversity. Finally, even the very text of scripture may have been reworked to fit the church's developing doctrines.[5] The church was as ready to make scripture fit its theology as it was to make its theology fit with scripture.

The loci or themes of systematic theology are indeed derived in a relatively obvious way from the content of the early creeds. However, there is no need to preface this commitment with some kind of privileged epistemology. Rather, we should look again at the fundamental role of the creeds in the catechesis of new believers. We can then see that the great and wondrous topics of systematic theology are part of catechesis or the work of spiritual formation. Who is God? What is the human predicament? How has Jesus Christ liberated us for salvation and healing? What is the nature and mission of the church? What is eternal life? These are precisely the issues the church confronts us with when we are baptized and initiated into the faith. More important, the church has very specific proposals that it wants us to take on board and weave into the very fabric of our thought

---

5. For those committed to an epistemic conception of scripture this discovery will be a nightmare to resolve because it suggests that the church was cooking its books to fit its convictions. Bart D. Ehrman clearly thinks that the church was corrupt in its operations at this level. See his *The Orthodox Corruption of Scripture: The Effect of Early Christological Controversies on the Text of Scripture* (New York: Oxford University Press, 1993). For the canonical theist it is entirely natural that the scriptural text should reflect the mind of the church.

and action. In this context the creeds operate as an indispensable map to help us find our way around the whole new world opened to us in the gospel and in conversion. As such the creeds are located in the canonical heritage of the church. That heritage consists of a vast array of materials, practices, and persons designed by the church and inspired by God to mediate salvation or the life of God incarnate in Jesus Christ and made available by the Holy Spirit. In systematic theology we focus on the world opened up by the creed and thus make no apology for the themes we wish to explore.

So what then do we do with those troublesome epistemological issues that immediately crop up? How do we deal with the issues of rationality, justification, entitlement, and the like that cannot be shirked? The answer is simple. We should recognize the validity of these questions but relocate them within a new subdiscipline within theology, that is, within the epistemology of theology. This may be radical for theology, but it is not at all radical in itself. We have plenty of splendid work on the epistemology of science, the epistemology of history, the epistemology of ethics, and the like, so this not something new under the sun. Epistemology of theology can take its place alongside these naturally.

One reason for taking this route is simply that nothing less than a new subdiscipline will do the job that needs to be done. Epistemological problems require extended and careful treatment. This does not mean that we cannot get on with our work in the meantime. We make all sorts of important decisions without having an epistemology to hand; so we can get on with our work in systematic theology. Nor does this proposal mean that we cannot propose relatively simple answers to epistemological problems; indeed, most epistemological proposals can be stated as simple imperatives or assertions: "Base everything on experience." "Assess every claim by reason." "Test all theological claims against scripture." "The poor and oppressed are a privileged source of truth in theology." "The pope is infallible on certain special occasions." "Everyone is the ultimate authority." "Truth is relative to social location." Whole epistemological traditions can be summarized in handy slogans. However, these simple proposals are never simply established; they are hard-won insights or illusions, and we cannot short-circuit their evaluation. We should face this fact squarely and invent a new subdiscipline to address the issues involved.[6]

---

6. As noted elsewhere in this volume, there are other good reasons for this move. When we ignore what we are doing in the epistemology of theology, it is all too easy for the canonical heritage of the church to be turned into abstract entities like "scripture" and "tra-

A Fresh Vision of Systematic Theology

We are now ready for a fresh vision of systematic theology. Formally, I propose that systematic theology be understood as the rational articulation and self-critical appropriation of the canonical doctrines of the church as related to the ongoing spiritual and intellectual formation of Christians in the church. We can fruitfully explore this proposal with a series of comments; there are six in all.

First, the work of systematic theology presupposes knowledge of the gospel, conversion, initial catechesis, and entry into the church. It is directed to Christians. It is focused on further intellectual and spiritual formation beyond the basic catechetical work that needs to become normal in the contemporary church. We should not be surprised that theology will not really make sense to outsiders, unless those outsiders are exceptionally sensitive and open. The gospel of the kingdom meets people in the street where they are, but folk need to be brought off the street if they are to understand and receive the riches of faith. Systematic theology is for those who have entered into the strange new world of the church or who are serious about entering this world. It is a further step beyond evangelization and catechesis. Premodern theology was correct on this.[7]

Second, the central subject of systematic theology is God in his work of creation and redemption. We can say this for this is the exact concern of the canonical doctrines of the undivided church. We move here from the formal to the material content of systematic theology. In the end systematic theology is about God. We are not speaking here about any and every

---

dition" and then used to solve epistemological problems. Usually one then gets the worst of both worlds: one misrepresents the canonical heritage, and one produces inadequate epistemologies. More generally, if we fail to do good epistemology, the church becomes hostage to philosophy, most especially to theories of knowledge. So every time the philosophers develop a new theory of knowledge there has to be a new systematic theology. When the philosophers get the flu, theologians get pneumonia. The current shift from modernism to postmodernism reveals this development very nicely; theologians are often scrambling to catch up with the stale theories that were hot in Paris in the 1960s or in Europe in the middle of the nineteenth century.

7. Ellen Charry's illuminating efforts to capture the pastoral dimensions of theology are exceptionally important at this point in the history of theology. See especially *By the Renewing of Your Minds: The Pastoral Function of Christian Doctrine* (New York: Oxford University Press, 1997). See also her penetrating essay, "Walking in the Truth: On Knowing God," in *But Is It All True? The Bible and the Question of Truth*, ed. Alan C. Padgett and Patrick R. Kiefert (Grand Rapids: Eerdmans, 2006), 144-69.

god; we are speaking about the triune God professed to be known and loved within the church. The overall goal is to come to terms with the full contours of the faith as it mediates salvation to the world. Love and life are fostered by the logic of faith.

Third, systematic theology is a form of faith seeking understanding. We begin the work of theology by taking testimony seriously. Initially we depend on the testimony of families and friends who bring us the gospel. Our trust then shifts to the testimony of the undivided church, for it is this church that has preserved the gospel and worked out the canonical heritage in which we are formed as Christians. The church testifies to the work of God in history and under God develops its canonical commitments. So we begin with the faith of the church and we enter into that faith to understand it more fully and deeply. This is often contrasted to understanding seeking faith, but we must handle this contrast carefully. In coming to faith we already have some understanding, and in seeking understanding we move to a fuller and richer faith. Perhaps we should say that all along the way there is both faith and understanding, each illuminating and increasing the other.

Fourth, implicit in this vision of systematic theology is the conviction that the new world opened up to us in the church is utterly real, and that in confessing its faith the church speaks the truth about this divine world. The church in faith declares as best it can the truth about creation, fall, and redemption. Indeed commitment to the truth was in part the driving force of the work of evangelism across the early centuries of the church's life. The church believed that the essential truth about God for the healing of the world had been given to it in all its mystery and fragility. Here there was a kind of bedrock conviction at work. The task of theologians was to unpack this truth with all the skill and flair they could muster. That this truth was rejected by the world, or that it was difficult to secure by public argument, did not inhibit them. It drove many of them to develop complex accounts of the relation between faith and reason, even though there was no agreement on this matter. Such epistemological work is secondary. Primarily, we stand in awe and worship in the presence of God. Then, in fear and trembling, and in company of the whole church in heaven and on earth, we seek to delineate what we see.

Within this work we should look to the canonical teachers of the church for help and illumination. Much of the work of theology is in fact pedestrian and commonplace. The regular work of theology needs to be distinguished from the very special gifts that God bestows from time to time on those in the articulation of the faith of the church. St. Symeon captured what is at stake with pleasing felicity when he speaks of those who "take the functions of the thighs since they carry in themselves the fecundity of the concepts adequate to God of the mystical theology."[8]

Fifth, systematic theology is pursued to the highest intellectual levels possible. It belongs naturally, therefore, in the university. In fact, universities in the West invariably grew out of the work of theology, for exploration of the faith inevitably involved all sorts of information and intellectual skill that needed extended attention and institutional support. Within the university systematic theology is an entirely legitimate field of inquiry. As such theology is more like geography than like physics; it is glad to draw on other relevant disciplines for its work. It is, however, a field of inquiry in its own right. Thus it should deploy its own special resources in divine revelation and in the ongoing wisdom of the Holy Spirit in its work. To be sure, theology will not find a place within the modern public university in the United States, but this is entirely a matter of contingent historical arrangements; it is not a matter of intrinsic necessity. Within the private universities and within those nations that still allow theology a place in the university, theologians should forthrightly pursue theology's own intellectual agenda; theologians must have the nerve to follow the evidence where it leads within their own field.

Sixth, within systematic theology we stand currently at a time of tension and renewal in the church in the West. We live for the most part in a pluralist world. We also live in a world that has to be reevangelized and where the church is in need of comprehensive renewal. There is tension because Christians still want to hold on to their older privileged position as chaplain to the culture and hence are tempted to go wherever the culture goes. There is renewal because without renewal we will not be able either to survive in a healthy manner or do the difficult work of evangelism. The systematic theologian, in my judgment, needs to keep a wary eye on these developments without becoming distracted or obsessed by them. In other words, we need to pay attention to the particular missionary situation in which we now find ourselves. We need sensitivity and flair in relating the canonical doctrine to a new missionary situation.

---

8. St. Symeon the New Theologian, *On the Mystical Life: The Ethical Discourses,* vol. 1: *The Church and the Last Things,* trans. Alexander Golitzen (Crestwood, NY: St. Vladimir's Theological Seminary Press, 1995), 43.

WILLIAM J. ABRAHAM

The Work of Systematic Theology

We are already embarked on an account of the tasks of the theologian, so let me tackle these topics more directly. The work of the theologian is manifold; there is not one task but many; and the different tasks will call for different sorts of methods. The challenge is to stay creative and versatile on all fronts. We can spell out the work of systematic theology in terms of four central tasks.

One task is expository. A theologian will expound, clarify, and articulate the canonical doctrines of the church. Here the work is primarily exegetical; the focus is historical. We seek to get hold of the central concepts and claims of the tradition. In this work, exploring the origins of this or that doctrine is very, very important. The challenge here is formidable in that most students who take up Christian theology have next to no initiation into the faith and are often discouraged from taking the tradition seriously.

A second task is hermeneutical. In this case the theologian goes beyond exegesis and ferrets out the deeper issues that lie beneath and around the canonical material. We explore the issues and questions addressed by the doctrine; we go beneath the surface of the tradition. We look at the alternatives that were canvassed and why they were received or rejected; we explore what insights may lie buried in material that was ultimately rejected. We look at ideas in the neighborhood of the canonical doctrines. We seek to explore how the doctrines hang together and relate to each other.

A third task is constructive. At this level the theologian makes proposals and suggestions for the church as a whole on how to best interpret and receive the canonical doctrine. The aim here is revision of understanding, reception, and application. So we propose how the church might better understand the Trinity, or better envision mission and evangelization, or better comprehend life after death. In some cases we pick up topics that remain unspecified or underdeveloped in the canonical heritage and expand on them, like atonement, or we resolve long-standing controversies, like the Augustinian-Pelagian debate on faith and freedom, that lie below the surface and have engaged some of the major theologians of the past. Or we suggest better ways to think of God's relation to the world; perhaps we think that some particular philosophical trajectory helps us here. Or we propose a better way to work out how to relate the gospel to the oppressed peoples of the world or to handle gender predicates as applied to God. The theologian sometimes works as a kind of physician or surgeon, seeking to bind up the wounds of the tradition. At other times he or she may work as a prophet, calling the church to radical obedience.

At other times he or she may work as an expert consultant, drawing on specialized skill or information to help the church sort through how best to think of the topic in hand. This is a delicate matter calling for great wisdom. Gregory of Palamas (1296-1359) provides a welcome word of advice on how to draw on ancillary disciplines:

> Is there then anything of use to us in [this] philosophy? Certainly. For just as there is much therapeutic value even in substances obtained from the flesh of serpents, and the doctors consider there is no better and more useful medicine than that derived from this source, so there is something of benefit to be had even from the profane philosophers — but somewhat in a mixture of honey and hemlock. So it is most needful that those who wish to separate out the honey from the mixture should beware that they do not take the deadly residue by mistake. And if you are to examine the problem, you would see that all or most of the harmful heresies derive their origin from this source.[9]

A fourth task is apologetic in nature. One part of this is to defend the church against objections and maybe even slander. In this instance the theologian assumes the role of a defense lawyer, seeking to clear the church of intellectual charges made against it. Another part of this is to explain and explore how the church grounds its convictions about God. This can go all the way from sorting out what is involved in the appeal to faith, revelation, reason, and experience, to working on full-scale theories of rationality, justification, and knowledge. This is where the spillover into epistemology is inevitable, and great care needs to be taken not to let this work get out of hand.

Keeping Epistemology in Its Place

When it comes to epistemological issues, some of this work has to be left to philosophy. Thus a theologian can and should assume a host of epistemological proposals that can be left to the work of philosophy. In this instance we are in the same boat as the historian, or the natural scientist, or the lawyer, or the ordinary citizens of the world. Theologians should not get

9. Gregory Palamas, *The Triads* (New York: Paulist Press, 1983), 28.

uptight about this sort of dependence; other perfectly respectable intellectual disciplines take this course without fuss or a bad conscience. Thus we assume that we can trust a host of cognitive capacities, dispositions, practices, and virtues. For example: we trust memory, perception, conscience, intuition, the laws of logic, induction, deduction, and the like.[10] We rely on cumulative case arguments, arguments to the best explanation, and the like. We assume the nurturing of intellectual virtues in the acquisition and maintenance of our beliefs. We presuppose the cultivation of attentiveness, of courage in following the truth, of persistence in holding on to the truth, of discernment, of wisdom, of fruitful curiosity, of discretion, of intellectual humility, of creative imagination, of teachableness, of foresight, of honesty, of consistency, of comprehensiveness in covering the relevant data, and so on. Equally, we take for granted in theology that we shall seek to eliminate intellectual vice. So we shall resist such vices as closed-mindedness, obtuseness, gullibility, superficiality, wishful thinking, self-deception, dogmatism, and idle curiosity.[11] Taken as a whole, these matters belong in epistemology proper. There is no need to sort out all these issues before we proceed. This is a standard that is not met in a host of disciplines, and there is no obligation to require such a standard in theology. We can help ourselves at the outset to all sorts of platitudes with a good conscience.

Theology will have its own substantial contribution to make to epistemology. In fact, doctrines of creation have figured prominently in the history of epistemology and are making a comeback in some circles at the minute through, for example, the remarkable work of Alvin Plantinga.[12] However, this work, too, lies squarely within epistemology and can happily remain there for now. What is especially needed is for the theologian to pay particular heed to those epistemological issues that are unique to theology. This is surely one reason why the issue of norm or norms in theology crops up the arena of prolegomena.

---

10. For a fine introduction to general issues in epistemology, see Robert Audi, *A Contemporary Introduction to the Theory of Knowledge* (London and New York: Routledge, 1998).

11. For a very sophisticated account of a virtue theory of knowledge, see Linda Trinkaus Zagzebski, *Virtues of the Mind: An Inquiry into the Nature of Virtue and the Ethical Foundations of Knowledge* (Cambridge: Cambridge University Press, 1996). For a more modest and accessible text, see W. Jay Wood, *Epistemology: Becoming Intellectually Virtuous* (Downers Grove, IL: InterVarsity Press, 1998).

12. Alvin Plantinga, *Warrant and Proper Function* (New York: Oxford University Press, 1993). For an equally rich contribution, see the volume by Paul J. Griffiths and Reinhard Hütter mentioned above.

Many of the norms taken up in this arena are general and fall into the general categories listed above. For example, consistency, comprehensiveness, coherence, salutarity, fittingness to situation, and the like are really general intellectual norms that are not unique to theology. Again we fall back into the arms of the epistemologist and should gladly welcome any help we can receive.

Other norms are not general. In particular, it is obvious that the topic of divine revelation is an issue of particular interest to the systematic theologian, a fact that is readily manifest in most volumes of systematic theology. I mean here revelation either of the nature and character of God or of the purposes and will of God. In the neighborhood of divine revelation we should also pay attention to the potential place of experience of God; both are normally contrasted with reason or inference. So it is appropriate for a theologian to explore to some level the nature and relations between natural theology, religious experience, and revelation. In turn this discussion will spill over into the relation between these phenomena and scripture and tradition. Given that these topics require extended discussion for their resolution, what is the systematic theologian to do? As already indicated, my main suggestion is to insist that these be relocated within a new subdiscipline of theology called the epistemology of theology, a field that will require the extensive and careful labors of both theologians and philosophers.

Does that proposal then rule out the inclusion of appeal to divine revelation, experience of God, or natural theology within systematic theology proper? The answer to that question is both a yes and a no. For the most part we can simply let these topics lie dormant, leaving them to be pursued in the epistemology of theology; we judiciously exclude any extended treatment of them and relocate them elsewhere. That is the yes. However, it is fanciful and unrealistic to think that we can avoid them altogether, or even that we should avoid them. Inevitably we shall find that we deploy epistemological proposals either tacitly or in an ad hoc manner in our work in systematic theology. We shall be drawn into epistemological matters by way of appropriate digression or by way of necessary explanation for other things we want to say. This is exactly as it should be, so we should relax and not be afraid to speak of divine revelation, religious experience, proper inference from features of experience and the world, and the like. Similar moves will occur when we deploy other kinds of philosophical considerations, say, crucial conceptual and material considerations about identity, action, meaning, contingency, necessity, and the like, so we should operate the same way here.

All I maintain is that we not make these moves on the cheap. So we recognize their place in our work; we gladly remember the constraints imposed on us by the aims of systematic theology; we come clean on the experts and authorities that we rely on; and we insist on appropriate and rigorous evaluation of all the philosophical assumptions we deploy. Failure to face the music here is one of the more embarrassing features of much contemporary systematic theology. The theologian needs to be on guard against sloppiness, moralistic hand waving, question-begging slogans, whistling in the dark, and outright self-deception. We should readily help ourselves to all the philosophical help we need in systematic theology, but we must do so with the clear acknowledgment that somebody somewhere has to foot the bill. Sooner or later, if we fail to do this, we will be confronted by the bill-collectors or mugged by their collection agencies.

Back to the Main Course

It is important not to be distracted by these epistemological digressions. In systematic theology the primary goal is to foster initiation into the full contours of Christian belief. The main course rightly focuses on those themes that over the years have emerged as constitutive of its content: the Trinity, Christology, pneumatology, creation, the human predicament, the church, salvation, and eschatology. The creed handed over in baptism is the critical point of entry into this world; systematic theology is the exploration and continuing enrichment of its nooks and crannies. At its core, systematic theology is a robust, rigorous form of university-level catechesis.

The language of catechesis will, of course, cause embarrassment. Moreover, the very idea of university-level catechesis will be greeted as a hopeless oxymoron. The worry here is at least twofold. First, it will be objected that this whole conception of systematic theology takes us back into a world from which theology was liberated in the modern period. Thus it takes us back into captivity to authority and tradition from which the Enlightenment has released us. Second, it will be objected that the language of catechesis with its associated notions of dogma, catechisms, rote learning, and repetition sends the wrong signal. It suggests the end of critical investigation and of fresh creative ventures in theology; it summons up ideas of intellectual laziness and musty Sunday schools.

I agree that the language of "catechesis" has its risks; others within canonical theism will find their own way to make the case that is at issue. However, I use the term quite deliberately precisely because it initially causes embarrassment. I want to embarrass the contemporary church and its theologians for their ignorance and shortsightedness in the matter of Christian initiation. Proper catechetical instruction is a very demanding enterprise intellectually and spiritually. We cannot reduce it to the thin, emaciated affair it became in the modern period when the church could rely on the culture of Christendom to carry the central themes of the faith.[13] Thus I reject the pejorative conception of catechesis that is the ruling prejudice of much modern theology. In the long haul we will have to relearn the art of catechesis even if it begins with titters, embarrassment, and shame all around. Drawing the term up into the heartbeat of systematic theology is one way to prompt the revolution that is needed. I seek to pull catechesis up to the level of systematic theology rather than to pull systematic theology down to the level of catechisms; the wary reader should take note of the reversal of direction that is at stake.

Happily, both the demands and the significance of catechesis are now receiving the attention they deserve. Paul J. Griffiths's comment is especially apt:

> Catechesis may be understood narrowly, as instruction in revealed truth as found in Scripture and in the tradition of the church. This is certainly part of its meaning: the catechist, taking her stand upon 1 Tim 6:20, understands herself as having been entrusted with a *parathēkē*, a *depositum,* that she must hand on by teaching it to others. In this sense, catechesis' primary function is to hand on information. But the act of catechizing may and should also be understood to include the transmitting of skills, among them skills of reading and responding to Scripture (skills not derivable from Scripture alone), and skills of worship. Catechesis, to use Gilbert Ryle's terms, transmits not only knowing-that (information), but also know-how, the capacity to engage in a form of activity, what Wittgenstein would call "knowing how to go on." It is a species of apprenticeship as well as a course of in-

---

13. Even then, this is a harsh judgment that does scant justice to our ancestors in faith. When students appear without the least understanding of the basic elements of Christian doctrine, it is very tempting indeed to send them out to read, mark, learn, and inwardly digest any old catechism and its scriptural notations that might lie to hand. At least they would have something in their heads if not their hearts from which to begin serious theological reflection.

struction, and of the ways in which the church recognizes this is to include mystagogy as an element intrinsic and proper to catechesis.[14]

As to charges of renewed captivity to authority and tradition, the very language deployed at this point gives the game away. We are back knocking at the door of epistemology and doing so in a selective and self-serving manner. The Enlightenment itself is now readily identified as a tradition or cluster of traditions in its own right, so it can no longer lay claim to special privileges given that its cover has been blown from a host of competing angles. So the nature of tradition and authority can be taken up where it belongs, that is, in the epistemology of theology. No doubt there will be contested verdicts on the losses and gains from the Enlightenment, but the bogymen and bugbears of the Enlightenment have long lost their spells and magic. We are liberated from the captivity of the Enlightenment and have no interest in returning to a Narrow Age dressed up in the language of a mere handful of intellectual virtues. The game of intellectual intimidation in the name of Enlightenment is over. Thus the first objection can be safely laid aside.

The second objection can also be readily dispatched. Retrieving and renewing the deep faith of the church is not the end of critical and creative investigation; it is the necessary first step in any critical and creative work in systematic theology. This work requires a full roster of academic skills and dispositions, not to speak of spiritual discernment and wisdom. Moreover, the labor does not end with the appropriation of the canonical faith of the church, for that heritage continues its course in the providence of God beyond the division of the eleventh century. Coming to terms with this history is a daunting challenge; the reception of the various materials, practices, and persons of the canonical tradition across the last millennium has much to teach us. Even the loss of the tradition and its corruptions has much to reveal to the discriminating eye and ear. Furthermore, there is much work to be done in the present in harvesting fresh insights, in supplying judicious commentary, and in exploring new vistas. It is simply mistaken to read this entire endeavor as lacking in intellectual challenge; I recommend that those who want an easy life look elsewhere for comfort and relief. Canonical theism offers systematic theology more than enough gains and trials to detain it for a generation and more.

14. Paul J. Griffiths, "How Reasoning Goes Wrong: A Quasi-Augustinian Account of Error and Its Implications," in Griffiths and Hütter, eds., *Reason and the Reasons of Faith*, 149-50.

Canonical Theism and the Life of the Church

WILLIAM J. ABRAHAM

Getting Our Priorities Straight

In 1935 H. Richard Niebuhr introduced his contribution to a clarion call to change in the church with an incisive historical comment on the ebb and flow of the relation between church and culture. He offered a cyclical theory of the life of the church with five recurring phases:

> A converted church in a corrupt civilization withdraws to its upper rooms, into monasteries and conventicles; it issues forth from these in the aggressive evangelism of apostles, monks and friars, circuit riders and missionaries; it relaxes its rigorism as it discerns the signs of repentance and faith; it enters into inevitable alliance with converted emperors and governors, philosophers and artists, merchants and entrepreneurs, and begins to live at peace in the culture they produce under stimulus of faith; when faith loses its force, as generation follows generation, discipline is relaxed, repentance grows formal, corruption enters with idolatry, and the church tied to the culture which it sponsored, suffers corruption with it.[1]

Niebuhr was convinced that the church of his day had reentered phase five (the corruption phase), mirroring the crises that had arisen in the Roman Empire in the days of Augustine and in the medieval world in the days of the Reformation. Thus the modern church had wedded itself to

---

1. H. Richard Niebuhr, "Toward the Independence of the Church," in H. Richard Niebuhr, William Pauck, and Francis P. Miller, *The Church Against the World* (New York: Willett, Clark and Company, 1935), 123.

forms of capitalism, nationalism, and anthropomorphism; the church was now at a point where it had to recover its independence and strike out in a new direction.

> The moment requires the church to stand upon its own feet, to do its work in its own way, to carry on its revolt against "the world," not in dependence upon allies or associates, but independently. . . . the revolt in the church against secularization of life and the system of "worldliness" points the way to the declaration of its independence.[2]

At the heart of this declaration for independence was a call to put Jesus Christ back in his rightful place in the life of the church. Negatively, this meant a clear resolution to avoid all efforts to collapse the faith into a sociopolitical program, whether nationalist, capitalist, or socialist. Positively, it meant coming to terms with the buried memory of Jesus Christ the crucified in such a way as to be able to say: "That which was from the beginning, that which we have heard, that which we have seen with our own eyes, that which we have beheld and which our hands have handled concerning the Word of life — that we declare unto you."[3] Beyond this Niebuhr was cautious and non-committal:

> Yet it is as futile as it is impossible to project at this moment the solution of problems which will arise in the future. If the future is pregnant with difficulties it is no less full of promise. The movement toward the independence of the church may lead to the development of a new missionary or evangelical movement, to the rise of an effective international Christianity, to the union of the divided parts of the church of Christ, and to the realization in civilization of the unity and peace of the saved children of God. The fulfillment of hopes and fears cannot be anticipated. The future will vary according to the way in which we deal with the present. And in this present the next step only begins to be visible.[4]

The soft predictions that Niebuhr ventured have not been realized. Certainly we have had the development of a new evangelical movement, a movement that peaked a generation ago.[5] We have also seen the rise of an

2. Niebuhr, "Toward the Independence of the Church," 148.
3. Niebuhr, "Toward the Independence of the Church," 152.
4. Niebuhr, "Toward the Independence of the Church," 156-57.
5. I have in mind here the movement that ran its course from the early 1950s until the 1970s and whose public face is well represented by the evangelist Billy Graham.

effective international Christianity represented by the "Next Christendom," depicted with great flair by Philip Jenkins.[6] We have not, however, seen the union of the divided parts of the church of Christ; on the contrary, we are in the midst of new divisions in and around issues of homosexuality. Nor have we witnessed the realization in civilization of the unity and peace of the saved children of God; on the contrary, we are in the midst of cultural, political, and religious clashes that have become radically violent in nature. More generally, the theological movement that Niebuhr and others ignited has run its course and has become something of a historical curiosity.

Canonical theists share Niebuhr's self-critical reserve about the collapse of the church into a sociopolitical program. Such programs invariably become idolatrous and fail to take seriously the depth of sin and the necessity of divine grace. They generally end up morally suffocating, theologically impotent, and politically obscurantist. Canonical theists also share Niebuhr's concern represented by his worry that the church all too readily aligns itself with norms of credibility that fail to do justice to the revelation God had given in Jesus Christ. We leave aside how far his penetrating and original suggestions on divine revelation resolve this worry.[7]

The most striking element of Niebuhr's analysis is the cyclical theory of change that undergirds it. Niebuhr thinks of the life of the church as a series of falls and restorations. Over against steady progress toward the kingdom of God on earth, there is an inescapable upward and downward flow in the fortunes of the faith. The great attraction of this narrative is that it can operate as a handy way of plotting our place in the history of the church and thus furnish a useful orientation for future action. However, internalizing narratives of rise and fall also harbors treacherous currents. Ironically, Niebuhr's narrative puts far too much store on the role of human agency in the life of faith. At the end of the day the critical emphasis is

---

6. Philip Jenkins, *The Next Christendom: The Coming of Global Christianity* (New York: Oxford University Press, 2002).

7. See his widely influential *The Meaning of Revelation* (New York: The Macmillan Company, 1941). I also lay aside his initial worries about the danger of identifying the forms of the church's life (its tradition, worship, prayer, and the like) with the God of faith. Niebuhr displays at this point in his theological journey a standard Protestant unease that canonical theists will reject. As I shall argue below, it is precisely a proper recovery of the varied elements in the canonical heritage that canonical theists see as crucial in the future life of the church. It is silly to play these off against the God of faith when they were designed precisely to mediate the power and grace of the God of faith.

less on the resources God makes constantly available and more on the human response to cultural change. In addition, embracing this kind of narrative can all too readily become a treadmill in which the despondent in faith engage in a constant search for the new thing that will somehow kick-start the new rise in faith that will begin the fresh cycle of withdrawal, outreach, relaxation, compromise, and corruption. It is easy to become caught up in running from one scheme to the next in order to find the final solution to the compromises and corruption of the church.

Canonical theists have gotten off the treadmill. They are wary of the anthropocentrism that comes with cyclical theories of change. Consequently, they are driven to a different agenda for the future. To be sure, human response does indeed matter in the life of faith, but the emphasis is not on our efforts to fix the church and the world or on our schemes to usher in a new era of withdrawal and renewal. The primary emphasis falls on the provision God has made in the church for the constant renewal of grace in every generation and in every nook and cranny of the universe. Canonical theists are convinced that the life of the church depends crucially on the life of the Holy Spirit working in and through the church's divinely inspired canonical heritage. Thus the future of the church depends on a sustained use of that canonical heritage in a spirit of emancipatory dependence on the energy, activity, and guidance of the Holy Spirit. Whether we are in for a Third Great Awakening or a new Dark Age, we need to keep our nerve and rely on the resources already in place. In this chapter I shall sketch what this priority means for the life of the church both generally and in some concrete detail.

Stated differently, my aim is to give direction to those who are drawn to canonical theism, and who desire to begin implementing this vision in the day-to-day life of the church. What is ultimately at stake for the canonical theist in reflecting on the life of the church is a reordering of its internal culture and practices. It is the life of the Holy Spirit mediated through the canonical heritage of the church that needs attention and implementation. If there is to be a new rise in faith, then this is as good a place as any at which to begin.

The Internal Culture of the Church

In thinking of change in the life of the church, canonical theists begin where they are rather than with abstract theories and principles. It would be wonderful if we knew exactly how best to map the place of the church in the varied cultures of the world, if we could specify aptly and accurately the church's current pathologies and pertinent cures, and if we could promise a splendid utopia up ahead. While maps, cures, and ideals have their place in our thinking about the church, they are secondary to the primary realities that deserve attention. We might think of these primary realities as background music that we constantly play and rehear.

One such reality is the good news of the gospel, the foundation of all our thinking and ministry. We believe unreservedly that God has entered into total commitment to the emancipation of the world from sin in Jesus Christ through the working of the Holy Spirit. We are also convinced that God has created a people over time and given that people the resources that are needed to flourish in every place and generation. This sense of divine success in Christ and in the life of his body provides a bedrock reality that cannot be shaken by the collapse of culture or even the failures of the church across space and time. Pentecost is an abiding reality that constantly renews confidence not in ourselves but in the promise and activity of the living God in our midst.

The gospel makes sense only, of course, against a backdrop of radical evil, spiritual dysfunction, and sin. Hence canonical theists are realists about themselves, the church they love, and the world. They expect to find tares within the wheat, sin in the midst of sanctity, corruption alongside faithfulness, and disease next door to health. Both individuals and communities have their own characteristic ways of sinning. This treachery emerges even in the reaction to and reception of the canonical heritage of the church. Consider how some show their appreciation for the beauty of liturgy by hiding it away in the recesses of a dead language. Think of how others seek to win converts to the gospel by systematically eliminating the call to repentance. Ponder the way the crucial office of episcopacy is turned into a means of raw power and self-aggrandizement. The catalogue of evils is a long one. Yet this is exactly what we should expect in any serious engagement with the human situation that is mediated in a host of ways through the canonical heritage of the church. Without the penetrating judgment and mercy of God we are doomed to ignorance or despair, given the contours of the human predicament.[8] Canonical theists readily take this in their stride.

---

8. This is surely one reason why we should heed the narrative of Israel so realistically yet hopefully relayed in the Old Testament. Failure to attend to this narrative will lead to inflated and disillusioning visions of the life of the church.

They can do so not just because they are rooted in the truth of the gospel but also because they are convinced that the grace and power of God that entered human history in Christ are mediated thoroughly and effectively in the resources God has so generously spread in, with, and through the great canonical heritage of the church. We can bear the truth in the end precisely because we know about divine mercy and intervention. The practices, materials, and persons of that heritage, illumined and energized by the Holy Spirit, really do work. As the Donatist controversy made clear, even incompetent agents can administer effective medicine. It is the range and effectiveness of the medicine that has captured the imagination of the canonical theist. In and through the resources of the church, God renews the church and makes saints continuously.

We can capture the main point at issue in this way: canonical theists will seek to foster a sense of both hope and realism in the culture of the church. They live within a horizon of faith that gives color to all that they do in the life of the church; they seek to cultivate both patience and enthusiasm, as they come to terms with the ecclesial reality they inhabit. The church, even when divided and broken, has a future in the hands of God; we live into the grain of providence wherever we are; hence we can relax and face whatever lies up ahead with dignity and grace.

The Practices of the Church

Given this spiritual reorientation in the life of the church, we can ask: What difference does canonical theism make to the way we operate and act? What do we do differently in the church if we take canonical theism seriously? I assume at this stage that we are immediately aware that the life of the church for the canonical theist will be rooted in worship, in a serious appropriation of the gospel, in a constant dependence on God, and the like. The issues before us concern the practices of the church. I want to explore how we may make fuller use of the resources God has given for the equipping of the saints in ministry.

On a practical level, I assume (as is the case with respect to the ordering of the internal culture of the church) that we all must begin where we are. We are not starting from scratch. Hence it will always help to conduct an informal audit of our practices, answering two obvious questions. First, which elements of the canonical heritage are we using, and which elements are we ignoring or neglecting? Second, are we inhabiting and deploying the canonical heritage of the church in the proper way, that is, as precious gifts of the Holy Spirit rather than, say, as mere tools that we can operate in our own strength and wisdom? Let me explore both of these questions briefly and by way of illustration; observant readers will note that the quality of the work involved is as important as the quantity of resources deployed. I shall interlace the answer to the second question as I answer the first, rather than taking the two separately.

Consider the ministry of evangelism. Much evangelistic practice takes the form of minimalist proclamation and invitation. Thus after seekers are presented with an outline of the gospel, they are invited to repent, to come forward and open their heart to Jesus, to recite a gospel formula, and the like. Of course, this sort of practice often has to be repeated again and again for it to work, but what is striking is how effective it sometimes is. So how much more effective would not the work of evangelism be if it involved a deeper presentation of the gospel and a really serious effort to enable new believers to take on board the full resources of the faith? Thus the recovery of robust forms of catechesis (within which, for example, the Nicene Creed would be handed over with skill and flair) is critical to the health of evangelistic practice. At present the intellectual formation offered tends to be reduced to the handing over of a reduced network of scriptural texts that leaves the convert bereft of the great narrative of creation, freedom, fall, and redemption. Converts have next to no idea who their God is, or who their savior is. Many never hear of the Holy Spirit. Serious engagement with the creed of the church would fix this overnight.

Moreover, receiving the creed would be invaluable in stabilizing the convert's use of scripture. At present many converts are often given the scriptures and then left to find their own way through the maze of texts received. Hence they readily fall victim to fantasy readings driven by an inflated vision of the status and origin of scripture, or they are left to rely on forms of scholarship that are driven by a functional atheism that has little or no ability to relate scripture to the life of faith. The great creed of the church arose precisely as a means of grace that provided an indispensable map for faith in the midst of a host of competing materials (including misleading and subversive gospels) that could never function on their own to do what the creed did. In time the church, using the creed felicitously, wisely weeded out the Gnostic material that has become so popular in our own day. Thus the church set appropriate boundaries to the scriptural canon, securing material that would truly make us wise unto salvation. Once the creed is in place, converts have precisely the intellectual and spiritual space they need to let scripture provide its own unique function as a means of grace in the church.

Consider, in addition, the ministry of preaching. It is in this arena that scripture comes into its own. Of course, scripture will have its own place in personal devotion, in group study, and in other settings. However, one way to think of scripture is to think of it as the official list of texts that are to be read and pondered in the context of worship week in and week out. Every other source deployed will therefore be secondary and subordinate to scripture. The canonical theist will approach the task of preaching with this in mind: in preaching we deploy the manifold, rich texts of scripture with a view to sanctification and healing. Without ignoring the obvious place of the distinctive gifts and personality of the preacher, the canonical theist will see the sermon not as a lecture or pep talk but as a medium of emancipation. Preaching will involve a host of speech-acts (assertion, exhortation, judgment, questioning, recommendation, and so on), but in and through those speech-acts the canonical theist will pray for and expect a Word from God in the present that heals the soul and rouses the believer and the church to deeper commitment and action.

Yet preaching was never intended to work on its own. As the practice of the church across the centuries makes clear, preaching operates alongside the sacraments. These draw one physically into the life of faith. Thus in baptism one is physically touched and immersed, making clear that there is a real burial and resurrection in Christian initiation. And the eucharist declares that one ingests the very life of God in the Spirit in the bread and wine of the eucharist. The full working of these gifts will always remain a mystery, but they are mysterious precisely because they take us beyond a merely intellectual and emotional experience into the participation of our bodies in the life of God. In the sacraments of baptism and eucharist we are incorporated into and sustained in the body of Christ. If these are neglected, the life of the church will be radically impoverished.

Consider further the use of icons. In the Spirit these operate at a host of levels that need not detain us here. Think merely of how they can function in confession and repentance. It is common in certain traditions for the believer to stand before an icon of Christ and a copy of the Gospels and there to confess one's sins to one's Lord and Savior. Words cannot capture how well this can bring home both the depth of sin and the mercy of God. Clearly icons expand the spiritual senses by incorporating sight into the process. We can readily extend the significance of this observation. Imagine someone haunted by the past, unable to set aside a network of sins that constantly hinder spiritual development. So a time is set for preparation; a careful inventory of sin is developed; there is a period of prayer and fasting. Then the great day arrives when the burdened conscience is released in a robust confession before Christ in iconographic presence, accompanied by a sensitive spiritual companion who stands with the penitent both in support and as an agent of absolution. Clearly, many have come to deep release without this means. However, it is obvious that a church without these means is setting aside an invaluable spiritual resource. Without this powerful visual aid, we are reduced to mere ears that hear; with it we are treated also as agents with eyes that see. Canonical theists will want, therefore, to explore the use and restoration of icons in the life of the church.

Canonical theists will also be concerned to plot the proper place of canon law or discipline. The problem addressed in this instance is that of waywardness and public disorder. Canonical theists will certainly insist on the inescapably personal and relational nature of church life. However, there can be no social organism across space and time without conventions, traditions, customs, symbols, and internal regulation. Every attempt to build a community out of the bare bones of personal relations has failed; even our everyday friendships operate in a context of convention and order. There are no deep relationships without context, and contexts are governed by discipline. Thus the church needs canon law to protect it from the whims of its members and the overreach of its leaders. Canon law, fragile and inadequate though it may be, constitutes the hard-won wisdom of the community. Of course, if we see it as a burden and constraint, then we will chaff and object to its presence and application. Canonical theists see it as an indispensable gift of the Spirit to be upheld and applied with good sense.

Similar considerations apply to the place of oversight and leadership. It is easy to see bishops, clergy, administrators, and other servants of the church as mere instruments of convenience or necessary evils. Against this we should see oversight and episcopacy as critical in the preservation and proper use of the resources of the church. To treat the practices that belong to this domain as exercises of power or as the mere operation of professional competence is to operate out of a secularist vision that poisons the inner culture of the church over time. True oversight has to be carried out by persons. It requires all sorts of delicate decisions that are determined not just by the content of moral and canon law but also by the particular circumstances of the moment. Thus persons in authority have complex obligations and responsibilities that call for the wisdom of God for their exercise. This can happen in a proper way only when they are elected in prayer and fasting. The way in which the offices of leadership and oversight are often pursued, that is, by means of political cunning and campaign (concealed in a cloak of piety and mock humility), is a scandal and a snare. We can surely limit this temptation if we see the offices of the church as genuine gifts of the Spirit with obligations and responsibilities that naturally fit such a high conception of the work involved. We can hope that fear and trembling rather than political and personal success (often dressed up as moral and ideological progress) will be more prevalent.

Once we think like this, we have an immediate point of contact with the place of canonical teachers and saints in the life of the church. Many of the great bishops of the church have in fact been great teachers and saints. It would be sentimental and unrealistic to think of all overseers and bishops in this light, for canonical teachers and saints will stand out conspicuously from the general mass of leadership and membership. Yet a church that participates in the memory of such figures will foster contemporary leaders who will thereby have a standard that inspires and corrects. Of course, the ultimate standard is Christ himself, but Christ, as teacher and perfect Son of God, is visible in the concrete lives of those set apart in the church as exemplary. This is why immersion in such models is not just a matter for the leaders of the church but is important for everyone. Hence canonical theists will seek to ensure that the church as a whole has appropriate access to their lives. It will surprise no one who thinks about what is at stake that great teachers and saints will sometimes be presented in a rhetorical dress and form that expresses an ideal that functions to inspire, rather merely depicting prosaic historical reality. Such sanctified exaggeration will in turn provoke a hermeneutic of grace that binds up the wounds of the great teachers and saints of the past. Naturally it is only through the guidance and ingenuity of the Holy Spirit that the lives of great teachers and saints can be appropriated in the life of the church.

An Objection Considered

Enough has been said to indicate the direction, ethos, and practices that the canonical theist will seek to incorporate into the life of the church, however it may be currently figured and formed in the particularities of his or her current situation. There is no recipe in advance for spelling out how the implementation of canonical theism is to be pursued; wisdom and patience will be indispensable. Such reserve is in itself an expression of the conviction that the life of the church depends on the guidance and assistance of the Holy Spirit. Even with this caution, we can have no illusions about the difficulties involved. For many the whole idea of canonical theism will become an even greater stretch than it currently is, once they begin to embody it in practice. It helps enormously at this point if they can track the way in which various elements of the canonical heritage are already in place in their own tradition. Canonical theism is an enrichment of what is already in place rather than an abstraction that has somehow to be applied from scratch. So embracing canonical theism involves attitude and disposition as much as it does accepting a network of theological and historical claims and implementing a raft of practices.

Even so, some will see in canonical theism one more version of orthodoxy in search of embodiment, and that in itself will be enough to cause dissonance and resistance. Worse still, they will be tempted to see canonical theism as one more ideology that represents in the end little more than a bid for power and ascendancy. Are we not back on the treadmill to find one more scheme that will fix the church once and for all?

Certainly, canonical theists are clear that the grounds and content of their claims are contested. They do have a set of doctrines and practices that are substantial. They also know that many hands are offering food in a time of hunger and starvation; we all need to be wary about the hand that feeds us. However, it is a mistake to conceive of canonical theism as either a recovery of orthodoxy or one more ideology in the life of the church, or as a quick-fix scheme to end corruption once and for all.

"Orthodoxy" is much too thin a word to capture what is at stake; it is also much too polemical. What is at stake for the canonical theist is a thick description of the life of the Holy Spirit in the church across space and time. This life cannot be reduced simply to right belief or orthodoxy. Doctrine matters, of course; indeed, the very specific doctrine enshrined in the Nicene Creed is read as constitutive of canonical theism. However, doctrine is not just right belief; it is one element in a medicine chest of resources that function in a natural and coordinated way with other elements. In addition, doctrine is seen as a precious gift of the Holy Spirit. To use it as a weapon, as a means to an end, is to court disaster; it is to run the risk of divorcing doctrine from its central purpose as a means of grace.[9]

---

9. I am not here saying that there is no place for polemic as a rhetorical strategy in the life of the church. It would surely be daft to put such constraints on the work of the Spirit. My aim is to dissolve a reductionist reading of canonical theism.

The term "ideology" is equally misleading. "Ideology" is generally taken to mean a theory invented (usually unconsciously) to mask the interests of a certain group intent on gaining power or even domination. The insight enshrined in this conception of ideology is a legitimate one. Human agency is subject to all sorts of self-deception, masking, and repression of power. Thus self-awareness and self-criticism are very important intellectual virtues. However, we need more at this point than hasty assertions of ideological commitment and partisanship masked as a call for the exercise of a thin list of intellectual virtues. Finger pointing and hand waving are cheap and easy; we need particular charges backed up by specific evidence and illuminating commentary. Suffice it to say at this stage that canonical theists reject the effort to redescribe their proposals as one more ideology. To do so would mean giving up on their claim that the persons, materials, and practices of the canonical heritage of the church are to be seen and received as gifts of the Holy Spirit. They are not ready to give up this claim because they are persuaded that this is the central truth of the matter; anything less than this description is reductionist and inaccurate. They are betting the store not on one more bid for power but on the resources abundantly made available by God in the life of the church.

It is this emphasis on the resources of God that dissolves the charge that we have here just one more scheme to fix the church once and for all. Such schemes presuppose a utopian vision of church life that is false; the church has always had to wrestle with the temptation of compromise and corruption. Human schemes to eradicate this temptation have never worked; and, even if we did secure success, we can be sure that it would not have come from one more human scheme. Canonical theism calls for a reorientation in the inner culture of the church and a bold redeployment of the means of grace through which the Holy Spirit has covenanted to work in all space and time since Pentecost.

Conclusion

In the nineteenth and early twentieth centuries, the church in the West was deeply preoccupied with two enduring challenges: the challenge of cultural credibility and the challenge of social and political change. In the first the question addressed was that of providing a persuasive presentation of the faith that would sustain cradle believers and win new ones. The solutions invariably involved a series of shotgun weddings and divorces with philosophers that have populated the church's ranks with more than enough illegitimate children who are tempted to another round of philosophical promiscuity. In the second challenge the question addressed was that of providing a social and political agenda that would embody the kingdom of God in the public arena. The solutions in this instance have involved a series of guided international tours from Russia to South America that show no signs of running out of fuel but whose airplanes have become prone to crash landings on poorly constructed runways. The challenges of credibility and social change continue to haunt the pulpits, seminaries, and hallways of contemporary churches. The constant effort to solve them by this or that philosophical agenda or by this or that sociopolitical agenda has become a treadmill that exhausts its users over time. Not surprisingly, there is acute dissonance, perplexity, and even alienation on the part of leaders and members. It is time to get off the treadmill.

Canonical theists are convinced that there is a better way forward. Their first priority is the reordering of the life of the church so as to recover its inner identity and practices as these developed initially across space and time. Once the church bets the store on this or that theory of knowledge or on this or that sociopolitical program, it sidelines its own best resources or abandons them as a snare and distraction. The abiding resource behind all the church's resources, of course, is simply the grace and energy of the triune God. This energy and grace are not hidden away in some heavenly La-la Land; they are made available in the mercy of God in the diverse canonical heritage of the church designed from the beginning as a constant well of renewal. One crucial element in the journey to the final victory of the gospel over evil is the patient reappropriation of the canonical heritage of the church, that network of practices, persons, and materials furnished by the Holy Spirit to mediate the power of God. It is a mark of the great generosity and ingenuity of God that these resources already lie to hand. The wisdom to use them aright is also abundantly accessible. All the children of God need the grace they provide; God's children need such grace now rather than in the distant future.

Contributors

William J. Abraham is Albert Cook Outler Professor of Wesley Studies and University Distinguished Professor, Perkins School of Theology, Southern Methodist University, Dallas, TX.

Frederick D. Aquino is Associate Professor of Theology and Philosophy in the Graduate School of Theology, Abilene Christian University, Abilene, TX.

Paul L. Gavrilyuk is Associate Professor of Historical Theology, Theology Department, University of Saint Thomas, Saint Paul, MN.

Charles Gutenson is Associate Professor of Theology, Asbury Theological Seminary, Wilmore, KY.

Douglas M. Koskela is Assistant Professor of Theology, Seattle Pacific University, Seattle, WA.

Mark E. Powell is Associate Professor of Theology, The Graduate School of Religion, Harding University, Memphis, TN.

Frederick W. Schmidt is Director of Spiritual Formation and Anglican Studies and Associate Professor of Christian Spirituality, Perkins School of Theology, Southern Methodist University, Dallas, TX.

Horace Six-Means is Assistant Professor of the History of Christianity, Hood Theological Seminary, Salisbury, NC.

Natalie B. Van Kirk is Canon Theologian at St. Matthew's Cathedral (Episcopal), Dallas, TX.

Jason E. Vickers is Assistant Professor of Theology and Wesleyan Studies, United Theological Seminary, Trotwood, OH.

David F. Watson is Assistant Professor of New Testament, United Theological Seminary, Trotwood, OH.

Index of Names

Index of Subjects

adoption, 80
aesthetics, 169
Africa, 108
African Methodist Episcopal Church,
    116
Alexandria, 52, 100, 104
Anabaptist, 112, 123n.12
anaphora/anaphorae, 68-71, 87, 99n.6
Anglicans, 45, 112, 123n.12, 136, 169, 201
antinomianism, 148
Antioch, 50, 100, 103
antiquity, 127, 231
apocalyptic literature, 246
apologetics, 6, 24, 55, 56n.30, 155
apostles, 97, 100, 103, 261, 267, 290, 303
apostolic
    age, 44n.3, 45
    communities, 267
    teaching, 49
    tradition, 31-33, 61
    witness, 55
Apostolic Constitutions, 65
apotheosis, 252
Arian controversy, 63, 78, 101, 133, 136,
    237
    Arianism, 66, 89, 106, 110n.44, 135
Asia Minor, 108
atheism, 143
Augsburg Confession, 112n.49

baptism, 3, 5, 29-30, 55, 59n.35, 63, 65-
    66, 73-96, 158, 163, 173, 177, 180-81,
    248, 250-52, 254, 291, 300, 310.
    baptismal initiation, 71
    catechumens, 69, 71
    chrismation, 69
    infant, 66
    liturgy, 86
    mystery of, 82, 84
Bethlehem, 135
Bible, 2, 4, 41, 44n.3, 58, 71-72, 135, 145,
    211, 213, 216, 231, 233, 236, 257
    authority of (biblical authority), 210,
        212-13, 215-16, 218, 220-21
    authorship, 226
    biblical canon, 68, 216, 290
    biblical criticism, 211
    biblical interpretation, 196
    biblical intertextuality, 77
    biblical stories, 127
    biblical studies, 226, 227, 240, 274, 276
    critical biblical scholarship, 224-43
    as inerrant or infallible, 16, 258
    as "list," 4
biblicism, 29, 266
bishop, xvii, 39, 47-49, 51-58, 60, 203,
    265, 311-12
    office of, 47-49, 60
    of Rome, 43, 56, 166, 209
books of hours, 162

Index of Scripture References

334